Power
to
Hurt

Books by Darcy O'Brien

Power to Hurt (1996)
A Dark and Bloody Ground (1993)
Margaret in Hollywood (1991)
Murder in Little Egypt (1989)
Two of a Kind: The Hillside Stranglers (1985)
The Silver Spooner (1981)
A Way of Life, Like Any Other (1978)
Patrick Kavanagh (1975)
W. R. Rodgers (1970)
The Conscience of James Joyce (1968)

Power to Hurt

Inside a Judge's Chambers: Sexual
Assault, Corruption, and the Ultimate
Reversal of Justice for Women

Darcy O'Brien

HarperCollinsPublishers

Photographs follow page 216.

HarperCollins books may be purchased for educational, business, or sales promotional use. For information please write: Special Markets Department, HarperCollins Publishers, Inc., 10 East 53rd Street, New York, NY 10022.

FIRST EDITION

Designed by Caitlin Daniels

Library of Congress Cataloging-in-Publication Data

O'Brien, Darcy.
    Power to hurt : inside a judge's chambers: sexual assault, corruption, and the ultimate reversal of justice for women / Darcy O'Brien. — 1st ed.
        p.   cm.
    ISBN 0-06-017959-7
    1. Lanier, David W.—Trials, litigation, etc. 2. Trials (Sex crimes)—Tennessee—Memphis. 3. Judicial misconduct—Tennessee—Dyer County. 4. Sex crimes—Tennessee—Dyer County. 5. Civil rights—Tennessee—Dyer County. I. Title.
KF224.L355O27   1996
345.73'0253'0976815—dc20
[347.3052530976815]   95-53683

96 97 98 99 00   ❖RRD H 10 9 8 7 6 5 4 3 2 1

In Memoriam
Amy Elizabeth Spain
(1965–1995)

They that have power to hurt and will do none,
That do not do the thing they most do show,
Who, moving others, are themselves as stone,
Unmoved, cold, and to temptation slow;
They rightly do inherit heaven's graces
And husband nature's riches from expense;
They are the lords and owners of their faces,
Others but stewards of their excellence.
The summer's flower is to the summer sweet,
Though to itself it only live or die;
But if that flower with base infection meet,
The basest weed outbraves his dignity:
    For sweetest things turn sourest by their deeds;
    Lilies that fester smell far worse than weeds.

—Shakespeare, Sonnet 94

1

Often when she needed to get away from family quarrels and other troubles, Vivian Forsythe would retreat to a spot on the Mississippi that for
her was the most peaceful place on earth. She always went there alone,
hiding in the tangled growth beside the water, where no one could see her
or hear her talking to herself and to the river, watching leaves and sticks
float away toward Memphis, wishing them well.

She had visited her hideaway since childhood. It must have been in her
from the beginning, the impulse to act, to escape if necessary, rather than
to lie there like a bottom feeder waiting for the hook and the net. After her
mother presented her with a brand-new Mustang for her fourteenth birthday, Vivian could drive to her secret outpost on a whim, sometimes when
she felt so anxious and defeated that it was either go there or die, or so it
seemed at certain desperate moments.

For her, one great attraction of that stretch of the Mississippi, a bend
that lay about ten crooked miles west of Dyersburg, Tennessee, was that
so few human beings lived anywhere nearby, and for good reason. You
could never tell when the great brown current might climb or burst
through the Little Levee and inundate the fields of cotton and soybeans.
There was not even a proper road there, only a strip of concrete, deeply
bedded so it would not wash away, called the "half-slab" because it was
merely the width of a single car. Usually splashed with mud and often
buried, it led more or less to nowhere.

The nowhere did have a name, Chic, Tennessee, pronounced "Chick."
It wasn't a town or even a village, not even a crossroads with a store—
only a handful of rickety frame houses and double-wide trailers here and
there, and three or four nice-looking barns diked up against the floods,

and the Free Church of God of Chic, a pretty white clapboard structure with a squat sort of steeple, marked by a red and gold sign. The way Vivian chose to read it, the sign proclaimed that there was a god of Chic. There was, too, as she knew from local history. The Chickasaws, after whom the place was named and whose arrowheads were always turning up thereabouts, called him the Father of Waters.

Vivian, who shunned church but did believe in the spiritual aspect of everything, sensed a divine presence out there where the power of the river, a mile wide when high and some ninety feet deep, was awe-inspiring. In love with the swirling brown god, she saw that the river was beautiful not in a picture-postcard way, but as terror is sublime. That current that nothing could stop made her feel as small as she really was and told her how trivial her sorrows were, measured by its might. Around her the thick trees, the cane and wild plants, and even the crops seemed to spring from primordial slime. When she stood atop the Little Levee with her feet squishing into gumbo, as locals called that mud, her spirits lifted at the sight of herons, egrets, and Mississippi kites; mallards and red-winged blackbirds; and every so often an eagle. The Moss Island Wildlife Refuge was near. From somewhere through the damp air came the calls of whippoorwills and mourning doves, the most soothing cries she knew. Her only fears were copperheads and cottonmouths.

When Vivian left home to enroll at Louisiana State University, five hundred miles south at Baton Rouge, she lost her paradise. The Mississippi ran there, too, but it wasn't the same for her. Every time she looked at it she saw only a river of tears, eddies of sorrows from home.

Her family had begun in Chic—that was another reason she was drawn to the place, Vivian knew, in search of beginnings and maybe ghosts, to remind her of what her father must have been like when he started out, strong and determined then. B. A. Forsythe had commenced his rise to wealth after World War II, when he was barely into his twenties, working other men's land in the southwest corner of Dyer County, where the Forked Deer and Obion rivers meet the Mississippi and where farming can be a torture and is always a gamble. He had been born there in 1925 in a house that had stood near the south end of the half-slab, or Chic Road. She had heard that a whorehouse, frequented by steamboat and tugboat crews but long ago demolished by the river, had also once flourished there, during a cruder time, or a more blatantly savage one.

The soil in those bottomlands is so rich from silt that it requires no fertilizer, and that means big savings; but when the floods come a farmer can be left with half a crop or none. Most planters avoid such risks, preferring the land that begins a mile or two inland on the protected side of the Big

Levee Road. Starting out with nothing but a pair of borrowed mules and a plow bought on a promise, however, B. A. Forsythe took what work he could get as a hired hand in those bottoms, then as a sharecropper, managing somehow to save a few dollars each month. By the early fifties he was buying up small parcels of land around Chic, inching his way up toward working for himself.

Vivian was named after him. His full name was Bivian Adair Forsythe, but he went by his initials, probably because Bivian sounded odd and might lead people to suspect that someone hadn't known how to spell. Vivian always sensed that she was his favorite, and she strove to be worthy of his affection, admiring him for what he had achieved through tireless toil. How he had saved enough to buy land, when most sharecropping wretches struggled to eat, she couldn't imagine. What must it have been like to stand behind mules, slogging across land that was often a swamp, felling trees in that heat, beating back growth so luxuriant that it might have been a jungle? From her own experience helping her daddy, which she did every year growing up, she knew that plowing there was tough enough with a tractor—and dangerous, with sinkholes a menace in that bottomless gumbo. She remembered a brush with death one sweltering afternoon when she was eight.

She was standing with her little brother watching the hired man plow a section near where Poorway Road meets the half-slab. He was trying to force the tractor up a muddy rise, and it would not go—it started slipping back. The tractor became nearly vertical in that ooze, wheels spinning deeper, and it looked about to tip. Out of some blind instinct to help, Vivian ran forward yelling, "Jump! Jump!" Her brother, scrambling alongside, pushed her down into a ditch as the machine, with the driver still clinging to it, flipped over backward and landed not two feet from her, wheels showering mud.

She never forgot the sound of his screams through the engine's wild roar—and then the silence, and how close she had come to being crushed herself. By the time B.A. arrived with his pickup and a rope and managed to pull the tractor upright, it was too late. The hired man, half-buried, was dead.

That was the first time, as she recalled, that she went off by herself to find her hideaway by the river, hours later when the sun was going down beyond the Missouri side and she could not get what had happened and almost happened out of her mind. Seeing the river, still moving, and hearing a flock of birds frantic with chatter and watching a big heron fly in a straight line a foot off the water made her feel better. She asked a blessing on her brother for saving her life.

Precarious as farming was in the bottoms and no doubt because of the risks, B.A. was in other ways cautious. Unlike most farmers, he avoided debt, making do with old Harvester equipment when others borrowed to finance the latest John Deere machines. He opened a general store near Chic, which brought in extra income and enabled him to buy seed wholesale. By 1960, when he met Vivian's mother, he owned more than three thousand acres of some of the richest farmland in the world—and the wettest. He could afford crop insurance by then, however, and was known as one of the wealthiest farmers in the county. Vivian figured that he must have been worth a million or so back then.

Soon he lost half of everything he owned. Hearing the story time and again, and bringing it vividly alive in her mind as she brooded about her family and herself, Vivian concluded that the seed of her parents' miseries lay in the nature of their beginnings.

B.A. first set eyes on her mother one hot day when she was standing alone in a cotton field, a sturdy, dark girl among the plants that were blossoming creamy white. He was thirty-six, with a wife and two sons. Judy Ann Reeves, who had been abandoned by her parents when she was eighteen months old, was then fourteen, and she was pregnant. The father of her baby had disappeared. She was living with her grandparents, who sharecropped on Forsythe land, in a shack on the Obion at the end of Poorway Road.

As someone who knew them in later years imagined it, "B.A. must've drug her up on the porch, washed out the mud from between her toes, and married her."

In truth, the nuptials were delayed. Judy had her baby, whom she named Donna; it was nearly four years before B.A. brought himself to leave his first wife and sons, go through the divorce that cost him half his assets, and marry Judy, adopting her daughter as his own.

In 1964 their own first child, a boy they named Adair, was born. Vivian Ann arrived on May 26, 1966, when her father was forty-one and her mother twenty. Her younger brother, Bradley, came three years later. By then B.A. was on his way toward regaining the level of prosperity he had lost in his divorce. He moved his new family from the village of Finley into a big five-bedroom house in a prosperous section of Dyersburg, a town of about fifteen thousand then, where Vivian grew up among the families of professional and business people and other well-to-do farmers as neighbors.

No farmer in that region lived on the land if he could afford a house in town, where his wife and children could dwell among respectable folks without dirt under their fingernails and engage in the close-knit life of the community. In this area there existed no landed aristocracy to which, as in other parts of the South, the growing white middle class could look with a mixture of deference, envy, and aspiration. Dyer County, settled during the 1830s by small farmers owning a few slaves or none, had never known the great plantations of the Tennessee counties bordering the state of Mississippi and of the deeper Delta. It embraced distinct social strata nevertheless; and B. A. Forsythe had risen from the lowest to the highest of them, lifting Judy to his level the instant he signed their marriage certificate. This being the South, albeit the Mid-South, the Forsythe land, as well as money, conferred status; lowest of all on the ladder were poor white men, or women, white sharecroppers or migrant workers, with neither land nor money. There was less stigma attached to being black and poor, since less was expected of a race considered inherently inferior; blacks themselves looked down on poor whites, who lacked even the legacy of slavery and discrimination to blame for their condition. That contempt for "white trash" crossed racial lines was bluntly expressed as the theme of many blues verses and street chants, caste analyses straight from the Delta bottoms:

> *My name is Sam, I was raised in the sand,*
> *I'd druther be a nigger than a poor white man.*

Vivian's mother and father, in their different ways, had come farther than any bank statements or changes of address could show.

Whether it was the age gap between them, or that her father had worked his way into prosperity without sharing that struggle with her mother, or a combination of these and less tangible, temperamental factors, Vivian could never be sure—but as far back as she could remember, there was tension and conflict between her parents, more than any she observed within the families of her friends. Their courtship must have been so romantic: the wealthy man sacrificing to rescue this waif he passionately loved; Judy, unlike her own parents, finding security for her child as well as for herself. But more often than not they were at odds, with Vivian and her sister and brothers caught in the middle. Sometimes the hostilities became physical, as epitomized by one of Vivian's early memories.

She must have been seven or eight then; it may have been the year the hired man died, not that spring but in the fall, when the land dried out. As usual during the cotton harvest, her father spent most days and nights at the farm, staying over in the double-wide mobile home he kept there, taking advantage of every waking hour, keeping an eye on things. Hands-on was the only way to make sure that everything was done right, that the seasonal workers earned their pay, that no one was stealing equipment or crops, to set the example of relentless hard work. As for the mobile home, he could easily have afforded to build another house there, but saw no reason to waste the money. In this he was no different from other successful farmers—or, out West, ranchers—who when it came to sweat believed in pulling on their Big Smiths and plunging in, expecting their families to do likewise and not put on airs. Here again, as a Dyer County farmer, B.A.'s attitude to manual labor contrasted with the old plantation mentality, where the definition of a gentleman included that he disdained to soil his hands. B.A. wanted his men to see that if the old man can work and live as we do, when there's planting or harvesting to be done, there must be no room on his place for a slacker.

Vivian, drawn to his energy, loved trailing along when her daddy issued orders and talked crops. She helped in the store and, as soon as she was strong enough, spent every summer on the farm, cleaning drains, helping with the spraying, doing all the chores, short of those requiring the strength of a grown man. She was eager for the day when her father would teach her to drive a tractor. It was her job also to mind her little brother—as she was on that cool autumn morning, playing hide-and-seek with Brad among the still-unpicked cotton rows when she heard shouts coming from the trailer.

Her parents were at it again. She heard their voices yapping like dogs at each other's throats and thought, *No, please.* She could not make out the words but did not have to; they were always variations on the same themes, money and sex. She understood little about either but enough to conclude that there was always too much or too little of one or the other and that her mother was asking for something and not getting it.

The voices grew more shrill. Vivian tried to distract Brad by running off some distance. She called to him, but he had lost heart for the game and started stumbling his way toward the ruckus. She decided that she had to do something.

"Wait here," she told her brother. "I'll be back."

"What're you going to do?"

"I'm going to make them stop."

"How?"

"Wait here."

Vivian ran toward the trailer and without knocking burst through the door. As she crashed in, her mother, letting loose something like a war cry, was lunging at her father and flailing at him with her fists. B.A. took hold of her upper arms and flung her against the wall as pots descended from a shelf.

Not again, was all Vivian could think. She rushed at them as they grappled. She snatched at her father's shirt and forced herself between them, using her hands as a wedge and yelling at them to stop fighting with each other.

"You get out of here," her father said as he backed off, panting. "This is between me and your mother!"

Judy began to cry.

"I'm not leaving till you stop!" Vivian said.

"He doesn't understand!" her mother said and retreated to the kitchenette.

Like a boxing referee, Vivian stood feet apart between them, holding out her arms palms up. She asked what this was all about.

"He won't give me anything," her mother said.

"You're bleeding me dry," B.A. said.

"Liar! Miser! You old man!"

"Not in front of Vivian!"

Vivian sat down at the table between them, buried her head in her arms, and cried. It was a strategy to make them quit fighting, but she meant it with all her heart, and it achieved its purpose. They kept on arguing, but more calmly and to defend to her their points of view, rather than to try to destroy one another.

It turned out that this particular argument was about B.A.'s refusal to consent to finance a designer boutique that Judy wanted to open in Dyersburg. She was asking him to buy her a certain building close to downtown and to advance her the cash for an inventory of exclusive fashions she planned to purchase in New York: cocktail dresses, accessories, the works.

"You know my taste," Judy said. "People are dying for this! Where can you go in Dyersburg to buy a dress? I mean something doesn't look like something Grandma would wear to God knows, the barbecue contest!"

"You can go to Memphis," B.A. said, "like you always has. Hell, what's wrong with Memphis? You been spending my money there for years!"

"I'm talking about real style," Judy said. "You wouldn't know. Do I have to move to New York?"

Vivian could hear the threat in her mother's voice and had heard more explicit ones, when Judy said she was leaving after spending plenty on clothing and jewelry.

As usual, B.A. bitterly complained about the bills before paying them and would let Judy have her way this time, too, Vivian was willing to bet. He would fuss and curse and say he was being ruined and then put up with just about anything, so as not to lose Judy. He had confessed as much to Vivian during many a sad, sloshed moment, saying he had no choice. Vivian had heard him accuse her mother of going out with other men. She would disappear for days sometimes, but she always came back.

"We'll talk about it later," B.A. said at last, and Vivian left to find Brad. There he was, crouched on the steps.

"What were they saying?" he asked.

"Mom's opening a store," Vivian said when they were out of earshot.

"Is it a toy store?"

"Maybe."

"Oh, boy!"

Her parents' fights took the fun out of a day. All at once she wished it were Monday and she were back in school. She resented her mother for always wanting things B.A. said he could not afford to give; it caused such unpleasantness—although maybe a dress shop was a good idea, for all Vivian knew. Maybe it would bring in money, and then her mother could have anything she wanted and there would be no more fights. That was Judy's argument, anyway.

Although she tried to remain outwardly neutral, Vivian almost always took her father's side in these disputes—not that by any means she approved of everything he did. She hated it when he was harsh with her brother Adair, a sweet, sad, quiet boy who did very poorly in school. His failures infuriated B.A., to the point of bourbon-fueled whippings. It frightened and sickened Vivian to hear the blows and her brother's cries and her father's curses, "You no-good lazy little shirker!" Judy never interfered. The odd thing was, Vivian noticed, that the angrier her father was at her mother, the likelier it was that Adair could expect a beating.

The frustrating thing about it was, there was no way that the beatings offered the slightest chance of making Adair into a better student. Everyone knew that he had something the matter with his head, probably the result of a blood clot to his brain when he was two that had been diagnosed as a stroke. Once Vivian, exasperated by his slowness, teased him as others had about being a "retard"; she felt guilty about her cruelty when she looked into his hurt eyes. Yet Judy and B.A. sent him away to military school, to learn discipline, supposedly. He was back home within weeks, having been taunted and beaten by other cadets.

As for Vivian's performance in school, she received straight A's but had the impression that her parents did not care about her grades one way or the other, since she was only a girl. If work on the farm earned her father's approval, her mother wished that she would stop acting the tomboy. When Judy managed to persuade her to put on a dress, Vivian made sure to spill something on it.

As she grew older, Vivian suspected, or hoped, that her father quietly approved of her academic accomplishments, even though he said nothing about them. With him she felt a natural affinity and rapport that she did not share with her mother. She and B.A. bore a strong physical resemblance to one another. Vivian and Bivian had the same fair skin, the same small mouth and delicate knob of a chin. He was graying and losing hair, but in photographs she saw that his had been a wavy dark brown, the same as hers. He remained quick in his movements and strong; Vivian could outrun most boys.

Judy Forsythe by contrast had squarish, rather broad features and straight, Indian-black hair and steady black eyes that were much darker than Vivian's or B.A.'s. Her complexion was that of a tribe native to the region, not red but the alluvial brown of the soil from which she had sprung. She was half-Irish and half-Cherokee, she told Vivian, who was inclined to believe that her mother envied her her pale, slender looks. Based on appearances, no one would have guessed that mother and daughter came from the same family.

But emotions between the two ran as deep and were as powerful as the mighty river, and as apt to flood.

2

What Vivian enjoyed most about growing up as a Forsythe was the freedom of it. When Judy opened Forsythe's House of Fashion at 427 Troy Avenue, she hired a woman to assist in the shop and mind the children. Vivian and her sister and brothers found more opportunities than ever to do as they pleased.

There were no rules at the big house on Lake Road, or none that could not easily be avoided, not even any special times for meals except, supposedly, after Sunday services at First Baptist. Vivian annoyed her parents by declaring that she thought churchgoers were hypocrites. What did people go to church for except to be seen, she argued. Wasn't it true that the organist at a certain prominent church was having an affair with the preacher?

"That's life," B.A. told Vivian.

"If that's life, I don't want any part of it," Vivian declared, and B.A. smiled at her.

"Well, honey," he said, "just you remember this. Jesus died for our sins."

"Don't make fun of me," Vivian said, and went into his arms for a hug. That was one of the moments she cherished.

The Forsythe children had no need for allowances, as they were free to charge what they wished at various Dyersburg stores. Occasionally B.A. objected when and if he saw the bills, as when his children charged eight dozen eggs at Halloween. As for Judy, she could be as generous to the children as she was to herself when it came to gifts, and thoroughly unpredictable.

On an early May day in 1980, at the house on Lake Road, Judy called Vivian to come outside. There was a surprise waiting in the driveway.

When she saw it, the new Mustang, shining silver in the sunlight, and rushed out to admire it, Vivian assumed that her mother had bought it for herself and wondered how B.A. would react, since the other family cars were hardly ready for the junk heap.

"Happy Birthday," Judy said. "What do you think?"

"Me? It's mine?" She protested that it wasn't even her birthday yet.

"It will be soon. Isn't it cute? You'll be the envy of every kid in high school!"

"Oh, Mom!" She ran to give Judy a hug. But how was she going to drive it? She was still thirteen for a couple of weeks, and not eligible even for a learner's permit until she was fifteen and a half. In Tennessee under-aged children could be granted permits to operate farm vehicles, but no one would believe that she was going to pull a plow with a sports car. And what would B.A. say?

"I'll handle your father," Judy said.

Her mother slipped on a hot-pink ultrasuede jumpsuit to drive Vivian to the licensing bureau, where she was very friendly to the examiner and kept up a steady line of chat from the backseat as Vivian passed her test and received her license, supposedly restricted for farm transportation. If Judy's performance was rather obvious, and if it made Vivian feel slightly odd to be allied with her mother to fool the authorities, she was much too excited about the car to dwell on any embarrassment. With the windows down and the radio rocking, she couldn't wait to show her friends.

Embarrassment was not a condition that anyone would have associated with Vivian by the time she graduated from Dyersburg High School with an impressive list of accomplishments behind her. Honor student, president of the student council, president of her sorority, Homecoming Queen—if her class had voted for Most Likely to Succeed, Vivian would have won hands down. She also played a dazzling shooting forward on the girls' basketball team that won the Christmas Invitational Tournament and reached the state semifinals in her senior year. A jump shot that she hit consistently from the corner and speed on defense earned her a starting berth throughout her junior and senior seasons.

As bright, popular, and vivacious as she was, there were those who avoided her company. She was also known as reckless, wild, a rebel as indifferent to proprieties and social barriers as she was to the speed limit. She knew that people called her a hellion, and she had no quarrel with that definition of herself. She was proud of it.

Even basketball, for all the discipline and diligence she devoted to it, she knew was for her an escape and rebellion of a kind. The complete concentration required on the court was the most effective way she knew to banish other thoughts, especially those involving anxieties and hostilities within her family. She also played against her mother's wishes.

Judy endorsed Vivian's social successes, especially those involving the sorority, which was linked to many of Dyersburg's well-to-do families, the country club set. Basketball, she made clear to Vivian, she considered a waste of time and beneath the dignity of a Forsythe girl; it was hardly feminine to work up a sweat in public. Her mother's disapproval egged Vivian on. There was a racial element to this mother-daughter conflict, too: Vivian was the only white starter on the team.

She often hung out with the black players after practice and on weekends, something no other white girl on or off the team did. With them she visited their clubs on the other side of the tracks, drinking and dancing till late, an incursion that only a few years before would have been unthinkable in that town for any white girl who did not expect to suffer ostracism from her own people. She was even rumored, falsely she said, to have a black boyfriend, but did little to discourage the talk, rather pleased if she managed to scandalize those she considered bigots anyway. Even her close white friends teased her about her basketball talents and associations, calling her "Black Girl." When it was only teasing, she didn't mind, even took it as a compliment, as she did when blacks poked fun at her "vanilla-fudge" skin. If the remarks became snide, however, she did not hesitate to fight back, her best weapon a sharp, quick tongue.

"You call me 'Black Girl'?" she snapped one day at a white boy who irritated her by the way he said it. "You call me 'nigger' if you want to. Let me ask you something, pinhead. What's your grade-point average? You going to college? I'd rather be black than a dumb redneck."

Although not unique in this, Vivian was also unusual in combining high grades with regularly getting high. Few Dyersburg students, as in any American high school by then, had not done drugs. Marijuana had not become the biggest cash crop in America only to supply old hippies; it was as common on campuses as chewing gum had been in the fifties. Vivian averaged about a joint a day, often lighting up in her room, with her windows open to lessen the smell, after finishing her homework, and combining pot and liquor at parties. Every so often she also tripped on LSD, which along with amphetamines, cocaine, various downers, and the grass was dealt regularly after school in the parking lot—again as was common in high schools around the country, as it had been since the early to mid-seventies. As for the liquor, she reveled in tearing around town or through the countryside in that Mustang with a half-pint handy, taken usually from the liquor cabinet at home, which was never locked.

If Vivian, largely because neither her studies nor her basketball seemed to be suffering, convinced herself that she could control her drinking and drugging, more or less, she did worry that the example she set for her little brother was doing him no good. By the time he entered high school he was stoned much of the time, and his grades, like Adair's, were hopeless. Neither of her parents seemed aware that Brad was turning into a zombie. When B.A.'s right-hand man discovered that Brad was cultivating a marijuana patch on the farm, B.A. went into one of his rages but, like Judy, who did not even seem particularly concerned, took no other action. Suddenly B.A. was growing old, at close to sixty too tired to play the stern father the way he had, not that he had ever been very effective in controlling the family. Vivian found him becoming vague, distant; she no longer had the talks with him she had enjoyed before—and those had usually been about the farm.

And now there were certain matters she could not discuss with him and probably never would. Others became her confidants. For a while, it was another man who played that role. He was old enough to be her father, or just, but she did not believe she thought of him in that way.

He was thirty-five, married with two children, and one of her teachers. The affair began during her sophomore year, when she was fifteen. It was not only that he gave her A's on all her tests and papers; she earned those. He wrote such flattering comments on them that she began talking to him after class. He told her that she was undoubtedly the smartest in the class, maybe the best student he had ever had. She wrote so well, he said, that she might consider becoming a writer some day. He often asked her to read aloud in class, to listen to the passion in her voice, he said, and, of course, her understanding. She caught every nuance.

They began meeting for coffee after school. Vivian was anything but naïve. Though still a virgin, she had come close to going all the way with one boyfriend and had enjoyed some intense summer evenings with another by the river in the Mustang. She sensed that these conversations, these coffee dates with her teacher, were leading somewhere, and that was anything but unthinkable. Her best friend was already having an affair with one of the high school athletic coaches and told Vivian all about it.

But the way her friend described that lovemaking, it was pretty much just sex; her friend knew that she was not the first and would not be the last girl this coach slept with. He was as notorious as some of the girls were willing and eager. Vivian felt otherwise about her teacher. He seemed sensitive and intellectual. It was as if he were looking into her soul when he took her hand under the table at the restaurant and squeezed it, gazing into her eyes. She could talk to him about things she could never discuss with her parents, on a level her friends couldn't reach, she thought.

One Flew Over the Cuckoo's Nest was one of her favorite movies and books, she told him. She identified with the character played by Jack Nicholson and did not think the story was merely about an insane asylum.

"What do you think it's about?" he asked her, taking her hand again.

"It's about the world," Vivian said, "don't you feel that? It's about my family, if you knew them. Sometimes I think I'm the only sane one, with a bunch of nuts. My mother especially."

"Tell me about your mother," he said. Their hands were resting between her knees.

"I don't suppose you've been to the House of Fashion? I'm not surprised. Not many people have, at least not to buy anything. I mean, can you imagine, opening an exclusive boutique in this town? My mother did it. It's killing my father. Maybe that's why she did it. Do you know that my father asked me to make sure there's an autopsy if he dies suddenly? Why do you think he would say that?"

"I wouldn't want to speculate," her teacher said.

Vivian explained that her mother's store carried only designer dresses and accessories. Judy selected everything herself on her buying trips to New York and Dallas, where she went several times a year. She might make a special trip just for shoes or handbags. It was crazy, Vivian thought. The merchandise piled up by the carload and nobody bought it. Her father paid the bills. He said it was breaking him. He was having to sell off land to keep pace. He was complaining that he had already lost hundreds of thousands of dollars.

She was proud of her mother, Vivian said, for the way she dressed, like nobody else in town. But the store was ridiculous. People were laughing at Judy behind her back. She was acting as if she was personally going to bring fashion to the boonies, and no one was buying.

"That's sad," he said.

"It's weird," she said. "It's *Cuckoo's Nest*."

"Have you told your mother what you think?"

"Are you kidding? Nobody tells my mother anything."

The store stocked furs, Vivian went on, for which there was zero demand, not at those prices. Her mother, believe it or not, disposed of them at garage sales and church bazaars. People snapped them up for nothing, with the original price tags still on them! Her father would stand there steaming and go home and drink. She didn't blame him.

"You want to see the store? Come on, it's closed now. I've got a key."

Vivian drove. It was getting dark, but inside the shop they could see, without turning on the lights, the racks of dresses, the alligator shoes and beaded bags and, toward the rear in the near-darkness, the furs. Laughing, Vivian slipped on a full-length mink and twirled for him. He dug his fingers into it.

They made love there on a heap of furs.

Vivian was sure she was in love. They returned sometimes to the House of Fashion and also made use of motels on the outskirts or in neighboring towns. She always drove the Mustang and a few times dropped him off at his house, a modest place in a new addition. She never actually asked him if he would, but she began to entertain fantasies about his leaving his wife and children to marry her, as her father had done. Mostly she did not think or care about the future with him, beyond their next meeting. When she was with him the world went away.

They took only sporadic precautions; summer arrived, and Vivian discovered she was pregnant. She wondered what he would say, what they would do, but did not hesitate to give him the news one evening at the House of Fashion. He was not pleased, that was obvious. He acted as if she had done something to inconvenience him; somehow she supposed she had. He said he had to get home right away.

Without offering her advice or any sort of help, he left town with his family soon afterward, to take a job in another state. She never heard from him again and made no attempt to contact him. She felt like a fool and guilty and angry with herself, not at him. It was all her fault, the way she looked at it.

She wanted to have the baby and keep it, figuring she would manage somehow, with her family's help. But when she confessed her condition to her mother, Judy would not hear of such a thing. There would be no such scandal attached to the Forsythes; Vivian must give up the idea of ruining her life that way, or of starting out with such a burden, as her mother had done. Urging her to keep the matter quiet, especially from B.A., Judy drove her to a Planned Parenthood clinic in Memphis, where a doctor performed the abortion before the end of her first trimester.

In the aftermath, Vivian's opinion of herself altered. The abortion lingered in her mind as a mistake or worse, perhaps a crime against God—she didn't know what to think, could not resolve her confusions about it, and sensed that she would never again feel innocent. She could not talk further to her mother about it, gathering that Judy wished her to behave as if nothing had happened. She considered seeing a psychiatrist or even a minister for counseling, but did not.

She did confide in two or three friends and learned that she was far from the only young woman her age in Dyersburg to have terminated a pregnancy that year, which brought some relief of conscience.

*   *   *

One of her friends whom Vivian believed she could trust to keep a secret
was Brenda Castain, a girl who was as poor as Vivian was rich and who
had problems with her own mother, with whom she lived alone in a small
house. One day during the summer before senior year she visited Brenda
and poured out her soul about her mother and all the things that were
making it hard to stay in Dyersburg.

"I've got to get out of here," Vivian said. "I'm going nuts. I've got to
get out of this frigging town!"

3

In the spring of 1984, Vivian made the decision to go to Louisiana State. Her parents seemed at most indifferent to the idea of her going to college at all, let alone that far from home; her mother suggested that it would be more practical for her to attend nursing school, to meet and marry a doctor, Vivian presumed, as if her scholastic achievements had been for nothing; her father said nothing much one way or the other. She announced her decision, hoping that her mother would finally get the message that Vivian was never going to join the Dyersburg social set. As for whether her parents intended to pay for her higher education, they did not say, one way or the other, when Vivian indicated that under any circumstances she was leaving and would work her way through school if necessary. She would apply for a basketball scholarship, if she proved talented enough at that level.

That was one of the bases on which she chose L.S.U. Wherever she went, there had to be a women's basketball program. Other than that, her decision was based on dreams. Another possibility had been the University of Southern California, which conjured up for her images of sunny beaches and glamour and sophistication. But she was frightened enough of the unknown to be wary of traveling that far away totally on her own. Those girls in her class who were going to college chose the University of Tennessee at Knoxville, Vanderbilt, or Old Miss, as the prosperous from Dyersburg had always done, exactly why Vivian wanted something different. That, as far as she knew, no one from Dyersburg had ever attended L.S.U. was for her a recommendation, along with her idea of Louisiana itself, which she imagined must be all rather like New Orleans. There was no one to tell her that Mardi Gras and Baton Rouge had nothing to do with one another. She joked that her decision was made when she learned that the legal drinking age for the whole state was still only eighteen. There she would be an adult and treated like one and on her own at last.

Just as she was concluding that she was actually going to have to experience this adventure entirely on her own, and at the height of her trepidations about it, her parents came through, and in a very big way. Of course they would pay for everything, they said. Not only that, they presented her with a new sports car—a 240SX—and two gold credit cards, with unlimited check-writing privileges.

By the time of her departure she had agreed to have her mother follow her down to Baton Rouge to help her find an apartment and get settled in; she was feeling a bit guilty about all this attention and about leaving her brother Brad behind. There was nothing she could do for Adair, but she and Brad had always been so close, and she continued to feel responsible for him. His problem with drugs was becoming a full-blown addiction; she suspected that he was selling marijuana to finance his habit; his grades were hopeless. But hanging around Dyersburg just for his sake, probably becoming more like him anyway, with nothing to do, was out of the question.

The Baton Rouge apartment Judy chose for her and lavishly furnished was not what Vivian had had in mind for her new life. She had envisioned herself as entering a sort of bohemian-intellectual phase, with rock and Delta blues playing and Faulkner on the bookshelves and new kinds of friends. Instead the place was new and so luxurious, with two bedrooms, picture windows, and vaulted ceilings, that in an odd sort of way it was as if she had never left home—as if her family and Dyersburg itself were just beyond the door or closer than that, inside her head. Other than registering for classes, choosing courses more or less at random, she hardly left the apartment for the first couple of weeks and as seldom as possible after that.

Maybe she should find a roommate, she considered, but did nothing about it. She did not know what was the matter with her, and she started drinking alone. Rush week came, her best opportunity to meet new people, but she sleepwalked through it. Her indifference or whatever it was must have showed; she was rejected by every sorority.

By November she was barely attending classes and was sinking deeper into boozy depression. She took off one night on a spin and wrecked her car against a tree. Her parents replaced the totaled sports car with a new Pontiac Grand Prix, accepting Vivian's assurances that it was just an accident and that she was adjusting nicely. In fooling them, she experienced a mixture of pleasure and guilt. Such emotion as she felt about anything was made up mostly of anger, but she could not figure out where that was coming from. Didn't she have everything she wanted? Had she come this far only to fail? The idea of complete and utter failure began to seem perversely attractive.

That Christmas vacation she managed to conceal her condition from her parents, who weren't asking many questions anyway. She realized how lucky she was when she talked to Brenda, who was working construction on a bridge for the highway department and whose only hope was marriage, but somehow Vivian didn't care.

It took another year and the help of a sympathetic academic guidance counselor before Vivian began to emerge from her funk. By the spring term of her sophomore year, she had compiled a cumulative D+ average and was prepared to be expelled. But her adviser, Kathleen Marshall, saw that Vivian's problems were emotional rather than intellectual. From talking to her and getting an earful about her background, Marshall told Vivian that she had gone away to college for no reason other than to leave home, even to defy her parents, who had ended up supporting her anyway, which canceled out any motive she might have had for striving to succeed. In high school she had accomplished all that she had for the flimsiest of reasons, to prove herself to her parents or even to defy them. Now she had no reason to do anything. Her best hope lay in a highly structured academic environment that would offer a new challenge. When Vivian said that her favorite courses had always been history and science, Marshall suggested that she enroll in Professor Douglas Owsley's "Introduction to Physical Anthropology," a notoriously difficult course that required frequent factual examinations, laboratory work, and a lengthy term project.

Professor Owsley's kindly but serious demeanor and his high standards struck just the right chord in Vivian. She quit drinking, except for the casual beer, stopped smoking pot, and began to enjoy the company of other students. The professor's own specialty was forensic anthropology, to which he often alluded in lectures, and Vivian found herself strongly attracted to this field. With its blend of anatomy, physiology, pathology, biology, chemistry, and cultural history, forensic anthropology seemed to provide Vivian with a way of looking at life and at humanity that was both stimulating and satisfying to her. If it was by definition a morbid sort of science, it also gave significance to even the most obscure, anonymous lives. In death, she saw, everyone was equal yet experienced his or her moment of drama, as revealed by the scientist.

On field trips that extended into the summer, Vivian joined Owsley's research team, which included students from other universities among its twenty members, at a dig in New Orleans. Construction along Canal Street had uncovered the cemetery of the city's antebellum charity hospital. Most of the bones Vivian and her colleagues dug up and examined in the lab proved to be African in origin, those of slaves. Identifying them, Vivian felt as if she were bringing the dead to life.

She became a fierce opponent of cremation. To burn bones to ashes, she believed, was to deny identity to the nobodies of this world, whose bones alone could speak for them. She imagined that one day someone like Professor Owsley might dig her up and be able to say, at least, that this was a woman.

She did wonder if her fear of oblivion and identification with the dead were unnatural, but what did that matter, if she had found what she wanted to do? When she applied for and received a grant to examine the site of an Indian massacre in Oklahoma with Professor Owsley and his team during the Christmas break, she decided that this must be her destiny. She would earn a doctorate in anthropology, specializing in forensics at the University of Tennessee, which happened to have the most highly regarded graduate program in the field.

She worried, however, about the coming holidays. The field trip would begin just after New Year's, but she did not want to risk spending the holidays in Dyersburg, which when she thought about it now, after the progress she had made, appeared to her as a kind of family crypt. When she called home these days, she heard nothing but one tale of woe after another, the latest being that Brad had been arrested for possession of marijuana with intent to sell. Rather than phoning again, to achieve more distance she wrote to her parents saying that she hoped they understood that she would not be home this year for Christmas, so she could get to Oklahoma early to begin her work there.

Her parents said no. Skeptical of her supposed new stability, they gave her a choice, either to come home for the holidays or to forget about returning to L.S.U., unless she could turn her skill and getting this grant, whatever it was for, into paying for the rest of her education herself. How were they to know, given her past performance, that this field trip wasn't an excuse for some romp?

She could hardly blame them for doubting her, frustrating though it was not to be believed. She had not been home for a year; if she told them that she was now earning A's again, they would doubt her until she could show them the transcript. She would have to spend Christmas in Dyersburg.

She headed for home with great reluctance, lingering to say good-bye to Professor Owsley and her new friends, dawdling around her apartment.

She pulled into the driveway on Lake Road in the middle of the night and went straight to bed, but she did not get much sleep.

The holiday atmosphere at home was not a festive one. A judge had reduced the charges against Brad to simple possession but ordered him committed to a six-week rehabilitation program at a local clinic, beginning in January. Brad was responding to that prospect by staying stoned. No one was in the mood to hear about Vivian's academic successes and plans. When she attempted to explain the importance of paleopathology to her parents, they responded as if she were putting on airs, showing them up, parading her so-called intellectual superiority before the rest of the family. What was this nonsense about her taking off to go dig for bones in some desert? Did she expect to support herself for the rest of her life that way? Her mother suggested that she enroll in nursing school before it was too late.

Her parents' preoccupation with dwindling finances had become acute. Vivian herself began to wonder whether it was fair for them to continue to pay her way through L.S.U. when her father was having to sell off more land, Judy was talking about having to go to work, Brad was headed for an expensive rehab, and the general feeling within the family was that of dissolution. No one expected help from poor Adair, who by now was working at Wal-Mart; Donna was setting the practical, female example by getting married and planning to raise her own family. Only Vivian had such grand ideas, which, within days of her return, seemed rather egotistical to her, or did some of the time—the pursuit of dreams at others' expense. What right did she have to set herself apart? Was she really that sure of herself, to ask for what no one else was receiving? She fought against this judgment, remembering what Professor Owsley had said at their last meeting, that she had talent for the work and a fine career ahead of her, if she would stick with it.

At least she was financing the field trip herself. She tried to concentrate on that, and she stayed away from the house as much as possible. Doing so, however, meant hanging around with old friends who were interested mainly in drinking and smoking dope and whose low horizons could not encompass ambitions such as Vivian's. Away from the teachers and students who thought of a future, not day-to-day, she fell too easily into old grooves, the desire to please and impress people according to their standards or the lack of them.

By New Year's, as she prepared in a desultory way to leave, having given up trying to explain what this field trip was about, she felt, weirdly, as disconnected from her new life as from the old; and she had lapsed into drink and pot, was more wasted than she had been in a year. As soon as she was back at work, she kept telling herself, she would clean up her act and pick up where she had left off, away from this hometown miasma.

On January 2, 1987, she threw her bags into her car. She had planned an early start but was so hung over that it was afternoon before she drove away. Some inexplicable lethargy weighed on her; she experienced less the thrill of escape than the sense that she was being banished to some unknown, foreign land. There were no farewells for her.

Leaving town, she started crying, convinced that no matter what choice she was making, it must be wrong, but that she had to make it anyway. On her way out she passed the former site of the House of Fashion, painful memories there, and hurried through Courthouse Square, past familiar liquor stores, the old fish shop, Dixie Auto Sales—and on toward Memphis.

In less than two hours she would reach I-40 and head west over the Mississippi, continue on through Arkansas, and arrive at the campus of the University of Oklahoma, where everyone would rendezvous. With her late start she would not make it before midnight. The journey seemed a long one. She never made it.

On the outskirts of Dyersburg, not fifteen minutes from home, she lost control of her car at about eighty miles an hour and rolled into a ditch. When she came to, a state trooper was trying to drag her out of the wreck. He asked her if she was all right, and she found that she could not speak, her jaw hurt so much.

For her parents, this crash was the last straw. There was no longer any question of her going back to college, not with this new wreck and the way she had carried on through the holidays. As soon as she recovered from her injuries, they insisted that she enter the drug and alcohol rehabilitation clinic, where she began her stay just as Brad completed his. She had no will to protest. A judgment had come down against her, maybe from God, that she had failed and was after all no different from anyone else. By the time she was released, the college term was half-gone, the field trip a long-lost chance. She wrote to Professor Owsley explaining what had happened but found she could not explain it and was too ashamed to try. She tore the letter up.

In the months that followed, Vivian's hope of someday returning to the university did not die, but it flickered within her, and she kept quiet about it. Eventually she did work up the courage to write to Professor Owsley, who urged her to return; and she enrolled in a couple of courses at Dyersburg State Community College, so she could at least accumulate credits toward a degree. Step by step, however, she reentangled herself in the life she had failed to escape. Her mother, who saw that the rehab program had not had much effect, asked her to leave the house. Vivian moved in with friends. She found various office jobs and then, by early 1988, was working as a barmaid and waitress at Chequers, a downtown hangout for the young. Although it was not a particularly rowdy place, Judy Forsythe expressed mortification when she learned that Vivian was dating a man she had met there.

His name was Charles "Butch" Archie. He was thirty-five, divorced, and he said that he was the owner of a large boat dock at Reelfoot Lake, the principal recreation spot in western Tennessee, about twenty-five miles north of Dyersburg in Lake and Obion counties. Vivian found herself attracted to Butch's outdoorsy good looks and his irreverent redneck humor. He started visiting Chequers nearly every night, once he and Vivian got to chatting. He would put away an impressive number of beers and play pool with her after hours. *If I am going to live in Dyersburg,* she mused to herself, *maybe for the rest of my life, a guy like Butch seems like the best of it.*

Soon they were heading into the night together in his pickup. If Butch was not exactly complicated, he was fun. Maybe it was possible after all, she told herself on a speedboat ride or in bed with him, to recapture something like the freedom she remembered from high school, or thought she did. At other moments she feared that she had drifted into not giving a damn, or wondered how much her mother's disapproval added to Butch's appeal. Whatever, after a few weeks she tired of worrying. They began talking about what it might be like to get married. She did most of that talking, she remembered later.

That May she realized she was pregnant. Again she told her mother. To get a reaction? Probably, Vivian thought. Judy strongly advised abortion again, but this time Vivian refused. Even when Butch denied being the father, Vivian insisted that she would not go through another abortion and would raise the child herself, if it came to that. On the Fourth of July, Butch relented, acknowledging paternity and offering to marry her. They moved in together. That October they became husband and wife in a civil ceremony performed by their next-door neighbor, an optometrist who, as B.A. once had been, was also a county commissioner invested with the authority to conduct the rite.

Vivian asked herself whether semiconsciously she had wanted to become pregnant. She had been taking birth control pills, but her state of mind, together with her drinking and pot smoking, made it unlikely that she would have noticed having missed a day here and there. She did not believe that she had done it to trick Butch but perhaps had wanted a baby to force a change in her life and to have something of her own to love. Hardly mature behavior, she knew, but so be it. To her, with all the problems it created, the pregnancy came as a blessed relief. She stopped drinking alcohol or taking drugs of any kind. She had a reason to live, she thought.

On January 13, 1989, Vivian gave birth to a girl, whom she named Rhiana Ashley. Vivian and Butch had disagreed over the first name. She had wanted to call her Rhiannon, after a Fleetwood Mac recording, a ballad Vivian loved sung by Stevie Nicks, about a powerful, mysterious woman. Rhiannon was the eternal feminine, the sum of all desires who eludes every man who tries to win her, a kind of psychedelic Lorelei. Butch thought the full name too weird, so they settled on the shortened version—and ended up calling the child Ashley, after that romantic Southerner the fictional Ashley Wilkes of *Gone With the Wind,* also Vivian's idea.

To escape the disapproving Forsythes, the Archies moved to Memphis, where Vivian found a job auditing accounts for a cardiologist, while Butch stayed home to care for the baby, more or less, and supposedly looked for a job. Vivian soon discovered that while he technically still owned the boat dock, its income went to creditors. When Vivian came home from work, Butch usually went out, supposedly to meet with his buddies. Vivian soon suspected him of cheating on her; they quarreled violently.

Vivian accused Butch of idleness and infidelity; he blamed her for tricking him into marriage. In the evenings at home alone with Ashley, Vivian wondered if she had again done something, like crashing her car the last time, to prove that her parents were right about her.

And soon she was on the phone to Judy with stories of depression and abuse. Hearing Judy say I told you so seemed just enough punishment; and yet, hearing that, she continued to believe that somehow she loved Butch, or could not admit her mistake, or was bound to him for powerful reasons beyond her understanding, such as that she deserved that punishment, too.

Their first anniversary came and went without celebration. Vivian told her parents she was giving up. On a Saturday afternoon when Butch was out, her parents drove to Memphis with a U-Haul trailer and took mother and child back to Dyersburg with their few belongings.

This reconciliation with her family only reinforced her sense of failure. Where was she to go from here? Had she only married Butch to make her parents rescue her? The thought did occur to her. Once back at home, she missed him as much as she resented him for his laziness and infidelity. Weeks passed; she kept putting off filing for divorce.

As another Christmas approached, Judy, alarmed by Vivian's inability to end her marriage, her listlessness, what appeared to be her clinical depression as she did little but sleep and dote on the baby, argued that some sort of intense therapy was in order. In Judy's view, Vivian was allowing herself to remain emotionally dependent on Butch, in the face of his utter irresponsibility.

Judy made inquiries among Dyersburg therapists and decided that Vivian needed help from the Crossroads Clinic in Chattanooga, which specialized in a popular theory called "codependency," offering therapy based on the hypothesis that patients could be weaned from neurotic attachments in which both people in a relationship fed destructively on one another. In her case, Vivian thought, the theory did not add up, since she might be neurotically attached to Butch, but he did not seem to give much of a damn about her. She was reluctant to separate herself for that long from Ashley, but she agreed to commit herself to a month's intensive treatment that would combine group therapy and one-on-one sessions with clinicians.

At Crossroads a different picture of her problems emerged for her, however, one that merged with her memory of what her counselor at L.S.U. had told her. Encouraged by her therapists, Vivian began to see that her emotional dependency was not on Butch but on her parents, especially her mother. So close was the emotional bond, for good and ill, between mother and daughter that Vivian was making virtually every decision in her life based on whether it would please or offend Judy—or so Vivian came to believe. She also concluded that her mother encouraged this dependency, at the same time that it was up to Vivian, somehow, to overcome it.

"You're telling me I need to grow up," she said to one of her doctors, who did not disagree with that blunt assessment. Unfortunately, Vivian was once again economically dependent on her parents. Until she managed to extricate herself from that bondage, the emotional tug of war with Judy would continue. Vivian saw more clearly and bleakly than ever what a price she was paying for leaving school—and how that, probably even the way in which she had managed to sabotage her field trip, had been yet another way to demand her mother's attention.

It was in the Crossroads scheme of treatment for the "client" to confront his or her codependent. When B.A. and Judy arrived at the clinic to take Vivian home, they agreed to participate in a final session with her and two therapists. The hour began calmly enough, with Vivian outlining what she believed she had learned about herself and her family. When she characterized herself as emotionally immature, her parents were happy to agree with her. The mood changed, however, when one of the therapists suggested that Vivian air any grievances she might be harboring.

Presumably that sort of invitation would be welcomed by many a

daughter with an imperfect mother, and as for Vivian, she tore into Judy
with the fury of an Electra. As her father looked on in silence—no one
could have guessed what B.A. was thinking, other than of the exit—
Vivian ran down a shocking list of accusations against her mother, which
Judy with equal vehemence denied, professing bewilderment at her
daughter's interpretation of events.

It was a trial with no judge, the plaintiff accusing, the defendant denying, the jury nowhere to be seen.

"You're telling me I'm lying?" Vivian asked. "You're the one who lies!
You've lied to all of us! I tell the truth, even if it hurts!"

In keeping with their professional roles, the therapists took no side in
this dispute. Neither did B.A. say anything, other than to comfort Judy.
When she saw how old and tired her father looked—he was still recovering from a stroke he had suffered some weeks before—Vivian relented.
She did not apologize, but said that perhaps there were some things best
forgotten, or at least forgiven.

Vivian, back at home again, went to work at a chiropractor's office, vow-
ing to save enough to move to her own apartment with Ashley. In March
1990, she filed for divorce; and in June, Chancery Court Judge David W.
Lanier heard the case.

Judge Lanier divided the couple's debts equally between them and set
strict guidelines for the father's visitation rights with the child. In the
words of his decree, the judge found that Mr. Archie had engaged in
"inappropriate marital conduct," without specifying what that was, and
directed that he be permitted to see Ashley only in Vivian's presence. He
also awarded Vivian child support, although a minimal amount in view of
Butch's current lack of income. She did not expect to receive much even
of that.

Shortly after the divorce hearing, Vivian collapsed at work with
abdominal pains. She was rushed to the hospital and operated on for the
removal of a burst ovarian cyst. Recovery would take ten weeks, the surgeon advised.

By the sixth week of her recuperation at home, Vivian's father began to
nag her about going back to work. He complained that she was accom-
plishing nothing by lolling around the house and ought to be getting on
with her life. He was getting old. He might die soon, he said, and then
what would happen to her and Ashley when he was no longer around to
support them? As it was, Judy would soon have to go to work just to keep
the premiums on his life insurance current. He had already sold off nearly
all of his farmland.

With a couple of glasses of whiskey, B.A.'s admonitions, which Vivian already took seriously, escalated to attacks, as he sat in his chair, flushed and frail, flailing the air with his stick. She was lazy and no good, he told her, the greatest disappointment of his life. Did she think the world owed her a living?

Weak from her operation, Vivian began job hunting again.

4

Vivian had already spent several days, early that September of 1990, showing her résumé to various attorneys and office managers when she met her old friend Brenda Castain for a drink at Chequers. Vivian had not visited the place for more than two years, since she had stopped drinking at the beginning of her pregnancy. These days she was still being careful with alcohol, avoided marijuana or any other drugs, and had kept away from Chequers because of its associations with Butch. Now, as she entered that dark, familiar place, she realized she had missed it, the long varnished bar and the shot-up highway signs and antique beer and whiskey posters, the smoky mirrors, the jukebox stocked with country and blues—current and old favorites, B. B. King, "Poke Salad Annie," the kind of music that made her happy when nothing else could. It was the only place in or near Dyersburg where you could meet for drinks without descending to honky-tonk: Chequers was more like a college bar, a place to get loose but short of blood and guts.

Its location, directly across from the courthouse, meant that customers on any given night would include legal secretaries, maybe a young lawyer or two, and working people of all kinds, just about anyone who wasn't a hardshell Baptist.

Brenda, who was still, and it was not only Vivian's opinion, possibly the most beautiful young woman in the county, had already ordered a pitcher of margaritas and two glasses. With her light mocha, satiny skin and round dark eyes and wonderful figure, she was certainly the most exotically attractive, with a family background that was unusual in that region. Her real parents, whom she had never seen, were from Latin America, she was not sure exactly where. Her adoptive mother had raised her, after that father had run off. She and Vivian had become close partly because Brenda, too, was a rebel, who believed that her mother had pressured her to use her good looks to ingratiate herself with the well-to-do.

Brenda was married now, with a son about Ashley's age. Her husband had a well-paying, managerial-level job with one of the several big industrial plants that had located in and around Dyersburg since the early eighties; but he required his wife to bring in extra money and was pleased that Brenda had landed a job with Judge David Lanier, who was known as the most powerful figure in Dyer County and a man of great influence throughout western Tennessee. Her position was a humble one, file clerk in the Dyer County Juvenile Court, over which Lanier, as chancery judge, had jurisdiction. But to her, as to all the women who worked at courthouse jobs, it was superior to just about any other kind of employment she could get in Dyersburg. It was certainly an improvement over what she had done to survive between high school and marriage—including construction work on a bridge near Chic that had washed out weeks after completion, a fiasco that greatly pleased and amused Vivian. And Brenda had recently applied to Judge Lanier for promotion to probation officer, which would be more interesting as well as more highly paid.

"You've got it made, Brenda," Vivian told her, "a job, a husband, security."

"The pay's lousy and the marriage isn't so great, either," Brenda said. "And Lanier can fire me anytime."

"Come on, look at me. God, have I screwed up!"

Vivian explained that she was trying to find a job with flexible hours, so she would not have to leave Ashley in day care all day long. But she was about to give up on that. It would probably mean letting her mother take care of Ashley part of the time.

"I'm a wreck," Vivian said. "My dad's given me notice. I don't blame him."

Brenda took a bottle of Valium from her purse and offered Vivian one. She took it, washing it down with her drink.

"I've got to find a way to go back to college," Vivian said. "I'll do it. I just need to get on my feet and get certain things behind me."

"You'll find a way if anyone can," Brenda said.

"Dr. Owsley wrote me, did I tell you? Remember my professor I told you about? He still believes in me."

"Why wouldn't he? Everybody still does."

"You must be kidding. Sure. Supergirl, broke with a kid and nowhere to go. I guess I'll take any job I can get."

"You wouldn't work in a plant. Not Vivian!"

"You don't know the way it is with me. I'll do anything."

"Well, what about working for Lanier?"

"He has an opening?"

"His secretary just quit."

"Why?"

"Who knows? Maybe she was fired. You could apply. Hey, if I get my promotion, we'd be working together! Probation officers have to report to the judge all the time."

Vivian was strongly tempted. Her mother and the housekeeper would have to take care of Ashley during the day, it was true, but maybe Donna would help out some of the time. At the moment there did not seem to be any other decent openings. She had meant it when she said that she would take anything, but a factory job was a pretty depressing prospect. You did not even need a high school diploma for many of the positions at Dyersburg Fabrics or Colonial Rubber or the World Color printing plant. For a woman without a college degree, even for one with some college, like Vivian, landing something at the courthouse was the best you could do, as Brenda reminded her. You could look nice, dress up for work; you were around professional people; the courthouse was the center of activity in Dyersburg; it was a chance to meet someone, maybe. What else could a woman do in their town? Ask for a loan to start a business? Out of the question.

"I can't even get a credit card without my husband's signature," Brenda said.

Vivian was well aware of all that. A woman could not even afford to get sick. When she had become ill this past summer, she had lost her job. The chiropractor had hired someone else the minute he found out that Vivian would be away for weeks after her operation.

"You think Lanier would hire me?" Vivian asked. "I did go to L.S.U. I'm a good secretary—"

"Come on, Vivian. Everybody knows you can do anything you want. Besides, you're pretty."

"Oh, yeah? I am? So what does that have to do with it? Oh, no, don't tell me. He's one of those, isn't he?"

The voices of the two women counterpointed, Vivian's a surge, a flood, Brenda's molasses-slow, so Southern.

"Let's say it's a big plus you're not a dog," Brenda said, pronouncing the last word "dawgh."

"You're trying to tell me something."

"Judge Lanier is a lech," Brenda said. "Everybody knows that. He fools around on his wife. He's a grabber."

"Oh, Christ. Did I ever have a job where some creep wasn't trying to put the make on me? Oh, well."

"He's a little more obvious than most. Everybody knows it."

"I didn't," Vivian said.

Brenda described how Lanier behaved with her. He was always patting her on the fanny and hugging her and nuzzling up to her like some big old jackass. He had even chased her around the table in her office once or twice.

"Give me a break!" Vivian said. "How do you handle that?"

"It's not so bad. I've learned to avoid being alone with him, is all." It was a bizarre situation, Brenda went on, considering how old and fat Lanier was, but she could handle it, and if she could, Vivian certainly could, too. He was more of a pain in the butt than anything else. And he did have his good points. He hardly ever raised his voice. He was pleasant to most people. His come-ons were more or less just a game, she thought. She had noticed that he tried to get his paws on other women, too. Everybody just had to put up with it. Probably he didn't even know what he was doing.

Vivian was surprised to hear this about David Lanier. She had known him and his family very well, she had thought, since childhood. The Forsythes shared a common stretch of green with the Laniers, a rolling, parklike expanse of maybe a hundred yards that joined their properties at the rear. She could remember skipping out the back door and over to the Laniers' for a dip in their swimming pool and hanging around with the Lanier girls at the country club. Leigh Anne, the older daughter, had been a cheerleader for the Dyersburg High Trojans when Vivian played basketball; the younger one, Robbye, had been friends with Brad for years.

Vivian recalled those summer afternoons at the Laniers' as idyllic—doing cannonballs into the pool, Mrs. Lanier, whom she remembered as a sweet woman, bringing out iced tea and sandwiches. Brenda had been there some times, too.

"Didn't Leigh Anne get you your job with her dad?" Vivian asked.

"She told me about it. She recommended me to him. She doesn't know how her father acts when she's not around."

"It would kill her," Vivian said. "Imagine having your father go after your friends. It's sad. Poor Leigh Anne, I feel sorry for her. Let's hear some music."

When Vivian told her parents about the courthouse opening, they were enthusiastic. B.A. was a longtime supporter of David Lanier, contributing substantially to his political campaigns over the past twenty or so years, from back in the days when the judge had been mayor of Dyersburg for seven consecutive terms. She decided to apply for the job.

As for Lanier's lusting after women, Vivian did not mention that to her parents, who would have dismissed it as idle gossip anyway. Besides, Brenda Castain might not be the most reliable source. She had a drug problem, as everyone except her husband seemed to know, and she may well have been exaggerating. Even if everything she had said was true, it sounded fairly harmless. Vivian imagined that Lanier, who was somewhere in his mid-fifties, was probably going through some sort of midlife crisis. He could easily have flipped over Brenda, who would tempt any man. That's what happened when you had movie-star looks. With Brenda around, Vivian figured, Lanier wouldn't be giving her a second glance.

She revised her résumé, adding a paragraph about her interest in forensic anthropology to impress the judge, and brought it down to the courthouse.

She knew from her divorce hearing where Judge Lanier's offices were on the first floor and was glad to be entering the building under different circumstances. It was a pleasing old red brick structure that dominated downtown with its tall entrances and graceful, fluted Ionic columns on all four sides. In its present form the courthouse had stood there since 1912, defining Dyersburg.

Judge Lanier was in court that morning. With no secretary on duty, his offices were locked. Vivian slipped her papers under the door.

5

A few days went by without Vivian's hearing anything from Judge Lanier. Assuming that her résumé must have been misplaced, she ran off another copy and returned to the courthouse to present it to him in person this time. The bell in the cupola atop the building tolled four as she climbed the steps of the west entrance; she was hoping to catch the judge as he left court or to wait for him until he was free.

Anxious to appear professional and businesslike, she was wearing a navy blazer, a gray pleated skirt, and low-heeled navy pumps, and she had had her hair trimmed slightly shorter than usual, just above shoulder length. She was somewhat more nervous than she had been the first time, because in the interim her parents had impressed on her what a powerful man Judge Lanier was, along with his brother, James O. Lanier, who only this past month had been elected District Attorney General for Dyer and Lake counties. According to B.A., the brothers, who were heirs to a political dynasty founded by their father in the 1930s, had feuded for years but between them more or less ruled the region, with close ties to the governor's mansion and the legislature in Nashville and to Tennessee senators and representatives in Washington. They controlled jobs, licensing, and civil and criminal matters of all kinds, and with both of them now in office, a person could find himself prosecuted by the one Lanier and tried, convicted, and sentenced by the other. No wonder B.A. and Judy liked the idea of Vivian's working for the judge.

The door was locked again, and his first-floor courtroom was also deserted. From a pay phone Vivian reached Brenda Castain at her office, which was in a different building a block off Courthouse Square. Brenda advised her to knock on the door of Lanier's chambers, where he was probably working alone. Vivian need not worry about disturbing him, Brenda said.

As Brenda instructed, Vivian found her way through the silent, high-ceilinged corridors to a door marked JUDGE'S CHAMBERS near the north entrance. She took notice of a large oil portrait hanging on the wall opposite the door. Framed in gilt, it was labeled JAMES P. LANIER, the judge's father, as B.A. had mentioned, dead now but still something of a local legend.

She knocked. Judge Lanier himself opened the door.

"Why, Vivian," he said, smiling. "What can I do for you?"

She had forgotten how big he was, at least six-two and quite overweight; his light brown, graying hair, swept up off his forehead into a feathery pompadour, added another inch or so to his height. His face was large, jowly and soft-looking. He was wearing his black judicial robe over a suit, with the jacket open to allow for his girth. Vivian, who was five-six, felt tiny.

"I hope you don't mind, Judge Lanier. I'd like to apply for a job."

He ushered her in. The room was small and dark, windowless, made cramped by a large, polished desk and bookshelves and straight chairs along the walls. He closed the hallway door. Another closed door across the room must lead, Vivian presumed, to the outer offices where she would work if she landed the job. Lanier, smoothing his robe behind him, seated himself in the big swivel chair behind his desk and gestured for her to take the armchair opposite him. Evidently she was to be granted a formal interview on the spot.

"It's nice to see you," Lanier said. "How are you getting on?"

Vivian handed her résumé across to him, saying that she had heard he had an opening for a secretary. Was there an application she needed to fill out? She'd like to do that.

"Why don't you fill it out right now?" the judge said, reaching into his desk and holding out a form. "Do you need a pen? It's an easy thing, very straightforward, no strain at all for you, I'm sure." His voice was mild, casual, not overly friendly but not intimidating, either. It was even, inflectionless, a single drawn-out note in the tenor clef, soothing in its way. His movements, too, were slowly drawn, as if hours were passing and everything were under control. Vivian's nerves subsided somewhat.

She completed the form quickly, the only sound the rustling of her papers as the judge thumbed through them, saying nothing. She glanced up once and caught him looking at her with his pale, deep-set eyes, and he smiled. Only that smile disconcerted her slightly, bringing to her mind for some unfathomable reason the image of a smirking Buddha.

"I guess you can see I've held secretary's jobs before. What I'm really interested in is forensics, you know? You can see, I studied forensic anthropology at L.S.U. One summer, it was fascinating, I—"

"It looks all right to me," he said, putting aside the résumé and staring at her with that grin.

Vivian noticed on the otherwise clean desk a lone color photograph framed in freestanding Lucite. It depicted four cheerleaders in miniskirts, and she recognized the girls from high school, one of them Leigh Anne Lanier, blonde and cute.

"How is Leigh Anne?" she asked. "I haven't seen her lately. I hear she's married and has a new baby. Does she still have that Mexican restaurant?"

"No," Lanier said. "They had to give that up. She's staying home with the baby now. We're trying to get a new restaurant started. I like Mexican food, don't you? I bet you like spicy food."

"Sure," Vivian said. "It's great. Nothing like a margarita," she laughed and regretted it, remembering having heard that David Lanier did not drink. She had the sense that it was time to go. "Well, thank you for considering my application. I think I could do a good job, I really do." She started to rise.

"Sit down a minute," the judge said, and Vivian obeyed. "There are matters I want to discuss with you. How are you getting along with your father?"

The question stunned her. She could only say, "Fine."

"Is that so?" he asked, still in that mild, even tone. "Because B.A. has been by to see me."

"He has? Why?"

"About you. He's very worried about you. He and your mother are concerned about you and your little girl, what's her name?"

"Ashley."

"Ashley, that's right. The concern is, Vivian, that you're not a very good mother."

"My father said that?"

"Tell me, do you have a boyfriend? Are you dating Bobby Coffey?"

"I have been out with him, yes."

"Do you think that's a very good idea, a young mother?"

"I don't know. I—"

"Your father is very concerned. How you're conducting yourself. I want to be frank with you. Your father told me that he and your mother were thinking about asking for custody of Ashley. I don't mean to upset you, but that's what your father said. He discussed it with me. On a hypothetical basis, of course. You know, B.A. and I have known each other a long time."

"I know. I don't understand. Give me a second to think."

"For the good of the child, I am sure he was thinking."

Vivian looked down at her hands, which had begun to sweat, and felt her collar sticking to the back of her neck. Ashley! Her father was talking about taking Ashley from her? What should she do? What did this mean, that her parents were planning to kick her out and keep Ashley at home? Would she end up working for Judge Lanier with Ashley taken away from her? Her father couldn't have meant that. Why had he gone behind her back, encouraged her to see the judge while stabbing her in the back?

Maybe her father was waiting to see whether she could land this job. Maybe everything depended on that. The person with the power to decide whether she could keep Ashley was sitting across that desk from her. Surely Judge Lanier would not take Ashley away! He must be warning her, to help her, that was it. She had to keep control of her emotions, that was the main thing. If her parents thought that she was incompetent, now was not the time to prove it.

"Judge Lanier," the words spilled out spontaneously in a voice that she could hear was cracking and shaking, "you wouldn't take Ashley away from me, would you? You wouldn't take my child? I know I haven't been perfect. But Ashley is my life!"

"Of course I can't discuss anything like that," the judge said. "I've only told you that your father came to me. There are laws. I am here to uphold the laws. I can't talk about this further. I cannot say anything about a case that might be before my court. I am the judge, and I hear cases, as the judge."

It took every effort not to burst into sobs, but there was no use pretending that she wasn't humiliated and wounded and frightened. She sat there with one hand over her face, the other gripping an elbow, slumped and hunched over. But at least she could keep herself from crying the way she always did, the way women were ridiculed for doing, losing control of their emotions.

"I still want the job," she managed to say into her hand. "I do hope you'll consider me, Judge Lanier. I know I could do good work for you."

"I am very sorry," Lanier said, "but you see, as it turns out, the secretary's job isn't open any longer." He let that sink in. "I don't know why you thought it was open. You were misinformed, it seems. I've promised it to another girl, a friend of . . ." and he named a local attorney.

Vivian felt that she had made a fool of herself. And why had he let her complete the application? So he could mark time until he could tell her what her parents thought of her? All she could feel was defeated.

"I'm going to be filling the position in a day or two. I am glad you came to see me, though," he said, tapping her application with a fingertip. "You should come see me again, anytime."

"Please keep me in mind," Vivian managed to say weakly. "I really do want to work."

She raised her head to gaze on that impassive, still oddly smiling face. He was leaning back in his chair against the wall, his left hand resting casually atop the knob of a third, narrow door, possibly to a closet. Her view was of the pillowy patch of flesh beneath his chin. She wanted to tell him about how hard she could work and how she could do just about anything from typing to using a computer to keeping accounts to driving a tractor, for that matter. But it was no use. He did not care to listen, she could tell. How awful it was, having no money. No one gave a damn about you.

"I would do anything for a job," she blurted, the tears starting. "I so much want to work! Honest I do, no matter what anyone thinks. I'd be a floor sweeper if I had to!" She burned with self-loathing, humiliated in her naked, obsequious pleading.

Sensing that she was about to lose her composure altogether and that this interview or whatever it was had ended, Vivian got to her feet, extended her hand across the desk, and thanked the judge for his time. At least she could manage a businesslike retreat. She was dying for some air. This somber, crowded room had become a dungeon.

He stood and took her hand in his, saying nothing. She withdrew her hand, or tried to. He held on to it, firmly. She pulled back again, thinking that he was trying to say something to her, a wordless gesture of reassurance, maybe, that he would never take Ashley from her? But when she pulled again and he would not let go, his smile vanished, his eyes so cold, she felt panic rising and tried to jerk free.

With his hand gripping hers up to the wrist, he snapped her arm to whip her around the corner of the desk, which jabbed her hip as she spun. In an instant he held her against him, grabbing her hair with his other hand and lifting her up to crush her mouth against his. She tried to twist her face away but could not, with his fist full of her hair, yanking at her when she moved, his right arm around her waist now, squeezing and dangling her off the floor.

Inching around, bracing his butt against the desk, he opened his legs and forced her up against his crotch, rolling her this way and that against himself. Her face free for a second, she cried out, "No, no!" but, wrapping his arms around her in a savage embrace, he hugged her with force enough to collapse her lungs, while he muttered, "No one can hear you, no one, no one."

Standing up, he lifted her by the elbows, wheeled with her, and slammed her down into a straight chair, cracking her head against the wall. Dazed, terrified, she saw him looming over her. He fumbled his robe aside and quickly unzipped himself and sprang his erect penis free. He jiggled it at her and moved it toward her face and, when she tried to turn aside, grabbed her hair again, pulling at it so hard she could hear the roots give way. He forced himself at her mouth, battering at her with it. She clenched her teeth and tightened her lips.

His thumbs went to the hinges of her jaw and pressed, his other fingers at her neck, holding her rigid. The pain was unspeakable, her jaw hurt so, as he pressed and pressed at both sides, harder and harder until her mouth came wide open and he was in her with his penis, poking, his pelvis working back and forth, thrusting it farther in, her head against the wall, back and forth until he was at the back of her throat and she was gagging as he stabbed, never letting up with his thumbs. She heard him moan and felt him spurt.

"You can use my bathroom if you like," he said, straightening himself, pointing to the door behind the desk. "You'd better. You're a mess."

She lurched into the bathroom. She took the soap, stuck it in her mouth to try to cleanse the filth, and rinsed out her mouth, trying not to look in the mirror, and splashed water on her face. *What has happened? How?* That was all she could think. She felt so dirty. *I have to get out of here.*

Hesitating, letting the water run, she considered trying to crawl out the small, frosted window. What if somebody saw her? What would she say? No one would believe her, and she did not want anyone to see her or know.

To leave, she would have to get past him. What if he grabbed her again? It took her a minute or two to get up the nerve. Finally she opened the door.

He was behind his desk, seated right beside her. Holding her breath, she hurried toward the hallway door and grasped it as she heard him say:

"Wait a minute. Let me give you something for your troubles."

Vivian turned her head to see him reach into a back pocket for his wallet.

She bolted, ran down the hall and outside, and stumbled down the courthouse steps. Thank God, no one had seen her. Thank God, she had parked her car near that entrance.

Vivian drove briefly in the direction of home, realized that she could not face her parents or Ashley, turned back in the direction of the courthouse, and took a sharp right at Highway 104. She headed straight west. With the sun in her eyes it was hard to see, but she knew the way blind.

She sped through Finley to the Big Levee Road, so straight and smooth and empty as a runway that she hit ninety all the way to Moss Island Road, where she squealed rubber making a sharp right turn that nearly sent her over the embankment. After that she made her way slowly through cotton fields that were white or a pale, Popsicle orange in the dying afternoon light, the blossoms nearly ready to be picked. She was glad, not exactly to be alive, but to have made it to the bottomlands again.

And then she was really there, at the far southern stretch of the half-slab. She got out of her car and toed the ground, dry and crunchy with silt at this time of year. She walked through the corner of the bean field and climbed the Little Levee to look across Blue Grass Towhead to the river.

She sat down atop the dry levee and talked to herself as she always had, running on like a brook, asking questions of the air and of the low, slow-moving river. She asked God for forgiveness and tried to figure out the meaning of her shame and did her best to banish images of David Lanier from her mind. She had the idea, or the hope, that if she stayed there long enough, what had happened might go away. She talked for a long while, until the sun went down beyond the Arkansas shore.

In the twilight she took off her shoes and made her way down to the river, because she wanted to hear it and feel the mud. She waded in, letting her feet, her ankles get wet, until the water, which was so gentle this time of year, reached halfway up her calves.

I am here where my daddy farmed, she told herself, *so he can protect me even though he couldn't or wouldn't.* She wished she could tell him everything, but knew she never could.

She stopped when the water going south was thigh-deep. All she could think about by that time was Ashley, and the river said to go home.

6

Several weeks later that fall, on a drizzly November afternoon, two FBI agents, one a male veteran and the other a female rookie, pulled into the parking lot of Crockett County High School, a cluster of new brick rectangles rising from the countryside about forty miles southeast of Dyersburg. They had chosen this rendezvous because it was remote yet easy to find, out on Highway 412 in the middle of rolling fields. Already harvested, the cotton plants stretched out brown and spindly and bare except for sparse tufts missed by the picking machines. Loose, dirty clumps of cotton lay wet along the margins of the highway and had drifted into the lot.

It was one o'clock, the students back in class. The agents found a space at the end of a row with a good view of the highway. They waited, their conversation punctuated by windshield wipers and chatter from the scanner.

The woman they wanted to talk to would be coming from Dyersburg, if she showed up. This was the second appointment they had scheduled with her. She had missed the first because, she said, she was afraid of Judge David Lanier. If Lanier found out that she was talking to the FBI, he would fire her and might do worse than that. She needed her job. She did not want trouble. She regretted having complained about him.

It had taken assurances of discretion and a great deal of persuasion over the telephone to convince this woman to reschedule her appointment. She had not been the one who contacted the FBI to begin with: the agents had sought her out on the basis of a tip.

Judge Lanier, along with his brother, District Attorney General James O. Lanier, was under FBI investigation for suspected political corruption.

Allegations had reached the Bureau that the judge was abusing his position by accepting kickbacks and bribes in return for judicial decisions; the recently elected DA had apparently secured thousands of votes by promising to reintroduce illegal gambling to Dyer and Lake counties and had hired a convicted felon as his chief criminal investigator, not a promising sign for vigorous law enforcement. Although the federal investigation was in its preliminary stages, information that this woman might be willing to confide damaging material concerning David Lanier had come from a presumably reliable source. Agents followed up on such tips, even anonymous ones, because about seventy percent of them called for action of some kind. People tended not to contact the FBI for frivolous reasons.

The only reason to have doubted the informant in this instance, who was not a paid snitch and was not bargaining for favors, was that he did have an ax to grind with Judge Lanier, who had fired him from a courthouse job. But you could find someone with a grievance against David or James O. Lanier under every rock in that part of Tennessee. Motives were irrelevant if the informant was telling the truth. That the woman was frightened of the judge enhanced the tipster's credibility.

They waited in the light rain, rubbing at fogging windows to watch for her. By one-thirty they were ready to give up when they saw a car veer into the lot and bounce over a speed bump. Special Agent Jerry Bastin flashed his lights and climbed out to greet the woman. He ushered her into the backseat and introduced his partner, Maryellen Donohue.

She really didn't have anything to say, the woman quickly announced as Bastin switched off the engine. She was beautiful, with her straight black hair pulled back into a chignon, a little damp from the rain. Her voice was soft and her speech was slow, pure northwestern Tennessee, but her looks indicated a strain of Spanish or Mediterranean blood, unusual in the region. She could have been Greek or Italian or Semitic, with luminous amber skin, full lips, and a strong, beveled nose—but there was nothing strong about her manner. She was trembling and having trouble catching her breath. Her big dark eyes looked scared. She clasped and unclasped her hands as she spoke and thrust them in and out of her raincoat pockets.

To give her time to calm down and to take care of the routine, Bastin asked her to spell out her name, Brenda Castain, and to give her date of birth, which made her twenty-five. He took notes on a legal pad.

There had been a misunderstanding, she insisted. She was there only because she was afraid that if she stood the agents up again, they might come looking for her, and Judge Lanier would know. She had only a few minutes to talk. She had to get back to work. If Lanier—

"Tell us why you're so afraid of Judge Lanier," Jerry Bastin said, setting his notes aside and twisting around from behind the wheel. "Has he got something to hide? Why don't you tell us about it?" She cast down her eyes and said nothing. "What kind of a man is David Lanier?"

"Vindictive!" she burst out. And then: "I didn't really mean that. I don't know him. I only work for him. You should ask someone else about him. I wish you would. Please leave me out of this."

"We've heard he's vindictive," Maryellen Donohue said. "You're not the only one who says so. We've already heard a lot about Judge Lanier, Brenda. What you tell us could confirm what we already know."

Agent Donohue, who was Brenda's age, was bluffing. She knew next to nothing about David Lanier, except that he was a political boss, and Agent Bastin knew only a little more than that. This was not their case, Dyer County not their territory. They were filling in for Bill Castleberry, the agent in charge of the Lanier investigation, who had asked them to help out because he was tied up trying to complete a different assignment. Castleberry, who had been gathering information about the Laniers only since September and who had not given priority to this case because of his other obligations, had been able to supply Bastin and Donohue with general background only. At this stage of an investigation, it was a matter of collecting whatever surfaced.

Brenda Castain said nothing, sitting there sighing, looking down at her nervous hands. Yet she no longer seemed anxious to leave. She had said that she could spare only a few minutes; ten or fifteen had already passed. The agents sensed that she wanted to talk and would except for her fear of reprisal. To try to encourage her, Bastin spoke of other cases in which people were reluctant to supply information to the FBI, only to discover that when they did, they were helped. That was what the Bureau was supposed to do, protect innocent people from the rotten ones.

"How long have you worked for Judge Lanier?" he asked.

"Since the first of the year. About eleven months."

"And how long has this trouble been going on?" Bastin knew this much from what Agent Castleberry had told him, that, according to the informant, Brenda Castain had been upset by the judge's sexual advances to her. What this had to do with the focus of the operation, suspected political corruption, was unclear, but Lanier had allegedly been after the woman for months, and she was distressed enough about it to complain to at least one friend. There were some lurid details, but it would not do for the agents to bring them up. Castain was a potential witness against Lanier, not a suspect in any crime. The initiative should come from her. Otherwise the agents could later be accused of trying to put ideas into her head. She had to make the accusations.

Finally she did, in a rush. Her voice breaking, she said that about a month after she had started working as a clerk at the juvenile court, Judge Lanier had begun making suggestive remarks to her and touching her in offensive ways. From the first he had put his arm around her and hugged her. She had not minded that, had thought he was merely being warm and friendly. Then the remarks had started, and the hugs got longer and tighter, and he had begun rubbing up against her and touching her in the wrong places. She could still tolerate that much, but eventually David Lanier had stepped way over the line.

"Like what?" Maryellen Donohue asked softly, one woman to another.

Speaking now primarily to Donohue and looking her in the eyes, Brenda described how the judge had tried to kiss her and had touched her on the bottom and rubbed himself against her breasts. He would start up as soon as he came into her office, leaning over her as she sat at her desk or intercepting her when she tried to busy herself at a filing cabinet. And then it got worse.

Sometimes he would call her into his chambers and shut the door. She tried to avoid that situation, the judge's chambers were so closed off, but he would insist. When she was alone with him, he would pull her down into his lap and shove his hand down her blouse. She would have to struggle to get free. The more she protested, the more it seemed to egg him on. She was afraid that sooner or later, he was going to take the next step.

In fact, he had already gone further. But she could not talk about that, or preferred not to, if the agents didn't mind. It was too embarrassing.

"We've heard everything," Donohue said, "believe me."

"Just last week or the week before, I forget, it was so horrible . . ." Brenda broke down and had to compose herself before going on. Bastin turned to stare at the windshield, sensing that his presence was making this more difficult. "He called me to his chambers. I didn't want to go in. There was no one else around. And he was in there. He was standing beside his desk, believe it or not, with his pants down. And his undershorts down. And he was masturbating. Right in front of me, I couldn't believe it!"

"What did you do?" Donohue asked.

"For a second I just stood there. I mean, it was so disgusting. I was so shocked, I couldn't believe this was happening. And then he asked me to come over to him and, you know."

"He asked what?"

"He said, 'Come help me.' Just like that. 'Come help me.' And he looked up at me. I told him, 'Stop it! Stop it!' And I ran out of there."

"What did he do when you ran?" Bastin asked.

"I don't know. I ran out of the building to my office. I was crying."

"Did you tell anybody about what had happened?" Donohue asked.

"Not then. Only later when I told . . ." and Brenda named the informant. Eventually she had also spoken to an attorney, who was sympathetic but explained that there was nothing he could do for her. He had to appear in Lanier's court frequently, the success of his practice depended on the judge, and with Lanier's brother now district attorney, there was really no practical place to turn. He advised her to keep her distance from the judge.

She had applied for a promotion to probation officer. She would still be working for Lanier, but the job would take her out and around, not as subject to the judge's whims. Unfortunately, it was strictly David Lanier's decision whether or not she would get her promotion. So far, he had not acted on her request. She had gone to him to ask him if he had made up his mind on whom to hire.

"He told me that I knew what I had to do to get the job," Brenda said.

"Meaning sex?" Donohue asked.

"He was very explicit," Brenda said. "You can't imagine. He calls me all the time. He wants to know what I'm doing, what I'm wearing. He calls me several times a day and at night. He says disgusting things. It's horrible when I have to stand there with my husband in the room and I have to listen to that garbage."

"You haven't told your husband?"

"I can't."

"Why not?"

"You don't know him. He'd blame me. Or he wouldn't believe me. He thinks Lanier's God, like everybody else does. All he cares about is that I get this promotion because it'll mean more money."

Bastin wanted to know if she could be sure that it was Judge Lanier who was making what she described as obscene calls. Brenda said that she could not prove it, the voice was muffled and strange, but who else would it be? Bastin offered to arrange to have a tape recorder attached to her phone at home and at work, to verify what Lanier was trying to make her do.

Brenda reacted with panic at this idea. What if the judge found out? What if her husband knew? Was Bastin thinking of using the tape as evidence in a trial? Would she have to testify?

Bastin said that if it came to that, of course she'd have to testify, and the judge would know about the tape then. He didn't have to find out about it now. Nobody did. There were techniques of surveillance. It would all have to be done with a court's permission.

"You'd want to testify, wouldn't you?" he asked. "I assume you want to see this man removed from the bench, if he's doing what you say he is."

For a while it had seemed that Brenda Castain had crossed a threshold and, having found powerful allies, was willing to cooperate. But all at once she reverted to her fearful state. She insisted that she could not possibly testify against Lanier. A tape was out of the question. Lanier would ruin her life. Her husband would be outraged, because his job was at stake, too. The agents did not understand how powerful Lanier was, and how vindictive. He controlled everything, he and his brother. You simply did not cross him if you wanted to go on working and living in Dyersburg. Nobody did. Nobody. She could not believe the things she had already said.

Switching gears, Brenda backtracked, saying that she was in an emotional state and hadn't meant to go this far. Lanier was not so bad after all. What man hadn't hit on women at work? She could handle him. He was just a big oaf in his way. What he had done was no worse than what other men did, only more obvious. She could accept it, like everyone else.

"But Lanier is a judge," Donohue interrupted.

Brenda grew adamant. When Bastin asked her if there were any other women the agents ought to talk to, she said no, she could not be responsible for starting something that could hurt a lot of people. She slid across the seat to get out.

Bastin tried to detain her with talk of doing what was right, with allusions to things like truth and justice, but he got nowhere; it was time to let her go. The interview had already lasted nearly two hours; the high school kids would soon be prowling the parking lot. He asked her to think things over and to call him and reminded her that the FBI was there to help.

She promised to call. She apologized for not being able to be more cooperative. She had made a mistake in complaining.

They watched her drive off in the rain.

On the way back to their office in Jackson, Tennessee, about a twenty-minute drive, Bastin and Donohue traded impressions. Maryellen Donohue was skeptical. How could a woman endure a creep like Lanier for nearly a year and still be angling for a promotion from him and then expect sympathy, let alone help? She seemed willing to put up with just about whatever Lanier did. If she were really that worried about him, she would quit, instead of complaining and then not being willing to do anything about it.

Jerry Bastin was more sympathetic. He said that he could understand why Castain might be reluctant to come forward. In the past year he had been dealing with a case that might be parallel, although on the surface it did not appear similar.

A sheriff, not in Dyer County, had been beating and raping male prisoners. It was surprising, or it had been to Bastin and Castleberry, how resistant the prisoners had been to talking about what had been happening to them. The victims had been willing to let the bastard go free. They were not only afraid but humiliated at having been raped, as if that branded them forever. They feared that people would think that they had asked for it or should otherwise have fought to the death to prevent it. Hadn't Brenda Castain said that her husband would blame her for anything the judge was doing? You never knew what suspicions and accusations went on below the surface of a marriage.

Maybe, Jerry Bastin speculated, Brenda Castain had not admitted everything that had happened between her and the judge. Maybe she had endured more than she was willing to talk about and felt that it was too late for her to quit. Or maybe Lanier had something on her that she was afraid might come out if she crossed him. There could be a whole can of worms here that Brenda for one reason or another was frightened to open.

Her fear, that was the principal impression Bastin had of her. She was a woman under the gun, that was obvious. Lanier was holding one gun, but maybe there were others, you never knew. Whatever, this was one scared woman.

Donohue agreed about the fear but attributed it to weakness. Women could not have it both ways, she argued. Either they came forward or they could expect the consequences. If they found a job situation intolerable, they should find another.

At any rate, this was not their case. Bastin and Donohue would dictate a report summarizing the interview. The FD–302—the standard form used by agents to record information that may later be used to prosecute and comprises the written history of every FBI investigation—would be typed up by a pool secretary in the Memphis office and forwarded to a supervisor, with another copy sent to the case agent, Bill Castleberry. Whether any supervisor would actually bother to read it was doubtful. Field agents or "street grunts," as they called themselves with pride, were skeptical about how much attention FBI management actually paid to the daily grind of an investigation.

But Castleberry would read the 302. It would be his decision as to what if any action to take on the complaint and to determine what if any relevance it had to the larger Lanier and Dyer County corruption investigation.

Jerry Bastin assumed that something would be done about Castain. But any sort of follow-up would be very difficult if the woman refused to help.

7

As important as they are as the building blocks of the narrative of an investigation, chapters in a case that may eventually be presented to Justice Department lawyers for possible indictments and prosecutions, FBI 302 reports have their limitations. They are meant to be an impersonal, objective summary of information conveyed during the course of an interview, expressing no opinions, interpretations, or evaluations of any kind. And they are summaries, at their best models of concise, concrete writing, but by definition incomplete, designed for easy reference to facts that are tied to a specific time and place. Unlike a trial transcript or a tape recording, they omit what the interviewing agent decides is extraneous and are therefore bound to be subjective, a product of the agent's judgment, depending on his or her intelligence and experience for their accuracy and relevance. The Brenda Castain 302, which was dictated by Jerry Bastin and, after being transcribed, approved and initialed by him and Maryellen Donohue, was a summary of a two-hour interview that covered only about three-quarters of a single-spaced typed page.

For all of its reputation as a high-tech, scientifically oriented agency, the FBI trusts its agents' judgments more than it does any theory, technique, or machine. Bureau policy forbids the use of tape recorders, for instance, during field interviews (as opposed to surveillance) of witnesses or suspects, and for several good reasons. The machine can malfunction, or it can be switched off at will during an interview, creating a false impression of completeness, perhaps concealing illegalities rather than revealing them. Likewise, a tape can break or be altered after the fact. The presence of a recording device is often intimidating to a subject, at the same time that it tends to distract the interviewer from listening with full attention and asking the right questions in spontaneous response to the mood and manner of the subject. The free interaction of personalities between interviewer and subject, moreover, can produce results that a machine might thwart, as a person may drop his guard and reveal more under the illusion that the interviewer cannot possibly remember everything that is being said. A subject may also be under the illusion that it is safer to lie when what one is saying is not being recorded, but this, too, works paradoxically to the agent's advantage. Lying to an FBI agent is a federal crime, which, once discovered, gives the agent extra leverage: the liar now has the choice of telling the truth or going to prison.

When Bill Castleberry read the Brenda Castain 302 he was as much aware of what must have been left out of the report as he was surprised and repelled by its contents. The material, which included Brenda's allegation that Judge Lanier had dropped his pants and masturbated in front of her in his chambers, was shocking, even to a veteran like Castleberry, who at forty-eight was entering his twenty-first year with the Bureau. He could not recall ever having heard before of such conduct by a judge, which was so outrageous as to invite disbelief. Nor, as far as Castleberry knew, had there ever before been any such complaints about David Lanier. Before deciding what if anything to do about the matter, Castleberry needed to talk to the interviewing agents.

He worked with Bastin and Donohue, along with four other agents, out of the Jackson office, which was located behind a steel door in the basement of the federal courthouse. With a population of fifty thousand, only an hour and a half northeast of Memphis on I–40, Jackson itself did not require that many FBI agents, who used it mainly as a base to pursue assignments in outlying counties and spent little of their time there. Castleberry's normal routine was to check in to deal with paperwork and phone calls for an hour or so each morning and then head out into the field. Usually he worked alone, making up his own schedule day by day and, often, into the night.

When he caught Bastin and Donohue at the office one morning, he asked them about the Castain 302 and quickly understood that the agents disagreed on the question of Brenda Castain's credibility. It wasn't a minor disagreement, either, but a considerable difference of opinion. Castleberry was inclined to give Bastin's view more weight because he was the senior agent, exactly Castleberry's age. Bastin's argument, that Castain was afraid to come forward out of a combination of fear and, possibly, shame, made sense. Castleberry had worked with Bastin on the case of the sodomite sheriff and remembered the reluctance of prisoners to admit that they had been raped. He also knew Jerry well and had a high regard for his intelligence and intuition.

Green as she was, however, fresh from FBI Academy training, on the job less than a year, Maryellen Donohue was a woman, with presumably special insight into this other young woman's character. And her lack of experience was mitigated by her background. She came from a New York law enforcement family, with her father and a couple of her male relatives cops. If she was new to the Bureau, as she was to the South, in a sense she had been in training all her life.

When she had arrived in Jackson several months ago, staying with the Castleberrys until she could find an apartment, Maryellen had seemed so young and naïve, Castleberry remembered. He and his wife had remarked privately that she appeared to have more in common with their daughters, one of whom was in college and the other in middle school, than with older agents. She could sit for hours watching movies, listening to music, or just talking with the girls. Bill and Patty Lea had felt as if they had adopted a new daughter. But that may have said more about their getting older than anything else. Maryellen was growing up fast under the pressures of FBI work. Her position, that Castain had compromised her credibility by hanging onto her job and seeking a promotion in spite of Lanier's behavior, had merit.

If the judge really was such a weirdo, Donohue said, did Castain need the FBI to help her quit? Why didn't she tell her husband about the harassment and get the hell out of there? If he didn't understand, he wasn't worth keeping anyway. And why had she refused to permit a tape to be placed on her phone? Nor had she contacted anyone in the Bureau since the interview, although she had been invited to do so. Maryellen would have been glad to counsel her, whether Castain was willing to cooperate further or not. Some people did not want help. She seemed to be willing to put up with a lot to keep that job.

And there was another problem, as all three agents agreed. Whether Brenda Castain should be believed or not, or deserved sympathy, sexual behavior was not a matter for the FBI to investigate, except in connection with another crime, one for which the Bureau had been given statutory responsibility by Congress and the Justice Department. They were not the sex police. There was not even a federal statute against rape, unless it occurred on federal property, certainly none against sexual harassment or indecent exposure that was supposedly taking place in a county courthouse. The sheriff who had been abusing prisoners was in another category, one that fell clearly under federal civil rights laws, as established by numerous precedents.

Castleberry wavered, uncertain whether to contact Brenda Castain himself and to do a background check on her. He regretted not having been present at the interview, so he could have made up his mind on his

own. In addition to his new assignment, however, as the agent in charge
of Dyer, Lake, and Lauderdale counties, with top priority to be given to
political corruption in Dyer, he was committed to wrapping up a lingering
savings-and-loan case in Trenton, over in Gibson County, which he had
cracked and for which he was still needed because of his expertise and
experience with bank fraud and embezzlement violations. Like most such
scandals, this one was enormously complicated to unravel, because these
white-collar criminals knew so many tricks, and it continued to occupy
about ninety percent of his time. That was the way an agent had to work,
concentrating on what was hot and seemed likely to lead to convictions,
having to let other matters slide until he could get to them. On the afternoon of the meeting with Castain, he had been grilling loan officers and
deciphering phony financial records.

In the end a combination of factors—the agents' conflicting views, the
pressures of other assignments, the priority given to political corruption
in Dyer County, doubt that the FBI had any business probing the sex life
of a state judge—led Castleberry to file the Brenda Castain 302 away in a
folder marked DAVID LANIER and to forget about it, more or less.

For the next month Bill Castleberry continued to be preoccupied with his
savings-and-loan case but was able to make an occasional foray into
Dyersburg to reacquaint himself with the territory, which he had known
well as a young man but had not visited in some thirty years. It was the
kind of assignment he always sought and usually had been able to land,
one offering the maximum in freedom and autonomy.

If there is a stereotype of the FBI agent—the Hollywood one, for
instance, a closed-mouthed automaton in a cheap suit, an armed bureau-
crat with a police mentality—Bill Castleberry did not fit it. He was a private sort of man and an inquisitive one, not only as a professional investigator but as a person with many interests beyond his agent's role. He was
an amateur botanist, for instance, able to identify and expound on the
species of flowers, plants, and trees throughout most of the United States;
he was a constant reader, of fiction for pleasure and of works on the history and theory of criminal behavior for professional reasons, among his
favorites being James Q. Wilson's *Crime and Human Nature* and anything written by Senator Daniel Patrick Moynihan, who nearly alone
among politicians he exempted from scorn; and he was passionate about
certain kinds of music, namely eighteenth- and nineteenth-century classi-
cal, Italian opera, and blues and jazz. Not that he was an intellectual snob,
he loved football and home cooking, but his indifference to television and
the movies bordered on distaste. He absorbed the news from newspapers
and confined his filmgoing to watching the occasional G-rated picture

with his family. Except for the pleasure Bill took in knocking back Jack Daniel's and beer in honky-tonks, someone not knowing what he did for a living might easily take Castleberry for a professor, the way he was constantly analyzing everything and everyone, including himself.

An incident that occurred during his first FBI assignment, in Phoenix during the early seventies, summed up his personality and attitude to life rather well, as he liked to say himself. The country was at the time riven by controversy over the war in Vietnam. Although he had never served in combat, Castleberry had visited Indochina often only a couple of years earlier, as a military policeman in the Air Force, in charge of rounding up deserters and ferrying them back to the United States. To that extent, he had firsthand knowledge of the toll this conflict was taking on American morale, and he had already decided that the war to save South Vietnam from Communism was a debacle. Ironically, his assignment in Phoenix that Saturday afternoon was to join some twenty other FBI agents in monitoring an antiwar parade and demonstration.

He was standing on a street corner downtown with several of his fellow agents, watching the parade go by.

"Why is it," Castleberry asked a colleague, "that they all look that way?" He noted the preponderance of beards among the male marchers, the denim work shirts and tie-dyed T-shirts, the beads, the women in granny dresses, the sandals, the Ben Franklin glasses, the Leninesque workers' caps. "I mean, this is Arizona, not Berkeley. Is it really about the war, or is this a fashion statement?"

And then, looking around at the other agents, he noticed that every one of them was dressed, as he was, in nearly identical clothes, the Sears Roebuck suits, wash-and-wear white shirts, and narrow dark ties that were the Bureau uniform then. They all looked as if they had sprung fully clothed, barbered, and shaved from the mind of J. Edgar Hoover, whose sartorial imagination was famously limited.

"Hey," Castleberry said, "you know what? We're all the same as them. Look at us. We're nothing but apes, too. Maybe we all ought to get together and have a costume party."

From the moment of that epiphany, Castleberry made sure to do his best, even as one of the ten thousand agents of the most highly disciplined faceless bureaucracy in the history of the planet, never to become a robot.

He had volunteered for his assignment to the three river counties in western Tennessee because he would be able to make his own targets and, for the most part, choose to work his own hours virtually unsupervised, on his own most of the time, in touch with his superiors mainly through 302s. And there were other reasons. He had been born just across the Mississippi in Arkansas but actually thought of western Tennessee as home. Most of his youth had been spent in Europe, where his father had been stationed in southern Germany as an Army officer; but when his father retired, Bill was still in his teens, and the family settled in Lauderdale County. He had met his wife, Patty Lea, there. She was a native of the small town of Ripley, and they both remembered Dyersburg, which was about twenty miles up Highway 51 from her birthplace.

Dyersburg, they recalled happily, was the one place in the area in those days where you could buy a six-pack or a half-pint on some Saturday night; all the neighboring towns were dry. Bill and Patty Lea liked to reminisce about those innocent days when they would race along country roads through the heavy, moist air with the radio playing Sinatra or maybe Elvis, and park by the river and sip beer through a straw— because, it was common wisdom, you got a quicker jolt that way. Thirty years later Pete's Place, a liquor store in a grungy building a block from the courthouse, was still there. Dyersburg, although it had sprawled, still seemed a pleasant, peaceful town and a thriving one. Cruising along those leafy, hilly streets, noticing how snug the houses looked and how much the people cared about their lawns and shrubs, hardly a weed and not a speck of trash in sight, he almost wished he didn't know how corrupt Dyer County was.

He was a stranger to the area now and worried about how he would make contacts, working alone. Not that there was any question of how to focus. The bull's-eye of his investigation had to be James O. Lanier, who had recently hired Billy G. Hall, a convicted felon, as chief investigator for the District Attorney's office. It did not take a genius to suspect that this chief investigator was about to become the DA's bagman for illegal gambling and other sources of payoffs, a role Billy Hall knew well how to play.

He had formerly worked hand-in-glove with a Dyer County sheriff who had pleaded guilty to numerous counts of fraud and abuse of office. Hall's previous responsibilities as a deputy included burning down bars and clubs whose owners made the mistake of leasing illegal gambling equipment from the wrong middleman, who was failing to kick back profits to the proper officials. The sanctioned poker machine distributor, linked to the sheriff, pleaded guilty to federal racketeering charges and to possession of a machine gun and a silencer, the latter designed specially, according to prosecutors, in a plot to murder the then-district attorney, who happened also to be the most vociferous political opponent of David and James O. Lanier.

Such were the most visible components of the legacy of corruption, poised apparently for revival, that Castleberry had to explore. The U.S. attorneys and the FBI had believed they had cleaned up Dyer County, but now many of the convicted were getting out of jail and, like Billy G. Hall, were regaining positions where they could start the mischief all over again. Castleberry felt rather like the proverbial U.S. marshal in some old Western. As a stranger in town, he was pretty lonely; no welcome mats were out for him, that he could see. He didn't even have an office there where he could make phone calls and collect his thoughts. He knew he was going to need some local help.

He thought his best chance for assistance probably lay in the Dyersburg Police Department, whose thirty-odd officers had the reputation of standing apart from the corruption that was rampant elsewhere. He introduced himself to Chief Bobby Williamson, who somehow had been able to keep his position running a clean department since 1969, and to several of the higher-ranking officers. They were not exactly unfriendly, but Castleberry thought he could detect the familiar standoffishness of local police toward the FBI, whose agents were often regarded as arrogant meddlers, understandably so, Castleberry believed. It was Bureau policy not to cooperate or share information with local law enforcement more than was absolutely necessary. Castleberry, who had a reputation within the Bureau as a maverick, refused to operate that way because he thought it unproductive, not to say stupid. To have any chance at figures as entrenched as the Laniers, he would need all the assistance he could get and was prepared to form mutually helpful partnerships. How to achieve that would be his first challenge. He would have to figure out which officers, if any, he could trust. After four months, he still wasn't sure, having found no opportunity to put anyone to the test.

On the morning of January 2, 1991, a Wednesday, he was at his desk in the Jackson office, examining documents related to the savings-and-loan case, when he took a call from a woman who sounded extremely agitated. She was from Dyersburg, she said, but was calling from the house of a friend in Memphis. She asked to see him as soon as possible in connection with a kidnapping charge that she could not discuss over the telephone. Without going into details, she indicated that the matter had something to do with Judge David Lanier and other prominent Dyersburg citizens. She could not meet him in Dyersburg, for reasons that would become apparent from the information she had to convey. She suggested an East Memphis location and identified herself as Judy Forsythe.

Castleberry, who had an appointment at the U.S. Attorney's office in Memphis at nine the next morning anyway, agreed to meet Mrs. Forsythe at a quarter to two Thursday afternoon in a parking lot adjacent to the intersection of Poplar Avenue and Kirby Parkway.

Who was Judy Forsythe? Castleberry had never heard the name before. This was a perfect example of why he needed local help. If he had man-

aged by then to develop Dyersburg sources and allies, he would have contacted them to get some background on Mrs. Forsythe and her relation to
the Laniers, whatever that might be. As it was, he could not be sure that
whoever he called might not tip off Judge Lanier or, short of that, be
indiscreet enough to permit the judge to find out one way or another. He
would have to hear what the woman had to say without knowing whether
she was reliable or, possibly, sent by the Laniers to mislead him.

Nobody at the FBI or in the U.S. Attorney's office was aware of any
recent kidnapping in the area, nor had anyone heard of Judy Forsythe.
After a morning spent discussing new allegations of corruption in Dyer
County—the sheriff's chief deputy for drug enforcement was supposedly
receiving payoffs from a dealer and planting drugs on citizens to create
opportunities for additional payoffs—Castleberry met Mrs. Forsythe at
the agreed spot and, at her suggestion, followed her to her friend's house
in Germantown, the suburb to which affluent whites had fled as the population of Memphis proper, swelled by migration from the deeper Delta,
had become increasingly black. He trailed her into a fairly new, heavily
wooded, and secluded development that took its exclusive tone from the
Polo and Hunt Club, an enclave of privilege that had once stood alone in
this rolling countryside and endured as an Old South vestige. Mrs.
Forsythe's friend's house sat well back from the road amid opulent land-
scaping.

She led him through a living room furnished with baroque antiques,
onto a glassed-in veranda that overlooked the garden and pool. They sat
down opposite one another in wicker chairs. A housekeeper served coffee
from a silver service.

On that day, with the temperature in the fifties, Castleberry was wearing a gray wool pinstriped suit that he happened to have bought at a
Germantown store. With his wire-rimmed glasses and close-cropped,
curly silvery hair and mustache, conservative clothes, outdoorsy tanned
complexion, a trim six-one, one hundred and ninety pounds, he could
have passed for one of the horsey set, fresh from chukkars and a steam at
the club, a long way and several tailors distant from that street corner in
Phoenix. His jacket covered the nine-millimeter German pistol he wore
on his right hip.

As over the phone, Mrs. Forsythe seemed agitated and fixed him with
burning eyes, evidently unsure how to begin.

"You said this had something to do with David Lanier?" Castleberry
asked offhandedly, deliberately appearing less curious than simply recep-
tive. It was his usual technique, when he knew little or nothing about the
subject of an interview, simply to allow the other person to talk, saying as
little as possible himself. Here I am, he intended his manner to project, an

FBI agent with many important things to do. You don't want me to be wasting my time, so start talking—and make it worth my while.

On October first or second of last year, she began, she could not be certain which, Judge Lanier had telephoned her residence twice. She answered one call; her "help" had taken the other.

The phrase "my help" struck Castleberry: Mrs. Forsythe wanted him to know, he gathered, that she was a woman of some means. He asked for the name of this person, whom Mrs. Forsythe identified as her maid.

Both times that he called, Judge Lanier had asked to speak to Mrs. Forsythe's daughter, Vivian Forsythe Archie. When she asked her why the judge wanted to contact her, Vivian, who eventually and, for some unknown reason, with reluctance called Lanier back, said that he had phoned because he had found her a job, with a Dr. Lynn A. Warner, a Dyersburg surgeon whom the Forsythes had known for many years.

Taking a deep breath and sighing, Mrs. Forsythe added that she had later discovered that within a week of that conversation, having accepted the job with Warner, Vivian had begun an affair with him.

"Do you mind if I take some notes?" Castleberry asked, reaching into the black leather briefcase he had with him. He jotted Vivian's and Dr. Warner's names down, thinking, Why is this woman so anxious to tell an FBI agent about her daughter's private life?

Soon Mrs. Forsythe was reeling off so many names that Castleberry had to ask her to slow down so he could keep things straight and get the spelling right. The more she rattled on about her daughter's sexual intrigues, the less he could see the relevance of any of it to an investigation into political corruption, except that this doctor and the judge apparently had some kind of business relationship as well as a mutual interest in Vivian Forsythe Archie.

The gist of her story, which took the better part of the afternoon to unravel, had to do with her fear that Judge Lanier would rule in favor of Vivian in a custody battle that Mrs. Forsythe and her husband were fighting with their daughter over their grandchild, Ashley. Mrs. Forsythe described to Castleberry how powerful David Lanier and his family were. She traced the Lanier ascendancy back to the founding father and indicated that unless one actually lived in Dyersburg, there was no way to understand how absolutely nothing got done without the Laniers' say-so, especially now that David's brother had become the district attorney. She had no real influence with the Laniers, even though her husband had always supported David politically. She was afraid that Vivian did have influence with the judge, for the worst, most unfortunate kinds of reasons.

Castleberry finally got the picture, that Mrs. Lanier was seeking the help of the FBI in her custody fight with her daughter. Mrs. Forsythe went to the extent of indicating that she feared for her personal safety, the matter had become so contentious.

Vivian, her mother said, was cross-addicted to drugs and alcohol and could not or would not act responsibly toward Ashley. After going to work for the doctor and beginning her affair with him, she had taken off with him and David Lanier late last October on a five-day trip to the Bahamas, leaving Ashley in her grandparents' care. Vivian's behavior had become increasingly erratic during this period. Most of the time she left Ashley with the grandparents, as during this escapade to the islands, when Vivian was alone with the two older men at a Nassau hotel. Was this any way for a mother to behave?

Castleberry said nothing.

Mrs. Forsythe described how, early last November, she had been taking care of Ashley when she noticed that there was something the matter with the child's arm, which was swollen with a bump on it and sore to the touch. She took the child to see Dr. Warner, who had set a broken arm of Vivian's when she was about six and taken out her appendix. At this time Mrs. Forsythe had not yet found out that Vivian was having an affair with Warner and had gone to the Bahamas with him and the judge. Otherwise she would certainly have selected a different doctor. Dr. Warner placed the arm in a cast.

Vivian, who apparently had not noticed the injury, insisted that it must have happened when Ashley had been visiting her father, Charles Archie, who had been with her the previous Sunday. Archie, on his part, insisted that Ashley must have broken the arm falling off a chair at church and claimed to have witnesses to the fall. Alarmed, Mrs. Forsythe and her husband drove Ashley to the Le Bonheur Children's Medical Center in Memphis, suspecting child abuse.

The Le Bonheur doctors reset the arm and placed it in a new, longer cast. They also called in Shelby County Social Services, whom Mrs. Forsythe informed that Vivian had violated a court order by leaving Ashley alone with the father and ex-husband.

Mrs. Forsythe handed Castleberry a copy of the hospital discharge sheet, dated November 16, 1990, which gave a summary of diagnosis and treatment, and which concluded that "it was determined that this child was indeed a victim of child abuse. She was placed in the custody of her natural grandparents. They will stay in Shelby County until the situation is further resolved."

Mrs. Forsythe added that she and her husband retained an attorney and obtained a court order giving them temporary custody of Ashley in Shelby County. Nothing, however, had been resolved. That was why she had contacted the FBI.

She and her husband, not wanting to return their granddaughter to an abusive situation, remained in Germantown with Ashley at their friend's house. But Vivian hired a Dyersburg attorney who was close to David Lanier and who arranged to have the dispute transferred back to Dyer County, where Lanier had the authority to rule on it. Surely Mr. Castleberry could understand how unjust this was, given all the circumstances.

Worse than that, Vivian, before coming to Germantown with her ex-husband to take the child, filed kidnapping charges against the Forsythes, absurd as that was. Judy and B. A. Forsythe not only had to suffer that indignity, but they had had no choice but to give the child up. They learned to their horror that there were warrants out for their arrest in Dyersburg. Sheriff's deputies were searching for them at home.

"Can you imagine?" she asked. "Do I look like a kidnapper?"

"A difficult situation," Castleberry said, thinking that the Forsythe family were not likely to be on friendly terms with one another for the foreseeable future. "I assume the kidnapping charges have been dropped?"

No, Mrs. Forsythe said, if he could believe it, they had had to return to Dyersburg and surrender at the police department. They were released, but a trial was set for the end of January in Dyersburg, before a city judge, not Lanier. But meanwhile the custody matter was very serious. Judge Lanier had turned that over to a referee, a lawyer who was a friend of his. Lanier would still make the final determination.

The situation, she insisted, was scandalously unfair. Here was Judge Lanier running off to the Bahamas with Vivian and getting her a job with Warner, with whom she was carrying on. Lanier, moreover, was involved as well with one of Vivian's girlfriends. On top of that, the judge was also dating a girl who at the same time was intimate with a male friend of Vivian's.

Castleberry had to ask Mrs. Forsythe to run through this lengthening list of characters again. If half of this was true, David Lanier was a busy fellow. There was more to Dyersburg than met the eye.

Mrs. Forsythe offered to supply audiotapes of telephone conversations among Vivian, Dr. Warner, and Judge Lanier to prove that the three of them were in league with one another. She also referred to a videotape, taken at the Memphis airport on behalf of Dr. Warner's wife by one of his outraged relatives, showing the doctor, Vivian, and David Lanier disembarking from a flight from the Bahamas.

Sensing that he had heard enough and that he had served whatever purpose he could, Castleberry rose to leave, pleading another appointment.

"Can you help us?" Mrs. Forsythe asked.

He expressed sympathy and the hope that the family could work out their problems. To him, it did not appear to be a situation over which the FBI had authority, but of course he would file a report.

On the drive home to Jackson, Castleberry lit a cigar and sifted through his mixed feelings. He was somewhat irritated at having wasted an entire afternoon, because it was obvious that the Forsythes' troubles were nothing with which the FBI could or should involve itself. Mrs. Forsythe's concern for her grandchild was genuine, of that much he was certain; at the same time, he suspected that animosity between Judy Forsythe and Vivian might lie at the bottom of the whole ghastly dispute, of which, predictably, the helpless two-year-old child was taking the brunt.

Mrs. Forsythe had not accused Vivian, exactly, of abusing Ashley, only of neglect, which was serious enough. But Mrs. Forsythe referred to Vivian, who must be a very troubled person, with such coldness. There seemed to be more hatred in her voice and eyes than worry. Was Ashley merely a pawn in a dispute between Judy and Vivian? That was his gut feeling. That Ashley had been abused was beyond doubt, or so the document from the hospital indicated. But for the grandmother to attempt to take the child from her mother, and for the mother to file kidnapping charges against the grandparents, indicated something like internecine warfare.

Where was Mr. Forsythe in all this, and why had he not been present at the interview, if he shared his wife's position? Perhaps he had fled the house, not wishing to involve the FBI. To get any kind of perspective on the entire hapless situation, the grandfather would have to be heard from, along with Vivian's ex-husband and God knew who else. Castleberry was not inclined to take much of what Mrs. Forsythe said at face value. Something about her, the more he thought about her, speeding home with the comfort of his cigar, made him think she was a fruitcake.

It was precisely the sort of situation that Castleberry did his best to avoid. To conduct a successful criminal investigation, you had to focus exclusively on what you were after, ignoring extraneous material that could only distract you from your goal. His assignment, he reminded himself, was political corruption, not the disintegration of yet another American family.

As for David Lanier's sexual involvements, they were equally irrelevant, although it was interesting that one name Judy Forsythe had dropped among so many others had rung a bell. She had said that the judge was intimate with one of Vivian's girlfriends, Brenda Castain. Was this a rumor based on Castain's charges of harassment, which must have spread around? Or had Judge Lanier finally bullied her into an affair?

Maybe Brenda Castain had already given in to Lanier when she complained to the agents six weeks ago, which might explain her reluctance to cooperate with the FBI, lest the whole humiliating business become public.

About Brenda Castain, Castleberry did not expect to find out and did not especially want to know. This was another distraction, no more an FBI matter than was the Forsythes' custody fight.

8

For all of Bill Castleberry's hypotheses, he could not imagine just how troubled and confused a person Vivian Forsythe had become, because he did not know what had happened to her. No one did. She had told no one about the incident in Judge Lanier's chambers, not even her mother. Nor had she discussed with anyone the specifics of her subsequent contacts with the judge or why she was so afraid of him.

On that evening back in September, after she had visited the river and had recovered sufficiently to summon up the courage to face going home, Vivian had rushed into the house trailing mud. Her mother demanded to know where she had been and, seeing her untidy condition, reached conclusions and began railing at her in unflattering terms. Vivian, saying nothing, picked up Ashley and carried her upstairs to the bathroom, locking the door. She ran a bath and sat Ashley down to play on the floor, talking to her, pretending that nothing was wrong.

She looked into the mirror and saw bruises at the corners of her jaw. Her jaw and neck were sore. She brushed her hair. It came out in clumps; her scalp hurt. She started to cry again but held back because of Ashley. *I am so filthy* was all she could think, looking down at her muddy feet but feeling dirty all over. She sank into the bath, talking to Ashley.

She stayed in the bath a long time, running the water again and again to warm it up, soaping and scrubbing at herself, wondering if she would ever feel clean again. When the water and Ashley's babbling began to soothe her a little, she thought, *I am going to be able to forget about this. In the morning I will hardly remember it. I had a bad interview, that was all. Maybe a bad dream. I will tell Mother that there was a misunderstanding and that the job wasn't open and I was sad and went for a walk.*

I am still here. Ashley is here. Nobody is going to take her away from me. That is all that matters. She talked that way to herself until there was no more warm water.

Vivian slept through the next day or stayed in bed, pulling the covers over her head and calling out that she was sick when her mother tried to wake her. She made up stories to herself about how she had spent the previous day—she had gone to a movie, or she was drunk and didn't remember anything, that was the best one—and told herself that when she finally did get up, nothing would have happened, except a couple of days lost out of her life.

That evening she took a phone call from Brenda and told her about the mistake, that there had been no job opening after all.

"I'm sorry," Brenda said. "You don't sound so hot."

"I think I have the flu," Vivian said.

Her mother, who had been listening, said that she had better start looking for a job again, or her father would be after her. Vivian said she would, as soon as she felt better.

"Was Judge Lanier nice?" her mother asked.

"Sure," Vivian said, afraid that if she badmouthed him, let alone told the truth, her mother wouldn't believe her and Lanier would hear about it and this would be the excuse to take Ashley away from her.

She imagined that there was a plan, or a conspiracy, to let her make one more mistake that would prove her worthlessness, kick her out of the house, and have Judge Lanier award custody to her parents. She would not be able to fight that because she would have no place to live, no money, no way of caring for Ashley on her own. Her only chance, she figured, was to make sure she was on her best behavior, she was so afraid. She forced herself to be extra-friendly to her ex-husband, letting him keep Ashley for a while on Sundays and concentrating on the better aspects of his character. Maybe she and Butch would get back together after all. He was Ashley's father, and they were a family no matter what, weren't they? You never knew what might happen. You couldn't expect too much out of life, that was the lesson she was trying to learn.

Once or twice she came close to telling friends about what had happened, because for all of her efforts not to, she could not stop thinking about it. If she told someone, it might go away at last, she hoped. But the words never came. A sense of utter shame and humiliation came over her and stopped her tongue. She didn't think anyone would believe her anyway, since they all knew that she was hardly a sexual naif. Vivian, the party girl, overwhelmed by a fat old man? Ridiculous. They might even laugh at her—that would be worse than anything.

She did bring herself to convey to Brenda and to a couple of others that for some reason she was afraid of Judge Lanier, without specifying exactly why. "I don't like his eyes," she would say, or, "I hate that silly grin of his, he looks like a fiend." No one paid any attention, except Brenda, who said she understood. She didn't like him either. Vivian got the idea that Brenda might have a secret, too. Maybe Lanier had done more than chase her around a table. But she couldn't bring herself to ask. Everything might come out, and he would know.

The days went by in a haze, as if she weren't actually living them. She went to a couple of job interviews, but being asked questions by a man in an office brought everything back in vivid, hideous detail, and she could hardly talk. They must have thought she was on drugs. She wished she was, or almost.

It was October. She came home one afternoon to find a message written by Loretta Dunivant, the housekeeper, saying that Judge Lanier had called and left his courthouse number. He had arranged a job interview for her.

She hated even touching the piece of paper with his name on it. She dropped it and went upstairs to cry. Was he crazy? Why would he think she would want to talk to him?

The next morning, her mother asked her if she had called Judge Lanier back. She cursed herself for not having thrown the message away. Maybe Loretta had told Mother about it anyway. No, Vivian said, she had not returned the call yet.

"Why not?" her mother asked.

"I've been busy. I haven't had a chance."

"Well, he called again this morning. He has a job interview for you. I talked to him myself. You'd better call him now. The interview is today."

"I can't. I'm busy."

"With what? What do you mean, you're busy? You've been lying around here."

"Later, Mom. Okay?"

"If you don't call him, your daddy is going to be mad. What is the matter with you? Judge Lanier is being so nice. Look at this," she said, holding up the message. "Here he is, Judge Lanier himself, going to all this trouble for you, and you won't even call him back!"

Vivian left the kitchen. Her mother followed her, insisting that she make the call. Vivian ran up to her room.

Within a few minutes her mother was at her bedroom door. Had she called Judge Lanier yet? Why would she insult a good man like him who was trying to do her a favor? She had better call him back at once, or her father would know it was the final proof that she didn't want to work after all. Vivian heard her mother's footsteps pounding angrily down the stairs.

When she heard her mother's voice once more, insisting, she burst into the hall, hurried downstairs, and dialed Lanier's number from the kitchen, with her mother and Loretta standing there.

"Hello, Vivian. How nice to hear your voice." So bland! His indifferent tone sent a corkscrew sensation down her backbone. "Did your mother tell you? I have a job interview for you. It's at twelve-thirty today."

"Twelve-thirty? Today? Where?"

"Come on down here, and I'll give you the details."

"I can't do that. Just tell me where it is."

"You'll need some background. You'll have to come here."

"I'm awfully pressed for time. I've got other interviews."

"That's all right. I can't talk now, I've got to go into court. Be here at twelve." And he hung up.

"Better start getting dressed," her mother said. "You don't want to be late. It's so good of Judge Lanier to help out like this, a man in his position. I hope you appreciate it."

Vivian could not believe how she had managed to entrap herself. She went up to her room to think. There was no way out.

Maybe she was being paranoid. It could be that Judge Lanier felt guilty about what he had done to her and was trying to make amends. Perhaps, like her, he was trying to act as if nothing had happened. If he got her another job, that would put the incident behind them and make everything all right. Wasn't that what she wanted, too?

She clung to the possibility that Lanier was remorseful, without fully believing in it, deciding to take no chances. She chose a dress that buttoned up to the top, in case he tried sticking his hands where he shouldn't, and decided to be late, so he would not have time to do anything except give her the address.

Fussing with her makeup until the last minute, pretending to have mislaid her car keys, she managed not to leave the house until twelve. When she reached the courthouse, she circled the square twice before parking outside the west entrance. As she ascended the steps, the big clock on the cupola said twelve-fifteen. She knocked on the hallway door to his chambers, sorry to see that everyone seemed to have left the building for lunch.

As before, Lanier opened the door himself, again in his robe and smiling, but as he said hello, the telephone on his desk started ringing. He went to answer it, leaving Vivian holding the door, standing halfway into the office, half in the hallway, hoping she could talk to him from that distance.

But as he talked on the phone, he motioned for her to come in.

The door shut when she let go of it. Deliberately, she chose the chair next to the door. He was on the phone for three or four minutes, talking to his wife, apparently. When he put down the receiver, he stood up and, coming out from behind the desk, began telling her that her appointment was with Dr. Lynn Warner.

As soon as he did, Vivian stood up, too, and felt behind her for the doorknob. He came toward her as he spoke.

"Dr. Warner has a secretarial-type position open because his daughter's getting ready to have a baby, but he feels like it might lead into full time."

Vivian turned the knob and pulled the door open a couple of inches behind her. He was getting very close to her as he continued to talk.

"Dr. Warner's office is at 503 East—"

"I know where it's at. He was my doctor—"

"Look, I've done you a favor. Now you do me a favor—" And suddenly he was on her, his hands thrusting out on either side of her head to slam the door shut, then grabbing her by the hair and smashing his huge body against her as she felt the knob jam into the small of her back. He pulled at her hair as she tried to jerk free.

"No! Please don't do that to me again!"

"Do me a favor!"

She pushed at his chest, but he spread his legs to give him more power and pressed his full weight against her, kissing at her face and neck, muttering, "I've helped you out. Now you help me out . . . ." She could feel his slobber on her face.

He pulled her to him, picked her up by her hair, and slammed her down into the chair. He exposed himself. His thumbs pressed into the pressure points. She began to cry. He gyrated and pressed harder as she whimpered.

"When are you coming back?" he asked when it was over. "Why not come back once a week?"

9

When David Lanier attacked her the first time, Vivian had reacted by trying to regain her composure as quickly as possible. If she had failed in
her efforts to forget what had happened, finding it impossible to escape
the images of that day or to ignore her sense that something very important within her had been killed, still she had managed to function, after a
fashion, and to conceal her inner anguish and fear of being found out. Her
heart was still beating. It felt smaller than before, about the size of a
bird's, but it was still there.

Now, with the incident repeated, the effect was different, not merely
twice as severe but complete, beyond any attempt she could any longer
make to comprehend it. The thought of trying to banish what had happened from her mind was not now relevant or conceivable. She no longer
had a mind, was not after that point aware of anything except immediate
sensations. If human beings are distinct from other species by an awareness of consciousness, she had lost hers and was not even aware of having lost it. She was like a game bird who, winged by a pellet, flies on but,
hit with another, falls, and can only drag herself along the ground, with an
instinct to fly again.

She made it down the steps and into her car mechanically, acting on
command from a source she neither knew nor felt. She had no feelings,
only reactions to invisible, incomprehensible signals, the way her car
responded to the turn of the ignition key.

She had an appointment. It was at twelve-thirty, which was so because
she had been told about it. That was why she was out that day. There
seemed no reason not to meet it. She would apologize for being late.
There were no alternatives, that she could tell.

Dr. Warner's office was less than a mile away, a block from the large Methodist Hospital complex. She drove at an ordinary pace, observing stop signs, signaling at every turn, remembering where to find a parking space, walking to his door deliberately, checking her watch to see that it was already ten to one. He was there, waiting for her. She said she was sorry for being late. It didn't matter, he said, he was glad to see her. Was she feeling all right? She was looking a little pale.

"I'm feeling fine," she said. In fact, she was feeling nothing at all. Someone might as well have taken a scissors and snipped all the circuits between her heart and her brain. She produced her résumé, handed it to him, and managed a smile because that was what you did.

"I really want to work, Dr. Warner," she heard herself say. "I'll do anything for this job."

"Of course I know you, Vivian. My goodness, it's been so many years. You have a very impressive résumé. You don't think you're overqualified, do you?" he asked cheerfully. She said nothing. "Can you start tomorrow?"

It seemed so simple. Why had it taken so long for this to happen? So many fruitless interviews and . . . "I promised a friend I'd baby-sit for her tomorrow because her mother's having a cancer operation," she heard herself saying, which probably wasn't very wise, it might irritate him. But he said that would be fine. He admired someone who kept promises.

At home she told her parents, who were very pleased, until she mentioned the baby-sitting. What did she mean, her father exploded, missing her first day of honest work! He grew purple-faced and took a swipe at her with his stick.

She was afraid he would have another stroke, but she did not react, except to say that she thought it was probably time for her to move out, with Ashley. Her parents seemed surprised, but they did not object. Vivian took Ashley into her arms and told her that she and Mommy were going to find a brand-new place to live, just the two of them. Wouldn't that be exciting?

The child only stared at her and reached out to touch her face. I love her, Vivian thought, but she didn't say it. The words did not come out. She knew that this was Ashley, whom she loved more than anyone or anything in the world. She was telling herself that, silently articulating it but not feeling it, or anything else.

She found a duplex on Ferguson Street, in the heart of town, and a day-care center, Kid's Zone, five blocks from Dr. Warner's office. She could leave Ashley there from six to six, if she liked, for ten dollars a day or forty-five a week, a big chunk of her salary, which was two hundred and fifty dollars a week. But now that she was working, her parents' attitude improved, and usually she brought the child to their house around seven and picked her up after work. Her mother seemed not to mind or, better, to welcome this arrangement, and Loretta was always there to help. Sometimes her mother complained that Ashley hadn't been given a bath or that her hair was in tangles or her clothes dirty. Vivian said nothing, because she knew this was true, but she could not seem to make herself do anything about it. She was all right at work. Dr. Warner said that she was doing splendidly—she even thought he overpraised her. After all, it didn't take much to answer the phone and keep track of appointments and cheer up waiting patients with her banter, which tumbled out of her mouth automatically, as if she had a tape in her head. But when she got home, she was listless, slow, and, more and more, depressed. It was all she could do to feed Ashley something and get her to bed. She started drinking in the darkness, beer at first and then whiskey, or whiskey and beer together. She got to sleep that way and did not dream so much— those terrible dreams! They were like dying, every night. David Lanier was in them, often in the form of a pale, fat snake.

She had been working for about ten days when it broke, the barrier that had formed inside of her. It was almost five; she was preparing to close up the office. Everyone but Dr. Warner had left when she was tidying up her desk to go and, without warning, it overcame her, a tightening in her chest that suddenly rose to choking sobs and gagging. She bent over, holding onto her desk, trying to force the emotion back, and rushed into the bathroom to cry and spit.

He was standing outside the bathroom waiting for her to come out.

"Vivian? What's the matter?"

"I don't know. I must be coming down with something," and she burst out again, hiding her face in her hands.

He put his arms around her. She cried into his shoulder. He wasn't much taller than she was. Her head fit comfortably onto his collar.

"I don't know what it is," she said. "Life's awfully difficult sometimes, isn't it?"

"Tell me about it."

"It's nothing. It's my divorce, it must be. I get lonely sometimes. I feel so sorry for Ashley. What can I do? Oh, never mind. It's nothing. I don't know why I'm doing this." She hated herself for her weakness. This wasn't professional behavior.

"It's all right. You'll be fine. You're doing a fine job here."

"Oh, thank you, Dr. Warner."

"Let me give you something."

He brought her a glass of water and a bottle of pills and told her to take two of them and asked her whether she had to go home right away. He wanted to do something to cheer her up. She said she guessed her mother could keep Ashley a while longer.

"You like to play pool, don't you?"

"Sure." She thought he wanted to take her to Chequers, which surprised her. She had never seen him in there. He wasn't exactly the Chequers type. It was okay with her; she wondered who else would be in there. Maybe that wasn't such a hot idea, but whatever he wanted would be all right, he was being so kind. She heard him call his wife to say that he had an emergency, which was sort of true.

She got into his car. When she asked if they were going to Chequers, he said no and laughed as if that were a preposterous idea. He was too old for a place like that.

"You're not so old," she said. "All kinds of people go in there. Well, maybe not doctors." He did appear much older than she had remembered him. His round face was deeply creased and his hair had gone gray and wispy. He had a long upper lip that with age made him look sad.

"I'm going to surprise you," he said. "Nobody knows about this place."

"I bet I do. I know every roadhouse from here to Tiptonville."

"You don't know this one."

He drove slowly through the square past the courthouse and down a block, past Pete's Place, and turned right alongside the old, run-down brick buildings in that part of town. Vivian knew nearly every inch of Dyersburg, but this was not among them. There was never any reason to go here, where the decrepit brick piles must have nothing in them but rats. The sun was going down. She made out a crude, hand-painted black-and-white sign posted over a doorway:

DYERSBURG SPORTS ARENA
CHAMPIONSHIP
WRESTLING
Fri and Sat   8:00 pm

"They must be kidding," she said, but he hadn't noticed.

He turned at the corner and into an alley and parked in a weedy, trashy lot, surrounded by the deserted buildings. There was not a sound back there.

"What is this? The back entrance to wrestling?"

"Come on. This is where we can play pool."

She couldn't imagine. He began to climb a fire escape that looked about to collapse. He motioned for her to follow, grinning down at her like a kid.

There were only two stories. At the landing he dug in his pocket and produced a key, and she followed him inside.

The first thing that caught her eye was a dented, rusty suit of armor standing in a corner. He switched on an overhead bulb and a gooseneck floor lamp. A vermilion painting of a matador on black velvet hung over a couch that had stuffing coming out of it. In the middle of the room was a pool table.

"Welcome to the Penthouse," Dr. Warner said.

"What is this?"

"Just a place. I'll show you around."

He led her to the kitchenette, a cubicle with a sink and a two-burner stove and a refrigerator, streaked with filth, that must have been thirty years old. Off the main apartment, so to speak, he took her down a dark, peeling hallway past two bedrooms that had nothing in them but beat-up dressers and mattresses on the floor, and into a third bedroom at the end that looked marginally more inviting and cleaner. There was an actual bed, queen-size, a cheap but new bureau, color photos of mountains Scotch-taped to the walls. Someone may have been in there with a dust mop. Dr. Warner announced that this was his room.

"What do you mean, yours?"

"David Lanier lets me use it. He owns this place. It was an old hotel, you can see. He calls it the Penthouse. David has a sense of humor."

"Judge Lanier?"

"What's the matter?"

"I guess nothing."

"You want to play some pool?"

"Okay."

Play pool was all they did that first time at the Penthouse. What bothered her more than anything else was that David Lanier owned it. But when Dr. Warner invited her there again, she acquiesced. They had a bottle and she drank enough of it to be able to go along with what she knew was going to happen after a game or two of pool. That became his code, "Do you want to play some pool?" Or "How about a game of pool today?" The only thing she asked of him was that he make sure Judge Lanier would not be at the Penthouse when they went there. A couple of times, when they had got to talking in bed and time had flown, Lanier was coming up the fire escape as they were leaving. She panicked when she heard his heavy clambering, and Dr. Warner escorted her out. She tried not to look at the judge and said nothing when he greeted her cordially but with ill-concealed contempt.

She did not break down in the office again. It happened all the time during the long evenings at home, which was worse, because Ashley noticed and what was a child to think, with her mother bursting into tears for no apparent reason? She did her best to hold back the sobs until Ashley was asleep.

What kept her from going entirely crazy with self-disgust, she told herself, was that Dr. Warner was so sweet—not that she enjoyed the sex or did not enjoy it. She felt nothing, and nothing was all right with her, the way she was. He seemed so grateful for the pleasure she gave him. He started telling her that he was falling in love with her, which in a way made things better and, in a way, worse. *I am nothing but his whore that he thinks he loves, the way old men do,* she told herself. *Or maybe he really does love me, which means I am doing something for somebody, and he is kind.*

They had long conversations in bed. He had had other affairs—she did not have to think she was taking him away from his wife, it was nothing like that. He wanted to hear about her lovers, and she told him, all the way back to her high school teacher—she wondered where he was and what had happened to him and whether he was still married, which she had to doubt. She spoke of her unhappy marriage and how things were okay between her and Butch, who was being better with Ashley. Finally, because he asked why she seemed to hate him so much, she told him something about David Lanier, first making Dr. Warner promise that he would never reveal it, because she could not afford to have the judge as her enemy, he was so powerful. Dr. Warner said he understood and promised.

She did not tell him the whole story but enough to make herself feel better, or so she hoped, having confessed the basic facts. She said that he had demanded that she give him oral sex in his office and that she had complied, worried about keeping custody of her daughter. She wished very much that she had not.

"I'm going to speak to David about this," Dr. Warner said.

She begged him not to. It was over. It was her fault. She made Dr. Warner promise not to say anything.

She wished she had not told him even that much, as far as it was from the whole truth, which was something that had to be buried forever.

Impressed with the medical knowledge she had picked up from her forensic anthropology work, Dr. Warner gave Vivian more responsibilities at the office, discussing diagnoses with her, letting her assist with physical therapy, permitting her to accompany him into surgery. They were almost like partners, she told herself. And, nearly every day, he told her that he loved her.

Toward the end of October, he asked her to take a trip to the Bahamas with him. She said no, she could not leave her child; but he argued that that was no excuse, she needed a break and deserved one. He insisted, over and over. At night, alone with Ashley asleep, Vivian drank and smoked pot in her bedroom with the window open and thought about the mess she was already in and how taking a trip with Dr. Warner would only make it worse. But when she was with him it was so hard to say no, he pleaded so, and she was weak, she was nothing.

She gave in and made arrangements with her sister and mother to keep Ashley for the five days. She did not say where she was going, and they didn't ask.

The day before they were supposed to leave, Dr. Warner broke it to her that David Lanier would be coming along. Lanier was advising him on an investment in the islands, Dr. Warner said, and had been there with him before. He hoped she wouldn't mind.

Vivian reacted strongly. It was impossible. She could not go anywhere with Judge Lanier. The trip was off, for her at least.

She could not do that to him, Dr. Warner said. He was paying for everything and had already made a deposit on the rooms. How could she think of canceling now? Was it only because of that little incident with Lanier she had told him about? If she was so anxious not to annoy the judge, backing out now would surely offend him. Lanier already knew she was coming. He knew they were having an affair. What else did he think they were doing in the Penthouse? She should think of it as an opportunity to be friends with him. She could use an ally like the judge. She really did not have any choice at this late date, from what Dr. Warner could see, not with the arrangements complete. He would be with her the whole time, he promised, and they could all be friends. That was the best way to handle it. She could even think of it this way, that she was going along to protect Ashley.

That first night in their hotel room in Nassau, Dr. Warner gave her an amethyst ring with a gold bracelet to match. She wore them down to dinner, after which the two men went into the casino to play blackjack. She watched them for a while and saw Dr. Warner give Judge Lanier money for the gambling. She guessed it must be payment for his advice on the box company or whatever business it was Dr. Warner had here. She played a hand herself and lost, said she was tired, and went up to bed. She took off the ring and the bracelet and thought how stupid and weak of her it was ever to have come.

When she woke up the next morning, she thought that what she should do would be to ask Dr. Warner for the money to take a plane home, right now. Instead she told him that she needed to be alone for a while, took a book with her, and left to go down to the beach. She passed Judge Lanier's room, which was right next to theirs, and hated to think of him in there. The days ahead in this place seemed long.

She waded in the clear water for a while and sat down under an umbrella to read but could not concentrate. It was Halloween and she would miss it with Ashley. *I have really gone over the edge now.*

"Good morning, Vivian. Have a good night's sleep?"

Judge Lanier sat down beside her in the sand. She said good morning. *He must have been watching me from his room,* she thought, *and rushed down here.* He was sniffing after her like a dog. Last night in the casino he had been awful to her, whispering to her that they should go up to his room. She had pretended not to hear. Now he was talking about how pretty the beach was.

He asked her how everything was going with Dr. Warner. She didn't answer.

"Look," Judge Lanier said, "I'm here alone. Don't you feel sorry for me? You're taking care of him. Why can't you take care of me, too? We could go up to my room right now. He'd never know."

"I am not *taking care* of that man," Vivian said. "I'm not what you think I am. He is the only one who's nice to me. I'm not taking care of anyone. I love that man. Please don't say that. If that's what you want, you should've brought someone with you."

"Well, if you want to be that way. But I'm alone. Why don't you call up one of your friends and tell her to come out here? She could fly here today."

"Stop it, please. I'm not like that."

"You know, a lot of women really care for me. A lot of very beautiful girls. Does that surprise you? I didn't have the time to ask anyone, unfortunately. You know that I've been dating Linda Pickering? Why don't you call her up and tell her what a good time we're having? She can fly out. I'll cover expenses, tell her."

"Linda Pickering is nothing but a slut," Vivian said, and she went back to the hotel.

Back at work the next week, Dr. Warner took Vivian to lunch at Que Pasa, a restaurant that had opened recently and was extremely popular among the legal community. At the next table were five lawyers and David Lanier. The judge kept staring at her as she picked at her food.

When the other men, including Dr. Warner, went to pay their checks, Judge Lanier lingered behind. He leaned over Vivian's table.

"When are you coming back?" he asked. "I told you, you can come back once a week."

Vivian stared at her plate. Lanier was making small noises in the back of his throat.

"You haven't told anyone, have you?" the judge asked. "You haven't talked to anyone about our little secret?"

"No," Vivian said, hearing a threat. "I have tight lips." She was instantly mortified by her unfortunate choice of words. Lanier emitted a sarcastic laugh.

In the car Vivian asked if the judge ate there often. It was an awfully chummy atmosphere, with him and those lawyers.

"David owns the place," Dr. Warner said.

10

The longer Vivian kept her secret, the more it gnawed away at her and impaired her ability to think clearly and to decide rationally on courses of action. She responded impetuously to one crisis after another, never sure of whether she was choosing the right approach or not, hoping that her devotion to her child would make things turn out the way they should. Underneath, she had come to place a very low value on herself, as if the few brutal minutes of Judge Lanier's assaults had transformed her into discounted merchandise.

She continued working for Dr. Warner even after their affair became known to his family. The doctor's wife, who, as if heaven-ordained, happened to have been Vivian's old Sunday school teacher, telephoned her at home and asked, "Vivian, what are you trying to do to me?" Vivian said nothing, unable to find any words that seemed both honest and appropriate, thinking, *I am a slut. What else would you expect of me?* After a silence Mrs. Warner told her not to come to work again.

But she did. Dr. Warner, advising Vivian not to listen to his wife, insisted that he had hired her and that he would be the one to fire her, if it came to that. She was under the impression that he, alone among everyone in the world, was protecting her, and that only he believed that she was worth protecting.

Their sexual relations, always more comforting than passionate, ended. She had never called him by any other name than Dr. Warner. She had considered the implications of that formality, psychoanalyzing herself; they were obvious, but she did not care about them. If he was a father figure, so what? Let her father worry about it, if he ever got the picture. B.A. could hardly object, since he had fallen in love with Judy when she was scarcely into her teens. People admired old men for having young women, but never the reverse. That was the world.

Dr. Warner's kindness, as Vivian saw it, and the salary and medical insurance that included Ashley kept her at work. The arrangement was as much as she could expect, more than most single women in Dyersburg had, so why crab about it?

But nearly every day, she despised herself, and she wondered when, if ever, she could get out.

To ease her stress, she complained of headaches, enough to persuade Dr. Warner to write her prescriptions for Valium—and then for a drug that was always handy at the office, meperidine, generic for Demerol. It was highly addictive, Vivian knew from reading physicians' manuals. Better to be hooked than not function at all.

Then came the sequence of events following Ashley's broken arm. Vivian's perspective on this unhappy interlude differed from her mother's. What mattered to Vivian was that her parents had spirited Ashley away from her, without her knowledge. For days she had not known where her child was and panicked. Somehow she could not accept that by leaving Ashley alone with Butch from nine in the morning until after eight that Sunday evening, she had been negligent.

Her resentments against her mother held sway, along with her belief that her attachment to Ashley must take precedence over all other considerations. She retained Charles S. Kelly, who was among Judge Lanier's inner circle of attorneys, to help her regain custody, and she filed kidnapping charges against her parents. If getting Ashley back meant relying on David Lanier to make that decision, she was willing to pay that price.

On December 3, 1990, Vivian, as part of the action to have the custody case returned to Dyer County jurisdiction, gave a deposition in Memphis, at the Juvenile Court of Shelby County. Under sharp questioning by her parents' attorney, who reminded her that she was under oath, Vivian readily admitted her affair and the trip to the Bahamas with Dr. Warner and Judge Lanier. She also acknowledged her problems with drugs and alcohol, describing herself candidly as an addict. She was now in control of this difficulty, she insisted, and had never let it interfere with her maternal responsibilities.

"Is Dr. Warner aware of your addictive history?" the lawyer asked.

"Oh, yes," Vivian said, removing from her purse a bottle of Valium that Dr. Warner had prescribed for her only the week before.

She also volunteered that she and the doctor had had sex in an apartment owned by Judge Lanier.

"Do you think it's an appropriate role model or an example to set for your daughter for you to be dating and going on trips with a married man?"

Vivian replied with an outburst against her mother that was so vehement that the legal proceedings had to be recessed long enough to allow tempers to cool. "I am not perfect," she said among much else, "and I have done many things that I regret." But the idea that her mother was a more appropriate role model for Ashley was, Vivian insisted, preposterous. Why should she, as the child's mother, be held to a higher standard than the grandmother, whose personal conduct had been a cause of anguish to her own children? Vivian testified that Judy had instructed her to make it look as if the family home had been hit by a jewel thief, by ransacking the master bedroom while wearing gloves, to avoid leaving fingerprints. She had cooperated, Vivian said, reluctantly, to gain favor with Judy, who had rewarded her with a two-carat diamond ring, reset at a Memphis store to avoid detection by the insurance adjusters. She assumed her mother had sold the rest of the jewelry supposedly stolen. And she accused Judy of another insurance scam, this one involving arson, the torching of the building that had housed Judy's fashion boutique, some months after its closing. While she took full responsibility for the mess she had made of her own life, Vivian said, she had certainly not had much of a maternal example to live by, in terms of honesty, clean living, or, for that matter, sexual restraint. Under the circumstances, it was not surprising, although not excusable, that she and her brother had both become involved with drugs.

Judy Forsythe denounced these accusations as products of a mind addled by alcohol and drugs, one that could no longer distinguish truth from falsehood. Vivian, Judy said, lied to cover her own failures, by pointing her finger at others'. Judy claimed to be motivated solely by love for her granddaughter and a desire to protect her from abuse. Why else, at her age, would she care to assume such responsibility, with her husband grown old and sick and both of them worn down by the troubles their two younger children continued to bring down on the family? This was not the first time Vivian had repeated these lies, Judy said, in an attempt to evoke sympathy. She felt sorry for her, but unfortunately the charges were of the kind that could neither be proved nor disproved. Such was the thanks she was getting for trying to save Ashley from harm and neglect.

The arson allegation, Judy would later explain, especially pained her. Far from profiting from the tragic fire that had leveled the building that had once housed the House of Fashion, she had donated the insurance payment to the Baptist church.

As Mrs. Forsythe later told Bill Castleberry in Germantown, this Memphis hearing resulted in transfer of the custody case from Shelby County to Dyersburg, a ruling that gave Judge Lanier jurisdiction over the matter. Judy's interview with Castleberry represented her last attempt to win support. With none forthcoming from the FBI, she concluded that David Lanier, because of what appeared to be his close relationship with Vivian, would rule in Vivian's favor: Lanier had, properly, recused himself from the actual decision; but it would still be up to him whether to accept or reject his referee's opinion. Judy Forsythe gave in, agreeing to let Vivian keep Ashley; and the kidnapping charges against Judy and B.A. were dropped.

It was no longer possible, Vivian knew, for her to continue working for Dr. Warner; she realized she ought to have quit the moment Mrs. Warner found out about the affair. But who would hire her, now that gossip about her personal problems was rampant throughout Dyersburg? She considered packing up and leaving town with Ashley, although she had no idea where she would go or how she would manage with the child; nor did she like the idea of separating Ashley from the family, whatever its defects. As much as Vivian resented her parents for what they had done, she was willing to admit that they may have thought they were acting in Ashley's interests. It was the way they had done it, spiriting her off without a word, that had driven Vivian to her strong response, as she told her lawyer. Charles Kelly sympathized with her and, appreciating her impossible job situation, offered her a position in his law office. It would mean occasional contact with David Lanier, but as there was no way to avoid him altogether in Dyersburg anyway, Vivian gratefully accepted. It did not escape her that having Kelly as her boss would be an excellent hedge against anything else Judge Lanier might do to harm her. Kelly, in addition to practicing in Lanier's court, also happened to be the judge's personal attorney.

Kelly cheerfully admitted in his gruff, blustery way that his career depended on keeping on good terms with David Lanier. As Kelly phrased their relationship, "I've got my nose as far up the judge's butt as I can stick it." Tall and slim, ruddy-faced with a grizzled beard, his black hair turning silver, Kelly had the narrow eyes of a hunter, was tough and profane and fond of his whiskey, and seemed a doubtful choice as Vivian's benefactor. He did not object to being known as a man who was fond of the ladies—between marriages only, of course, as he joked about himself. The rumor, naturally, was that he had not hired Vivian Forsythe for her typing skills.

But she trusted Kelly because he was such a straightforward rogue, the opposite of Judge Lanier, so refreshingly unhypocritical that he was unlikely to pull any surprises on her. On his part, as Kelly told friends, he sympathized with Vivian for several reasons. He was not a native of Dyersburg, having moved there some twenty years before from Memphis, and he retained a skeptical view of the tight little society that scorned someone as unconventional as she, or as he. Privately he could see as much merit to Judy Forsythe's position about Ashley as in Vivian's in the women's dispute, but he admired the way Vivian had fought for her rights to her child.

Kelly was used to fighting for his own survival. His latest close scrape involved a plane he was buying on time. To keep up the payments, as he explained when questioned by federal officials, he rented the plane out. He had been as surprised and chagrined as could be, he said, when he found out that it had been seized in Colombia while it was taking on a load of cocaine, after having delivered a load of machine guns. He had to explain as well how there was no connection between this incident and his happening also to be the attorney for a man under investigation by Bill Castleberry as the biggest narcotics dealer in western Tennessee.

As for his relationship with David Lanier, Kelly cultivated that by hosting a weekly penny-a-point gin rummy game at his big, contemporary stone house in the hills, overlooking his duck pond and the cattle farm where he raised Charolais. Judge Lanier was a regular at that game, where he was the only player who did not drink, so he usually won, which meant that he would be in a good mood in court the next day. Lanier always quit when his winnings reached fifty dollars, which was the legal limit for a friendly game. The judge's scrupulousness about this particular law was, to Kelly, very funny, but he kept his amusement to himself. David Lanier had no sense of humor, not about anything.

One day at work in Kelly's office—he had his own building, several blocks from the courthouse—Vivian was asked to carry some papers over to Judge Lanier's. She had performed that task several times before, always dreading it, praying that she would find Lanier on the bench or otherwise safely occupied. If she had to encounter him, he invariably stared at her and smirked and, if he could manage it, whispered to her about their secret, reminding her of the power he held over her. On this day Vivian doubted that she had the strength to face him.

She picked up the papers, however, and was walking out the door when she saw Charles Kelly and could not hold back her anxiety.

"Do I have to do this?" she blurted out. "Do I have to take this stuff to Judge Lanier?"

There were three other women working at their desks. They all looked up.

"What's the matter?" Kelly asked. "Don't you like David?"

"I hate him. I absolutely hate that man!"

"Any particular reason?"

She said nothing further.

Kelly believed he understood. Other women who had worked for him had joked or complained about the way the judge ogled and touched them and made suggestive remarks. Some were cynical in reaction, others more offended, Vivian manifestly one of the latter. She was standing in the doorway trembling with rage.

Kelly told her that if she felt that strongly, she did not have to deal with the judge by herself anymore.

Another of the secretaries volunteered. The sun was out, but she put on her raincoat and made a great show of buttoning it up to the neck. Everyone laughed, even Vivian.

Other than the incomplete version of her experiences with Lanier that she had conveyed to Dr. Warner, that was the closest Vivian came to revealing her secret. Back in November, when Brenda talked to her about being interviewed by the FBI, Vivian had considered confiding in her friend but decided to wait to see what action the agents would take. If they came to her, she determined, she would spill everything, and she urged Brenda to cooperate.

When the Bureau did nothing, both women gave up hope of outside help. Brenda, who had let Vivian know that Lanier was becoming more and more demanding, went on working for the judge and, Vivian could tell, began getting more heavily into drugs. For a while the two women did not see much of each other. Vivian was disturbed by what was happening to her friend, who had become a bundle of nerves and depression and whose predicament reminded Vivian too much of her own.

By that spring Bill Castleberry was wrapping up his savings-and-loan case and had begun to focus on the family scandal that was the justice system in Dyer and Lake counties. Although, contrary to expectations, illegal gambling machines had not yet reappeared in the territory, deals were being made for them and signs were everywhere that the Laniers manipulated the courts, law enforcement, and certain attorneys. Most alarming were indications of connections between District Attorney James O. Lanier and the drug trade. Complaints, some of them made anonymously, poured into the U.S. Attorney's office in Memphis; the Dyersburg Police Department warned that its efforts to combat certain kinds of crime, especially narcotics violations and juvenile offenses, were being compromised by the DA. Evidence mounted that James O. had placed an "ear" within the ranks of the Tennessee Bureau of Investigation, which offered to assist the FBI in a corruption probe. To that end, a fresh TBI recruit with no direct ties to the territory began training.

As he had hoped, the assistance Castleberry gave to the Dyersburg

Police Department began to pay off when a federal grand jury indicted Bobby Upson, a sheriff's deputy who had been planting drugs on people to extort payoffs. (The Upson case was made easier by the deputy's ineptitude. His own drug-sniffing dog jumped on him when the deputy was about to search a car, in full view of several DPD officers. He fended off the animal, which was only doing the job for which it had been trained, and then miraculously discovered drugs under the dashboard—where, obviously, he had just planted them.) Upson later confessed, after lying to a grand jury.

Chief Bobby Williamson welcomed Castleberry's help in federalizing this prosecution, which enabled the DPD to do an end run around the corrupt district attorney. Williamson now introduced Castleberry to his most trusted officers, initiating a true local-federal alliance, as Castleberry had sought.

Castleberry also joined the Western Tennessee Crime Investigators Association (WTCIA)—becoming the first and only FBI agent to do so. At this group's monthly lunches, held in different towns throughout the territory, he was able to mingle and swap information with municipal, county, and state officers, who came together to help each other out. He encountered resistance to his presence, understandable in view of the Bureau's longstanding policy of isolation and aloofness, but gradually made inroads.

At the April WTCIA lunch there was much talk of James O. Lanier's latest move. On the morning of the eleventh, the Dyer County District Attorney assured a gathering of reporters that he was a fair and forgiving man. Hatchets had been buried, he said, after a bitter election campaign; relations were now amicable between him and elements of law enforcement who had opposed him.

But that afternoon the truth came out. He convened another, very different kind of meeting with some forty investigators representing the sheriffs and police of Dyer and Lake counties.

This second assembly took place at the Dyer County courthouse, in the second-floor courtroom where the Circuit Court normally met, adjacent to the DA's offices and directly above David Lanier's Chancery and Juvenile Court. It was lost on no one that the Laniers now occupied the entire building.

It was a different James O. Lanier that afternoon. In a fiery speech the district attorney, who was a swaggering six-foot-four and spoke in a raspy monotone that someone described as having the effect of a steel file on a molar, warned that from now on, he and he alone would be running the show.

"I know who you are, you Horner-loving sonsofbitches," James O.

snarled, referring to his defeated opponent, former district attorney Jim Horner, the most vocal and persistent political enemy and critic of both Laniers. "I want you all to notice that I am tape-recording this meeting. You can take out your tape recorders, too, if you want to, because you'd better get down everything I say, and some of you may be too stupid to remember it." He added that the doors were locked and that his chief investigator, Billy Hall, was armed and standing guard outside.

Anyone who did not follow the rules as he was about to lay them down would be fired instantly.

He was ordering, effective immediately, a halt to all undercover operations of any kind. Any such activity would be directed by the DA's office or would not take place. Any and all police raids, for any purpose, would have to be cleared beforehand by the DA's office. A search warrant issued by a judge would no longer constitute authority to do anything. Nor was any matter to be brought before a grand jury without the DA's prior approval.

There were other restrictions decreed. Shaking his fist, his eyes slits, his face blazing red, James O. shouted that he would tolerate no defiance. Or, as he phrased it:

"Anybody that doesn't do things my way is going to find himself useless as tits on a boar-hog."

Everyone got the message. James O. was reserving all police power to himself. It amounted to a criminal takeover. He and his accomplices would henceforth be immune to scrutiny, and he was prepared to pick off his enemies one by one from then on.

As the demoralized investigators filed out, James O. took Chief Bobby Williamson aside and instructed him to fire Captain Stan Cavness, who was head of Youth Guidance, the DPD juvenile division.

David Lanier, Williamson knew, was behind this move. The judge had long wanted Cavness fired and had spread false accusations about him, charging him with child molesting. The former DA, Horner, had cleared Cavness, bringing in the Tennessee Bureau of Investigation, which had determined that the disturbing allegations were without foundation. Had the chief not stood behind him, Cavness's career would have been over despite his innocence.

Here was proof that the Laniers, after decades of bitter feuding between the brothers, were consolidating their interests. Stan Cavness was David's nemesis, not James O's; but now, when Cavness approached the DA, offered his hand, and expressed hope that they could work together, James O. shunned him, calling him a "lying no-good sonofabitch."

Williamson refused to fire Cavness. James O. visited him twice,

demanding the firing. To try to placate the Laniers, Williamson shifted
Cavness to a supervisory position so he would not have to testify in court
and could remain out of the Laniers' sight. That was not good enough.
James O. appeared again at the chief's office.

"It looks like you won't fire Cavness," the DA said, "so I'll have to
indict him."

"On what charges?" Williamson asked.

"Molesting children in the community."

"I haven't heard any complaints like that," the chief said. "Stan was
cleared of that, and you know it."

James O. was relentless. He said that he would launch an investigation
that would prove Cavness had been involved with at least one underage
girl and possibly others.

Williamson still refused to fire him. He worried what would happen
next.

These circumstances encouraged Williamson to cooperate with Bill
Castleberry. The FBI and the TBI—although the state agency might itself
be vulnerable to the Laniers' influence—were his only hope to salvage
the integrity of his department. He would try to "go federal" with as many
cases as possible, the only reliable prosecutorial avenue left open to him.
Other than David Lanier, there was another state judge in Dyersburg, Joe
G. Riley of the Circuit Court, who handled criminal matters other than
those involving juveniles. Riley was honest, but District Attorney Lanier
decided which cases to bring and which to prosecute vigorously. All civil
and juvenile matters went before Judge David Lanier.

Rendering officers inoperative when they refused to abide by his
wishes had been Judge Lanier's way with the law for years, as the chief
explained to Castleberry. His style was less confrontational, most of the
time, more devious than that of James O., but it had the same result, the
subverting of justice to ends of personal power.

Williamson had endured as chief for twenty-two years by means of his
own political savvy. His integrity was absolute, but he protected it by cultivating behind-the-scenes support from the Board of Aldermen, who held
power over the appointment of the police chief. He was willing to risk his
own job rather than to betray one of his officers, and that loyalty ensured
the allegiance of his department. He had also fought to bring his officers
under civil service protection. Courthouse employees, by contrast, were
hired and fired at David Lanier's will—which made for constant turnover
and an atmosphere of dread.

Both Laniers were famously vindictive. Back in the sixties, when
David was mayor of Dyersburg, he persuaded the Board of Aldermen to
fire the previous chief of police. When a newly elected board reinstated

the man, Lanier criticized and harassed him until he was hospitalized from nervous exhaustion. That was when Williamson took over. No one expected him to last.

As for David's war against Stan Cavness, that had been going on for fifteen years. Cavness, too, had been driven to nervous collapse at one point, and had resigned. But the chief welcomed him back when he recovered. Now the combined power of the Lanier brothers had forced him to the sidelines again. Getting rid of one or both of the Laniers would be the only way for Cavness and the department as a whole to function effectively again.

And there was much for the department to do. Dyersburg, for all its placid, bucolic appearance, had some serious crime problems, like every other small American town by the beginning of the nineties, most related to narcotics. A street in the black section just west of downtown was known as Crack Alley, where the Special Response Team expected sniper fire every time they went after dealers. Now the dealers, like the gamblers, would have protection from the top, or many of them would, as raids and undercover operations were stymied. Dyersburg was on its way to becoming wide open as it had not been for sixty years, because the Laniers had joined forces.

"I've never had a brother that treated me like a brother," James O. told the chief in demanding Cavness's firing. "But David and I are together on this."

11

The police chief's only hope to get rid of one or both Laniers lay with federal intervention, as he and everyone else concerned were very much aware, because Article VI, section 6 of the Tennessee Constitution stated unequivocally that judges and attorneys for the state could be removed only by a two-thirds majority vote of both houses of the General Assembly, or state legislature. The Laniers' political connections made successful impeachment of either of them unimaginable.

Chief Williamson gave Bill Castleberry use of an office in the secure basement area of headquarters. By early 1991 the agent was spending more time making phone calls and exchanging information at the bunker-like DPD building on Market Street, which had been built in 1974, than at his FBI desk in Jackson. He parked at the rear and entered discreetly through a back door.

Castleberry quickly came to understand that this federal investigation would be far more difficult than any previous FBI sweep of Dyer County had been. In 1985, after a highly publicized federal crackdown, Sheriff Tommy Cribbs had pleaded guilty to twenty-two counts, including brutality toward prisoners, threatening witnesses, possession of illegal firearms, and defrauding insurance companies and the county treasury. Convicting the Laniers would require more complex detective work. Compared to them, the former sheriff had been something of a clown, if a dangerous one.

Although it had taken the federal government to nail him, Tommy Cribbs was such a wild man that his downfall had been only a matter of time. His eccentric behavior attracted the attention of Geraldo Rivera, then a controversial reporter for ABC-TV's *20/20* newsmagazine, who devoted an entire segment of the program to Cribbs, presenting him to the nation as the archetype of the berserk Southern sheriff.

Contrary to redneck clichés, Cribbs's excesses had little to do with racism. Like his father before him, the admired and respected, kindly but tough Sheriff John Cribbs, Tommy always captured around ninety percent of the black vote, which in Dyer County meant fifteen percent of the total electorate. He explained that his popularity with the blacks stemmed from "treating them like human beings." Timely donations, a couple of hundred dollars, to collection plates at black churches helped, too. As for other minority groups, there were none, in any significant numbers, in Dyer County.

The rest of his support came from farmers who appreciated the way Cribbs controlled petty thievery—"When Tommy was sheriff, I never had to worry about missing the battery out of my tractor"—and from the network of folks for whom he did favors, including the gamblers with whom he was in cahoots. His philosophy of government, which like his job he had inherited from his daddy, was, "Live and let live, and whatever you say, say nothing." This meant keeping the boozers, bootleggers, dope dealers, gamblers, prostitutes, chiselers, and other crooks on one side and the churchgoing, law-abiding people on the other, and letting each live the way they chose, going after miscreants only when there was contact between the territories. It worked. As one attorney said, "Plato never thought of better."

Tommy Cribbs's lunatic personal behavior, however, compromised his effectiveness as an officer of the law, as power and liquor went to his head. He attacked prisoners, business owners reluctant to kick back profits, and members of the animal kingdom, indiscriminately. "When Tommy's drunk," the saying went, "he hates everything that's alive." Unlike his father, who was known for his compassion toward people in trouble—the old man once took off his boots and gave them to a boy arrested for stealing, so the poor, frightened kid could "learn to walk tall"—Tommy's investigative techniques tended toward the brutal. His inquisitorial approach included interrogating suspects while seating them, naked, on a block of ice; pressing a gun alongside their heads and firing it, as a broad hint; and sticking the muzzle of a pistol into their mouths.

Firearms were Tommy's thing. He would sooner shoot a fly on the ceiling, and often did, than swat it. He decimated a flock of geese that were resting on a pond beside the Highway Patrol station simply because they were there, and they annoyed him, and he did not much care for state troopers, either, so he thought he'd shake them up a little.

Students of the Cribbsian psyche traced his passion for killing to his youth, when his father assigned the boy the task of providing enough fish and game to feed the prisoners, freeing up money allotted by the county for that purpose to be applied to other needs. Young Tommy became a skilled jailhouse cook, praised for the heaps of possum, venison, squirrel, waterfowl, catfish, and other delicacies he whomped up day after day.

It was his compulsion for cooking and eating what he killed—by gunshot, or by dropping a barrel of nails into a river and blowing it up with dynamite, a custom of fishing frowned on by sportsmen but productive— that hastened the end of his law-enforcement career. Tommy, who was a talented raconteur and, when on the sober side of drunk, a charming fellow in a rough-edged country way, enjoyed telling the story of his downfall, not minding that it made him seem like a man with the appetite of a coyote.

Back in June 1984, Sheriff Cribbs was driving around with a buddy of his, chugalugging a few beers, when all at once he was overcome by a powerful hankering for venison. Deer hunting was out of season, however, so, not wishing to set a bad example for his constituents, he forsook the banks of the Forked Deer River, his native hunting grounds, and headed across the bridge over the Mississippi to the Missouri side in search of prey.

After an hour's fruitless stalking, with nary a deer in sight, Cribbs, growing impatient, weak with hunger by then, spied a solitary sheep munching in a field and shot it—or her, as it turned out—dead. He heaved the bloody carcass—he had fired several rounds into the beast—into the trunk of his car and sped homeward in anticipation of a feast.

Back across the river it struck him that his wife might not be in the mood for mutton, or not in this woolly form. He began scouting for a good place to settle in for the big feed.

Unfortunately for the sheriff, it happened that the sheep, whose name was Heather, was no ordinary sheep but the pride and personal pet of a circuit court judge whose farmhouse lay just over a hill from the spot of the killing, and who called out the law when he discovered his beloved ewe missing and noticed a trail of blood leading down the highway. That was one irate judge.

Tennessee troopers took up the chase when the drops of blood trickled over the state line. They led right up to a door in a modest motel hidden away in the countryside. Inside, the posse came upon the sheriff and his friend, and what was left of Heather.

Cribbs was hovering over an enormous pot rigged atop a flaming can of Sterno, shaking pepper into a bubbling stew. Evidence abounded that he had butchered Heather in the motel room, leaving an unholy mess, as if a multiple homicide had occurred there.

Caught redhanded, Cribbs could only grin and say, "You boys want to stay for supper?"

The publicity attached to this and others of Cribbs's adventures, brutalities, savageries, and chicaneries embarrassed most of the citizens of Dyer County, who were engaged in promoting a progressive image of Dyersburg and its environs, emphasizing their fine school system, low taxes, absence of labor unions, proximity of superhighways and the big river, cheap housing, plentiful churches, and other attractions in what had become a highly successful campaign to lure new businesses. Appalled when their sheriff appeared on national television, they feared that people around the country would think this yahoo representative of them.

Few felt sorry for Tommy Cribbs when stealing a sheep, not to mention using a motel room as an abattoir, turned out to be a felony, to which Cribbs and his dinner guest pleaded guilty, at the same time that the sheriff admitted other, more serious crimes. He professed remorse and was his own best analyst, perceiving that political power had corrupted him into believing that the rules of civilized behavior did not apply to him. Even he agreed that he deserved to be put away for a spell.

In the federal lockup the former sheriff made friends with a former governor of Tennessee, Ray Blanton, who was also an inmate there having been convicted of selling pardons. They were of one mind on this, Tommy Cribbs told his son when the boy talked of running for sheriff himself, that getting elected was no fun anymore, the way the feds came snooping around.

Tommy Cribbs asked one of those feds, Bill Castleberry, for help once Cribbs was out on parole. More than anything else he wanted his hunting license reinstated. Castleberry advised that he was an FBI agent, not a game warden, but was glad to listen to what Cribbs had to tell him about the history and politics and underground economy of Dyer County. In the process of lending Cribbs an ear, hearing him talk about the days of his father and how the Laniers had come to power, Castleberry gained a deeper sense of the differences between Cribbs and the Laniers. The behavior of David and James O. threatened the corruption of the entire criminal and civil justice system in the region, whereas Tommy Cribbs had merely been a self-destructive aberration. The kind of corruption the Laniers were fomenting was like an internal disease—invisible, difficult to diagnose or treat, lethal to the rights of honest citizens to make a decent living, encouraging cynicism from top to bottom in their society. They validated the old saying that a fish rots from the head down. Where Cribbs had been easily spotted and relatively easily excised, a raw good old boy who enjoyed grabbing cottonmouths with his bare hands and milking their poison for the fun of it, whose faults hung out like his beer gut, the Laniers were slick, secretive, deftly manipulative, a challenge to catch in the act.

They had been fooling so many people for so long that it seemed impossible to understand, until Joey McDowell, a Dyersburg police detective with whom he soon became friends, reminded Castleberry that "lots of folks believe in professional 'rasslin,' too." This was a piece of wisdom Castleberry kept in mind as he pursued men who time after time over the years had received the endorsement of the electorate, and whom Dyer Countians had come to accept as being as indigenous as cottonwoods.

Between them the Laniers had held numerous public offices—mayor, judge, public defender, representative to the Tennessee legislature, and now district attorney general. In skillfully crafting their positions, each brother, like all professional politicians, presented to the public his own particular front. They were alike, yet different.

David's facade had much to do with public religion. He was a pillar of the Church of Christ, a severe Protestant denomination, with two million members nationwide, that clung to a concept of true Christianity, that is to say a faith and ritual meant to emulate original believers, of the sort that hid out in catacombs. On the logic that pipe organs could not have existed in ancient Rome, let alone Gethsemane, services in the Church of Christ forbade musical instruments as an interference between the human voice and God. David was known as a strict adherent to his church's strictures, especially those against cursing, tobacco, and the imbibing of alcoholic stimulants. Charles Kelly, for instance, a man not known for piety, remembered that David was so religious that he had sulked during a trip to Las Vegas, had withdrawn from the blackjack tables, when he caught his wife taking wine. None of David's card-playing cronies had ever seen David sip so much as a beer. And the judge never cursed or smoked.

Yet it was common knowledge in Dyersburg that David's piety did not encompass marriage vows. As a "fucker-arounder" was how he was known. When he joined another dozen or so sinners in public confession one Sunday in early 1991, a Church of Christ ritual that meant coming forward to the chancel and standing in silent penance, everyone assumed that David Lanier's broken commandment was the seventh. The news that Lanier had participated in this ritual quickly spread through the town and became exaggerated. People were saying that he had actually named his partner in adultery; disputes arose as to which of his women he had publicly disgraced.

By the time Bill Castleberry entered the scene, Lanier was spending most nights in the downtown apartment he called the Penthouse. He took some meals at the family home on Starlight Drive, where Joan Lanier's attentions to her garden, touching in view of the disarray in her marriage, earned a "Dyersburg Beauty Spot" award, as a sign in the front yard proclaimed. Joan was now alone, with one daughter married and the younger child, Robbye, staying with her dad, off and on, in the Penthouse.

Few had visited the inside of this apartment. The two-story building that housed it looked overdue for the wrecker's ball, an argument for urban renewal. Old-timers remembered it from the twenties, thirties, and early forties as the Palace Hotel, in fact a whorehouse. The Palace was the hub of Dyersburg's former red-light district, where ladies of joy wearing kimonos and ostrich feathers beckoned from the windows of what was now the judge's pied-à-terre. Lanier had bought the entire building in the early eighties and now shared it with two other tenants—a beauty shop on Main and the wrestling arena, nothing but a makeshift ring and some folding chairs in the old lobby on Cedar.

It was by any definition a dump. Why anyone would choose to live there was a mystery. One of Lanier's gin rummy cronies followed him up the fire escape one afternoon and kidded him about this decrepit aerie. Lanier merely grinned, like some sneaky adolescent happy in his secret world.

If the few people afforded glimpses of David Lanier's private life found it sordid, the public Lanier's act was so respectable that, like a dinner jacket, it deflected curiosity about the human being within. Dyersburg was a mannerly town, distinctly Southern in its respect for decorum, its citizens accustomed to overlooking private vice in the interest of outward order and appearances. Geographically it was part of the Mississippi Delta, if that somewhat nebulous entity may be considered to begin at Cairo, Illinois, where the Ohio joins what Mark Twain called the crookedest river in the world. Culturally speaking, however, Dyer County lay too far north and its population was too white to be linked to the land where the blues began.

To hear live blues, rhythm and blues, and basic rock, you had to go to Memphis and farther south where blacks outnumbered whites; traditionally the Delta was said to begin in the lobby of Memphis's Peabody Hotel; it was the black gospel singers of Tupelo, Mississippi, who gave that Delta soul to Elvis Presley. For its predominately white inhabitants, however, Dyersburg offered many advantages: near-full employment, a low cost of living, a very low rate of violent crime, and a general cheerfulness owing to this peace and prosperity. The blessings of the river, a plangent fertility, meant growth and renewal were in the very air—especially when the late spring sun blazed and every living thing began to sprout. Dyer was the number-one soybean-producing county in the state. When those pods swelled and the cotton bolls were about to burst and it was almost time for the annual Dyer County Barbecue Contest, featuring pulled shoulder and ribs and whole hog smothered in sauces from sweet

to hot, hickory smoke and honeysuckle filled the air, and who cared who
was doing what to whom?

In a less engorged locale David Lanier might have been more closely
watched, but in Dyer County being priapic was not considered aberrant.
There were eighty Christian churches in Dyersburg. On a Sunday salva-
tion, not repentance, was the message. Such talk of hellfire as had once
been the kindling of sermons had long since been dampened by the
gospel of positive thinking and success. And David Lanier, like his father
before him, was living proof of the power and the glory of a family that
knew how to play the game of life for what it was worth.

Every so often Judge Lanier had his hair permed, into curlicues resem-
bling the tendrils on peas. The women who fingered his head to perform
this operation joked among themselves that it was the judge's way to cel-
ebrate a new sexual conquest. At the salon in the Dyersburg Mall the
chitchat was that when David Lanier preened, it meant that some desperate girl had awarded him a blow job. When he arose from the chair with
ringlets glistening, they said that he looked like the Goodyear blimp in a
wig. Absurd though they thought him, they made any excuse to escape
jury duty, to avoid his stares and gropes.

The public David Lanier exuded power and self-confidence. Behind
the bench he was a potentate. His ill-founded rulings and imperious
demeanor in his courtroom so irritated and offended one out-of-town
attorney, himself the boss of another northwestern Tennessee county or
two, that he compared Lanier to Charles Laughton playing Henry VIII
and vowed, after one infuriating afternoon of litigation, never to appear
before "that arrogant sonofabitch Lanier" again.

In and around what he preferred to refer to as "my" courthouse, Judge
Lanier was lord of all he surveyed. Lawyers, his inner circle of them and
beyond it, complained among themselves about his capricious, ignorant
way with the law, but all complied with the economic necessity of kow-
towing to him. Short of assassination, they longed to get rid of him.
When, in 1987, a vacancy occurred on the Tennessee Court of Criminal
Appeals, nearly all of the forty-seven attorneys of Dyersburg, three of
whom were women, united in a campaign to lobby the governor to ele-
vate David Lanier to the higher court. They wrote letters, made phone
calls, traveled to Nashville to pull strings. Under the guise of praising him
for his judicial temperament, acumen, and the sagacity of his decisions,
they did all they could to kick him upstairs. To one another they justified
this cynical ploy by reasoning that Lanier would do less harm on the
higher court, where clerks would pursue the research he disdained and
other judges could outvote him.

At first the scheme seemed to be succeeding: Lanier made the short list of gubernatorial nominations. The governor may have seen through the strategy, however, because he eventually appointed another judge to the post. In 1990, when a new vacancy opened up, Lanier failed to gain nomination. His unopposed reelection to the Chancery and Juvenile Courts meant that the attorneys of Dyersburg had to accept that he would reign until 1998 or longer. They took recourse in courtroom humor, calling him Judge Big Head or, more often, King David.

His brother James O. Lanier's facade consisted mainly in the pretense that he cared about law and order and the public good and was a devoted family man. Insiders knew to the contrary that he was in league with crooks and that his family life was a shambles, quite apart from his feuds with David. He had disowned his only son, James E. Lanier, mostly because the young man had shunned his father's dirty brand of politics but also because Jimmy had made the mistake, in his father's eyes, of marrying a Roman Catholic—and one from Halls, to boot, a Lauderdale County town that had a majority black population. "That whore from Halls," her father-in-law referred to her when he mentioned her at all, after she had once innocently accepted a ride to Dyersburg with some other Halls women. When the young woman lay dying of cancer, James O. refused to speak to her or to his son. Jimmy subsequently remarried; James O. continued to shun him.

The typical adjectives attorneys, policemen, and others who knew him chose to describe James O. included "mean," "vicious," "brutal," "treacherous," "egomaniacal," "ruthless," "vindictive," and "psychopathic." He was also a wife-beater. Jimmy remembered hearing his mother's cries and the blows his father rained on her. One terrible night that continued to haunt him into adulthood, Jimmy ran downstairs in response to his mother's screams and wrestled a revolver away from his father to keep him from shooting her.

James O., however, was generally considered to have the better legal mind of the two brothers and was something of an intellectual, albeit of a specialized variety. To a certain extent he was a Civil War scholar, with particular focus on the career of Nathan Bedford Forrest, the Confederate general who had coined the phrase "got there fustes' with the mostes'." That prior to his military service Forrest had been one of the busiest slave traders in Memphis, whose business included reselling freed or escaped men and women captured in the North and sent down the river, was nothing James O. held against him. He admired Forrest, whom most historians hold responsible for the slaughter of surrendered black Union soldiers at Fort Pillow, for his ruthless guerrilla tactics as well as for his postwar activities, including the killing with an ax of a black freedman known as an agitator, and election as the first Grand

Wizard or supreme commander of the Ku Klux Klan. James O.'s regard for Forrest, amounting to hero worship, did not include the general's later repudiation of the Klan.

James O.'s unreconstructed devotion to the Old South, which was hardly unusual in the region but perhaps more vigorous than most, was also manifest in the name he chose for a political newsletter he wrote and published clandestinely. Called *The Copperhead,* it took its title from the term for Northerners who had supported the Confederacy and the cause of slavery. In its pages James O. denounced his enemies and spread lies about some of them. In one issue he falsely accused Lyman Ingram, a popular attorney and ally of Sheriff John Cribbs, of murdering a man who had tried to assassinate the sheriff. Other than attacking him as a political rival, James O. reviled Cribbs because of the support the sheriff received from blacks.

One man in history other than Nathan Bedford Forrest merited comparable admiration from James O., namely Adolph Hitler. Lanier was too shrewd a politician to trumpet his pro-Nazi enthusiasms publicly, but family members and, indeed, anyone visiting his house became vividly aware of them. James O. boasted of owning one of the country's largest private collections of books and memorabilia connected to National Socialism. This was no disinterested scholar's archive, but evidence of his enthusiasm for aggression as a virtue and for the cause of Aryan supremacy. Visitors to his library beheld a shrine honoring the Third Reich. Among the books stood mannequins dressed in SS, Luftwaffe, Gestapo, and other Nazi uniforms, along with bloodred flags emblazoned with swastikas and display cases exhibiting iron crosses, firearms, military documents, and other keepsakes of that gruesome era.

Bill Castleberry gathered background on the Laniers from the police and other sources. He was particularly struck by James O.'s affinity with Adolf Hitler. When Castleberry was a boy growing up on the American base at Augsburg, in south-central Germany, his father had made a point of taking Bill and his brothers to visit the extermination camp at Dachau, where hundreds of thousands of Jews and other victims had been subjected to medical experiments, subhuman barracks, starvation, and death by gunshot, beatings, and disease, their bodies incinerated in specially designed ovens. The sight of that row of brick-and-steel ovens, their doors standing open, left an indelible impression on Bill. He often thought that his decision to devote his life to the pursuit of justice had been fixed by that ghastly scene at Dachau, that revelation of what human beings can and will do to one another if permitted to become a law unto themselves. He had not fully understood it then, but it had ended his innocence, and years of investigating abuses of power etched the dark lesson more deeply in his mind.

He accumulated as much information as he could about the Laniers because he knew, apart from his natural curiosity, the value of understanding the subjects of an investigation as thoroughly as possible, to define their weaknesses and strengths so as to be able to gauge how they might react to various sorts of pressures when applied. As to their weaknesses, the Lanier brothers' family background suggested intriguing hints. As different as they were in style, education, and social origin from Tommy Cribbs, the Laniers shared a common failing with him, an instability of character that derived from the perils of inheritance. Like Tommy, David and James O. had come into their power because of their father, rather than earning it on their own; and like the sheriff's son, they appeared to be incapable of managing it prudently, driven by whatever demons of filial inadequacy to destroy other people, and perhaps themselves, rather than to create and maintain a political machine that, whatever its corruptions, functioned for the benefit of many people other than only themselves. David and James O.'s father had been a political boss in the old tradition of benevolent despotism, while his sons, from everything Bill Castleberry came to understand, wielded and clung to power only for its own sake.

The patriarch, the revered James P. Lanier, began his professional life as a high school teacher and then a principal in Dyer County during the Great Depression. By all accounts "Mr. Jimmy," as he was known, was a gregarious man with a considerable talent for public relations. In 1938 he was elected county clerk, at the age of thirty-one, and held that position for the next twenty-three years, transforming it into a power base from which he controlled the politics of Dyer and other river counties. Mr. Jimmy developed close ties to the famed Boss Ed Crump of Memphis; between them they consistently delivered the votes of western Tennessee to Democrats of their choosing. James P.'s influence reached through the state capital at Nashville to Washington, where senators and congressmen were indebted to him, and he became a close adviser to five Tennessee governors in succession.

Generally well liked and respected though he was, James P. kept power with methods common at the time that had little to do with conventional democratic process. That is to say, he took certain precautions against losing elections, either his own or those of candidates chosen for his slate. The men who collected the ballot boxes in the forty precincts of Dyer County were on his payroll. Opposition candidates often tallied no votes whatever. A farm couple once complained that they had voted Republican, yet the Democratic candidate had captured the district two hundred votes to none. Their votes were duly recorded, and from that time on the opposition always received exactly two votes in that precinct. Everyone seemed satisfied. On another occasion, all the ballots in one box were filled out in the same handwriting, with identical purple ink. James P. castigated the hireling responsible for his lack of imagination in faking the ballots, but word of that particular fiasco never reached beyond the bank vault where the votes were counted. A man who had been present remembered the day forty years later.

However, delivering the vote, rather than outright cheating, was the key to James P.'s political longevity. He paid drivers fifteen to twenty dollars per car to haul voters to the polls, rounding them up from cotton fields and gins and fabric factories, rousting them out of bed, gathering them from fishing holes, and delivering them back when they had fulfilled their civic duties. They came willingly, voting for Mr. Jimmy and his slate of candidates because they believed, correctly for the most part, that they owed their livelihoods to him, along with the improvements that kept coming with the federal and state money that James P. summoned at the snap of his fingers. Roads and bridges were built, the levee was strengthened, the school system improved, all because of Mr. Jimmy and his power. Few squawked that he and his cronies raked something off the top.

A courthouse veteran remembered the day in the fifties when he was hitching a ride into town and Mr. Jimmy himself picked him up. If he didn't mind, Mr. Jimmy said, they would take a little detour, to complete some business he had pending. They stopped beside a road construction crew, and the foreman came over and handed James P. a fat envelope, which Mr. Jimmy opened, displaying the contents to his passenger.

"Three thousand dollars," Mr. Jimmy said, fanning the bills. "Ain't that pretty? You cain't build nothing in this county lest I say so. This here's how I'm gonna make my boy David a millionaire."

Mr. Jimmy knew that the hitchhiker would absorb this lesson in political science and assumed, rightly, that he appreciated what most people who voted for James P. or Huey Long or Boss Crump or other bosses like them all over the country understood, that the despot who brought jobs and civic improvements deserved a cut of the spoils. Unfortunately, in showing such favoritism, excessive protectiveness, and generosity toward his younger son, Mr. Jimmy was sowing the seeds of the Lanier dynasty's eventual change from a means of distributing benefits to many, while paying off a few, to something that benefited only the few. By pampering one son and shunning the other, the old man was creating two malignancies, one a spoiled solipsist and the other a resentful mass of anger with the ethics of a Hitler.

It was common knowledge that James P. favored David over James O. Years after his death, veterans of Mr. Jimmy's era remembered how the father had "coddled David, keeping him a boy," in the words of one survivor of Dyer County intrigue over seven decades. "That's why David has this King David complex of his that everybody knows about. All he has ever wanted to do is climb a ladder so everybody can kiss his damn ass while he's looking down at them. That man is one cold sonofabitch. Except for those daughters of his, he don't give a damn about nobody. He don't think he needs nobody, and old James P., he made David that way. Spoiled him rotten. Now, James P. himself was another story. Father and son, different as night and day."

If James P. was beloved because he helped the community, David was so indifferent to the public good that during the fourteen years that he served as mayor, there was little or no economic growth in Dyer County. Some people believe that David worked behind the scenes with established businesses to lock newcomers out, in order to keep wages down and maintain power. A boom, persisting into the nineties, began only after David lost the mayoralty election in 1979; after that the population grew by nearly a fourth in ten years. His father, or so went the folk belief, would have adjusted better to changing economic realities, whereas David cared only about his personal power. In the heyday of James P., an ordinary citizen who was out of work went straight to the County Clerk's office or to James P.'s house out in the country, where everyone was welcome. The old man would promise to put in a good word for the supplicant, who when the job came through knew whom to thank, or thought he did. No one ever dreamed of asking David Lanier for that kind of personal attention, unless something more than a vote was offered in return.

Unlike his father, David was never observed actually enjoying himself—in public. At social gatherings, which he tended to avoid, he clung to women. A bright, attractive woman who, everyone believed, maintained a delicate balance between obligations to her husband and her employer, the judge, often advised David to forsake the company of women at parties and try to mingle with the men, whom David seemed to avoid, as if from fear of contamination. James P., by contrast, had made masculine conviviality the hallmark of his politics, the granddaddy gladhander of them all.

To oil his Nashville, Memphis, and Washington contacts, James P. built a hunting lodge on the banks of the Forked (pronounced FORK-ed) Deer River, a rough-hewn bunkhouse that slept forty, where political bigwigs piled in for a week at a stretch to shoot ducks and smoke hogs and drink and pee on the trees and swap stories and in general raise hell. That was how the old man made the milk of human kindness and money flow.

When David Lanier went hunting, he preferred the company of his daughters, who loved him for that and accepted his silences but could not swing a deal for a mile of new road.

James P.'s power remained absolute until 1961 when, in the aftermath of change that followed John F. Kennedy's election, the patriarch was defeated by a local businessman.

James P. was back in office five years later as general sessions judge. Like the county clerkship, this was a minor post, not even a court of record, an administrative job—but with it he regained a political leverage of which he made the most. At that time he told a newspaper reporter that he had never been a political boss.

"I never told anyone how to vote," he said, "although I sometimes offered advice."

In 1974 James O. Lanier, then a state representative, stunned everyone by supporting his father's opponent, who won. James P. died of a heart attack two years later.

Upon his death, James P.'s political machine split between James O. and David. Their feuds gave some leeway to their rivals for power, the Cribbs family, until Tommy's flameout left the field again to Laniers. By that time David was secure and supreme in his judgeship, which he had acquired in 1982 with only thirty-four percent of the vote, having been opposed by several candidates. Shrewdly, he had counted on lingering fealty to the Lanier name and the absence of any provision for a runoff. His percentage of the vote was an accurate indication of the strength of his legacy. Most of those who cast ballots for him did so out of loyalty and affection for the surname. But David had learned this much from James P., that once in office, he would capitalize on it.

"If you think I had power as mayor," he told a local attorney, "wait till you see what I can do as judge." In 1990 he ran unopposed for a second eight-year term.

And by then, with James O.'s promises to gamblers common knowledge, and with both brothers in office, the Justice Department could neglect Dyer County no longer. It wasn't like the old days.

12

The week after James O. Lanier's courthouse putsch, Joey McDowell, who resisted being absorbed into a police state, asked Bill Castleberry for a meeting. Urgent, he said it was. What he had to tell was so sensitive that they had better not meet at police headquarters. No one could be certain that James O. didn't have a spy there.

They met at Joey's house on Troy Avenue. McDowell, a third-generation cop whose father, Joe, an honest and kindly man, had been appointed sheriff to succeed the disgraced Tommy Cribbs, ranked up with Stan Cavness on David Lanier's enemies list. Like Cavness, Joey had hung on to his detective's job only because of Chief Williamson's loyalty and shrewd politicking—and his own in-your-face brand of toughness.

Castleberry arrived before eight in the morning, parking around the corner from the yellow frame house, where Joey had grown up. Joey's wife, Carol, who taught fifth grade, was just leaving for school with their boy and girl. Castleberry had met her before and knew that Joey confided in her and that she was smart as a whip, like her husband.

"Must be something important," she said as she hurried out, "for the FBI to get up this early."

The house, tidy and pretty but too small for a family of four, was crammed with antique furniture, one of Carol's passions along with her herb garden, edged with shells and stones from trips the family took. It was the sort of home, Castleberry thought, and the sort of family, like his own, that could keep a cop sane.

Joey McDowell was, barely, young enough to be Bill Castleberry's son. At thirty-six, a stocky five-foot-nine, his trim beard and his hair, which he brushed straight back from his brow, already turning pepper-and-salt, McDowell came at you straight on, a no-bullshit kind of guy. His message was in his fierce eyes. To encounter him was to instantly find yourself fighting the urge to confess, or to imagine that he already knew everything or would soon manage to extract the truth from you one way or another. Unlike Castleberry, who had fired his gun only once in the line of duty during all his years with the FBI, McDowell had been forced to do so often and recently, in September 1990, had shot and killed a burglar who had lunged with a knife at another policeman.

They made an impressive pair, this unlikely partnership of special agent and local detective, the one as smooth-talking and calculating as the other was blunt. They understood each other and became friends as soon as Chief Williamson introduced them.

Joey showed Bill to the dining room table, where a large tape machine was set up. Joey pushed the play button.

It was a two-way conversation. One voice was Joey's, a gravelly drawl as distinct as the sound of an eighteen-wheeler shifting gears. The other voice Castleberry could not identify. It was slow, low, and monotonous, and it kept posing the same question, over and over: "Did you find papers?" To which Joey replied again and again that all the evidence was in the hands of the chief of police.

"It's about Tony Bowers," Castleberry guessed, referring to a Tennessee Bureau of Investigation agent who had killed himself a week before. "Who're you talking to? Is that James O. Lanier?"

"You got it," Joey said. "He always sounds like that. He keeps at you. It could drive you nuts."

Castleberry listened further to the droning monotone. "It sounds like he wants to get his hands on some evidence, *real bad.* And you don't want to give it to him," Castleberry said.

"You're damned right I don't."

McDowell explained. The FBI agent, Bowers, had been crazy over a personal situation, as everyone knew, because the woman he loved was running around on him. Bowers had committed suicide by ramming his pickup at about seventy miles an hour into a concrete bridge abutment, with the barrel of a shotgun stuck in his mouth.

McDowell learned that the victim had been found with his head blown off, clutching the shotgun, his thumb depressing the trigger. The impact with the bridge would have killed him anyway. Bowers had doubled his bet on death.

"Why would a cop want to die that bad?" McDowell asked. He started up the tape again. "Now listen to this."

Joey: You think Tony was dealing?
James O.: No. He was covering up.

"Okay," Castleberry said. "To answer your question, a cop kills himself when he's betrayed his badge—if he's a good cop. Was Tony Bowers a good cop?"

"The best," Joey said. "He was covering up for somebody he loved, and he couldn't handle that, and he killed himself. But there's more. The truth is that that sonofabitch James O. killed him. It was James O. drove him to kill himself."

McDowell described how he had gone from the crash site directly to Bowers's house and there discovered notes and letters that amounted to a kind of diary revealing the extent of James O.'s treachery. Because he was taking kickbacks and payoffs from drug dealers, James O. needed to know about TBI investigations and raids before they happened. Rather than risk trying to corrupt an agent directly, he had seized on Tony Bowers's known weakness for this woman, who had the moral principles of a cottonmouth. He had put her on his payroll and persuaded her to pump information from Tony and relay it. James O. had known about every raid in advance, which was why none of his drug connections were getting caught.

It wasn't only her sexual betrayals that made Bowers want to die, it was that through her he had betrayed his agency. Maybe he figured he couldn't live without her anyway, but it was his own guilt that made him pull that trigger. And James O. had set it all up.

The woman must have tipped James O. off to the incriminating evidence—or maybe Tony himself had, before killing himself. McDowell couldn't say, one way or the other. But the situation now was, James O. was out to get McDowell.

"That was why he called that meeting," Joey said. "That's why he's stopped all investigations. That meeting came exactly three days after James O. asked about those letters. He panicked. He's lost his ear in the TBI. Next thing he'll do, he'll indict me on some phony charge."

Meanwhile, the evidence was safely locked up but useless. The DA was not about to investigate himself.

"And this is where I come in," Castleberry said.

"What are the chances of a federal indictment of James O.," McDowell asked, "knowing what you know now?"

Castleberry thought. There was not enough yet, but this was indeed a big break.

"For the first time," Castleberry said, "I think he's makeable."

"We've got to stop the sonofabitch," McDowell said, "before he gets somebody else killed. I hear Tony's partner is real messed up over this."

*   *   *

By June 1991 Castleberry had established a network of paid and unpaid informants, most of them consisting of people in difficulty with the law who believed that cooperating with an FBI agent might help them. Socially they ranged from high to low but were mostly low, minor players within the criminal class, their contact with the agent perhaps the only thing in their lives that made them feel important. Keeping them talking was its own kind of art.

Castleberry prided himself on his ability to communicate with people on all social levels, altering his accent, vocabulary, and manner appropriately, always aware that in the South, you caught more flies with honey. He understood that if he could not talk to people on their own level and in their own language, they would volunteer nothing.

Non-Southern agents sometimes found this approach difficult to accept or emulate. Many were frustrated to discover that a harsh, nasal Yankee voice could itself be an impediment to investigation. Only this past year, a fellow from New York, with a successful record above the Mason-Dixon line, caused problems because nobody would talk to him. Castleberry asked a certain woman who, he knew, had plenty to say, why the New Yorker had upset her and caused her to clam up. The woman, whose associates included some of the roughest characters in western Tennessee, replied: "Why, that sonofabitch don't know how to talk to a lady!"

Castleberry enjoyed most this part of his work, getting to know a region by exploring every inch of it and, especially, talking to ladies and gentlemen of all types. He cherished these contacts, and the absolute freedom he had to roam as he wished, far more than actually gaining convictions, the only true measure of an agent's success. He often felt sorry for the people he nailed. Few of them were evil, just ordinary folks who had strayed and been caught; and making a case almost invariably involved exposing innocent people's lives to the pitiless workings of the criminal justice system. His record of convictions made him one of the most highly commended agents in the Bureau, however, at the same time that his sometimes unorthodox methods meant that his personnel file was very thick.

Privately Castleberry admitted that he sometimes interviewed people, or lingered in their company, largely for the pleasure of hearing them talk and learning about their lives. An obese hog thief from Lake County, for instance, who had a few contacts on the lowest, most petty level of the drug trade was unlikely to produce much information of value. But Castleberry was entranced by his bizarre accent and dialect, which was that of a white raised in the bottoms among blacks and who turned one-syllable words like *hog* or *seed* into drawn-out, mournful riffs, the music of the soil: "haawguh"; "sheeadszuh." A sad-eyed, sweet big lump of a man, he was a concert all by himself.

Some informants received cash payments, as little as five or ten dollars in return for some minor tip, others larger amounts. These were the official informants, the amounts paid to them always recorded, their identities and reputations for reliability checked and cleared with FBI headquarters in Memphis, becoming part of the growing file on David and James O. Lanier.

There was another type of informant, however, on which no file or record of any kind was kept. According to FBI regulations, this category of informant did not exist; agents were forbidden to make use of them. But every successful one did.

These were people who for one reason or another, often out of a desire to make amends for a dishonest life, volunteered on condition that nothing be known of their cooperation. In Castleberry's view, they were motivated by conscience into a form of deathbed confession, as if getting right with God through the intercession of the Federal Bureau of Investigation, perhaps the last government entity that most people believed remained free of corruption. Usually they were men in late middle age—say a businessman who had done his share of tax evasion and other corner-cutting, who was coming to terms with mortality and wanted to exit on a positive note.

The relations between an agent and such a person had to be one of absolute trust—which was why the Bureau officially barred such arrangements. They involved an agent's operating beyond supervision, than which nothing was more abhorrent to Bureau management, "the suits," as field agents among themselves referred to supervisors.

Castleberry had shunned every opportunity to ascend in rank—and in pay—to management. He had no wish to trade his freedom for a desk job. Although he kept his supervisors informed as required in every other respect, he was soon making quiet use of a Dyersburg informant who knew a great deal about the Laniers but would discuss them only under a guarantee of secrecy. Castleberry referred to this person, if at all, only sporadically in his notebooks under the generic title of "Source." Who Source was and what Source revealed over many months were matters known only to the two of them.

How Castleberry discovered this person and why they decided that could trust one another were questions he would have found difficult to answer. Somehow each sensed that the other wanted to be on the level. Neither was a moralist, yet each believed in the moral principle of loyalty. Each had reasons—one professional, the other personal as well as professional—for wanting to see the Lanier dynasty fall. At the same time, each viewed the Laniers with curiosity, even with fascination, together with a certain cynical, detached amusement, up to a point. And they shared a contempt for the Laniers stemming from sympathy for their victims, irritation at the way one family controlled the territory, and distaste born of long acquaintance with their type, men whose selfish lust for power made others' lives miserable.

At first, before their acquaintance became something that was almost friendship, Castleberry had to play guessing games with Source, who parried with feints and nods and hints, rarely volunteering so much as a clue. "You're off base," or "Try that," Source might say, or "Bullshit." Occasionally Source, who, being Southern, still practiced storytelling as a conversational mode, would spin an illustrative tale. It was from Source that Castleberry gained appreciation of the degree of bad blood between David and James O. Lanier, which persisted in spite of their current, expedient cooperation.

The brothers usually passed each other on the street or in the courthouse, Castleberry learned, without speaking, communicating only when politics required it. Understanding this, Castleberry imagined the possibility of driving a still bigger wedge between them—playing one off against the other—maybe inducing David, for instance, to rat on James O. To make this strategy work, it would be necessary to produce incriminating evidence against both.

What was the origin of the brothers' mutual animosity, Castleberry asked Source one day. Had there been some single event such as a quarrel over money or property inherited that had set them at odds?

It was a good question, apparently, because it set Source to talking.

Not long ago, Source had been having a few drinks with James O., reminiscing about former times. When James O. alluded to "that goddamned brother of mine," Source asked how the family rift had begun. Did it go back to 1979, when James O. had supported David's opponent in the mayoralty election? David charged "irregularities" in the voting when he lost the office he had held since 1965, but James O., who happened to be attorney to the election commission, certified that David had been defeated by five votes. David filed suit, a judge ordered a new election—and David lost that one by more than five hundred votes, a result that suggested that the electorate thought he was being a poor loser.

Or did the animosity date from further back, when James O. had supported James P.'s opponent? Or further, to 1958, when James P. had pressured the draft board, which had issued an induction notice for David, into delaying his swearing-in until the boy could graduate from the University of Tennessee Law School and pass the bar exam? That ruling was denounced as blatant favoritism. And when David eluded the Army altogether by joining the National Guard—in direct violation of the law, which stated that no one could join the Guard after receiving an induction notice—three members of the draft board resigned to protest James P.'s "political interference." James O., who had completed his military service without special privileges, must have seethed with resentment against his father and brother.

"Hell, no," James O. replied to Source, "it goes back farther than any of that horseshit. I can't remember a time when David and I didn't hate the sight of one another. Yes, David was a daddy's boy. He was always sucking up to the old man, too. James P. fell for it. He thought David hung the moon. James P. even tried to stop me from running for representative, the first time I did. Came out for my opponent, how do you like that? Momma always favored me, though, God love her. I was pretty damned bitter when she died."

Source knew that story, or as much of it as anyone but David did. The first Mrs. Lanier, after James P. divorced her in the late sixties to marry his secretary, committed suicide.

David never talked about his mother's death, Source said, not to anyone. It was generally believed, however, that David himself had discovered her unconscious but still breathing, clutching a drained bottle of rat poison.

The rivalries must have been programmed into the family genes, James O. said. There was nothing anybody could do about his and David's feuding, which extended into every area of their lives. They were only speaking to each other now because they had to.

"I'll tell you how bad it is," James O. went on in his corrosive, contemptuous drone, snarling out the words in a vituperative indictment of David and, intentionally or not, of himself. "David has always tried to prove he's better than me. Sonofabitch, take women. Every time I had one, David had to have her, too. He wanted to prove he could get in any woman's pants I could. He's always been out to show that he can have more pussy than I can, the sorry asshole."

To Source, this analysis of fraternal dynamics, genetics aside, offered much insight into David's general character as expressed through his sexual appetites. It was all power, all competition. The judge seemed to get a special kick out of going after other men's women, not only his brother's. A regular at Charles Kelly's gin rummy games had told Source that David was constantly getting up from the table to make private phone calls. While he was gone, everyone would try to guess what woman he was telephoning.

On one occasion it turned out that he was phoning one of the other players' wives. She later confided to her husband that David had tried to put the make on her by telling her that her husband was occupied playing cards and that now would be the perfect opportunity for a little loving visit. David said that he could cash in his points and be over in five minutes with no one the wiser.

The wife had fended him off. Her husband was angry when he found out, but he was too beholden to Lanier to challenge him.

"David doesn't even *like* women," James O. scoffed. "It all goes back to his rivalry with me, nothing but competition. Now is that not one hell of a reason for a man to unzip his pants?"

Still targeting James O. and his narcotics connections, sensing that he was getting close to being able to present enough evidence for an indictment, Castleberry also began accumulating material against David Lanier, the most promising of which involved a complex investment scheme in a Mexican restaurant called Que Pasa.

It seemed that Judge Lanier owned a building that had previously housed a restaurant. A construction laborer named Robert Ponder, who was new to the Dyersburg area, had asked the judge to help him get backing to open a new restaurant there. Lanier had given him a list of potential investors, but when Ponder had no luck raising the money, the judge cosigned a note for twenty-five thousand dollars with a local bank, and a Dr. Lynn A. Warner put up another ten thousand.

All this was perfectly legitimate, but Castleberry, through his various confidential sources, heard that Judge Lanier then went to several additional people, including attorneys practicing in his court, and suggested that they put up guarantees of a thousand dollars each, or more, to underwrite the judge's personal investment. In return for their backing, these investors would receive a twenty-five percent discount on burritos or whatever was their choice of food at Que Pasa.

Aside from the questionable propriety of attorneys becoming financially entangled—in the riskiest of all businesses, a restaurant—with the judge whose decisions determined the success of their law practices, there was another wrinkle, which turned the scheme into a political payoff to Lanier. The guarantors assumed responsibility for the bank note but were not to share in profits, if the restaurant made any. The deal was a one-way street, to Lanier's sole benefit. What Robert Ponder would get out of it, if anything, was unclear, presumably a matter between him and the judge.

Yet the purchasers of shares seemed to think the deal worth making, or perhaps had no choice but to think so, if they wanted to go on practicing law in Dyersburg. They must have acted under the presumption that they were doing a favor for the judge and could expect favorable treatment in court in return. As for their discount on food, they would have to consume a mighty big heap of beans to break even—and quickly, from what Castleberry understood was the tottering financial condition of Que Pasa.

Castleberry gathered that the Que Pasa scheme was typical of the way David Lanier operated, quietly, leaving no paper trail, extracting or extorting favors from people over whom he had leverage. Although written records of the guarantees were few, there would be ways to persuade the attorneys involved to enlighten a grand jury about them.

FBI informants also made allegations against David Lanier of other, more conventional types of judicial misconduct, such as the soliciting of bribes to fix real estate and other kinds of cases. James O., however, remained the primary target until, late that spring, the word spread that the district attorney was not looking well.

James O. had been rumored to have been ill the previous year but had boasted of having been given "a clean bill of health" by his doctors on his way toward winning the election. Until now he had betrayed no signs of slowing down, or letting up. By the end of June, however, he was showing up at the office only once or twice a week. Then he stopped coming to work altogether, delegating authority to the assistant DA.

Finally the truth came out. James O. let it be known that he was dying of brain cancer, with only a few months left to him, at most.

James O., who was just shy of sixty years of age, must have known how ill he was all along, Source told Castleberry, and Joey McDowell was of the same opinion. He had run for district attorney out of ego and spite, knowing he would never live out his term, making promises he did not know or care if he could keep, to savor one more triumph on his father's grave and to wield power to the end. He must also have enjoyed getting close enough to his brother to make him feel the heat and to force him to share that power. Like his hero, Hitler, James O. would die in office.

He instructed that his body be cremated, "so they won't know whether I'm really dead or not," as he told a deathbed visitor before his expiration a year after his election as district attorney. He must have been thinking, or so the visitor surmised, of how for many years after the end of the Third Reich people wondered whether Hitler was alive and well in South America, poised for a comeback.

In a last attempt at reconciliation, his son had tried to patch things up, only to be rebuffed, ordered from the house with a roar and a warning not to expect a penny of inheritance. James O.'s will, written by himself in an emphatic longhand, left ten thousand dollars each to his two daughters "from the proceeds of my World War II collection," as he identified the Nazi archives, which he estimated to be worth at least fifty thousand dollars. The balance of his estate went to his widow, whom he instructed to "honor my wishes to disinherit my son, James E. Lanier, by not bestowing anything of value to him during her lifetime or at her death."

Nothing from his estate was to go to his only son, "since he chose to take his part by thievery during my lifetime, leaving me heavily in debt and taking full advantage of my misplaced blind trust in him." Whatever debt James E. may or may not have incurred, none existed by the time of James O.'s death. "I forgive him for what he did, although I will never understand how he could so easily cast aside a relationship of which I was so proud. My disappointment in him as a person and a son will go to the grave with me."

The emotional impact of this vituperation on the son was considerable but would have been greater had he not been in conflict with his father for so many years. "I have no idea why he hated me so," James E. said of James O. He had married a Catholic; he had left his father's office to practice law on his own. His principal transgression, so far as he could make out, had been to accept an appointment as assistant district attorney under Jim Horner, a position from which he resigned when James O. defeated the incumbent. Not only was Horner James O.'s and David's avowed political enemy, but at the time James E. accepted the appointment, James O. was holding down the job of public defender. The family monopoly meant that a defendant could be defended by one Lanier and prosecuted by another, in the court of a third—a situation that encouraged further family conflict, not to speak of raising ethical concerns. His Uncle David had always been decent to him, James E. said, further enraging James O. and intensifying fratricidal competition.

James E. vowed never to run for public office himself. His ambition was to gain appointment again as assistant DA one day, to prosecute crooks rather than connive with them.

"One Lanier down, one to go," a Justice Department official was reputed to have said after James O.'s death in August 1991. By that time the investigation had taken an unexpected turn.

13

Castleberry admitted to a twinge of regret at missing the opportunity to expose such an unpleasant character, one of the few criminals about whom he could discover nothing redemptive. And shifting the focus to David Lanier meant rethinking the entire case. David, Castleberry believed, would prove a more elusive kind of fish.

The judge appeared to confide in no one; no one claimed to know him well. In the several weeks since he had begun poking around the territory, Castleberry had yet to discover a man who called himself David Lanier's friend. The key to nearly every investigation was inside information. The more a man kept to himself, the tougher it was to get the goods on him— or as the old saying went, there are very few deaf and dumb folks in prison.

Still, no investigation was ever entirely fruitless. What he had already learned about the territory, the many contacts he had made, would at least be a starting point. When, around the middle of June, Castleberry learned that James O. was failing fast, he retrieved the file on Judge Lanier from the Jackson FBI office and went through it item by item, searching for some departure point.

There were not many: some material concerning Que Pasa; the lengthy and bizarre 302 report about his encounter with Judy Forsythe and her conflicts with her daughter; follow-up information on Dr. Lynn Warner's investments in a Bahamian box factory. Dr. Warner was also an investor in Que Pasa. A background check on him indicated, without proof but with intriguing implications, that he had been the subject of an inquiry by Methodist Hospital involving the alleged performance of unnecessary surgery. Judge Lanier among his other duties heard workmen's compensation cases, an area notorious for fraud. That link ought to be examined.

Castleberry reached the last document in the file, the earliest in terms of date of entry, November 1990, the 302 from Jerry Bastin and Maryellen Donohue's interview with Brenda Castain. The final sentence stood out.

Castain had requested a promotion. Judge Lanier, she claimed, had made his decision contingent on her sexual compliance.

There had been no FBI contact with Castain since.

A phone call to the Dyer County Juvenile Court confirmed that Brenda Castain was still employed there. And she had been promoted.

Castleberry wondered whether he should contact Castain. He thought not, given that she had evidently compromised herself. If she had been willing to submit to Lanier's sexual demands, she might be useless as a source. If she resented him, she could be angry, like any disaffected sexual partner a prime prospect for betrayal; but she might care so much about retaining her job that she would tip Lanier off and cripple the investigation.

Thinking about Castain gave Castleberry a new angle on David Lanier. It was a matter of having identified the target's weak spot and jabbing away at it until it began to bleed—or did not, depending on how things turned out. The judge's weakness was apparently women. The Castain 302 offered evidence that Lanier was abusing his position by extorting or coercing sex from an employee. Stories and hints Castleberry had picked up from Source and others strongly indicated that Brenda Castain was not the only such employee.

Castleberry began by talking again to Source. As usual, he visited Source's house at night, discreetly. Over several drinks he asked if Source knew of any women who were likely to have been involved sexually with Judge Lanier over a period of time and who had also worked for him, in a position to have some inside knowledge of his professional conduct.

Source came up with several names of present and former female employees. Of them he considered that of Linda Pickering the most promising, for several reasons. She was no longer working for Lanier, for one thing, so she would not be jeopardizing her job by talking. If Lanier had not had sex with her, he had certainly tried, because, according to Source, she was a knockout. And David had at least tried to give the appearance that he had succeeded with her. It was Source's opinion that David had paid Linda Pickering for sex and probably was still doing so. Castleberry had the impression that Source had a more thorough knowledge of Linda Pickering's activities than was being revealed that night. If Judge Lanier was involved in prostitution, that was a matter worth pursuing. Castleberry put Linda Pickering at the top of his list.

He went to Joey McDowell with the same question: "Who can tell me the names of women who have worked with Judge Lanier or around him, who may have had sex with him, or whom he would likely go after?"

"Well," Joey said, "I can tell you." He supplied four names: Sandy Sanders, who was now working as the supervising youth services officer; Sherry Cooper, who was now Lanier's personal secretary; Brenda Castain; and Linda Pickering.

"Okay," Castleberry said, "which of them are attractive, you know, above average? Most tempting, let's say."

"All of them," McDowell said. "Attractive young white female, that's the number one qualification."

Of course Lanier didn't have to advertise to fill these jobs. They were the most coveted in Dyersburg for women without a college degree, and the judge hired and fired as he wished. Castleberry was gaining a new appreciation of Lanier's judicial prerogatives.

Of all of them, McDowell knew Linda Pickering best, because she lived only a few doors up the street from him. She also happened to be among the two most attractive, according to Joey, among his four names; and she was on Source's list. Castleberry asked McDowell if he thought Pickering would agree to be interviewed.

"I'll set it up," McDowell said.

They met at Joey's house at three in the afternoon on Tuesday, July 2. Linda Pickering, who was dark-haired and, it was the word that came first to Castleberry's mind, ravishing, was extremely nervous from the start. She had walked over to the McDowells' so as not to leave her car outside. When Castleberry asked for her place of employment and her work telephone number, she asked him please never to call her there. Her employers were two men who were close to David Lanier, and if they knew she was talking to the FBI about him, they would certainly fire her.

She described how she had gone to work for the judge in August 1987, as a juvenile probation officer. At that time she was twenty-six and married, with a child. She was dating another man, however, which eventually caused her divorce.

About two months later, Lanier telephoned her at home, asking if he could come over to her apartment. He was being playful and was obviously propositioning her, and she politely said no. When he asked if her boyfriend was there, she realized that Lanier knew about her affair and was using that as leverage to get her to give in.

She recalled that after that, Lanier became obsessed with her. He repeatedly told her that if she was seeing another man, she could see him also. He phoned her at all hours, at work and at home, and invited her to accompany him to a judicial conference in Paris, Tennessee. When she refused, he persisted, and he told her that if she did not go with him, she would have to resign. "We are not going to get along" were his exact words.

The next time he summoned her to his office, she put a tape recorder in her purse. When he told her again that she would have to quit and that he was giving her one last chance to go with him to the conference, she refused, and he handed her a letter of resignation to sign, which stated that she "desired to relocate." She signed it, just to get away from him.

"I promise you that you will have a hard time getting another job in Dyer County," Lanier told her.

When she left to go to the juvenile office building, to clean out her desk, the judge followed her there, and ordered the other women working in her office to leave. The two of them were now alone. Lanier approached her, she became frightened, and she pulled out the recorder and threatened to scream if he touched her. He backed off.

After that she had had difficulty finding a job. She had learned from the personnel manager of a bank that Lanier had made negative remarks about her. She was anxious to do nothing to jeopardize the position she had finally landed.

Castleberry studied her closely as she recited her story, and he was not entirely comfortable with it. The sound of her voice rang occasionally false, notably when she was describing how she had denied Lanier her favors; her speech was studded with hesitations; she held her hands spread out before her most of the time, as a shield; and there was the almost cringing position of her body. These and other signs that Castleberry always looked for indicated to him that she was lying or, more accurately, was not telling the whole truth. No one ever did, but she appeared to be holding back something significant.

She was most convincing when describing Lanier's obsession with her, his jealousy over other men, his phone calls. Castleberry believed her when she claimed that Lanier had driven by her house at all hours to check on her; she had named a neighbor whom she said would corroborate this. Where she seemed to be hedging was in her description of her responses to this obsession. If she had made a tape and threatened him with it, where was it? Lost, she said.

Castleberry asked her if she could name any other women who may have been approached by Lanier. She mentioned Brenda Castain, Sandy Sanders, Sherry Cooper, and a fourth, longtime courthouse employee.

Castleberry thanked her and let her go, asking her to keep this interview to herself, if she would.

McDowell agreed that Linda Pickering had been holding back. Certain details, such as that Lanier had docked her last paycheck by a hundred dollars because she had used a courthouse machine to record him, rang true as an instance of petty vengeance; her story that he had given her back the hundred when she threatened him did not, somehow. Her account in its essence was believable, but at certain points she had sounded rehearsed.

It did not seem worthwhile, however, to interview her again, to pressure her to reveal more. She did not seem to be a likely person to reveal anything about Lanier's professional shenanigans. Linda Pickering's strong suit was apparently not inquisitiveness, which may have been one reason that the judge had picked on her.

Still, the picture she had provided of a man obsessed to the point of stalking her encouraged Castleberry to think that further inquiries along this line might be worthwhile. And what she had not said might be equally significant, the more he considered the matter. Why would two allies of Judge Lanier hire Pickering, if Lanier had prevented others from giving her a job? It didn't add up. Was she not as much on the outs with the judge as she had let on? Who were these employers of hers?

McDowell knew who they were. The business was a home nursing service owned by Dr. Lynn Warner and Charles "Bubba" Agee, an attorney.

Castleberry exclaimed that Dr. Warner was turning up all over the place. And Agee was the name of one of Warner's partners in a cardboard box factory in Nassau, the Bahamas, where Lanier, according to Judy Forsythe, had visited with Warner and Forsythe's daughter. All these connections were as intriguing as they were mysterious.

Castleberry wanted more women's names. McDowell suggested a possible source.

The next week, at eight-thirty on a Thursday morning, they made a surprise visit to Ben Beveridge, the man who had originally supplied Brenda Castain's name to the FBI, who lived in a village near Dyersburg. They decided to catch him by surprise because, Joey advised, he was now frightened by the possible consequences of what amounted to an act of informing.

He did appear nervous that morning but revealed that several other women had also complained to him about Lanier's behavior when he, too, had been working for the judge—before he was told to resign or be fired. Others had confided in him since, expressing outrage and fear. Brenda Castain had been the most upset about the judge's sexual advances but had since withdrawn into silence.

He now named five additional women. At the top of his list was Mary Haralson, who had quit several weeks ago as Lanier's secretary and had not been able to find another job since. She believed that the judge was blackballing her.

Haralson's was among three new names Beveridge mentioned. Castleberry's master list had lengthened to seven. Beveridge was not sure whether Mary Haralson had quit or been fired—with Judge Lanier it usually amounted to the same thing.

Castleberry asked for Haralson's address and phone number. He didn't know the exact address, Beveridge said, but he knew the house, which was out in the country and hard to find. He would be glad to show it to them.

With McDowell in the passenger seat, Castleberry followed Beveridge's pickup into the country. He had not decided whether Haralson should be the next woman he would contact, although that she was no longer working for Lanier made her a candidate. They would see where she lived and then decide on the most diplomatic way to approach her for an interview. The main thing was not to tip off Lanier—under the possibly dubious assumption that Linda Pickering had not already done that.

Castleberry pulled up behind Beveridge as he slowed, approaching a small clapboard house, painted white, that stood alone at the edge of an empty pasture. The grass was high, luxuriant and sweet-smelling on this summer morning, the temperature already past eighty, the air thick with moisture. You could feel everything growing. This was Castleberry's favorite time of year. He loved the heat, the verdancy of his Tennessee. A fresh morning like this out in the countryside reminded him of the summers he had spent painting schoolhouses up and down the river counties, putting himself through Memphis State, shirtless and sweating and working like crazy for a pittance, dreaming of the baloney sandwich his mother had made him that would taste like manna for lunch. He had been in the best shape of his life then and could not have been happier. He felt nearly as good now, stubbing out the first cigar of the day, cool in a polo shirt and khakis, his jacket neatly folded on the backseat. McDowell was casual, too, in a short-sleeved shirt and jeans. Too bad they weren't going fishing. Joey was a guy he would like to go fishing with.

Beveridge stopped and pointed.

Castleberry was waving thanks for the help and was ready to return to Dyersburg when he saw Beveridge getting out of his truck and striding toward the house.

"Uh-oh," Castleberry said.

McDowell shouted "Not now!" but Beveridge was already on the porch, knocking on the door. "He wants to help, damn it," McDowell said.

"He wants to play FBI," Castleberry said.

No one was answering, but there were two cars in the driveway. Beveridge knocked again. They must still be asleep, McDowell groaned.

"We're going to scare the shit out of them," Castleberry said, and considered speeding away, but that would look even worse. Nothing like being awakened by the FBI. This was a royal fuckup.

A young man, his hair ratty, wearing only a pair of white briefs, opened the door.

"Good morning," Castleberry parodied whatever Beveridge was saying. "Get your pants on, son. The feds want to talk to you."

The nearly naked fellow looked past Beveridge to the road, where Castleberry and McDowell sat in the big, dark blue Chevy Caprice sedan, with its two aerials sprouting from the trunk lid.

"We might as well play it out," McDowell said.

They climbed the porch steps and introduced themselves. Castleberry asked if Mary Haralson was in and could he have a word with her. She was still asleep, the young man said, but he would get her.

She came out alone, wrapping a robe around her nightgown, rubbing at sleep. Linda Pickering had been striking in one way, a stunner. Mary Haralson was, if not quite beautiful, appealing in another. Coltish, with long straight cornsilk hair and cornflower-blue eyes, her face dusted with freckles, she was like the morning, was all Castleberry could think. Her voice was so soft it floated away on a puff of breeze.

She asked how she could help. Were they looking for someone? Had something happened? She showed no fear, no trace of alarm. Innocence knew itself and proclaimed itself. Reluctantly Castleberry barged ahead.

"If you don't mind, Ms. Haralson, we'd like to ask you a few questions about your employment with Judge David Lanier."

With that her aspect changed radically. Clutching her hands together, anxiety dancing in her eyes, she asked the men if they would mind stepping over to the corner of the porch, and she closed the front door before joining them. Ben Beveridge, accepting that his tour of duty as a special agent had ended, retreated to his truck and drove away.

Out of prescribed routine and in the hope of nudging this awkward situation onto a more businesslike plane, Castleberry asked for her date of birth—she was twenty-five—and her Social Security number and the dates of her employment with Judge Lanier, which had lasted less than three months, earlier that year.

She said that it would be very embarrassing and hurtful to her marriage if she had to talk about these matters now, with her husband so near. He might come out on the porch at any moment. She was afraid of what might happen if she told everything she knew. She was completely unprepared for this.

"I understand," Castleberry said. "I'm sorry we showed up without calling ahead. It was a mistake."

"I need some time to think about what I'm going to do," she pleaded.

"That's just fine. Why don't you give Mr. McDowell here a ring when you decide, or you can reach me through the Jackson FBI office."

She thanked them and hurried inside.

"That was some strong reaction," Castleberry said in the car. "We hadn't even said what we wanted to ask her about. She knew."

"She's scared to death," McDowell said. "What in hell did that bastard do to her?"

Whatever had happened, she had not been able to tell her husband about it. That certainly narrowed the possibilities.

By the time they reached Dyersburg, Castleberry had begun to realize that because of the way Mary Haralson had reacted, everything had changed. He felt a certain satisfaction in his instincts. Digging up that Brenda Castain 302 had been the turning point. Blindly after that he had followed a scent that was definitely leading to something, even if he remained unsure of what it was.

Now he needed to step back and think through a strategy—where to go next, what women to see, when to make the moves that would expose what they were after to Lanier.

He had been working too intensely on too many different things lately to make sound choices—twenty-eight days and nights without so much as a Sunday off. His savings-and-loan case had threatened to come unraveled again and had demanded renewed attention; he was helping the FBI get the goods on Kenny Fowler, the big-time narcotics dealer; bank robberies in the area had meant chasing fugitives; an escaped federal prisoner had forced him to spend several nights prowling through fields fending off snakes and chiggers; plus the Laniers.

It had been like that for nearly a year, it seemed. He had been earning his salary, and he had piled up a lot of vacation time. He was going to take Patty Lea and their daughters to Holden Beach, North Carolina, where they would visit with his brother, a professor of psychology at the University of South Carolina, and his family, for the last two weeks of July. There he would lie on the sand reading a book and contemplating the web of intrigue that Dyersburg was gradually revealing itself to be.

And when he got back, he would offer his analysis to the U.S. Attorney's office and listen to what they had to say. The whole question of the propriety or even the usefulness of peering into the corners of a judge's sex life was uncharted waters for him. For all he knew, he might be completely off course, in terms of what an FBI agent was permitted by statute to do.

He had a feeling, however, that Mary Haralson's anguished face had become a beacon.

"By the way," he asked McDowell as they were passing through Courthouse Square, "are there any ugly women in Dyer County?"

"Bottom-dwellers are ugly as a mud fence," McDowell said. "Want to see some?"

Back at DPD headquarters, Castleberry and McDowell had a talk with Bobby Williamson, to let him know what direction the investigation was taking. Williamson did not flinch, but he reminded them of what was on the horizon once the judge found out. Castleberry had better know what he was doing, because if this didn't work, if they set off a fire that didn't burn up Lanier, David would be apoplectic, and he would have his revenge, you could count on that. Joey McDowell and Bobby Williamson would spend the rest of their lives out picking shit with the rest of the chickens.

McDowell, sort of smiling, reminded Castleberry of what another FBI agent had said about him, that he was a great agent, but that he was also like a mule who kicked down the barn to get at his feed and afterward couldn't figure out how to put the boards up again. When old Bill investigates, the other agent had said, you sure as hell know he's been there.

"I'll tell you what," Joey said. "If we don't get rid of King David with what we're doing, you and I and the chief here can climb up on the roof of the courthouse and hold hands and jump off." His voice was low, steady, and had greater impact for being controlled, like a short left hook.

"I don't want to hold your hands," Castleberry said. "I'll hold one of them, but I want a bottle of Jack Daniel's in my other."

"All right," Joey said. "And I'll have a bottle of George Dickel in mine."

Castleberry contemplated the risk McDowell and Williamson were willing to take. For the FBI agent, failure here would be frustrating and maybe embarrassing; but for these men it would mean the end of their careers. Joey would have to pack up his family and leave town.

Joey was giving him one of those fierce stares. He looked like the mind reader on a carnival poster.

"I'll say this, Bill," he said, lingering over each word, shaking his finger. "If you are gonna shoot the king, you had better kill him. You had damn well better kill him."

14

By the end of his holiday Castleberry had decided that he had to pursue the matter of Judge Lanier's treatment of female courthouse employees. For the agent, this was an unprecedented situation. He was not following a lead to a crime known to have been committed, because there was none. He could not recall ever before conducting an investigation on some impulse as vague as it was compelling. But to leave Mary Haralson stranded, so to speak, on her porch seemed unthinkable. He could not stop ruminating about this woman, who had been too frightened to talk. He had a feeling, and no more than that, that what she had to say would point somewhere, toward an end that remained unknown. He was going to permit himself to be led by an inner voice, which told him that if he did not follow his instincts, he would live to regret that decision.

At the same time, he would follow up on the tangible evidence of corruption, giving the investigation at least two prongs. This trip Lanier had taken to the Bahamas was intriguing. Who had paid for it? Had it been merely a lark for two middle-aged men and a young woman, or did it harbor legal ramifications? If the funds had come from Dr. Warner or other investors in this box company, the excursion could amount to buying the judge's goodwill, a bribe by any other name.

Castleberry returned, however, to a flurry of problems with other cases. He had to cancel a meeting about Lanier with U.S. attorneys when his supervisors asked him to join a team of other agents working an extortion case in another small western Tennessee town. His assignment was to impersonate the victim, who happened to look like him. For a few days he drove around in a big BMW and left a bag of money at a drop site, hoping that no one would take a shot at him. Motoring in style had its pleasures, but was not what he wanted to be doing.

Finally he got some help with the Lanier case when the new Tennessee Bureau of Investigation agent assigned to him completed training. It was good to have the TBI involved, even though the state on its own would never prosecute the judge, given Lanier's political connections.

Steve Champine, thirty, an Army Special Forces veteran, quickly proved his value. Together he and Castleberry smuggled a prisoner out of a county jail, without the sheriff's knowledge, and spirited him to a motel, where they debriefed the jailbird about drug trafficking and payoffs. The information was vital, and they returned the prisoner to his cell safely, thanks to a cooperative source. Castleberry welcomed a partner who did not mind engaging in imaginative operations—an athletic, powerfully built young man as smart and alert as he was tough. And Champine could take some of the heat off Joey McDowell, who could work more effectively behind the scenes.

It was Joey who provided the next promising lead.

One evening early in September, Linda Pickering telephoned the McDowell house in a panic. Joey sped to her house right away. Her place had been burglarized.

When Joey arrived, a man Linda introduced as her fiancé, a manager at a local plant, was with her, comforting her. She was beside herself.

There had been a break-in, from the looks of the kitchen door. Why did Linda suspect Lanier, Joey asked her, since she had told the FBI that she had not had anything to do with the judge for more than a year?

As McDowell and Castleberry had deduced, Linda had not been candid with them. Now, tearfully, encouraged by hugs from her new man, she admitted that Lanier had initiated a sexual relationship with her nearly three years earlier. It had continued, she found it difficult to admit, until early last week, when she had finally had the nerve to tell him that she would no longer see him.

She told him the truth, that she was planning to get married again, wanted to clean up her life, and was fed up with the way he had treated her, holding her job over her head to make her give him sex. She had told the man she loved everything, she informed the judge, had nothing further to hide, and refused to deceive her love and future husband.

Lanier had reacted sullenly but appeared to accept her decision. The next morning, however, he telephoned as she was leaving to take her child to school and to go to work, and he made a frightening demand of her.

He told her that a gun had been stolen from the juvenile court office and that he wanted it back, to "run the numbers" on it. He instructed her to go to the police station and to ask Joey McDowell for the gun. He did not describe the weapon but implied that Joey would know which gun it was.

Without saying anything about it, Joey at once concluded that Linda must have told Lanier about her interview with the FBI and himself. So Lanier was enraged and trying to threaten him, through the woman who had just rejected him.

Linda said that she was scared and that she and her fiancé agreed to tell McDowell about this strange request for a gun. They were about to do so when she discovered the break-in.

More likely, McDowell thought, she had not planned to say anything, until the burglary had frightened her into calling him.

But why would Lanier want her to fetch a gun from Joey? It was such an odd request. Had the judge finally cracked?

Linda was afraid that Lanier was trying to set her up. What if the judge killed Joey with the gun, leaving her fingerprints on it but none of his own? She would be framed for murder!

"That's a pretty disturbing idea," Joey said, "from my point of view, too, you can understand." Had Linda been watching too much television, he wondered, or was she making sense? Was Lanier angry enough at him to kill him? The answer was yes, but that did not mean he would actually do it.

From his car Joey fetched a recording device, which he attached to Linda Pickering's phone. He told her that if she wanted him and Bill Castleberry to help her, she would have to be completely truthful with them from now on. In the meanwhile, he believed that Lanier was more angry with him than he was with her. If the judge called again, they would have it on tape.

Lanier did telephone, the next morning, and Linda gave Joey the tape. Listening to it, he was no more enlightened. He heard Lanier's voice telling Linda to get a stolen gun from McDowell, who would know which gun it was, and bring it to the judge's chambers. Joey had no idea what if any gun Lanier was talking about.

The judge was threatening him, was all Joey could conclude. "I know what you're up to," Lanier must be saying, "and if you don't stop now, you're dead." Whether he meant it literally or figuratively, the implications were unpleasant.

McDowell contacted Castleberry and told him that things in Dyersburg were heating up fast.

On the afternoon of September 11, Castleberry, accompanied by Steve Champine, interviewed Linda Pickering again, this time at her fiancé's house. She wanted to talk with her fiancé present, she said, because they were now in this together. Castleberry agreed. He noticed at once that Pickering's manner had changed. She was nervous but straightforward this time, with no defensive gestures or evasive speech patterns. She had not been completely truthful before, she said, because she feared damaging publicity about her sexual relationship with Judge Lanier, which had gone on for about three years, ending only about ten days ago.

Lanier had, as she had explained previously, used her extramarital affair with a young Dyersburg man as leverage to persuade her to have sex with him also. (Pickering named the former lover. Castleberry said nothing but recognized the name, which had surfaced in connection with drugs.) After her separation from her husband, Lanier had broken her resistance, beginning with "flirty" talk and furtive embraces in his chambers. These had had more of a repellent than an attractive effect. When he suggested that his knowledge of her ongoing affair with the young man would be ample grounds to award custody of her child to her ex-husband, however, she weakened, and succumbed when the judge said that if she did not, he would fire her.

At first he gave her gifts of lingerie and other "stuff" in return for sex. Eventually she accepted as little as fifty dollars or as much as two hundred, always handed to her in large bills after sex. "Here, buy yourself something with this," he would say.

Except for one trip to Las Vegas with him in 1989, the sexual acts always occurred in Lanier's chambers, once or twice a week on a regular basis. He would summon her when he was in the mood, and she would have to drop whatever she was doing, such as interviewing a parolee, and hurry over to his chambers. She was ashamed of her low behavior, but she had felt trapped.

He had fired her when she refused to accompany him to the out-of-town judicial convention. It was one thing to go to his chambers and give him what he demanded, another to be seen in public with him, around people who would spread the news. Lanier wanted to show her off to the other judges.

On her own, she found that she could not get another job. A personnel officer at a bank had confided to her that Lanier was blackballing her. Desperate, she went back to him and resumed exchanging sex for money, which was her only income at that time. She was also afraid to date other men because of Lanier's threats about her child custody, his jealousy, and his following her around and driving past her house. He called her at all hours, from phone booths and from the place he called his Penthouse. She was a nervous wreck.

She begged him to help her get a real job. Finally he told her that he would recommend her to some friends of his, but only on one condition. She would have to agree to let him make a videotape of herself having sex with him.

He would give her three hundred dollars for that, he said, along with the job recommendation. She consented. She remained more ashamed of this incident than of anything else. He videotaped her performing oral sex on him, with the machine resting on a bookcase, one afternoon in his chambers. He gave her the money, and she got the job.

"What happened to that videotape?" Castleberry asked.

She had pleaded with him to give it to her, afraid that he would show it around. He agreed, but only if she would meet him out of town. Earlier that year she had met him at the Best Western motel in Paris, Tennessee, had sex with him there, and took the videotape in return. Later she cut the tape up and destroyed it.

"Did you look at it first?" Castleberry asked. "To see if it was the same tape?"

"No," she replied. "I didn't want to see it."

The next day, Castleberry drove to Memphis to brief Assistant U.S. Attorney Stephen C. Parker, who had been assigned by U.S. Attorney E. Hickman Ewing, Jr., to handle most political corruption cases and whom Castleberry had come to like and respect. Parker, thirty-seven, was a former Memphis policeman who had decided to go to law school and become a prosecutor when he watched his friend and police lieutenant die after being gunned down while trying to make an arrest. The incident was key to his intense motivation. Parker openly and happily admitted that he still thought more like a cop than a lawyer, an attitude that naturally endeared him to Castleberry, but he had a highly successful record of convictions during his three years as an AUSA. He considered himself a protégé of his boss and mentor, Hickman Ewing, who was virtually unique among U.S. attorneys across the country in having no political party affiliation. Ewing had been appointed during the early days of the first Reagan administration, when Attorney General William French Smith set standards of merit rather than politics for U.S. Attorneys, an innovative policy modified by French's successor and subsequently abandoned. Ewing, who had started the initial investigation of Dyer County corruption back in 1982, led all U.S. attorneys in corruption convictions and had urged Parker and the FBI to go after the Laniers, who like other Democrats considered both Ewing and Parker crypto-Republican zealots. Ewing's indictment of the Memphis State basketball coach, however, who was a local icon, was incurring the wrath of the U.S. congressman from Memphis, Don Sunquist, who was a Republican. Parker felt that Ewing's days as U.S. attorney were already numbered, because of Sunquist's clout in Washington, and hoped to indict David Lanier before Ewing was forced out, as a last victory for his tenure.

Parker, a tall fellow with unruly graying brown hair, a dark brown mustache, and a ready grin, was a highly charged, emotional man, who spontaneously revealed his feelings—in complete contrast to Castleberry, who almost never lost his cool and like an English actor projected whatever image a situation demanded. Castleberry's natural demeanor, like his view of the world, was ironic; Parker's, consistent with his intense religious faith, swung widely from boyish enthusiasm to gloom; but once committed to a case, he was fiercely tenacious. When Castleberry brought him up to date on the Lanier case, Parker slumped in his chair.

"We've got no case, no case at all," he moaned, "if women accept money for sex."

"I had no idea you'd be so supportive," Castleberry said.

Castleberry knew Parker well enough not to give up that easily. He launched into a lengthy defense of the investigation, citing different angles he was pursuing. As for the women, he was only at the beginning there. Mary Haralson had not told her story yet; Linda Pickering, he admitted, had in effect become a prostitute, but Lanier had turned her into one, and her story checked out. Motel records confirmed her account of an out-of-town rendezvous. Lanier had been a spider, catching her in his web, tying her up and sucking her blood.

"That's real eloquent, Bill," Parker said. "You should've been a trial lawyer. But there's no federal statute against imitating a spider. Or against sex. Or videotapes."

"A judge? *In his chambers?*"

"How many jurors would take the word of a prostitute over a judge? She took the money, she did his bidding willingly, she consented. Get real."

Castleberry persisted. Without quite forbidding him to pursue the sexual angle, Parker reminded him that they would need or ought to have much more in the way of bribery and extortion evidence to make a strong case, and he urged Bill to concentrate on those and relegate the women to the background. He was sure Lanier had acted like a sonofabitch toward them, but it was too bad; that sort of thing was not a federal matter. The women ought to sue Lanier for wrongful dismissal in state court, if they had grievances.

"They're afraid of him," Castleberry said. "He runs the county." Parker did not respond. "What about Brenda Castain? Shouldn't we follow up on her? She filed the original complaint."

"Okay," Parker relented. "Just don't get carried away." He was smiling broadly now. "Like you're capable of doing, so I hear."

Castleberry showed Parker the list of women's names obtained from McDowell, Beveridge, and Source—without, of course, mentioning the existence of the secret informant. Several of the women still worked for Lanier, and one of them occupied a high courthouse position and, Castleberry had been told, knew as much as anyone about David Lanier. Parker was uncomfortable about her and the others still employed, who might either lose their jobs or tip off Lanier if interviewed, so he and Castleberry walked down the hall to Hick Ewing's office to ask for his advice. Ewing gave his approval to further interviews but cautioned that they were far from having sufficient evidence in any area for an indictment.

In the end it was Bill Castleberry's reputation as an agent that caused Parker and Ewing to give him the benefit of the doubt, for now. His success rate was such that assistant U.S. attorneys vied for his help on their cases. A less experienced and proven investigator would not have been able to win Parker and Ewing over to acknowledging the possible importance of the women.

Driving back to Jackson that afternoon, Castleberry was feeling rather down. He was dissatisfied with the relatively meager results his work had so far produced. And he questioned whether he had pressed his argument with the attorneys less from conviction than from the challenge of winning their support. That was always a danger when you were mostly in the dark about a case, relying on hunches and impressions.

15

Presently David Lanier reacted. He sent word through the Memphis FBI office that he wished to speak personally with whoever was investigating him.

Castleberry telephoned Lanier's secretary, whose name happened to be on Joey McDowell's list, and arranged an appointment with Lanier for the next day, Wednesday, September 18, at half past noon, saying that he would be accompanied by a TBI agent. The secretary, Sherry Cooper, who sounded friendly enough, told him not to appear at the main office, where she worked, because she would be out to lunch, and it would be locked. He was to go to a door marked JUDGE'S CHAMBERS, and to knock.

Castleberry had not expected this development. It meant that Lanier knew more about what was going on than anyone had supposed—although the more Castleberry thought about it, the less surprising it seemed. Linda Pickering had still been involved with Lanier when they had first interviewed her. Her relationship with him was based on money and fear, the best reasons in the world to inspire candor. And their approach to Mary Haralson had been inept. By now she must have talked to her husband; and he might have talked to others, leaking word to Lanier inadvertently.

Unexpected though it was, Lanier's response could also be an opportunity. Castleberry found it significant from a psychological standpoint and prepared for the meeting thoroughly. His guess was that Lanier was engaging in a show of strength, a preemptive strike, by summoning the agents to his lair. Up till now Castleberry had devoted months of thought to the judge but had observed him only from a distance, striding magisterially down the courthouse steps, squeezing his bulk into a faded gold

1966 Mercedes that blew black smoke. From everything Castleberry had learned about him, Lanier intended to intimidate his adversaries and had no doubts that he could do so.

Castleberry relished the challenge. He woke up on Wednesday with adrenaline pumping. Habitually he left the house having misplaced his car keys, and Patty Lea found them for him, a ritual sealed with a good-bye kiss. This morning he kissed her having forgotten nothing.

He met Champine at DPD headquarters at ten. They spent the rest of the morning in the basement conference room with Joey McDowell and Stan Cavness, discussing Lanier's personality and how best to confront it.

Cavness recalled his earliest run-in with David Lanier, back in 1975, when David was mayor and Stan was a reporter for the Dyersburg *State Gazette,* the daily that had long been critical of the Laniers, to no effect. Someone had leaked to the paper documents from City Hall that were very damaging to the mayor, who even then behaved like a monarch.

The city, Cavness learned, had hired a Memphis engineering firm to recommend a site for a new water tower. Of ten locations proposed by the city the worst, according to the experts, was a plot out on the Highway 51 bypass, behind the Volunteer Inn, a motel in which Mayor David Lanier was a partner. This site, the engineers stated, lacked sufficient height and had unsuitable soil.

The documents recorded that Lanier had also owned the land behind the motel where, as the mayor had just announced, the city was going to build the tower in defiance of the engineering studies. Only days before its purchase by the city, Lanier had quietly sold the land to a business associate of his, for an inflated price that drove up the amount the city had to pay. The city's acquisition was approved, without any public hearing, on the day a six-hundred-thousand-dollar grant to build the tower came through from the federal Department of Housing and Urban Development.

"The people of Dyersburg have been mistreated," Stan Cavness quoted an anonymous HUD official in the *Gazette*'s front-page story exposing this scandal. "We tried to stop the project but were overruled by our superiors, for some reason." The implication was clear, that David Lanier had been the primary beneficiary, in pocketing cash for land that had been rejected by a team of respected hydrologists.

When the article appeared, Stan Cavness got his first taste of what it meant to buck a Lanier. The mayor, infuriated, summoned the reporter and told him icily, "You don't cross me, hear? Don't you know who I am? You can't come into my town and cross me," he said, alluding to Cavness's not having been raised within the city limits. "I'll get you one day."

David Lanier had hounded Stan Cavness ever since. At the time of this first challenge to power, Cavness had been only twenty-one, buoyed by youthful self-confidence, idealism, and naïveté. He actually believed he had taken on the mayor and faced him down. When David won reelection to a sixth term by a two-to-one margin, however, Cavness got a lesson in who held the power in Dyersburg and decided he might accomplish more good in the world by becoming a cop. Observing the way parents abused their power over their children, watching the police trying to deal with child abuse cases, had drawn him into joining the DPD.

Cavness had the appearance and the disposition of a clean-shaven Santa Claus. As he recounted that first run-in with David Lanier, however, his fists clenched in anger. He tried to lighten the mood by telling another Lanier anecdote, this one from his early days on the police force.

One night he and his partner answered a distress call from a roadhouse. A bar whore nicknamed Tucson, who had a lot of miles on her, had started a fight. There she was, wildass drunk, slashing the air with a broken bottle, like some flipped-out granny in a miniskirt. When Stan grabbed her, she stomped on his big toe with her spiked heel. That eliminated any kind feelings for her, and he placed her under arrest.

At the jailhouse she demanded her right to a phone call, and Stan complied, loaning her the coins himself. Without having to look it up, she dialed a number.

"Hello, David," she said, and proceeded to complain about her brutal treatment at the hands of the police. Then she held out the receiver to Stan and said, "The mayor wants to talk to you." Stan came to the phone.

"Officer Cavness?" the voice said. It was Lanier, all right.

"Yessir, Mr. Mayor," Stan said into the phone.

"I want you to release this woman, Tucson."

Stan, his toe still smarting, indignant, decided not to let Tucson know what the mayor was asking him to do.

"That's right, Mr. Mayor," he dissembled, "she's being charged with assaulting an officer and resisting arrest."

"You didn't understand me," Lanier replied. "I told you to release her."

"We'll see that she's locked up safely, sir."

"Officer! I am ordering you to release this woman!" Lanier shouted into the phone. When Stan kept up his ruse, the mayor hung up.

Lanier contacted a police captain, who released Tucson that night. But Cavness wrote up his report exactly as events had transpired, and when Lanier got wind of that, he demanded Cavness's resignation, for the first of many times.

Then as now, in an extremely tense confrontation at the mayor's office, Chief Williamson backed Stan. Lanier threatened to file suit on behalf of the city against Cavness if he did not quit. The mayor backed off, how-ever, when Cavness swore that he would testify that Lanier must know Tucson awfully well, since she knew his home phone number by heart and had started talking to "David" without having to identify herself.

Cavness, whose father had been a wandering Baptist preacher and who had been fascinated all his life by how people could be moved more by the perception of power than by its actuality, had learned from experience that standing up to Lanier could shake the tyrant, if not topple him. The trouble was, hardly anyone ever dared challenge him—not that Cavness blamed them.

"He's the coldest, most unfeeling man I've ever met," Cavness said. "Look in his eyes, there's nothing there. He's like a Mafia don. The only human beings he cares about are his children." For his daughters, Lanier would do things that he never considered doing for anyone else. He lived with the younger one most of the time now; he had set the older one, Leigh Anne, up in a Mexican restaurant with her husband—this was before Que Pasa—or so everyone assumed.

One day Stan and other officers ordered food by phone from the place, and who delivered it but Judge Lanier, on his lunch hour! There was the great man, carting tacos to cops! It made him seem almost human.

"Did you tip him?" Castleberry asked.

"Thought about it," Cavness laughed.

Joey McDowell was rather skeptical of the nature and degree of Lanier's affection for his daughters, however devoted Robbye and Leigh Anne were to their father. To Joey, this was by and large another exten-sion of Lanier's power relationships with everyone, even if he did volun-teer for taco duty. Joey reminded Stan of the time when they had been juvenile officers together and Lanier had instructed them to go "find" drugs on Larry Johnson, the young man to whom Leigh Anne was then engaged to be married. The judge had at first been roundabout with his request but had become explicit when McDowell and Cavness refused to comply.

"You all catch anybody you want to catch," Lanier had sputtered. "Why can't you catch somebody I want you to catch? You go find drugs on that boy!"

The officers protested that they had no probable cause for a search of the young man or his car.

"I'm giving you probable cause," the judge said, "right now! I know what probable cause is, and when I say you have it, you have it!"

Exasperated with them, he said that he would have the sheriff take care of the matter. One of Tommy Cribbs's deputies then arrested Johnson for possession of marijuana.

It was not that Lanier had thought the boy wasn't good enough for Leigh Anne, McDowell explained. It was all a typical Lanier power play. The judge hadn't cared who his daughter's husband was, so long as it was crystal-clear who was boss.

"He got that boy into trouble to get him out of it," Stan Cavness elaborated. Lanier had bailed Johnson out himself, the day of the arrest. "The next thing you knew, the judge was down at the jail giving the poor kid a lecture. 'Don't you ever forget I'm doing this for you' and so on. I think even old Tommy Cribbs must have been disgusted by it, he'd never do a thing like that to one of his own."

"Not unless he was drunk," Joey interrupted.

"That boy sure did get the message," Cavness continued. "He was over doing chores at the Lanier house the next day. David had himself plenty of free labor from then on. And when Leigh Anne and Johnson got married, Lanier set them up in that restaurant. They owed everything to him, and that's the way the judge wanted it."

It was during that time that Lanier added McDowell to his enemies list. Joey and Stan together had created a program they called Dyer County-Dyersburg Metro Juvenile Department, or Metro Youth for short, beginning early in 1982, under Lanier's predecessor as judge, a fine old man who had been in office for nearly fifty years. McDowell and Cavness were commissioned as both sheriff's deputies and policemen. They formed the new department to cope with a huge caseload, over six hundred arrests annually of boys and girls under the age of eighteen and twice that many complaints. Both had training in juvenile law, and both knew that conventional methods were neither helping the juveniles nor reducing juvenile crime in the community. Metro Youth combined law enforcement with psychological counseling and intensive work with parents, who were usually the root cause of problems. When it came to sentencing, they prepared recommendations based on a comprehensive knowledge of a youth's background, with detailed plans for follow-up supervision and counseling.

The program worked. It quickly became a model for the state, and Joey and Stan traveled throughout Tennessee helping other cities set up similar departments.

"It was the most fulfilling thing I've ever done as a cop," Joey told Castleberry and Champine. "Then David Lanier got elected judge, and he destroyed it."

Metro Youth was a threat to Judge Lanier's power. He made it clear that he and he alone would control which cases were prosecuted and what the sentences would be, without any advice or background supplied from officers, social workers, psychologists, psychiatrists, clergy, or anyone else. Piece by piece he took apart something that had united the community to address problems that were otherwise intractable. Metro Youth had even solved at least one murder that made Joey angry to remember and that was never far from his mind.

"This little boy," Joey said, "we found him dead in a dresser drawer. We rushed him to the hospital, but it was too late. I'll never forget the sight of him. He had this tiny little shrunken-up body and this great big head; he was five years old, with bruises and scars and cigarette burns all over him, especially on his head. My God, it was awful." Joey had to light a cigarette and sip some coffee to go on.

Stan explained that the whole episode, which took Joey on a chase after the parents, all the way to Oklahoma, was especially tough on McDowell because his own daughter, Anna, had been born the day before they found the boy. Joey had been present at the birth, and then the next day, in the same hospital, he had to watch the autopsy of that little boy. At first the doctors couldn't tell whether he had died of asphyxiation or internal bleeding. It could have been either.

"The parents killed him," Joey went on. "They were gypsies. They roamed around earning money telling stories and stealing, you know, had all their other four kids into it but not this one. He was half-black, and they hated him for it, called him a corky and kept him locked up or made him lie on the floor of the car out of sight. I guess the mother'd gotten herself knocked up. He was her disgrace, being black.

"He would've starved to death before they suffocated him, but his sister, she was only six, kept him alive sneaking him half her hamburgers. She led me to a motel room they'd stayed in where they locked him in a closet while they ate. His sister told me she'd snuck him food in there. I found some bread crumbs and a sandwich wrapper."

The mother pleaded guilty to first-degree murder and received a life sentence; the father got thirty-three years, for second-degree murder.

"I guess the mother closed the drawer on him," Joey said. "They should've executed both parents, the way I see it. We found homes for the kids who survived, but they'd seen it all, the beatings and the torture and the killing. That little girl who fed him, she had goodness in her, didn't she? But what chance does she have in life, after that?"

Joey and Stan agreed that they might never have solved the murder and could not have helped the other children without their Metro Youth program, which Lanier soon scuttled.

"Lanier would shout at us and throw us out of court," Stan said. "He banned us. He'd refuse a case if we brought it, either one of us. He ruined it all."

Finally Lanier fired them outright. In a unique show of solidarity against the judge, their entire staff quit with them. Lanier didn't care. He liked it. He hired his own staff after that.

"Stocked his stable," Joey said. "Attractive white females only need apply."

Other stories followed, but Castleberry could not get his mind off that little half-caste boy—and the officers' reaction to him. The murder had occurred eight years before but obviously haunted them, especially Joey. Here were two officers who cared deeply about their work, about human beings, examples of what every cop should be. He had watched Joey work with his Special Response Team, whose two black members functioned as equals along with the other tough guys, toward whom Joey acted as brother, uncle, father, coach, and commander. And Castleberry had seen Joey at home with his wife and kids, as close a family as could be, uncommonly so for a policeman's. Now he understood that fierce look Joey had, those haunted eyes. The pain good cops carried around with them was something terrible. And these were the guys David Lanier had tried to ruin.

It was time for Castleberry and Champine to face the judge.

As instructed, they entered the courthouse at the north side and found the door to the judge's chambers, pausing to examine the portrait of James P. hanging on the hallway wall opposite. The painting would have been the first thing a woman saw when leaving the judge's office by that exit. No doubt David Lanier himself had directed that it be placed there.

Castleberry commented on how respectable the patriarch looked, like a college president, bespectacled, benignly authoritative in a blue suit, above a bronze plaque extolling his service to the county and the state.

Castleberry knocked, firmly. They waited. At last the knob turned, the door moved inward about an inch, and stopped. Castleberry pushed it open—just in time to observe His Honor settling himself into the chair behind his desk, smoothing his black robe.

The obviousness of this ploy struck Castleberry. Having left the door slightly ajar, Lanier must have scurried across the room and behind his desk, so as to be seated regally as the agents entered. He ought to have employed a footman. Apart from its transparency, there was something childish about the maneuver, which reminded Castleberry of how a pubescent boy would improvise to prevent his mother from catching him in a forbidden practice. If Brenda Castain was to be believed, the analogy was not far-fetched.

"I am Judge Lanier," he intoned, drawing out the words.

"David," Castleberry replied without missing a beat, "I am Special Agent Bill Castleberry of the FBI. And this is Special Agent Steve Champine of the Tennessee Bureau of Investigation."

Castleberry had decided beforehand that he would try to disconcert Lanier by ignoring his title and addressing him by his first name. This encounter would be a test of nerves and wills, of who could throw whom off balance. Especially after the stories he had heard that morning, Castleberry was determined to get the jump.

Lanier did seem to be taken aback at this irreverence. There was an interval of silence as Castleberry, wishing to imply an air of utter indifference, let his eyes range over the degrees on the wall behind the judge, the books, a photograph of high school cheerleaders on the desk. No photo of Mrs. Lanier, he noted.

Without being invited to do so, Castleberry seated himself in a straight chair against a bookshelf. Champine followed his example.

The silence lengthened. Castleberry became aware of how small, how confining the room was, no larger than nine by twelve, he estimated, and how dark and oppressive without windows. He conjured up the energetic activities that supposedly had taken place in there. Where? And how? To achieve actual intercourse, the desk must have come into play. To accomplish the act lying down, without rearranging the furniture, participants would have had to grapple on the brown-carpeted floor along the narrow aisle between the desk and the chairs that lined one wall—a space barely sufficient for someone of Lanier's girth. Maybe he had sat in a chair during that videotaping, with Linda Pickering kneeling—Castleberry repressed the image, which to him was more emetic than erotic.

Lanier was staring at him, vacant-eyed, wearing an odd grin, the right corner of the upper lip raised to show some teeth. Castleberry attempted to mirror this smirk or sneer, without much success, he feared. He was sure that he must look like some overly friendly goofball or a man with loose dentures, not the image of contemptuous mimicry he was trying to project. Whatever, Lanier broke eye contact. When he finally spoke, he kept his eyes lowered or wandering around the room.

"I have no wish to engage in any question-and-answer session at this time," he said.

"Okay," Castleberry offered cheerily.

"I welcome the opportunity to meet the agents investigating me. That's the reason I called the FBI, for a meeting."

"That was my understanding," Castleberry said. "So here we are."

"All of the allegations against me are false. They are politically motivated."

Castleberry did not reply to that. Which allegations was Lanier referring to? Ones that had not surfaced yet? He waited, staring at that big face as hard as he could, for Lanier to identify what charges he was talking about.

But the judge said nothing further. A standoff.

"Okay, David," Castleberry said, rising. "Glad to meet you, also. And I'm sure we'll be seeing more of each other."

There were no handshakes.

Outside, after an interview that had lasted maybe five minutes, Castleberry asked Champine for his impressions.

"That guy is scared," Champine said.

"Yeah, I thought he looked a little wobbly. But it's our job to find out what he's afraid of."

16

To discuss the Lanier interview and to figure out what to do next, Castleberry drove Champine to Barham's, a barbecue restaurant out on the bypass that was rarely crowded at lunch. At the counter he ordered his usual sandwich, a thick hand-cut slice of smoked baloney topped, Memphis-style, with coleslaw and lashings of hot sauce, and a tall glass of unsweetened iced tea that you tapped yourself from a cooler. He rarely missed lunch, a ritual that lent structure to improvised days and provided a refuge in which to think. Champine shared his aversion to fast food joints, on culinary as well as atmospheric grounds. A modest, family-run place like Barham's accommodated their mutual fondness for real barbecue and seclusion. They settled into a corner table at the rear.

Castleberry said that he believed their performance in the judge's chambers had earned them at least a draw. Champine had the knack of making his silences eloquent, and Bill had sparred coolly and effectively with Lanier. Now was the time to gain the momentum somehow, letting Lanier know that he had failed to intimidate them: "I want him to know we're not going away. I want him to be thinking about us, day and night. How?"

Halfway through his sandwich, he had made up his mind.

"It's time for a full-court press," he said. "Time to go all out. We're launching a surprise attack. We'll let him know his little mind game didn't work. And this will be therapeutic for us, you'll see."

In excited monologue he laid out his scheme.

By two that afternoon they were on the sidewalk in front of the Baird-Brewer Building, a three-story brick structure dating from 1918, vaguely

romanesque in style, that had once been a hospital and now housed the
Office of Criminal Investigation of the Juvenile Court. They were still
within Lanier's domain. This was the building, a block north of the courthouse, from which Joey McDowell and Stan Cavness had been driven
after watching Lanier wreck their Metro Youth program. Three women
who happened to be on Castleberry's list worked there now.

The women would be surprised to see them. This time Castleberry had
not phoned ahead for an appointment. There was some risk in this tactic,
with its element of shock.

The advantage of an unannounced visit by an agent was that sometimes the impact of saying "FBI" and flashing a badge induced candor. If
the target wasn't there, however, the technique often backfired, causing
panic, making a potentially valuable witness flee or clam up, perhaps
from fear of being caught in some irrelevant crime. Everyone had something to hide. Letting a subject think unhurriedly about the prospect of
talking to an agent could be more effective, a kind of courteous seduction.

In this instance Castleberry chose surprise because his primary purpose
was to rattle Lanier by means of what amounted to an invasion of his territory, signaling him that he had failed to scare the agents off, whether the
women talked or not.

They climbed the stairs to the second floor and found the office of the
Youth Services Officer at the far end of the hall. A sign on the secretary's
desk identified her as Tina Brock. She was on the list.

"Is Sandy Sanders in?" Castleberry asked. He was looking quite official that afternoon, having dressed for the judge in a dark suit, white shirt,
and red tie; Champine was similarly attired. They brought out their
badges, or "badged" her in police parlance, and their IDs with photographs. Tina Brock said that Sandy Sanders was with someone but
would be free shortly.

"Fine," Castleberry said. "Tell her we're not in a hurry. We'll talk to
you first. And is Brenda Castain in? Good. Ask her to stick around. Is
there a room we can use? We'll need some privacy."

Tina Brock led them to a small room down the hall. Champine took
notes as Castleberry informed her that they were conducting an investigation of Judge David Lanier. Was Ms. Brock aware of any sexual harassment of female employees by the judge during the nine months that she
had worked for him?

She had heard many rumors, even before she had taken this job. And
on her first day at work, the judge had come over from the courthouse
and said to her, in a way that had upset her, "People will think you're my
girlfriend." If this was meant as a compliment to her looks, she did not
appreciate it.

Because of what she had heard, she had been afraid that something like this might happen. She immediately told him, "I'm not that kind of person. I don't go in for that sort of thing." She was forthright because she believed that he was testing her to see how she felt about sexual activity.

"And how did he react to that?" Castleberry asked.

"He must have gotten the message. He didn't bother me after that." She added that working in this building, she had little occasion to visit the courthouse.

The interview was brief. Sandy Sanders was waiting for them when they returned, and she asked them into her private office. Her manner was cordial, if nervous. Castleberry had the impression that she had been hoping to see them.

Sandy Sanders was the supervisor of this division, with Tina Brock, Brenda Castain, and a male probation officer under her. As she explained her duties, which did not include hiring or firing anyone—the judge reserved that authority for himself—she was serious, even grave as she looked directly at the agents. Behind her desk she held her head high and projected physical and emotional strength. She gave her age as thirty-one and was the first of the women for whom, Castleberry thought to himself, the word *girl* would be not only demeaning but nondescriptive.

"I am a very religious person," she volunteered to his first question about harassment. "I believe that I was placed here for a reason."

Although Castleberry's own membership in the First Methodist Church of Jackson was mostly nominal, retained for his daughters' sakes, he had no objection to divine intervention, if it was on his side, and hoped Sandy Sanders's profession of faith meant commitment to the truth. She assumed the earnest, fervent demeanor of the born again, her eyes bright and steady, as if she were ready to witness for Christ. What she seemed most interested in conveying, however, was less a description of David Lanier's behavior than her refusal to capitulate to him. She wanted Castleberry to know that her religious principles had kept her free from sin or even from temptation—yet she seemed to be soft-pedaling whatever it was that Lanier had tried with her. Castleberry had to ask her to start her story over two or three times, and to be more specific about matters she obviously wished to avoid discussing. Finally she became more direct.

When Lanier first interviewed her for the department-head job, she made a point of saying that she was a conservative person with "old-fashioned beliefs." Probably for that reason, Lanier ended up giving the position to someone else, although Sanders was better qualified, with ninety-six hours of college credit in criminal justice studies. She was disappointed, because the position fit her interests and talents perfectly. Married, with two children, she wanted to help troubled kids, and she fervently believed that God had chosen her for this kind of ministering.

Two years ago last May, Lanier called her after the person he had hired, a man, had left, and asked her if she was still interested. When she said yes, he said there were certain matters he needed to clear up first and told her to come to his chambers for another interview.

It was a very disturbing session. Lanier told her that he had heard certain rumors, that she had been telling people that if the judge tried anything with her, her husband would give him a whipping, beat the living tar out of him. What did she have to say for herself?

The accusation caught her so much by surprise, and was so unjust and untrue, that she had lost control of her emotions. Protesting that she had never said such a thing and never would, she burst into tears, and was so embarrassed at this loss of composure that it became worse. She had sat there in front of him, humiliated. He had let her go without saying whether she had the job or not.

A few days later, he called again. By then she was not sure at all whether she wanted to work for him, or should, but when he offered to hire her, she accepted.

"It was a challenge," Sanders said, angrily and seeming on the verge of tears again. "I believe a person should meet challenges, not back away from them."

And then he hit on you, Castleberry said to himself, knowing what must be coming. This guy was some manipulator. But had he broken Sandy Sanders?

Soon after she had started work, she continued, Lanier had begun touching her "in certain places." Her job entailed frequent visits to see him at the courthouse. She was responsible for recommending the disposition of cases, although he often ignored her advice, and preparing the docket for the judge. It was when she was alone with him that Lanier put his hands on her.

Castleberry asked her if she would mind elaborating. He hoped it wouldn't be too painful, but a more specific description of what Lanier had done would be very helpful.

"He grabbed my breast and my buttocks," she said, "and he tried to kiss me, numerous times."

"Always in his chambers?"

"Yes, except once he followed me down the aisle of his courtroom and squeezed my behind as I was going through the door. I think he wanted people to see him doing it, to humiliate me. It did."

She kept thinking that her resistance and obvious displeasure would make him stop, but shunning him had the opposite effect. It seemed to excite him. Finally, after a few weeks of this, she confronted him.

"Did you tell anyone about what was going on?" Castleberry asked.

"I discussed it with my husband and with some members of my church. People advised me to quit. I'm not a quitter. I wanted to have it out with him."

"So you did?"

"He finally did something that got me so upset and angry that I did."

Sanders described how she was sitting in a chair in Lanier's chambers, deliberately having chosen the one closest to the door, during one of their weekly meetings to discuss the docket. He had come around from behind his desk, slowly at first, listening to her report, and suddenly he had lunged at her, pinned her into the chair, and forcibly kissed her on the lips.

She had managed to struggle free and bolted from the courthouse and back to her office, where she broke down in sobs.

When she calmed down, she was furious. She rang his number and told him that she had to talk to him, now, and he said to come over.

Back in his chambers, she calmly but forcefully told him that she appreciated him as a person and as a judge, and that she hoped he appreciated her as a human being. She wanted him to know that she was happily married and a churchgoer, and that she was devoted to doing right and living right. She did not appreciate what he was doing to her.

"How did he react to that?"

"He looked at me, and he said, 'I'm sorry. I'm sorry.'"

She accepted his apology, or tried to; it was difficult. She had wanted to be forgiving.

He had not been sorry, as she found out. After that, the attacks stopped, but he began harassing her in other ways. She had never received a raise since, not for almost two years, although everyone else had. He chipped away at her authority, taking this and that responsibility away from her, until she was reduced to everyone else's level, although she was by title still their supervisor. He had been trying to force her to quit, without firing her outright, by making her job unpleasant. He had never criticized her work before. Now he was nitpicking about everything she did. He was trying to get her to crack emotionally, but she had made sure never to let him know how his demeaning actions were affecting her. She knew that when she had broken down in front of him before, he took it as a sign of his control over her.

It had been a battle of wills, these past months. She was suffering, her nerves were raw, she was not being paid properly—but she refused to quit. By now, she was sure, he hated her.

As he and Champine were leaving her office, Sandy Sanders cast Castleberry a look that seemed to say, "Well, now I've told you everything. I've bared my soul. What are you going to do about it?"

He wished he knew. He believed every word she had said, and he admired her strongly for her character. But still, had Lanier broken any laws? Sanders could sue Lanier, but what lawyer would take her case, and who would believe her over a judge? Her case would be stronger if he had fired her, as Lanier must know; even then the odds against her winning would be tremendous, the cost prohibitive.

Brenda Castain was waiting for them in her office. She crouched behind her desk, as if trying to hide.

Here was the woman Castleberry had most wanted to see, the original, the only complainant. If she had given in to Lanier, as her promotion last December, about a month after Bastin and Donohue had talked to her, suggested, at least she had actually gone to the FBI, reluctantly or not. Castleberry was hoping that, like Sanders, Castain had been waiting for outside help and would prove eager to cooperate. She had had more than an hour to realize that she was no longer alone, that other women were being interviewed, too.

But no, Brenda Castain could hardly speak, she was obviously so scared. Her tortured face, beautiful as it was, reminded Castleberry of a prisoner's. Her skin was greenish; her nervous hands were puffy, outsized in relation to her other features, a possible indication of drug use. She averted her eyes, so he could not see whether her pupils were dilated.

What she had told the agents before had been true, Castain admitted, although she may have exaggerated, she had been so upset back then.

"And now?" Castleberry asked. "What's been happening since then?"

"I don't have any problems now," she said. "Everything is fine."

"What do you mean, fine? Judge Lanier isn't harassing you? He isn't doing anything you object to?"

"No. My only problems are with my husband."

She explained that somehow, within two days of her having talked to the FBI agents last fall, Judge Lanier had found out about it. He had known about everything she had said.

She must have talked to someone who had informed Lanier, Castleberry was certain, unless Lanier had a source within the FBI, which was extremely unlikely. But Castleberry said nothing. Brenda Castain added that she had finally told her husband about the situation and that this had caused her a lot of problems.

"What kind of problems?"

She had nothing further to say, except to repeat that she no longer was having any difficulties with Judge Lanier, who was behaving like a gentleman toward her.

"Thank you," Castleberry said, and ended the interview.

Outside, Castleberry turned to Champine to ask what he thought about Brenda Castain. Champine said she was terrified, freaked out—and lying.

"Absolutely," Castleberry said. "That sonofabitch is still making her give sex to him, I'd bet on it."

Even though Tina Brock had claimed having suffered only a minor irritation from Lanier, she admitted that she had heard enough rumors to put her on guard; Sandy Sanders had provided concrete examples of harassment and of what amounted to assault; Brenda Castain was hiding something, probably a lot, and had previously provided serious, even grotesque examples of harassment and, possibly, extortion. The pattern was distinct, whatever the variations in the women's statements. Everywhere you looked, Lanier was after one woman or another and had caused at least some of them serious distress.

But where were the actual crimes?

"Back to the courthouse," Castleberry said. "Let's turn up the pressure some more."

They walked straight into Lanier's office and introduced themselves to the secretary, Sherry Cooper, who was on the list. They said they would appreciate a few minutes of her time.

She stalled them. Friendly, bubbly, an appealing little bundle of energy, she apologized in her honey-tongued drawl for being so terrifically busy just now, having to clear things up before the end of the day. Her desk was clean; the phone was silent, but she sighed at being so far behind.

"That's okay," Castleberry said. "We'll be back in the morning. How would nine-thirty be for you?"

She agreed. *Have a pleasant night's sleep,* Castleberry was thinking. *And be sure to tell your boss about your plans for tomorrow. And please don't try to bullshit us.*

In the hallway Castleberry suggested that they take the opportunity to make sure everybody in the building knew that they were there. He and Champine made the rounds, sticking their noses into offices, greeting people with, "How are you today?" and "Nice to see you." Everyone knew who they were. Reactions varied from forced smiles to hostile stares.

"We're going to make a point of showing up here every day," Castleberry told Champine as they left. "I want Lanier to feel like a man adrift on a raft with great white sharks circling."

There were eight motels in and around Dyersburg. Of them the Holiday Inn, on the bypass at the intersection of highways 78 and 51, was the largest and most attractive. It served as the town's social center, where civic groups held their meetings, the prosperous met for buffet lunch after church, and out-of-town businessmen gathered with locals to promote the area's decade-long prosperity. The occupancy rate was high, but Joey McDowell had befriended the manager, who could always provide a room for any officer in need of a neutral place to conduct interviews and make phone calls.

Late that afternoon, figuring that the sooner he could interview as many women as possible, the more pressure it would place on Lanier, Castleberry took a room at the rear on the ground floor, where visitors could come and go without attracting attention. He telephoned Source to ask for a meeting to introduce Steve Champine, who knew of Source's existence but no more than that, and to go over the lengthening list of names. On Castleberry's assurances that Champine was trustworthy and that there was a bottle of whiskey waiting, Source agreed to come to the Holiday Inn after dark.

By the time Source arrived, Castleberry had arranged with Joey McDowell and Chief Williamson to have the basement conference room at the DPD available all the following day, on the assumption that the women would be more candid away from their offices. They could enter from the side parking lot through a tunnel that led straight to that room, so that no one would see them. At the same time, the secrecy and police atmosphere would create pressure on them to loosen their tongues.

"You're on the right track with that one," Source said of a new name on the list, Cathy Kiely, about whom no one knew much of anything but who had been Lanier's secretary for a suspiciously brief period a year ago. At the other extreme was a woman who had worked in the court-house for years. Source advised that she might be the key to the whole case.

When Source left, Castleberry telephoned four women and scheduled appointments with them at two-hour intervals the next day. He let them know that they had no choice but to appear. None sounded pleased about that.

Before leaving the motel, he phoned Steve Parker to update him and to ask for legal guidance. How useful was the evidence accumulated so far? Hadn't Lanier committed a crime if he had extorted sex from Brenda Castain, even if she had, finally, willingly succumbed?

"I don't think so," Parker said.

Heading for home around nine that night, Castleberry was anxious. By what he had done that day and by lining up more witnesses for the next, without knowing what if any crimes he was investigating, he had put himself out on a limb. What he was doing might even be illegal, since agents were no longer authorized to go on fishing expeditions, as in the seventies, when illegal searches and other transgressions had blackened the FBI's reputation. There had to be probable cause that a crime had been committed for an agent to run around disrupting lives, frightening people, and compiling sensitive files of 302s.

Leaving Dyersburg, he stopped at a barbecue stand, Hog Heaven, for a sandwich and a soda to take out.

It was a clear, cool night. Out in the countryside he pulled his car onto a dirt road, stopped, and killed the engine. In the silence and darkness he looked at the stars and munched on his sandwich and tried to decide what to do. Nearly all of the women had something to hide, he was sure; none wanted to talk. He would have to make them open up, one way or another.

17

Castleberry and Champine need not have worried, if they wanted news of their presence to spread. Dyersburg may not have been any more prone to gossip than other towns its size, close to twenty thousand by then, but word of mouth was an unusually efficient medium of communication there. Why this was so was not difficult to understand.

For one thing, this was the South. Southerners, other than the type who dwells in a hollow with shotgun propped on windowsill, talk more than other Americans—converse more often and at greater length than, say, residents of Vermont or the Dakotas, and with disarming intimacy. And for another, the channels of gossip in Dyersburg flowed freely because there was so much to gossip about. In 1990, as locals learned from Paul Harvey's popular daily radio program, originating from Chicago and heard by millions nationwide, Dyer had the highest ratio of divorces to marriages of any county in the United States, surpassing even Clark County, Nevada, of which Las Vegas is the seat. If citizens were embarrassed by this publicity, they were not surprised by it, knowing that multiple marriages among them had become commonplace if not the norm. One secretary at the courthouse kept busy doing nothing but trying to monitor delinquent child support payments. Who had been spotted running around with whom was what made phone lines hum. And David Lanier played the lead in a soap opera that had been watched for more than twenty years.

The minute the agents left his chambers, Judge Lanier was on the phone to his lawyers. His secretary, meanwhile, was at lunch speculating with her colleagues from the courthouse and City Hall about what the agents might be after. By that afternoon, the word was out, to the alarm of many and the curiosity of all. As soon as Castleberry terminated the interview with Brenda Castain, she called Vivian Forsythe.

At work at Charles Kelly's office, Vivian could not speak freely. She agreed to meet at Brenda's house.

Vivian had still not told Brenda or anyone else about her experiences with David Lanier. Her initial reaction on hearing about the kinds of questions the agents had asked Brenda was terror. Would she be next? What would happen to her, what would Lanier do to her if she told the truth? Lanier would convince everyone that she was out of her mind and do as he had threatened, take Ashley away from her. Her parents, she had no doubt, would believe Lanier. Nor had her behavior during the past few months done anything to assure them that she was capable of being on her own and a responsible mother.

Holding down a job and taking care of Ashley as a single mother had proved too much for her without her parents' help. Her victory over her parents in the custody battle had been a hollow one, she soon realized. Their spiriting Ashley off to Memphis and hiding the child there, as Vivian saw events at the time, had enraged her, goaded her into extreme response. In retrospect she understood better why they had done it. Then she had been utterly out of control, as she had been ever since those hideous instances in Lanier's chambers. Hysterical, irresponsible, volatile, drinking and drugging, running off with Dr. Warner and the judge to the Bahamas—she had even abandoned Ashley on that favorite children's holiday, Halloween, last year.

Having won back custody of Ashley, Vivian had been able to manage on her own for only a few weeks. Still in rebellion against her mother, she was relying on her ex-husband more and more to share child care responsibilities, choosing to believe that he had had nothing to do with hurting Ashley's arm—the alternative being to accept that her mother and the Memphis doctors had been right in suspecting abuse. She left Ashley with Butch the entire weekend during the middle of March, entertaining the idea that his willingness to care for his daughter should be encouraged and might even mean a future for them as a family, divorced or not. On that Monday morning, March 11, 1991, Butch brought Ashley home, and Vivian dropped her off at day care on the way to work.

That afternoon the day-care center called to say that Ashley was experiencing pain urinating. Vivian immediately brought her to see Dr. Joseph Connell, a pediatrician, who took a urine sample. The results of the urinalysis came through the next day. Dr. Connell's office informed Vivian that she was to bring Ashley to a pediatric clinic immediately. A social worker would meet them there.

In his report, the examining physician at the clinic stated that the urinalysis performed at Dr. Connell's office had noted some dead or inactive sperm present in the sample. A complete physical examination showed no evidence of any bruises, contusions, or abrasions on any areas of Ashley's body; likewise, there was no evidence of vaginal or anal penetration, and wet smears taken of these areas and examined under a microscope were negative. The findings of the urinalysis, however, indicating suspected sexual abuse, were "very significant" and should be "pursued."

No one could say with certainty who had abused Ashley or when or where the abuse had taken place, and the social worker, however, after extensive interviews with Vivian and her ex-husband, reached no definite conclusions.

Vivian, believing that her inability to cope as a single mother was now an inescapable, humiliating fact, and that she had only one option left, explained the situation to her mother, showing her the clinic's report, and moved back into her parents' house with Ashley. From then on she adhered strictly to the original stipulation of her divorce agreement, not forgetting that it had been ordered by David Lanier, that Butch was never to see Ashley unless Vivian was present. It was many weeks before she let him see the child at all, although he protested his innocence. Could someone at the day-are center have been responsible, if not an adult then some precocious boy? It was possible. Vivian did not know what to think.

Or to do. She continued working; she knew she had to prove herself anew; she tried to repress her suspicion that her mother now had what she had wanted all along, total control over her and Ashley—and how could she complain when, through her own carelessness and impetuousness, she was dependent on her parents again? The atmosphere in the house, so full of rancor and resentment, her father depressed by age and the loss of his beloved farmland, plunged her into deeper depression. More and more, little by little, she surrendered Ashley to Judy Forsythe's care, or to the housekeeper's. You were right all along, she knew her inaction and indifference were saying, I'm a failure, I was never any good. On weekends she slept past noon. She kept pills and a bottle close.

She started seeing more of Brenda Castain again, drawn by old ties and, more, by the dim satisfaction of being around someone who was in a worse situation—far, far worse, as Vivian soon learned—than she. One night in 1991 at Brenda's house, when Brenda's husband was out and her little boy was asleep, Vivian watched in sickened fascination as her friend injected herself with meperidine, jabbing the needle under a toenail, so as not to leave a mark. This depressant was the only way, Brenda said, she could cope with the nightmare her life had become. She only wished she had a stronger drug.

Back in December, Brenda said, after she had given up on the FBI, she had capitulated to David Lanier. The judge had known about her drug

habit, which was nowhere as bad as it had become since but was sufficient to cause a positive result on drug tests required for her job. Lanier
knew she needed extra money, for her habit and because her husband was
after her to earn more. She was clearing less than two-fifty a week.
Instead of asking for a promotion, she ought to have quit, no matter what,
with the way the judge was behaving and demanding sex from her.

Yet if she had resigned, he would have exposed her as a user and taken
her child away, she felt certain of that. Her husband would never have
stood by her. She had felt trapped.

That was when she surrendered. For months now, she had been giving
Lanier sex on demand. He summoned her to his office whenever he felt
the urge, often two and three times a week. And he telephoned her constantly, demanding to know if she was seeing anyone else, reminding her
that he knew about the drugs, driving by her house, badgering her.

Drugs were her only escape, as much as they were her curse also. Her
husband suspected, because she was so listless at home. Sometimes she
used cocaine to snap her awake.

Brenda's tale of horrors renewed Vivian's loathing for Lanier—and her
fear of him. Here was her best friend, who spent her days investigating
and counseling juveniles, nearly all of whom had drug problems themselves, then running home to smoke or snort or shoot up, after giving
Judge Lanier a screw or a blow job—and trying to deal with her child.
And with her husband, who had been furious to learn that Brenda had
talked to the FBI.

Far from sympathizing with her, Brenda's husband had accused her of
leading Judge Lanier on. If she did not behave herself and keep her job
and get a promotion, her husband had threatened, he would leave her and
take their son with him, as he was sure Judge Lanier would permit.

Someday she would get caught, Brenda said she feared. One day the
end would come. For now she could only try to survive. She was adept at
not showing the effects of drugs in public. No one at the office suspected,
she didn't think, except for Lanier.

Vivian believed it. She had never known the extent of Brenda's dependency herself until now. And she of all people understood that a person
could be thoroughly addicted and still function. Hungover or half-crazy
from pills at Charles Kelly's office, she performed her tasks with her
usual efficiency and dispatch. Kelly said she was one of the most skilled
secretaries he had ever had. It was all a game.

That night when Brenda told her everything, Vivian watched as her
friend inhaled a line of coke, to freshen up before her husband came
home, she said. Why not, Vivian told herself, what do I have to lose? I'm
already wrecking my own life, why not go all the way down? She also

told herself that she had a stronger will than Brenda's and would never permit herself to get trapped in so totally degrading a situation. Hadn't she tried to fight Lanier off, rather than give in to him? Hadn't she avoided him and refused his disgusting advances since? No, she could never be as weak as poor Brenda. She asked for some coke and sniffed it up through a bill. *At least I'm not shooting up,* she thought.

She had forgotten how coke's affect on her was less a high than a leveling out of anxiety. She gave Brenda a twenty for some to take home in a Baggie.

That had been the beginning of an accelerating descent. Weeks limped past for her with increasing dreariness and dissolution. She kept telling herself that any day now she would pull out of this spin, but soon she was drinking every night and drugging almost as often.

She could see, as if through a thick pane of glass, herself running away from Ashley, escaping the house at every excuse, leaving her daughter with family members or Loretta, the housekeeper. Even Vivian's sister, with whom relations were edgy at best and who was anxious not to let her forget that irresponsible jaunt with Dr. Warner, was caring for Ashley now, once or twice a week. "I love you," Vivian told her daughter when she held her, but she despised the sound of her own voice and knew she was giving up.

She thought of visiting the river as she always had, but did not, fearing what it might tell her. She could see herself floating away, like a stick on the stream, giving in, giving up. Do I want to die? She often asked herself that question. Increasingly the answer came up yes.

By that September afternoon when Brenda called her, frantic about the FBI's visit, Vivian had not thought for nearly a year that there would ever be an investigation of Judge Lanier. Brenda was frantic about what might happen. Would she be exposed? Would she be fired, lose her child? Or would, of all things, the FBI save her? She could no longer imagine that.

Nor could Vivian, but she decided that evening, letting drugs take hold, that if the FBI ever came to her, she would tell the truth. She would let whatever was going to happen, happen. If they were talking to Brenda and others at her office, they would be interviewing more women. But what were the chances of their ever getting to her? No one knew about her and Lanier. Should she tell someone, Brenda maybe, now? Or go to the FBI herself? She did not have the courage to do that. How did she know that it would accomplish anything?

No, she would watch the drama play out. She would try to regain her equilibrium, try to be a better mother, cling to her job and lie low as the judge and his lawyers maneuvered—until, she was sure, the agents would go away and Dyersburg was the same as always and Lanier was in his courthouse, snug and smart as a shithouse rat.

18

One by one throughout that day, September 19, 1991, women made their way down that dark tunnel, where Steve Champine waited to take them through the steel door and into the dungeon—that was Joey McDowell's sardonic term for the basement conference room, and it stuck. He understood what it would be like for these women, many of whom had never been inside a police station before, to be confronted by government agents. The questions asked them would be acutely embarrassing. None of them wanted to be there; all of them would be frightened. But that was the way it had to be. How else could they be induced to tell the truth?

The first scheduled interview was with Sherry Cooper. Rather than telephoning her, Castleberry and Champine, for maximum effect, showed up again at her office promptly at nine-thirty.

"We can talk here," Castleberry said, "or if you prefer, you can come to the police station. That might be more comfortable for you," he added, expecting to unnerve her and shake her loyalty to the judge with this last somewhat sarcastic touch.

But Sherry Cooper did not seem in the least bit fazed.

"Fine," she said, as if they had asked her out for a milkshake. "I'll follow you guys over."

And so she did in her car, a distance of five blocks. In the conference room she remarked on how pretty the day was, a hint of fall in the air.

Her insouciance bugged Castleberry. It was as if she had taken the initiative away from him. What was the point in being an FBI agent if the witness did not respect his position? He fixed her with his fiercest glare, removing his glasses to give her the full whammy of his dark blue eyes, which he knew could express any emotion he chose and which he considered his greatest interviewing asset. He counted on being able to manipulate a subject with those eyes, making a person see kindness or doubt or impatience or unknown and dire consequences.

Unless Sherry Cooper was being utterly truthful, which seemed preposterous in the light of what other women had already revealed about David Lanier's habitually predatory behavior, Castleberry soon felt that he might as well keep his goddamned eyes shut, for all the effect they were having on her. David Lanier was like family to her, she said. She had worked happily for him as a secretary and paralegal for nearly three years, except for two brief periods, and had never had anything to complain about. She was a very close friend of the judge's older daughter, Leigh Anne, and had been since childhood, so she had known all the Laniers forever. Leigh Anne had told her about the job opening to begin with and had recommended her for it.

"Have you ever heard any rumors about Judge Lanier harassing women?" Castleberry asked, in a tone that meant, "We know you have, so you better tell us about them."

Here she gave in, but slightly. She had heard stories about Lanier, she admitted, as everyone had. But she was so close to the family that right at the start she had warned him, in a perfectly friendly way, that she would not put up with any nonsense. She had been sexually harassed on a previous job and would never tolerate it again. The judge had never given her any trouble, nor had she ever seen him bothering anyone else.

"I have to warn you, Ms. Cooper," Castleberry said, "that it is a crime to lie to a federal official."

She was aware of that. If the judge was up to something, she had no way of knowing about it. She did not have a key to his chambers; as far as she knew, no one did, other than Lanier himself. If he wanted to see her, he buzzed her, and she always knocked before entering. As the agents knew, there was a private door to the chambers, so she never had any idea who was in there. And a filing room separated her office from the chambers.

Castleberry advised her that she might have to give testimony before a grand jury. If she was lying to him and later contradicted herself under oath, that was one crime. If she lied to the grand jury, it was perjury. With her job and her paralegal training, she replied, she was well aware of all that.

"Would you be prepared to submit to a polygraph examination?" Castleberry asked.

"Sure," she said. "No problem."

And she jounced out of the dungeon, perky as ever.

Castleberry pronounced Sherry Cooper an enigma. If it had not been for what Linda Pickering and Sandy Sanders had revealed, he would have believed Cooper, or almost.

By one o'clock, having seen two additional women, the agents were becoming increasingly discouraged. One subject manifested and professed an ignorance so complete as to make her potential testimony on any subject useless. The other, middle aged but girlishly and expensively dressed in flouncy polka dots, effectively dismissed the agents as impertinent meddlers in her private life, revealing absolutely nothing about it. A courthouse veteran of nearly ten years' standing, she was now in an important administrative position and very much aware of her rights. She knew nothing of any sexual harassment by David Lanier, against her or anyone else, she said rather airily. Castleberry had reports that many people assumed that she had been sexually involved with the judge, had been seen holding hands and playing footsie with him on out-of-town trips, that sort of thing. Without mentioning these stories, he asked her flat out whether she was or had been having an affair with the judge. Never batting an eye, she effectively terminated the interview.

"Since when is sex between consenting adults considered harassment?" she asked. "I had no idea that consensual sex was any of the FBI's business."

He politely thanked her and told her she could go. A whiff of what smelled like expensive perfume lingered after her. Knowing that he had been bested, he petulantly lit a cigar. At least he could outstink her.

He was impressed. He admired her for having put him in his place. It was frustrating, because he had been advised that this woman probably knew more about David Lanier than anyone else did, but he doubted that he would ever get her to cooperate. She was too confident, self-possessed, and aware of her rights. He was just irritated enough to consider interviewing her husband but dropped that idea.

The agents broke for lunch at the Cozy Kitchen, a popular café, aptly named, half a block from the courthouse. As usual it was crowded at the lunch hour, the long center table lined with old men who gathered there every day and who lowered their voices as Castleberry and Champine passed on their way to fill their trays.

Castleberry had gained three or four pounds lately from too much barbecue and too many late-night whiskies when he could not sleep, trying to figure out Lanier. As he grew older, he worried about the FBI's rigorous biannual fitness tests. It could be embarrassing, huffing and puffing around a track behind men half your age. Except for some hearing loss in the upper registers, the result of hours on the firing range before the Bureau decided that earplugs were a good idea, he remained fit, but he had to watch his weight. His father, a hard worker and a hard drinker, a fun-loving man adored by his family, had died of a heart attack at fifty.

Today Castleberry passed up the fried chicken, chicken-fried steak, and fried pork chops smothered with rich brown gravy in favor of vegetables, which in good Southern style were several and fresh. Champine followed suit.

The tables were close together, the other patrons manifestly all ears. The agents fell spontaneously into an improvised code to discuss the case. Lanier became Darth Vader, or "the Darth," ruler of the evil empire. Castleberry said that he and Stevie Wonder, as he dubbed Champine, were going to have to do better with the interviewing if they were ever going to nail the Darth. Champine said that maybe Castleberry would have to live up to the nickname he had in the Bureau. Another agent had told Champine that Bill, because of the way he had conducted an interview during a certain case in the past, was known as the Prince of Fucking Darkness.

He might have to, Castleberry sighed, but these were women, and they weren't even criminals. The whole situation was bizarre, disturbing, and confusing. There were no guidelines, and there was nowhere to turn for advice. He supposed, reluctantly, they would have to get tougher.

Cathy Kiely, who was scheduled for two o'clock, was a divorced mother of two. According to Source, she was a statuesque blonde, a "Miss America type." Supposedly Lanier's wife had been furious with him for hiring Kiely as his secretary. The young woman had lasted only a week or two; no one knew why. Perhaps Mrs. Lanier for once had prevailed.

Kiely lived up to Source's description physically; emotionally she was very shaky. Her hands trembled; she had trouble remembering her birth date, which put her in her early thirties; and she had to fumble in her purse for her Social Security card to provide the number. She said that she had been unable to sleep last night after Castleberry's phone call. She would rather be almost anywhere than sitting before the agents.

Castleberry bore in. Why had she quit working for Lanier? Had he fired her? Had he harassed her?

She burst into tears. Castleberry kept at her. Whom was she protecting? What was she holding back? He jammed her with questions and underlined the usual warnings about lying to an agent or to a grand jury.

She protested that she was terrified of Lanier and his power—but she talked. Her story was virtually identical to Sandy Sanders's—the same come-ons, the same groping and squeezing—except that he had not desisted when she protested. On the day of her interview for the job, Lanier had come out from behind his desk and hugged her, saying, "I hope you don't mind. We're very friendly around here."

At the time she had laughed, to humor him—a big mistake, which had given him the wrong signal. Within a few days he became relentless in pursuit. When she resisted, he belittled her work, accusing her of not even knowing how to answer the phone properly. When one day he grabbed her and rubbed up against her, she quit.

Castleberry was unable to get her to give specific details of Lanier's actions, and he ended the interview feeling somewhat uncertain about her. He believed her story, but somehow he suspected that he had not heard the whole of it. It seemed a bit odd that she had gone back to Lanier for a recommendation for a job in Nashville; he had agreed—on the condition that she let him take her out to dinner in Nashville and sleep with her; she angrily refused. What had she expected of him, after the way he had treated her? And why was she so reluctant to cooperate now?

Frustrated, Castleberry was prepared to play Prince of Darkness with Mary Haralson, but she disarmed him by thanking him for letting her have so much time to prepare for this ordeal. It had taken her these several weeks, since that July encounter on her porch, to calm her husband down, after she finally got up the courage to tell him the real reason that she had lost her job with Lanier. Her husband had wanted to kill the judge, or to give him a good beating.

"Tell him to leave punishment to the courts," Castleberry said.

Haralson remained frightened of Lanier, she said. She had finally landed a new job, with a bank. Lanier had been over there, checking up on her, and was friends with the president, she believed.

Castleberry assured her that this interview was confidential. He did not tell her that if matters developed the way he hoped they might, she would have to repeat whatever she told him now in court.

Mary Haralson, who was now a month shy of her twenty-sixth birthday, had become friends with Lanier's daughter Leigh Anne, because their husbands were hunting buddies. The two couples socialized together, and she had been swimming at the judge's house on Starlight. She had heard rumors about Lanier's womanizing and harassing of female employees but assumed that her friendship with Leigh Anne, who recommended her for the secretary's job, would prevent trouble.

To preclude any misconceptions he might have, she mentioned during her interview that she was a church member and happily married. For the first month on the job, everything had gone smoothly.

Then the suggestive remarks started. She mentioned one day that she was going to begin jogging again.

"Joggers always look unhappy," he said. "I can relieve your tension and I'm sure you can relieve mine."

One afternoon she buzzed him and said that there was a gentleman waiting to see him.

"There's a gentleman back here waiting to see you, too," Lanier replied. To her the remark was blatantly sexual, less from the words than from the tone in which he uttered it.

Whenever she asked for time off to run an errand, he would make snide remarks, such as, "When you're ready to take the whole day off, maybe you can do something for me." Or when she asked for a couple of hours to attend a school assembly at which her son was to receive an award: "You can have days off to lie around the pool in your bikini, if you'll do me a favor." This sort of banter made her feel cheap. She put up with it because she needed the job and because it was such a good one, even though the pay was not great. And what would she tell Leigh Anne if she quit? Her reasoning was stupid, she now realized, but she had felt trapped.

About ten weeks after she had started work, Lanier summoned her to his chambers late one afternoon. After a minute's idle talk, he came out from behind his desk and grabbed her and started kissing her on her neck. She broke free and ran from the building. She ought never to have come back, but she did. She thought no one would believe the truth.

Within a day or two he came after her again. She was in his chambers when he snuck up on her during a break in a trial. He stepped behind her and pressed her up against a filing cabinet.

Castleberry asked for a more specific description. How had he grabbed her?

She admitted that she could feel him "moving his hips around" and that she could feel his penis against her buttocks. She immediately turned around, pushed him away, and warned him to stay back, in a loud voice. He told her to be quiet, because the door to the courtroom was open and someone might hear. If he was worried about that, she said, he had better keep his hands to himself.

After that he kept his distance but began denigrating her work, nitpicking about everything and criticizing her personal appearance. He accused her of having come to work in jogging clothes, something that she would never do. His constant carping, rather than encouraging her to quit, made her feel a failure, and she began to believe that there was actually something the matter with her. Now she was sorry that she had not told her husband about what was going on, but she was afraid of his reaction and of disappointing him. Her salary was important to them both. She was distressed enough to borrow money from another woman at the courthouse, to buy a new dress for work, hoping to appease Lanier.

If she needed extra money, the judge told her one day, she should come to an Amway meeting that was being held at his house that night. In her spare time she could become a distributor for the cleaning products company, which relied on home salespeople; his wife was one. She went, to please him.

Afterward he asked her if she was going to join up, and she said no, she did not have the money for membership, which cost more than a hundred dollars. That was no problem, he said. He would give her the money. They could work out a pleasant and easy method of repayment that would not cost her a penny. She told him that she resented the suggestion.

She had been working for him for about three months when, shortly after the incident in which she had yelled at him, he called her in and told her that "things are not working out." She told him that he was getting rid of her only because she refused to have anything to do with him sexually, but he denied that. She gave him her keys and left.

When she was unable to find another job, she realized that she would never get one in Dyersburg without a reference from Lanier, because of his power and his being her last employer. She gathered the courage to go see him in his chambers. "I can't do anything for you unless you do something for me," he told her. When she questioned whether she could trust him, he got up from his desk, put his arm around her, and asked if she was offering him a bribe.

She called him "disgusting." He pulled her to him and started trying to kiss her. She extricated herself, ran into the hallway, and dashed upstairs.

To her shock he followed her, caught her on the landing, and asked her, "Are you wired?" She said she did not know what he was talking about.

Castleberry asked about his visiting her at the bank where she now worked. It had been about a month ago, she said. He had come in on a Saturday, surprising her when almost no one else was around. He sidled up to her desk and told her that she owed him a favor because without him she would never have landed this job. She said that she owed him nothing, that she had landed her position on her own. He pranced out, as if he had scored. He made her feel so weak, and she was frightened. She thought of the time he had asked her whether she was afraid of him, and she had said no.

"You should be afraid of me," Lanier had said, running his hands down the edges of his robe. "I am a judge. People are supposed to be afraid of me."

Had there been any other contacts with Lanier, Castleberry asked, since her firing? Other visits? Phone calls? He was thinking about what other women had reported of Lanier's persistence.

He was also thinking about how abject Mary Haralson appeared, slumped over in her chair, talking to the table. Castleberry had long ago given up hunting for sport. He would gladly eat what someone else shot, but he no longer liked to kill things himself. In his youth, though, he had loved the autumn ritual of shooting doves. She reminded him of one—a young dove hit, bloodied, fallen to earth with a thump, glassy-eyed and ready for plucking and the pan.

She had received two obscene phone calls, Mary Haralson said, at home at night, shortly after Lanier had fired her. The voice was male. She could not say whose it was. Yes, it could have been Lanier. She could not say for certain.

Of course it was Lanier, Castleberry wanted to say, but restrained himself. If Mary Haralson chose to believe that these calls were coincidental, let her. He pressed her about them. She was reluctant to discuss them. He bore in on her, sensing that this was important. She became upset, but he kept at her.

"What did the voice say?"

It was muffled, she said, incomprehensible at first. She had asked if the caller had the right number. Then he became clearer and called her by her name.

"He said, 'Mary, do you enjoy sex?'"

"Those were his words? That's what he said, 'Do you enjoy sex?'"

Her pale gold hair, streaked with red, was falling around her face. She thought she had said enough.

"What were his exact words?" Castleberry asked.

"He told me that he had a ten-inch dick and asked me if I'd like to suck it."

19

Once they knew that the FBI was in town, Vivian and Brenda telephoned each other constantly with news of the agents' whereabouts, obsessed by what everybody was talking about, the investigation of David Lanier. After that day in the dungeon, word of which spread in spite of the efforts at discretion, Castleberry and Champine became so well known in town that even the clannish old men at the center table in the Cozy Kitchen acknowledged them one day during the first week in October and invited them to join the group for lunch. Castleberry was surprised and somewhat heartened.

"What's going on with the feds and David Lanier?" one of the veterans asked him. "You all got something on the judge?"

"Well, sir, it's hard to say," Castleberry said cautiously as he unloaded his tray of beets, beans, and tomatoes. He had no idea whether the fellow was for or against the judge or who else might be listening.

"I'd say the judge is in a whole lot of trouble," the old man offered, and Castleberry smiled, not contradicting him but keeping silent. This was indeed encouraging. If only the Justice Department would agree!

That was all that was said about the case that noon. For the next hour the agents swapped opinions with the elders on the state of the cotton harvest and the condition of the levee.

By this time Castleberry had begun to hope that the grand jury could soon be persuaded to issue subpoenas for courthouse employment records, which would make finding Lanier's possible victims an easier, more systematic matter; subpoenas were not forthcoming, however, because Steve Parker remained undecided about which federal statute made the judge's behavior a clearly criminal offense.

Meanwhile, Castleberry turned up two more women who claimed to have been assaulted by Lanier. The identity of one of them was passed to him by a "hip pocket," FBI patois for a casual, one-time informant who volunteers a piece of information gratis, for whatever reasons—in this case resentment of Judge Lanier. This hip pocket was a friend of a friend of a woman who claimed that Lanier had grabbed and abused her when she came to his chambers to present an idea for a juvenile social welfare program.

The witness, whose name was Janet Thomasson, entreated with Castleberry not to force her to appear at the police station, suggesting instead that they meet during off hours at the Shoney's restaurant on the bypass, where there was a banquet room that would not be in use and could provide privacy. He and Champine met her there at nine in the morning on Thursday, October 3.

Thomasson, who was thirty-five, was yet another example of the attractiveness of the women who seemed to swarm around the courthouse hive. In this instance the look was urban sophisticate. Tall, very slender, with high cheekbones and huge dark eyes accentuated by a ton of makeup, she wore a tailored wool jacket with exaggerated shoulder pads and might have come from a *Harper's Bazaar* shoot. She was also extraordinarily nervous, obviously a highly strung person, who made it clear that she would rather be doing almost anything than having to talk about an incident that had come close to deranging her. Castleberry sensed at once that he was confronting someone on the edge and kept his bad cop act in check.

Thomasson described how she had presented herself to Lanier in his chambers one day the previous June, trying to get his approval for a program she had devised to help juveniles by educating their parents to family responsibilities. After hearing her out, briefly, Lanier grabbed her as she was gathering up her books, papers, and purse to leave, wrapping his arms and legs around her, forcing kisses on her and shoving his hand between her legs. He had let her go, she believed, only because she went into a state of absolute panic—she had a horror of constraint of any kind, and her furious and frantic response may have frightened him.

She had told only one person, her best friend, about this attack, because she knew how powerful Lanier was and that he could ruin her life if he wished. She was terrified at having disclosed the incident now.

As similar as the details of Thomasson's account were to those of other women, she was the first to report being assaulted so abruptly by Lanier, without so much as any of what might be called a break-in or softening-up period. She had met the judge only briefly once or twice before. To Castleberry Thomasson's story, which was completely convincing, indicated the degree of impunity with which Lanier believed he could act, and he wondered how long Lanier had been behaving this way.

It was Joey McDowell's view, seconded by Stan Cavness and Chief Williamson, that Lanier had always been a womanizer—there were stories about him and his women back when he had been mayor, and there was his rather comical relationship with the lady called Tucson. But everyone agreed that Lanier had become worse since becoming a judge—much worse than anyone had known, as Castleberry's probe was showing. There was a clear pattern emerging of an obscene alliance among the law, power, and sex, a merging of practical, psychological, and biological forces that for Lanier produced an extreme aphrodisiac effect. Castleberry began to sense that he was dealing here with something that lay beyond familiar analysis or even rational understanding. That courthouse harbored a kind of monster, who answered to no one.

Even Stan Cavness's own secretary, incredibly enough, had recently been pursued by the judge. A senior in high school, she was employed part-time in the Youth Guidance office in a work-study program that involved being present during hearings in juvenile court. The judge spotted her in a back row and gave her his lopsided grin and what she described to Cavness, apologizing for her graphic language, as an "eat me" look. Soon she discovered that he was following her around town, sometimes in his Mercedes, on other occasions in a battered red-and-white pickup. She saw him staring and grinning at her when she came out of Kroger's supermarket, in traffic, at the mall, almost everywhere she went. He had even followed her to her parents' house in the well-to-do "Pill Hill" or physicians' residential section of town.

Because she worked for a police captain who loathed Lanier, the judge's stalking was more of a joke to her than anything else, although from time to time she found herself becoming spooked by it. She was eager to cooperate when Cavness asked her if she would be willing to wear a wire, let Lanier approach her, and obtain possibly incriminating dialogue from him. She was not yet seventeen, and Cavness relished the idea of catching Lanier trying to a seduce a juvenile, which would be sweet compensation for the misery the judge had caused Cavness by falsely accusing him of that crime.

Lanier suddenly stopped bothering the girl, however, when he followed her to work one morning and learned who was her boss.

Were Lanier's female prey numberless? It began to appear that they were. Shoot an arrow into the air, Castleberry said to Joey McDowell, and the odds are that it will fall on a woman who at one time or another has been harassed, or at least that, by David Lanier.

Joey took up the challenge. He was long past his days as a traffic cop,

but he promised to catch a female speeder and ask her whether she had
ever been harassed by David Lanier. Castleberry dared him.

Joey tried it, out on the bypass. The woman, who he estimated was
about thirty—he didn't even bother asking to see her driver's license,
going straight to the point—said that indeed, yes, she had been hustled by
the judge during her divorce proceedings. She hated Lanier for that and
thought he was a disgrace to his office.

"Drive carefully," Joey told her, letting her go and leaving her wondering what on earth all that was about.

"They're back!" Brenda, feverish with excitement, was calling Vivian at
work. She had just seen Castleberry and Champine walk in the east
entrance to the courthouse. They had not been around for a few days, or
at least she had heard no reports of sightings, and had begun to hope that
maybe the whole investigation had gone nowhere and they were giving
up on it. Vivian took the opposite view. The more trouble anyone could
make for Lanier, the better she liked it, little as she could believe that he
was ever in any serious jeopardy.

Vivian, at Charles Kelly's office eight blocks from Courthouse Square,
was removed from the center of action. Brenda, in the Baird-Brewer
Building and frequently reporting to the judge at the courthouse, always
knew when the agents were around, as they had been most days for weeks
until recently, either actually talking to people or just being there to carry
out the strategy of intimidation.

"Tell me again what the FBI guy looks like," Vivian said. "I swear I
saw him coming out of Shoney's the other day."

"Pretty tall," Brenda said. "He's kind of a Carl Perkins type?" She was
referring to the singer and songwriter, the author of "Blue Suede Shoes,"
who was a local hero because he had been born and raised in Tiptonville,
in Lake County. "Curly silvery hair. Hip glasses. Cool. Handsome dude."

"That's him, I'm sure of it. And there was a tough little guy with him."

"That's the TBI guy."

"What're they up to in there, do you suppose?" Vivian asked.

"I'll find out," Brenda said. "Call you back."

What Brenda learned that day, October 10, 1991, was that Castleberry
had served Dyer County Executive Don Dills with a subpoena requiring
him to turn over personnel records of the Dyer County Juvenile Court
Office, the Youth Services Office, the Criminal Court, the Law and
Equity Court, the Probate Court, and the Chancery Court, dating from
January 1, 1982, to the present, with a week allowed for compliance. He
served a similarly inclusive subpoena on the Master (or chief administra-
tor) of the Court, Saundra "Sissy" Nale, and requested from her a floor

plan of the courtrooms and the rooms adjoining them, the purpose of which was to study the configuration of Judge Lanier's offices, so as to verify witnesses' accounts of how they had been cornered and assaulted by him.

Assault, rather than harassment, was now the operative word for Castleberry. What Janet Thomasson and others described could no longer, it seemed to him, be adequately conveyed by the weaker word. Without legal guidance, simply from his commitment to get the language right so as to have maximum effect on the Justice Department, he began writing in his 302s that David Lanier had assaulted this or that woman in his chambers, dropping harassment from the reports.

He had a subpoena for Lanier, too, requiring him to supply his own employment records, which were the most important, because they covered most of the witnesses who had been discovered so far. He and Champine were informed that the judge was at home for lunch.

"We'll pay him a visit," Castleberry said. "I hate to disturb his meal."

Mrs. Joan Lanier answered the door of the fifties-style house with its manicured lawn, flowerbeds, and shrubs, a picture-perfect image of domesticity that contrasted with the idea Castleberry had of the so-called Penthouse, according to Source's vivid description of that place.

Mrs. Lanier took one look at the agents and turned her head to call her husband:

"It's the FBI!"

"She stole my line," Castleberry muttered.

The judge accepted the subpoena without comment.

Within a few days of the subpoenas' delivery, the Dyersburg *State Gazette* printed a front-page story about them, saying that "Federal Bureau of Investigation Special Agent Bill Castleberry specifically requested the personnel records of female employees of Chancellor David W. Lanier," referring to the judge's official title in the chancery court. This was the first word by any media of the investigation and the first hint of its new focus. U.S. Attorney Ed Bryant, who by then had replaced E. Hickman Ewing, had no comment, except to say that "the subpoenas speak for themselves." Memphis and Jackson television channels, seen in Dyersburg, broadcast the news that night.

Steve Parker, with Bryant's approval, had received the authority to issue the subpoenas from the grand jury as part of the broad corruption probe. As yet no definite route to prosecuting Lanier on the women's charges had surfaced. Before his departure from the U.S. Attorney's office, Hickman Ewing had told Parker that there might conceivably be a civil rights angle to the case, but that approach had its perils. Parker also worried that he might get himself into the position of arguing that Lanier had extorted sex from some of the women, which would mean trying to prove that sex was something of value—a prospect that had the earmarks of a legal morass. He could end up saying in effect that all women who gave sex were engaging in a form of prostitution, which was the line some radical feminists took in analyzing marriage as an economic institution. He could imagine the reaction of a jury of Southerners to that!

But Parker was now looking for any way to advance the case on the sexual grounds. His change of mind, actually as much a change of heart, had come about because Bill Castleberry had finally convinced him to meet some of the women face-to-face, to hear their stories.

One day during the first week of October, Castleberry had spotted Parker in a hallway at the Federal Building in Memphis and buttonholed him. Castleberry took the 302s on Mary Haralson, Janet Thomasson, and others out of his briefcase and asked Parker to read them, at once.

Parker stood in the hallway, glancing through the reports. He remained skeptical of any legal recourse for these women, but he could see how serious their charges were, and listened as Castleberry insisted that the 302s could not convey the full impact of the stories. Parker had to meet the women.

Castleberry's emotional pitch worked. To Parker, Bill seemed different from the man he thought he knew—taciturn, precise, thorough—an aggressive investigator, many said overly so, but more calculating than emotional. The word "Machiavellian" was often associated with him. Now he was acting like some recruit who had just discovered that there was after all actual evil in the world.

Parker was scheduled to be in Jackson that week on an unrelated matter at the federal courthouse there. Castleberry said that he would have a few of the women available for interviews. "They don't know it yet, but they'll be there," was the way he put it. "I'll drive them there myself if I have to. I'll run a goddamned shuttle service."

A few minutes later, Parker encountered Amy Spain, a bright young assistant U.S. attorney, only a year out of law school and therefore about the same age as most of Lanier's employees. It occurred to Parker that having Amy along to help evaluate these women might be useful. Castleberry had warned that they were reluctant to talk, frightened of Lanier and embarrassed by what he had done to them. With Amy present they might feel more comfortable, and she would add a woman's point of view. Parker also respected Amy, who had turned down offers from several powerhouse Memphis firms to work for the Justice Department at half the pay, and was glad of the chance to include her in one of his cases. She agreed to accompany him to Jackson, which happened to be her hometown.

Even Castleberry's emotional pitch did not prepare Steve Parker for the impact of the two interviews the agent was able to arrange on that first, breakthrough day. Castleberry himself was taken aback by the degree of emotion the sessions evoked.

He had expected, as was nearly always the case, that having told their stories once, the witnesses would find it easier to go through the events again. In fact, he had worried that they would have become emotionally subdued by now and would fail to impress Parker and Spain with the degree of psychological damage they had suffered. Exactly the opposite occurred.

Mary Haralson appeared on the verge of collapse before the attorneys, weeping, frequently having to stop to recover herself, so distraught that Castleberry had to leave the small office where the interviews took place several times, the display of anguish was so painful to watch. He found himself feeling unaccountably guilty, as if he were responsible for putting her through an excruciating experience again. *It's in a good cause,* he told himself.

Sandy Sanders was also tearful but angrier, possessed, as it were, of Christian righteousness, as she described Lanier's grabbing at her and his more subtle denigrations and punishments since.

Castleberry thought he understood why the women had become more intense about their experiences. Talking to agents in their hometown had been one thing. Now they were revealing themselves to federal officials in a strange place and must feel doubly exposed. The reality of the possibility of having to go public with their charges had sunk in.

Those two interviews were enough for Steve Parker, who said he would ask for subpoenas immediately and would interview the rest of the women as soon as possible. Castleberry expressed confidence that more witnesses would turn up once he was able to verify the identities of every woman who had worked for Lanier during the past few years. And, he said, he would not be surprised to find other witnesses, such as Janet Thomasson, who had never been on the judge's payroll but found themselves vulnerable to him anyway.

It was somewhat of a surprise to both Parker and Castleberry that Amy Spain was not as sure as they were about the importance of proceeding. She emphasized that they still had no clear idea of what if any federal statute Lanier had violated, unless it was a seldom-used one that gave employees the right to sue for sexual harassment. There was obviously no question about the emotional damage Judge Lanier had inflicted on these women, Spain argued. But why had they not quit their jobs? Mary Haralson admitted that she had hung on until Lanier fired her. Sandy Sanders was still employed by the judge.

"If I'd been in their shoes," Spain said, "I would have been out of there after the first incident. I would never let anyone treat me like that." And how would a jury react?

Steve Parker's seniority, however, made his reaction decisive. Now he prepared to use the grand jury as his investigatory arm, the most powerful weapon for any federal prosecutor. In many states and local jurisdictions grand juries functioned mainly to hear evidence as presented to them, to decide whether to issue indictments. Parker preferred to take advantage of the broad subpoena powers of the federal grand jury, which, in effect, became an investigatory weapon of the Justice Department, enabling the prosecutors to acquire documents and to compel testimony that would otherwise be beyond their reach. Once the grand jury agreed that a crime or crimes may have been committed, its powers to gather evidence were virtually unlimited.

The wisest thing an American citizen could do was to stay clear of the federal system of justice. Once targeted, whether as a subject of possible indictment or as merely a witness, a man or woman could forget about most of the Bill of Rights. It was up to the sense of fairness and the discretion of prosecutors and agents to determine what and how much of a person's private and professional life was to be hung out to dry.

As for David Lanier, Castleberry and Parker felt that all of this couldn't happen to a nicer guy.

Amy Spain's more cautious, even tepid reaction to the women, which persisted as others came in for interviews in Memphis, concerned Castleberry, who had assumed that a woman would empathize more readily with the witnesses than a man would. He attributed her skepticism partly to her being new to her job and therefore cautious—and perhaps also to the self-consciousness she might feel about being a neophyte and female in a world inhabited mainly by men. And he recalled Maryellen Donohue's similar skepticism.

Although there was an age gap of some ten years between Amy and her, Castleberry also thought about his elder daughter, Laura Lea, an English major at Union University in Jackson who was considering law school. He felt a twinge, imagining Laura being exposed to the sordidness of a case such as this and to the vicious competitiveness of lawyers. As for his younger daughter, Christa Ann, who was still in middle school, he habitually referred to her as "my baby" and had not yet begun to envision her as an adult. Now, observing what the women of Dyersburg were enduring, Castleberry understood that his protectiveness toward his daughters might not be such a favor to them. Raised Southern-style to believe that a man's role was to protect the women of the family, having kept even his wife innocent of the ugliest of his cases, having cherished home and family as his oasis from the nastiness of common existence, he began to question whether the barriers he maintained around these women weren't certain to give way, sooner or later, before the filthy tide of modern life—as they had for Amy Spain. Amy was coping with her new knowledge, it seemed, but would his daughters be as able?

He did wonder sometimes why someone both as bright and as feminine as Amy, who like his daughters came from a close, stable family, had chosen a field as fraught with human degradation as that of a criminal prosecutor. He was willing to bet that Amy's parents must have wondered, too. Did the privilege in which Amy had grown up help to explain the lack of rapport he sensed between her and the women now traipsing into Parker's office to bare themselves?

Amy, whose only sibling, a brother, was finishing medical school, came from a family in which achievement was the norm. Her father was the head of his own accounting firm; her mother was a contractor and a designer and builder of upscale houses. The Spain family home sat on a corner lot off Country Club Lane in Jackson. Amy had attended private schools, including Old Hickory Academy, and had always been an honor student, through college and as editor of the law review at the University of Memphis. Her parents and relatives had predicted that she would become a lawyer from the age of ten, when she would stand in the center of a room arguing current events with adults.

Amy, quiet and very hard-working, was never a snob—but partly it was a matter of style, this distance between her and the women she was now evaluating. With her shiny, bobbed brown hair, her pretty but studious face, her self-contained manner and understated, tasteful suits, she would not have looked out of place in any big-city law firm, the best of which in Memphis had recruited her. Only her obvious squeamishness over the raw sexual details and language evoked in these interviews—along with her mild, genteel accent—identified her as Southern. But outwardly Amy was as different as could be from the witnesses, from Janet Thomasson's overdone makeup to Mary Haralson's country drawl to Cathy Kiely's beauty pageant looks and comportment.

To hear these other women speak, to watch the birdlike fluttering of their hands, to see the way they sat and stood was to think of organdy and lace, of stuffed animals and dolls and small-town beauty parlors, even of rural Sunday schools and of what goes on by the river on hot nights heavy with honeysuckle, barbecue, and sweat. Amy was none of that. Amy projected her sweet nature but, equally, an independence of mind and being—whereas these other young women were manifestly preened and groomed for a world run by rude, rough-handed men who preferred girls to women and liked their women to act like girls.

There were exceptions. Sandy Sanders was businesslike and, though shaken, defiant of Lanier. Amy seemed to identify with her more than with any of the others.

Something Amy had said about Lanier's behavior stuck in Castleberry's mind. "If my boss ever did that to me," she proclaimed matter-of-factly, "if he ever tried to touch me, I'd quit on the spot and not wait to get fired. I'd stay with my parents until I got another job." Did she appreciate that these women could not rely on parents, or that for a Dyersburg woman with a family to support and not much education, a courthouse job was an achievement not lightly to be abandoned? Had she comprehended the power David Lanier had to wreck their lives if they defied him?

Of all the women he interviewed, Steve Parker was most enthusiastic about Brenda Castain as a potential trial witness. He noted that Brenda had been the first and only woman to initiate a complaint, even reluctantly, and that her original FBI interview eventually changed the entire investigation. He believed her when she insisted that she had fended off Lanier and that the judge had left her alone since her promotion.

Castleberry remained convinced that Brenda was lying. He could not prove this, however, and kept his opinion to himself. A certain amount of tension had developed between him and Parker, and Castleberry did not wish to risk increasing it.

Parker was irritated by Castleberry's habit of getting up and leaving in the middle of interviews, wandering around the building or going outside to smoke a cigar. Castleberry did not enjoy being confined in an enclosed space, unless he was in control of the situation. And besides, he had heard the women's stories already and did not see the necessity of enduring these painful accounts again. He also felt that it was better for the women not to have someone present who, in several instances, had pulled their statements out of them and whom several of them clearly resented and blamed for their present embarrassing and frightening predicament.

A quiet struggle of wills went on between the two men, one that reflected the occasional tensions between the Justice Department and the FBI. Parker asked Castleberry to furnish 302 reports of this new round of interviews. Castleberry did not agree to this. He could not, he maintained, because it was specifically against Bureau policy for an agent so much as to take notes of a meeting between a witness and attorneys. He continued to leave in the middle of these sessions, getting under Parker's skin.

Castleberry resented, and Parker knew this, being asked to perform as what amounted to a secretary for the Justice Department. Get your own stenographer, he was saying, without actually articulating it.

Yet he did not wish to antagonize Parker, whose abilities he respected, who was known as sympathetic to FBI agents, and upon whom the future of the case depended. They reached a compromise of sorts, with Castleberry attending half the interviews, Champine the other half. Parker gave up asking for 302s, and Castleberry, adopting a policy of silence, withdrew behind his G-man's poker face to observe what these lawyers would make of the material he had accumulated and to which he continued to add. If they did not care to ask his opinions of the witnesses, he would not offer any. With both men, enormous professional pride entered into this battle of nerves between them. If Parker chose to believe in Brenda Castain's honesty, Castleberry thought, let him take the responsibility for that.

It was shortly after Parker expressed his enthusiasm for Castain that a member of Joey McDowell's Special Response Team was driving along Cedar Street in Dyersburg one night when the officer happened to hear the word "cocaine" drift in over his scanner. He was heading toward a raid on a crack cocaine house east of downtown when the word reached his ears. He stopped and quickly adjusted his receiver, to which a recorder was attached, to pick up the frequency and heard a male voice discussing the price of drugs.

There was no time to listen, however, because the officer had to hurry ahead to the location of the planned raid, and the voice quickly faded out, but it stuck in his mind. The man had sounded exactly like Judge Lanier.

"It's Lanier, I swear it's got to be," he told McDowell back at the station as the men were removing their flak jackets and cooling off after the night's excitement, which had netted a dozen arrests. "You got to listen to this tape."

Joey did, and he agreed that it was Lanier all right, talking to someone about drugs. Joey asked for the exact location where the signal had been picked up. It was Main and Cedar, within a block of Lanier's Penthouse. The judge must have been talking on a cordless phone.

The next day he checked with Castleberry to make sure that it was legal to intercept and record a cordless call without a court order. He was thinking about listening in some more.

It was legal, Castleberry said, but he wanted nothing to do with it. His strong belief was that recording the calls of someone who knew he was under investigation was always a mistake. The suspect was likely to make self-serving statements that could contradict other evidence; tapes were subject to challenge anyway, because they could so easily be faked; and the whole idea was dangerous because of the courts' sensitivity about privacy issues. If McDowell wanted to try something on his own, that was up to him, but he should clear it with Steve Parker first.

Parker affirmed that the courts had ruled that there is "no presumption of privacy" with a cordless call, because of the nature of the technology, in which the sender broadcasts its signal over one of only ten AM wavelengths. Anyone with a scanner was free to listen in. He was not asking him to do it, but if McDowell did make tapes of Lanier's conversations, Parker wanted copies of them.

Castleberry strongly believed that the repercussions might not be worth the risk. If the prosecutors received tapes, they would be subject to discovery by the defense, as mandated at any trial.

Joey McDowell and Stan Cavness, however, could not resist the chance to contribute whatever they could to Lanier's incrimination. They set up a scanner-recorder outside the Penthouse, less than a hundred feet from the door, found the frequency, and let the voice-activated tape roll. Concealed, the scanner could be left there twenty-four hours a day, which it was for more than a week.

The most significant conversations were between Lanier and Brenda Castain. They revealed that she was involved in an ongoing sexual relationship with Lanier, who, while listening to her desperate accounts of the collapse of her marriage, her fears about losing custody of her son, and her drug addiction, ordered her to appear at his chambers at specific times to give him sex. She also worried about lying to the FBI and the prosecutors.

Lanier professed not to be worried. How would anyone know the truth, as long as they kept their secrets between them? He did not specifically instruct her to continue to lie to federal authorities, but the implication was obvious.

McDowell, knowing their importance, tried to hand the tapes over to Castleberry, who refused to touch them, however pleased he was to have his suspicions about Castain confirmed. If Parker was that anxious to have them, he should ask Steve Champine to deliver them to Memphis, Castleberry said, leaving the FBI uninvolved.

Parker did just that.

And he was embarrassed about his misplaced faith in Brenda Castain. With his experience as a Memphis street cop, he had believed that he could tell at once if someone was on drugs, particularly if the addiction was as severe as Castain indicated hers to be. Drug use was also a matter that was personally sensitive to Parker, whose mother had been addicted to tranquilizers and who had died, he believed, because of them.

"I thought Brenda was the sweetest, most innocent thing I'd ever seen," Parker admitted to Castleberry, who appreciated his honesty as he mocked and laughed at himself for his misjudgment. Both men were relieved that the truth had come out now. A surprise like that during a trial could sink a case. Someone would now have to warn Brenda to tell the truth before the grand jury. There was no consideration of any recriminations against her. She was in enough trouble.

As for Amy Spain, her skepticism about Castain for not having quit her job with Lanier long ago looked more impressive, as did Maryellen Donohue's original doubts.

But Brenda had not received her promotion until last December, Castleberry reflected. Maybe if he had acted sooner on the 302 and gone to see her, she would have been saved from the tragic mistake of giving in to Lanier. Certainly she would have made a more convincing witness. It was a gloomy moment.

20

Was it mere coincidence, or did the David Lanier investigation develop when it did because intangible social and historical forces converged to make it happen?

Bill Castleberry had been under the impression that his own bull-headed, impulsive, and maybe reckless and foolhardy initiatives had set in motion a process that kept gaining momentum, no matter how many surprises and disappointments occurred, to some uncertain end. Vivian Forsythe, still keeping a low profile at the law office while her friend Brenda's life came unglued and her own seemed about to do the same, watched as the agents drew closer. Castleberry and Champine walked in one day to interview Charles Kelly behind a closed door. Kelly was his usual cocky self afterward, but Vivian thought he looked nervous, and everyone in the office was spooked. Brenda called to say the FBI had discovered her addiction, she didn't know how, and she was terrified they would throw her in jail. She knew that at the least she would soon be out of a job. Yet Vivian still felt weirdly isolated from what was going on, sitting in the middle of it all with her secret.

And then, suddenly and all at once, the entire country was talking about sexual harassment. On Monday, October 7, Anita Hill, an obscure law professor at the University of Oklahoma, met the media to announce that she was willing to testify before the U.S. Senate Judiciary Committee that Judge Clarence Thomas, nominated for the U.S. Supreme Court, had behaved improperly toward her ten years before. By Friday virtually the entire country was watching her testimony, followed on Saturday and Monday by Thomas's denial and defense of himself, the cross-examination of Hill, and a parade of witnesses contradicting each other. The national debate over who was more credible, the law professor or the judge, began, to continue unabated and indefinitely despite Thomas's confirmation by the Senate on October 15.

The Charles Kelly law office may have been typical of workplaces around the country, but the discussions of Hill versus Thomas that flourished there for weeks had an added edge because of the proximity of Judge David Lanier. Vivian kept quiet, although she joined with others in the laughter about Long Dong Silver, the porno film character to whom Thomas had supposedly alluded, and the errant pubic hair on the Coke can to which Thomas, so Hill claimed, had referred, upsetting her. Vivian had to agree with the other secretaries that if such things had truly bothered Anita Hill, she must have been a very naïve, sheltered young woman. Vivian could only think that if that had been all that Judge Lanier had done to her, she would not be complaining on national television.

But Vivian was less sanguine about Clarence Thomas, and more sympathetic to Anita Hill, when someone linked the Supreme Court nominee to David Lanier by way of a casual witticism. She heard from Brenda that a young woman working for Judge Lanier had found his chambers unlocked one day—a unique circumstance, from what anyone could remember—and had wandered in to have a look around. Shoved under the desk she noticed a sleeping bag, certainly an odd item to discover in there, although one with which Brenda was all too familiar. When the curious employee looked closely at the judicial robe hanging in a corner, she noticed that the inside of it was splotched down the front with what appeared to be stains of semen.

Later, without mentioning why, she asked the judge if he would care to have her take the robe to the cleaners. He replied with a sharp "No!" Since then that symbol of office had been referred to behind Lanier's back as "the Judge Thomas robe."

Vivian appreciated the humor, but the grotesquerie of it made her sick, intensifying memories she had tried and failed for a year to repress. She could no longer scoff at Anita Hill, either, as most of her co-workers did, although she found it impossible to understand why Hill had followed Thomas from one job to another, if he treated her with contempt and his remarks bothered her so much. Vivian had been hit on by one man or another at every job she had ever held, until this one. What would Anita Hill have done if Clarence Thomas had thrown her against a wall and forced himself on her?

For Castleberry, as for Steve Parker and Amy Spain, the Hill-Thomas hearings were a bad omen from the start and worse when opinion polls showed that six out of ten Americans believed Judge Thomas and thought Anita Hill was either lying or exaggerating, for a combination of personal and professional motives. When the Senate confirmed Thomas's nomination, in effect vindicating him, or saying at least that Hill had failed to prove her charges beyond a reasonable doubt, worries about the Lanier case multiplied.

It did seem that without planning it they had become swept up in a national tidal wave of concern about sexual harassment—yet harassment was not really the issue with Lanier. Castleberry had to wonder whether from the beginning he had been acting unconsciously as the agent of some invisible dynamic of social change. He certainly had never before paid much attention to women's issues—except as the influx of female agents within the FBI, and there still weren't many, affected his own work. Personally he welcomed additional female agents, whatever problems resulted. And there were some. It was common knowledge among senior law enforcement officials that male-female pairings among agents do create hazards. In high-anxiety, fast-action cases involving, say, stakeouts or undercover work or the pursuit of fugitives, adrenaline had been known to fuel sexual energy. The excitement could quickly turn partners into lovers, with tangled results in personal lives. Without ever having been a social activist, Castleberry accepted the necessity of risks and complications women would bring to the Bureau, along with their advantages and positive attributes.

Yet here he was in the midst of a women's cause, trying to bring a male oppressor to justice. Had he been moved to do this by a hidden hand? A shifting plane of history of which the Hill-Thomas imbroglio, into which feminists had hurled themselves, was the most visible evidence and the noisiest? And which seemed to have dealt women a defeat?

The most troubling aspect of the majority of the public's rejection of Anita Hill, as an indication of what might lie in store for the Lanier prosecution, was the emphasis placed on her long silence before coming out with her charges. She had waited ten years, having told only one person at the time of the alleged harassment, or so it appeared, a witness who could not even swear that Hill had mentioned Thomas by name when she complained about her boss. But at last she had come forward, writing to the Senate committee, wishing to remain anonymous but finally agreeing to make her charges public. None of the Lanier witnesses had taken any action against him on their own. Some had complained to a friend, Sandy Sanders to church members, but none had gone public. Some had even concealed their distress from their husbands.

Lanier, like Thomas and his supporters, was already complaining that the investigation of him was nothing more than a political vendetta. If most of the public believed that about the attempts to derail the Thomas nomination, would they not draw the same conclusion in this case, since

Lanier was a Democrat, the new U.S. Attorney a Republican, and most of the women could be perceived as harboring various personal grievances against him? If Hill was doubted by so many, what were the chances that a jury would believe the far more shocking accusations against a judge by these women, who were not exactly law professors?

In Parker's utilitarian office, he hashed out the implications of Hill-Thomas with Ed Bryant, Amy Spain, and Bill Castleberry. How could they prevent the Lanier case from merging in the public's mind with a quagmire so messy that only a militant feminist on one side or a misogynistic right-winger on the other could be certain what to think? Hill-Thomas was exactly the sort of scenario Parker would never have embraced as a basis for prosecution, a situation in which he himself could not see a clear right and wrong and would be unable to paint the oppositions starkly for a jury.

Castleberry knew now that his only hope for retaining the prosecutors' support lay in scaring up additional witnesses. But where were they?

To Castleberry's surprise, a lead to another witness came from Parker himself. A Dyersburg lawyer who was among those signing guarantees for Que Pasa contacted the U.S. Attorney's office to offer his cooperation. To Parker, it was obvious why this man had suddenly discovered his conscience. He must have known that the agents had already interviewed Charles Kelly and other attorneys and figured he would be next on the list. Better not to appear to be hiding something.

In the course of discussing Lanier's business dealings, Parker asked the attorney if he knew anything about the judge and sexual harassment.

"You'll find that's David's biggest handicap," the lawyer said, a subject of concern within the legal community for several years. "And if what I heard he did to Patty Wallace is true, he's guilty of more than harassment."

"Who's Patty Wallace?" Parker asked.

The lawyer said that she was a woman whom everyone liked and respected. She had never worked directly for Lanier, but supposedly he had done something pretty outrageous to her a few years ago. She was now secretary to the county executive.

He had never heard of her either, Castleberry said when Parker reached him at home that night, but he must have encountered her when he delivered the subpoena to her office. He would be in Dyersburg tomorrow, to pick up the employment records and make an attempt to interview the judge, and would call on Patty Wallace, too.

Castleberry was praying that the records would yield something. He would turn them over to a team of agents with accounting backgrounds, who faced a huge task, because everything was in alphabetical order, ten years' worth of names, and, far from being computerized or even typed, handwritten.

Having no other leads, Castleberry had been going over his file of 302s again to see whether he might have overlooked any names of potential witnesses. He had come up with only one, culled from one of the earliest reports, dating from nine months back. He did not see much of anything there but planned to ask Vivian Forsythe at some point whether she knew anything about Dr. Lynn Warner's business dealings with David Lanier.

"Don't make me do this, unless you're really going to do something about it."

That was what Patty Wallace said, quietly and firmly, as she led Castleberry and Champine into the conference room of the county executive's first-floor offices at the courthouse. She had already handed over the subpoenaed documents, including David Lanier's, which Castleberry surmised the judge had fobbed off in order to avoid further contact with the agents. When Castleberry told Wallace that he wanted to talk to her about Lanier, she had reacted with outward calm, but her eyes had flashed. Then came her remark.

What could he say to her? It's not up to me? I have no idea what the Justice Department will decide?

"We wouldn't be here if we didn't intend to do something," was the best he could manage.

She was a fairly tall, slender, stately woman in her mid-thirties, wearing tweed slacks and a long-sleeved silk blouse, with meticulously clipped curly brown hair swept up. As she stared at him with unblinking, slightly protuberant eyes, the words that came to Castleberry's mind were *dignified* and *proper*.

If she had not been such an imposing person, regal in her manner of speech and bearing, Castleberry would not have known what to make of her story, which on the face of it was extremely hard to believe. Three years earlier, she was unsure of the exact date but could pinpoint it from records, she had been employed as secretary to the circuit court clerk. She had never worked for Judge Lanier, but on that day Judge Riley was out of town and Lanier substituted for him on the circuit bench. Her boss, T. J. Jones, also happened to be out of town at a conference, so it was up to her to perform the duties of the clerk in the courtroom.

At nine o'clock, bringing the case data with her, including two or three large law books, she took a seat to the left of Lanier, behind the bench. Almost at once, Lanier placed his left hand on her thigh. She was wearing slacks that day. Lanier began rubbing his hand up and down and, as he opened proceedings, leaned over to whisper to her.

"Don't worry," he said, "I can do anything I want up here. No one will know, because I'm the judge."

As the case dragged on through the morning, Lanier became more and more bold. She had her legs crossed, but he jammed his fingers between them and moved his fingers back and forth, "against the most private parts of my body," Wallace said.

Unlike most of the other women, Patty Wallace did not burst into tears as she described what Lanier had done to her. Nor did Castleberry have to prod her for details. Lanier had continued touching and rubbing her until about thirty minutes before the break for lunch.

She had not known what to do about it, other than trying to press her legs together. No one could see what was happening, because the bench rail in that courtroom was high, with no openings toward the spectators. Nor could she see what Lanier was doing with his other hand, beneath his robe.

"This went on all morning?" Castleberry asked.

"Until about eleven-thirty," she said. She did not know what to do, between trying to perform her job properly and deciding whether to get up and leave. If she had, she said, the proceedings would have come to a halt, and she was afraid that no one would believe her if she tried to explain her reasons. Lanier was a powerful man. She also worried that he would take out anything she did in recriminations against her boss, to whom she felt great loyalty.

At last, Lanier had to sign some documents, and as soon as he removed his hand she took the opportunity to place books on her lap. She held them there when he tried to remove them.

She had seen Lanier come up to other women at the courthouse and fondle their breasts and buttocks, but she realized later that she must have been in shock when he actually touched her behind the bench, she had been so utterly surprised and humiliated.

When T. J. Jones returned from the conference, she told him at once what had happened and said that she refused ever to go into court with David Lanier again. Jones said this was "okay" and that he did not expect her to put up with that kind of treatment. He said nothing to Lanier, how-ever, so far as she knew, and a few months later she quit, after five years at the job, and took a far less interesting one at the Dyersburg airport. She had not been able to forget about what had happened or to bear the sight of Lanier around the courthouse, and she lived in fear that he would try something else with her. She missed the legal atmosphere, however, and later took a job at Charles Kelly's office until landing her present position, where she had been for about three months. As long ago as the incident had been, she remained afraid of Lanier.

With the Anita Hill precedent now in mind, Castleberry asked Wallace if she had told anyone else about the incident. She had, she said, informing two other women in the office about it immediately after it happened, and she named them. She had never told her husband about it, however, not even to this day, because he was very protective of her and volatile. She was afraid that he would kill Judge Lanier, or punch him at least, as a matter of honor.

Champine agreed, when they discussed the interview outside, that Wallace was as believable as the events were astonishing. They went back inside to check the height of the bench rail in the second-floor courtroom and found it as she had described, high enough to block anyone's view, extending nearly all the way across the width of the room, in either direction from the judge's elevated perch. One would have had to walk around behind it and get on one's knees to see what was being done.

Castleberry was now prepared to believe, or at least to entertain the possibility of another story he had up till now considered too wild to be credible, and which he doubted anyone would ever verify, that Lanier had persuaded a woman to hide under the bench—in his own courtroom, not this one—and perform fellatio on him during a trial. As the woman had already denied that the judge had so much as harassed her, there did not seem to be much point in questioning her about this incident. And if she admitted it, she would only cast doubt on Patty Wallace's story of having been assaulted, which Castleberry entirely believed. If one woman admitted to having performed such an act willingly, would a jury believe that Wallace had been coerced?

There was a serious problem with Wallace's statement—the more than two hours that she admitted Lanier's assault had gone on. Her manifest sense of outrage and propriety and devotion to her job convinced Castleberry and Champine that she had indeed been in shock and had not known what to do without disrupting court and inviting disbelief. In retrospect she had made a mistake in not jumping up, perhaps feigning illness, as soon as she could accept what was actually being done to her. But to watch and hear her describe it was to believe in her as the sort of person who would cling to the helm while the ship went down, if duty required it. But would a jury understand this?

Castleberry went to DPD headquarters to phone Steve Parker and gave him the gist of Wallace's story.

"That's a no-go," Parker said. "Bill, come on, get serious! No jury in the world will buy it!" Parker believed in the story himself—but would it hold up?

"Wait till you meet her," Castleberry said. "Champine agrees with me. He's no pushover."

"You guys have lost your minds. All these women are getting to you. How are we going to make this work in court?"

"Just see her," Castleberry said.

After a break at the Cozy Kitchen the agents walked back to the courthouse and requested a word with the judge. Lanier deigned to grant them an audience in the filing room, where Castleberry asked him if he would be willing to answer questions about allegations that had been made against him. It was his right, and this was his opportunity, to provide the agents with information.

Lanier said that he would want his lawyers there, and in the agents' presence he told Sherry Cooper to phone Charles Kelly, Charles "Bubba" Agee, and a third attorney, Ralph Lawson, whom Castleberry had yet to interview.

The lawyers appeared within minutes. Whatever else they had been doing paled in importance to attendance on the judge. Castleberry was prepared for this eventuality. He welcomed it, because he had a surprise for the lawyers.

"I have to warn you gentlemen," Castleberry said, "that you may be facing a conflict-of-interest situation if you continue to act as attorneys for Judge Lanier."

The three lawyers looked at each other and at Lanier for guidance. None was forthcoming.

"What conflict of interest?" Kelly asked.

Castleberry assumed that Kelly must know of exactly what conflict; if the other two attorneys did not, they would find out soon enough. It was called Que Pasa. All three had been guarantors. There was now proof of their backing, because the restaurant was failing, the note was due, and their checks had come in to cover it. Now was Castleberry's opportunity to prey on their fears of being involved and to neutralize their effectiveness as counsel.

"I mean that you may be called as witnesses before the grand jury or in a trial, in any indictment and prosecution of Judge Lanier," Castleberry said. "You may wish to consider that."

Their consternation was evident. Lanier looked furious.

"We need to confer," Kelly said.

"Please go right ahead. We can wait."

"It's up to the judge to decide any conflict," Kelly said, to which Castleberry did not respond.

Castleberry and Champine took pleasure in the confusion that ensued.

The judge and his three counselors left the office and huddled in a corner of the hallway to discuss their dilemma. Castleberry already knew, from Source, that Lanier had tried to anesthetize half a dozen local lawyers as potential witnesses against him by announcing that, whether they knew it or not, they were all his personal attorneys and that every conversation or dealing they had ever had with him was therefore privileged.

Castleberry could not hear what Lanier was saying to this trio in the hallway. The four men clustered together, babbling and gesticulating. Probably they were discussing Que Pasa. It was a rather impromptu way of convening a conference that might bear heavily on their client's future, not to speak of the lawyers' own. The agents savored the moment. It was as if they had sprinkled Lanier and his cronies with cayenne pepper.

Finally they returned. Kelly announced that he would not permit his client to answer questions at this time.

Would the attorneys consent to separate interviews, Castleberry asked, to acquaint themselves with some of the problems they and their client might be facing?

Kelly said that he had already been interviewed and had nothing to add. The others asked him for time to think matters over. Lanier retreated into his chambers.

"Let them stew awhile," Castleberry said to Champine on the court-house steps. "They're going to worry about how to cover their asses." He had accomplished his intention, to induce an anxiety attack, and was hoping that somebody would now do something stupid.

Champine asked Castleberry for his current opinion as to whether the sexual charges would ever reach the trial stage.

He had been more optimistic, though never certain, before the Hill-Thomas fiasco. Too many of the witnesses were tainted beyond credibility, even Patty Wallace, honest though she was. What if Anita Hill had claimed to have permitted Clarence Thomas to touch her in that way for a couple of hours in a courtroom, without having said boo?

The more he thought about Patty Wallace, the more he began to consider her the litmus test for Steve Parker. If Parker could be persuaded to interview Wallace and ended up believing in her, he might go for the other witnesses, too—if only he could discover an appropriate statute.

21

On a Tuesday afternoon six days later, October 22, Vivian was at work when she heard one of the other secretaries say, "They're here again. It's the FBI. They're coming in."

Vivian started to phone Brenda, to tell her that the agents were about to interview Charles Kelly again and to ask her if she knew what was going on, but hung up when the agents entered. Vivian heard Charles Kelly mutter "goddamn *federales*" under his breath as he emerged from his office before he greeted them cheerfully, joking with them about whether they were in need of some legal advice. He was wearing boots that day, acting every inch the Champagne cowboy, as Vivian had heard his new young wife call him.

When the older agent asked if they could talk to him for a minute, just one question, Kelly ushered them into his office and shut the door.

Everyone was quiet, trying to eavesdrop, but Vivian could hear nothing. The agents' presence in town always made her nervous, although she did not share in the hostility toward them that she gathered most people felt, especially around the courthouse. From Brenda and from others, Vivian understood that a good number of those they had interviewed would like to see them run out of town on a rail. Sissy Nale had said that if this was an example of what an FBI agent was like, snooping around and asking impertinent questions about people's private lives, parading about as if he had a mission from God and swaggering through the hallways of the courthouse disrupting everyone's business and setting the whole town on its ear—if this arrogant bully Castleberry was your typical FBI agent, she no longer felt like saluting the American flag.

No one seemed to be able to talk about anything except the investigation. Vivian, although she told no one this, felt that if the one thing the agents accomplished was to put a scare into David Lanier, it was worth it. She just wished that for once she could see the bastard squirm, but everyone said that he was taking the investigation in stride, business as usual, whatever that meant! Other than Brenda and the other women in the juvenile department, she did not know what women the agents had interviewed, but she knew about the subpoenaed records, and that they did not include her own name.

Vivian did understand, however, the panic and pain the agents were causing. Only that morning Brenda had called, sounding hysterical. The agents had appeared again at her office and this time had served her with a subpoena to testify before a grand jury next month. Was she going to have to tell the truth now about everything, the sex with Lanier, her addiction? That would be the end of her job and her marriage. The agent had said that grand jury proceedings were secret. Was anything, really?

At that moment, with the agents still in talking to Kelly, Vivian asked herself what she would do in Brenda's position, and at once she knew. She would tell the truth, and not only because it was so dangerous to lie under oath. Actually, she had given the question a lot of thought over the past few months. She had never reached the point of deciding to come forward on her own, but if the agents came to her, she would tell everything. What did she have to lose any longer, other than her job? She clung to that, even as the rest of her life swirled out of control. She was doing more drugs. She was no longer a good mother, if she ever had been. She couldn't stand looking at herself in the mirror. She felt like giving up. At least before she collapsed altogether she could tell somebody the truth, go out in a blaze.

But they would never find her. Probably she was just trying to flatter herself and make herself feel better, saying she would ever do anything that took strength. Right now the main thing she craved was a joint, or more than that.

The agents came out of Kelly's office. Vivian kept her head down, waiting for them to leave. But they did not.

They walked straight over to her desk.

"Mrs. Archie?" the older one said. "My name is Bill Castleberry and I'm with the FBI. This is Special Agent Steve Champine of the Tennessee Bureau of Investigation. Do you prefer being called Mrs. Archie, or Ms. Forsythe?"

"It doesn't matter," she said, still not looking up, unable to breathe. "Vivian's fine."

"Okay, Vivian. We'd like to ask you a few questions, if you don't mind. Mr. Kelly said we could use this office over here."

"All right," Vivian said. She stood up and gripped the back of her chair to steady herself.

"And I need to give you this subpoena."

Vivian took the sheet of paper. At first she could not make her eyes focus. Then she read the words:

> You are hereby commanded to appear and testify before the Grand Jury of the United States District Court at the place, date, and time specified below.

Commanded to appear!

Back at DPD headquarters after hearing Vivian's story, Castleberry and Champine remained stunned as they relayed to Joey McDowell the gist of what she had told them. Among the three of them, only Joey was not wholly surprised by the degree of Lanier's brutality, as Vivian had described it in hideous detail. She had broken down frequently but managed to get through the account of both incidents with no prompting whatsoever.

"I told you all that bastard is capable of anything," Joey said. "Still is, too. I'll say it again. If you're gonna shoot the king, you'd better kill him. You gonna call Parker?"

He thought not, Castleberry said. He wanted Steve to get the full impact, straight from Vivian Forsythe. This was going to put the case on a different plane. This was not harassment, and it was not assault. It was rape. Vivian herself had agreed that that was the only word for it.

He was not even going to put the details into the 302. He would make it just one line, something like "was forced to have oral sex with Lanier on two separate occasions in the judge's chambers," period. That would certainly get Parker's attention, without giving away too much beforehand.

There was only one potential problem with her story that anyone could see. Not the phenomenon of oral rape itself, they were all familiar with that, and so would Parker be, although it would undoubtedly be a shock for Amy Spain. A rapist, as McDowell, especially, knew from his vast experience with abuse cases, can apply pressure to the hinges of the jaw, forcing them to open, the same way anyone can force a dog to take a pill.

No, the one problem was that it had happened twice. How can you get raped twice by the same person? People might be skeptical. But Vivian had been so persuasive, so convincing to the agents, that anyone would believe her, they thought—if only she conveyed the same emotion the next time she told the story.

"Don't worry about that," Joey said. "Mark my words, she'll be getting more emotional, not less. I've seen it happen, every time. You better just pray she doesn't go cuckoo on you. I know the whole Forsythe family, every one of them, and I want to tell you, that is not the most emotionally stable group of people you'll ever meet. They've had their problems, believe me."

Castleberry remembered again his interview with Judy Forsythe—that meeting he had dismissed as pointless and that now, only because he had read that 302 again, had led to the most important witness so far. He had gone into the meeting with Vivian hoping to hear something about Dr. Warner and Lanier and instead had heard a real horror story.

Charles Kelly let Vivian take the rest of the afternoon off after her interview. She went home and, without speaking to anyone except to say she felt sick, crawled into bed, hoping to fall asleep, but she could not. She kept looking at the subpoena, which commanded her to appear at the Federal Building in Memphis at nine-thirty on the morning of November 1. Only a week away! Mr. Castleberry had said something about meeting with U.S. attorneys before that, or had he said that the November 1 date wasn't necessarily exactly when she would be called? She couldn't remember, she had been in such a state.

Lying in bed, she felt numb. All these months she had wondered what would happen and how she would feel if she confided in someone, other than the sanitized version of events she had told Dr. Warner. Would the truth make her free? She had no idea now, feeling nothing, as if someone else had done the talking to the agents, or that she had dreamed it.

By six it was getting dark. The numbness began to give way to a rising anxiety, alternating with the most vivid recollections she had had in months of the incidents in the judge's chambers. When the phone rang and her mother shouted up "It's for you," Vivian ran to take the call—anything to get out of her own head.

It was Brenda. She had shown her husband the subpoena and confessed everything to him. He had packed a bag and left, taking their son with him and calling her a whore. Vivian said she'd be right over, as soon as she fed Ashley.

Giving the child dinner, Vivian kept bursting into tears. Everyone asked her what was the matter. She could not talk, would not, and left without saying where she was going.

Brenda was puffing frantically on a joint and had already done some other drug, Vivian could tell when she arrived, and started to cry hysterically. She held Brenda in her arms and rocked her.

"They came to see me, too," Vivian said. "They gave me a subpoena, too." She started to fill Brenda in on the interview and was longing to tell her that they were soul mates forever and that Lanier had done terrible things to her as well—but Brenda was out of it for now. She must have been speedballing again, Vivian figured, mixing a downer with cocaine or some other upper in the same dose, which could scramble you like nothing else. Brenda kept mumbling about her absent son and death.

Vivian went into the kitchen to make some coffee—what else was she to do? There, lying on the sink, she saw the needles and the vial of Mepergan, another brand name for meperidine, for which Brenda had a source at the hospital. It was what they had given Vivian last year when they wheeled her in for her operation to remove the ovarian cyst. She knew women who would fake illness just to be brought to the emergency room for a shot of it. Dilaudid was supposedly even more powerful; Mepergan, she had often heard, was, however, possibly the most addictive of all drugs, worse in that way than morphine, which was one reason the latter was preferred by physicians for longer-term use. Vivian picked up the rig and went back to where Brenda was lying on the couch.

A big step to become an IV user. Vivian was ready.

"Help me," she asked Brenda. "Help me find a vein." She wanted to get to that alpha state, right now.

22

Suddenly the witnesses started to proliferate. It was the grand jury subpoenas that did it, that and Castleberry's persistence in returning to women who had not been cooperative the first time, inviting them to the dungeon and asking them again and again to name others' names. Here was made manifest the power prosecutors derive from a grand jury, behind it the explicit consequence of a possible five-year jail term and a two-hundred-and-fifty-thousand-dollar fine for perjury—a potent truth serum. By the second week in November, when the hearings were in full swing, the list of witnesses with either first- or secondhand knowledge of Judge Lanier's abuses had lengthened from the four or five of weeks ago to nineteen, with the anticipation that the number would swell.

Some of these women changed their stories radically from their first interviews—from outright denial to detailed accounts, many verifiable from outside evidence, of being harassed, stalked, and assaulted; others provided vivid additional material. One told of finding dead roses in her car and strewn across her porch when she rejected Lanier's advances. Several described his driving past their houses repeatedly and how they had received obscene phone calls from a man who sounded white and middle-aged but with a muffled voice that they could not positively identify as Lanier's but that certainly could have been his. Another had been terrified to open the curtains of her basement apartment one morning to find the judge on his hands and knees in the bushes, peering at her through the window. Another described how she had visited Lanier's chambers, at his invitation, to discuss her divorce settlement, and the judge had unzipped his pants, exposed his genitals to her, and asked her to give him oral sex.

Still another, named Jennifer Gallagher, who worked at the Dyersburg City Hall and had child custody and child support matters pending before the judge, said that he had called her for months, asking her to "come see" him and to accompany him on trips to Atlantic City and Florida. She had resisted. He had called her at work five and six times a day, until the switchboard operator and others began to assume that she must be involved with him. Finally, she said, she had visited his chambers, where he had grabbed her, opened her blouse and slacks, pulled a sleeping bag out from under his desk, and pushed her down onto it, forcing intercourse.

And then there was Vivian Forsythe, who was every bit as convincing to Steve Parker and Amy Spain as she had been to Castleberry and Champine. She poured out her story again in Parker's small tenth-floor office, where he sat behind his desk with Amy, Bill, Champine, and Ed Bryant crowded around, quiet as mourners at a grave. Castleberry did not walk out during this session, as Vivian wept through her account. Joey McDowell was right. Vivian was if anything even more emotional this time—and she looked terrible, as if she had not slept in weeks.

Parker, alerted by his previous misjudgment of Brenda Castain, asked Vivian to stay to talk to him alone after the interview proper was over. She sat in a heap before his desk, trying to dry her eyes.

"You have a drug problem, don't you?" Parker asked, as gently as he could. His heart went out to this woman who had endured so much and more to tell the truth. He could see how close to cracking she was.

Vivian admitted it, drugs and drink, too. She had always been reckless, she said, but everything had become worse since the incidents with Lanier and now the investigation. She was in very bad shape, she knew it.

"We can help you," Parker said. "We can get you in a program."

"I'll be all right," Vivian said. "I'm better now."

"Is everybody being all right? Are you being treated fairly?"

"Mr. Castleberry is nice," Vivian said, crying. "He's a nice man, isn't he?"

"Sure he is," Parker said. "I want you to let us get you help. I want you to think about that. Have you told your family about your problems or about what you're doing here?"

"Oh, no," Vivian said. "I couldn't do that!"

Parker made sure that Vivian had his office and home numbers. She already had Castleberry's.

She had been able to identify with Sandy Sanders from the start, but now Amy Spain was moved by two other women, Patty Wallace and Vivian, the former because of her dignity and the latter because she wore her heart on her sleeve, blurting everything out in an entirely convincing way, as frank about own faults, including her drug problems, as she was in describing the rapes in brutal, sickening detail. Amy instantly liked Vivian for her candor and obvious intelligence, and sympathized with her. Most important to Amy was that she saw Vivian as someone a jury would believe.

When Vivian testified before the grand jury during the third week in November, Amy had a chance to talk to her alone, in the law library on the tenth floor. Theirs was not a long conversation, but it was sufficient for Amy to hear something about the Forsythe family background, including Vivian's accusations against Judy Forsythe concerning insurance fraud and Brad Forsythe's drug addiction, which by then was so advanced that it would surprise no one if he overdosed. Amy believed that Vivian had had serious difficulties in coming to terms with what she described as her mother's sexual mores and that, in this as in so much of her personality, Vivian was torn between identifying with her mother and rejecting her. A spontaneous, loving young woman came through; her concerns about her younger brother, for instance, seemed entirely genuine, but her addiction was equally obvious. Like Steve Parker, Amy worried about Vivian's chances for survival, even during the next few weeks. Parker, Spain, and Castleberry discussed her and agreed that Vivian was suicidal. What could they do for her, other than hope?

As for Patty Wallace, as Castleberry had hoped, Parker and Spain were completely won over by her manifest integrity. They were surprised only when she told them that she was not informing her husband yet about her cooperation with the prosecutors and the grand jury, for fear that he would react violently against Lanier. Her husband would have to find out sooner or later, Parker told Wallace, unless, of course, the case never went to trial. That was exactly why she was still keeping him in the dark, Wallace replied. If the candor she had already granted and would continue to display before the grand jury came to nothing, her husband would almost certainly decide to carry out justice on his own. "You don't know my Barry," she said.

Amy Spain's appreciation of Patty Wallace's and other women's situations in relation to Lanier deepened when the FBI team scrutinizing courthouse records provided breakdowns of courthouse salaries. Patty Wallace, for instance, had been receiving about fifteen thousand dollars a year, gross, and approximately twelve thousand per annum in take-home pay in 1988, the year in which she claimed the judge had assaulted her. Other employees made less, with no prospect of substantial rises in pay levels, other than adjustments for inflation. They had no civil service protection, and their health insurance covered only themselves, not their dependents.

Wallace's husband, as a United Parcel Service driver and Teamsters Union member, had a bigger salary and family-inclusive benefits, so that together they earned an income that, in an area with a relatively low cost of living, fit any definition of middle class. They had recently purchased an attractive new house in a semirural development to the west of the bypass. They could not have done this without her salary, however; and if Patty divorced, with two children in school, she would find herself in desperate straits, as several of the other witnesses obviously were. To be female and to have Judge Lanier as an enemy in Dyersburg was obviously a dangerous thing, indeed a formula for destitution. It was fear of the judge, as much as loathing of him, that had led her to quit her courthouse job rather than risk another confrontation with him, returning to a different courthouse position, and one that required no contact with Lanier, only years later.

Even as a beginning Justice Department lawyer, Amy Spain's salary was at least five times that of any of the witnesses, and came with far greater benefits and security. She was also single, with a close and prosperous family behind her. Once she became acutely aware of the contrasts, her sympathies for many of the Dyersburg women enlarged accordingly. She saw that an awareness of economic and social realities was as much a key to comprehending the importance of the Lanier case as was knowledge of the law. Patty Wallace was putting her own and her family's security at risk by what she was doing, yet her controlled, almost aristocratic demeanor, accentuated by her slender jeweled hands—she wore two antique rings on the right hand, another on her left ring finger, and her gold wedding band on her left forefinger—symbolized her independence of spirit. Neither she nor any of the others had had anywhere to turn for help until now. How, Amy Spain began to ask herself, can we possibly let a woman like that down?

Far from all of the women interviewed evoked a sympathetic response from Amy Spain, nor from Steve Parker, Ed Bryant, or the agents. Some prevaricated, some were hostile, and a few flat-out lied. One of these last, a woman who had been quoted by two co-workers in her office as having bragged that she had given David Lanier "the best blow job of his life," admitted having said it but claimed that she had meant it as a joke, and regretted it as having been "in poor taste." No one believed her, but no one could shake her from her claim never to have had anything sexual to do with the judge. This sort of personality and language continued to disturb Amy Spain, who admitted to Parker and Castleberry that until this investigation, she had never so much as uttered the word penis in public before in her life, "let alone with a bunch of you macho males sitting there!"

The vulnerability of the women was apparent from the start of the grand jury hearings, which were front-page news in every paper of the region and led TV news broadcasts. The agents ushered the witnesses down a back stairwell of the Federal Building after the women testified, and the media did not disclose their names; but word of who some of them were quickly got around Dyersburg, and recriminations began.

Several received frequent hang-up calls. Patty Wallace kept a record of these and noted as many as five or six in a single day, on her answering machine or when she picked up. Many of the women reported noticing a certain coolness, or iciness, developing toward them among townspeople, including colleagues at work. It was a subtle matter, they told the agents and the prosecutors, but definitely there. They did not think they were being paranoid.

Castleberry tried to reassure them, saying that once people truly understood what Lanier had done, they would side with the witnesses. He did not tell them how long that process would take, however, given the slowness with which the judicial system moved, nor was he at all sure he believed it, but he felt that his job was to shore up their faith. To be completely honest with them would have meant saying, "Don't worry, it'll get much worse, before it ever gets better—if it does."

And it quickly did get worse for one of the women. Mary Haralson was one of the first to testify. One day later in November, the personnel officer at the bank where she worked called her in to tell her she was fired.

The reason he gave was transparently specious, that because she was having to take so much time off to testify in Memphis and was being so distracted by the Lanier investigation, she could no longer perform her job properly. She had no doubt what power lay behind her dismissal, but there was nothing she could do about it. She said nothing, and cleaned out her desk.

She began looking for another job immediately. By Christmas she was still out of work.

Publicly Lanier remained sanguine. Only days before the grand jury hearing began, he was claiming to a reporter that he had never been informed by federal prosecutors that he was the target of any investigation. He continued to insist that he would conduct his courts as usual. The last time he looked, his term as judge had another seven years to run. Everything would go on as usual.

On the first day of the grand jury hearings, however, Mrs. Joan Mills Lanier, represented by attorney Ralph Lawson, filed for divorce from her husband of twenty-eight years, David W. Lanier, on the grounds "that the defendant is guilty of such cruel and inhuman treatment, including the act of adultery, toward the Plaintiff as renders cohabitation unsafe and improper." With remarkable speed, the hearing in the matter was held and the divorce granted on November 7, in Gibson County, with Mrs. Lanier receiving a settlement that was by any standard generous. She was entitled by law to half the couple's property; but Judge Lanier also agreed to convey to her "his remaining one-half interest in the same tracts or parcels of real estate enumerated before the Court."

Castleberry understood, from Source and others, that virtually all of Lanier's assets were in real estate, urban and rural. The prosecutors and other observers throughout the community considered the divorce a sham. Some said so privately; others, including Joey McDowell, were vocal in their skepticism. Donna Whittle, the reporter covering the story for the *State Gazette,* phrased the matter carefully in her front-page account: "Sources close to the grand jury investigation have suggested the divorce may be an attempt by Lanier to protect financial assets from civil litigation that could stem from the probe."

Those believing that the divorce was a financial ruse were encouraged in this hypothesis by scrutiny of the date and exact time of filings by plaintiff and defendant. Their action coincided with the start of grand jury hearings in Memphis; Judge Lanier's acceptance of Mrs. Lanier's financial demands, as listed in her complaint, was not merely swift but previous, having actually been filed fifteen minutes *before* her petition, indicating an unusually quick and amicable meeting of minds between contending parties and giving rise to suspicions of ulterior purpose. And the elapsed time between the initial filings and the final divorce, exactly one week, rivaled Mexican promptness as to speed of dissolution.

Sham divorce or not, scarcely a person in Dyersburg, excepting perhaps victims of the judge's erotomania, or lust, blamed Mrs. Lanier for trying to hang on to what she could, given what everyone knew she had endured in her marriage, her well-known dutifulness as a mother, her obvious distress, and the fall in income she would experience were the judge to be sent to jail. People as diverse and as different in their approaches to the law as Chief Bobby Williamson and former sheriff Tommy Cribbs, who remembered Joan and her twin sister from long ago, when the girls grew up near the banks of the Forked Deer, considered her blameless and felt nothing but compassion for her. "She deserves every penny" was how one man phrased it. "She earned it just cooking lunch for that pig."

The shift of assets to her name did make the possibility of success in any putative civil suits by victims remote, as there did not appear to be any sure way to prove the divorce bogus, given that the judge had admit-

ted adultery, that his wife had sued him on those grounds, and that she
could argue that the pressure brought on by publicity, not the fear of
indictment and conviction, had prompted her action. As for the worth of
David Lanier's estate before he turned his assets over to his wife, no one
could say, except as a rough estimate. A search of real estate records filed
with the county revealed properties in David Lanier's name worth in
excess of a million dollars. Whatever liabilities he may have incurred
were known to his banker and not part of the public record.

At the beginning of the grand jury hearings, Steve Parker and Amy Spain
were still wrestling with the problem of finding a sound legal basis for
bringing federal charges against David Lanier. Their discussions had narrowed to the area of civil rights, as derived from Title VII of the Civil
Rights Act of 1964. They had in mind a criminal action that might, if it
were successful, be sufficient to force the judge from the bench and open
the way for the women to sue him on their own.

To proceed with any civil rights litigation, the U.S. Attorney's office
for the Western District of Tennessee had to obtain clearance from the
Justice Department in Washington. It happened that Albert Moskowitz,
Deputy Head of the Criminal Section of the Civil Rights Division of the
Department of Justice, was in Memphis as Parker and Spain prepared
their presentation to the grand jury. Well known to the prosecutors
because of his successful record in civil rights actions around the country,
Moskowitz had also been in Memphis for several weeks earlier that year,
helping another assistant U.S. attorney win the conviction of a Shelby
County sheriff's deputy who had beaten a drug suspect to death.

Parker and Spain discussed with Moskowitz the evidence against
Lanier, outlining their legal approach, which involved combining the
intent of two separate statutes. Moskowitz was impressed with the evidence, and he thought their legal strategy ingenious—but he did not favor
it. He felt strongly, after mulling the matter over for a couple of days, that
a procedure derived from the Constitution itself, rather than from Title
VII, would be more effective. They were dealing here with actual physical assault. In two or three instances, notably the incidents involving
Vivian Forsythe and Jennifer Gallagher, the assaults might prove to have
been felonious; the others certainly qualified as misdemeanors. If felony
charges were brought, they would be talking about rape, by any other
name.

Parker, Spain, and Moskowitz agreed to try to prosecute Judge Lanier
using the same criminal statute under which the sheriff's deputy had been
convicted of murder: U.S. Code 18, § 242, "deprivation of rights under
color of law." This statute, which had been on the books for over a hun-

dred years, had been enacted during Reconstruction and derived from the Thirteenth and Fourteenth Amendments, which abolished slavery and established the rights of citizenship. It was one of the two principal laws under which civil rights prosecutions were brought by the federal government. (The other, § 241, covered conspiracy.) § 242 read, in part:

> Whoever, under color of any law, statute, ordinance, regulation, or custom, willfully subjects any inhabitant of any state, Territory, or District to the deprivation of any rights, privileges, or immunities secured or protected by the Constitution or laws of the United States . . . shall be fined not more than $1,000 or imprisoned not more than one year, or both; and if bodily injury results shall be fined under this title or imprisoned not more than ten years, or both; and if death results shall be subject to imprisonment for any term of years or for life.

The term "under color of law" as constructed by the courts referred to any such criminal action as described that was carried out by a person representing himself or herself as an officer of the law or a public official acting under the authority of the law. The rights referred to in the statute included the right to personal safety. Under both these definitions, Moskowitz argued, § 242 should apply to a state judge who had violated the "bodily integrity" of these women, as fundamentally guaranteed by the Constitution itself.

Parker and Spain were delighted that Al Moskowitz had come up with this constitutional approach. Because criminal civil-rights prosecution was what he did, and because he thought that this was a most important and potentially a landmark case, Moskowitz accepted Parker's invitation to join the prosecution team, for however long it would take to see the case through.

Moskowitz's endorsement and help were the biggest boosts of morale Parker and Spain had enjoyed since embarking on the Lanier investigation. He had already proved the suppleness of his mind by redirecting their legal strategy. Not the least of the advantages of Moskowitz's approach was that it would help to distance the Lanier case from the Hill-Thomas controversy, which, far from going away, seemed to be intensifying in the wake of Judge Thomas's confirmation.

Al Moskowitz was forty-five, a slight, articulate man with a receding line of light brown curly hair, and round horn-rimmed glasses that lent him an owlish look above his brown mustache. His usual expression in repose was marked by a faint, closed-mouth smile that, with his quizzical eyes and a slight tilt of the head, seemed to ask, "Are you sure you know what you're talking about?" He was manifestly bookish. He seemed to

have been born in his rumpled dark suit; it was not clear that he had ever
been out of doors. If the tall, demonstrative Parker could have passed for
an athletic coach, Moskowitz was the professor, and Amy Spain his student.

In fact, Al Moskowitz almost became a professor. He had earned an
M.A. in Latin and Greek literature from the University of Michigan, after
majoring in English at the City College of New York, and he began his
professional life teaching classics at an exclusive private school near
Kansas City. As he told the story, teaching began to depress him when he
noticed how much better the students were able to dress than he could on
that salary and when he watched them leave to enter a world that seemed
to be slipping away from him. When he decided to get married and start a
family, he left to earn his law degree at the University of Missouri, and
for five years was a public defender in Kansas City until, having developed a passionate interest in civil rights, he joined the Justice
Department.

"We'll make a great team," Parker told him exuberantly, throwing his
arm around him. "The Jewish Yankee, the mannerly Southern belle, and
me, I'm the token redneck. I just know you're not gonna want to go hunt
squirrel with me, but we'll get along anyway."

As sure as he was that if Judge Lanier was going to be indicted, it
should be under U.S. 18 § 242, Moskowitz was far from confident of success. As he warned Parker and Spain, the case should go ahead on this
basis, because it was the right thing to do and the only avenue that he
could see that might lead to a conviction. But they were taking a big risk.
He knew this area of the law better than any other, as well as anyone did,
and he also knew its history, which was not in the least encouraging.

The statute, originally enacted to protect freed slaves from the reintro-
duction of slavelike conditions, by controlling the Ku Klux Klan and
white supremacist law enforcement, had for decades been used successfully to convict police officers who physically assaulted suspects or prisoners with unnecessary force. What had begun as a law to combat the
highly successful attempts by Southern whites to keep emancipated
blacks in thrall had evolved into the most effective means the Justice
Department had of protecting all citizens from the abuse of power by law-
enforcement personnel everywhere in the country.

It pleased Moskowitz to think that this law might now be shown as an
effective weapon on behalf of women's rights. Hadn't Lanier essentially
reduced many of these women to the condition of sex slaves? And hadn't
he used his position as judge to accomplish this "under color of law"? The
historical symmetry of the idea, that a statute enacted to protect one
oppressed group and extended to others might now be applied to achieve

justice for women, was a satisfying prospect to Moskowitz, who was a modest man but liked to imagine when he took pride in his work that he was contributing something to the cause of individual freedom in America.

But there was a problem.

Moskowitz broke the news to Parker and Spain during a strategy session in the law library of the U.S. Attorney's office. The three of them sat at the big table with their books and yellow legal pads.

In the entire history of § 242, there had been only one previous attempt at prosecuting a sitting judge for civil rights violations. And that attempt had ended in absolute failure.

In 1986, a Texas state judge had been indicted for violating the civil rights of several prostitutes by extorting sex from them in exchange for lenient sentences. Moskowitz remembered the case well, because he had been close to it. The jury, unimpressed by the testimony against the judge by the prostitutes, who had twenty-nine convictions on various sex and drug charges among them, acquitted the defendant on all the civil rights charges.

The jury did convict the judge on related mail fraud counts—but the U.S. Supreme Court threw out those verdicts a year later. The judge walked out a free man, even though his own son had testified against him.

Needless to say, there were numerous parallels to the Lanier case in this singular precedent. The Texas judge appeared to have been nearly as libidinous as Lanier; like Lanier, he had allegedly used his power to coerce or persuade sex from women. And the jury—a Southern one, it had to be noted—had disbelieved the principal witnesses, undoubtedly because they were women of compromised virtue.

"Many of our witnesses aren't perfect," Parker said. "What're we going to do about it?" Exactly as in the Texas case, Lanier had gone after women, many of them with big problems. That was his leverage. If they weren't already prostitutes, he would make them into ones. Some had fought him off, but all had kept more or less silent.

Parker was plummeting into dark thoughts. He envisioned Linda Pickering or Brenda Castain before a churchgoing jury of Memphians, typically people who kept Bibles by their bedsides, the sort of folks he met at his own church every Sunday, who believed as he did but had never learned to forgive as he had—because, living good lives, they had never been exposed to the extent of iniquity in the world, as he had.

One of the precautions he intended to take, Moskowitz said, was to interview each of the women himself. He would have to evaluate each woman's credibility on his own, and try to make sure that there were no hidden bombs that could go off during the trial to blow up the case. The women's secrets.

"Bill Castleberry's not going to like that," Amy Spain said.

"Bill's already complaining," Parker agreed. "He says we're raking these women over the coals. He thinks that if they have to keep repeating their stories, some of them aren't going to make it."

"Castleberry will have to understand," Moskowitz said. "I am not going to be put in the position of putting on witnesses I'm not sure of myself."

Parker thought about Vivian Forsythe. She had managed, barely, to get through her story another time before the grand jury. It had been touch and go. Tears were one thing, but Vivian had been on the verge of collapse. Parker had skated her over the most delicate sequence in her narrative, the account of how and why she had returned to Lanier's chambers, to be assaulted a second time—and how she had still not told her parents or anyone about what had happened. Parker had been unable to gauge the jury's reaction to this.

Vivian's narcotics problem, whatever she was on, was now obvious to anyone alert to the signs. Her hands were the size of softballs.

She had tried to hide them by folding her arms, but Parker had seen them and was appalled—as Castleberry had been, who was not permitted to enter the jury room but had noted the hands while driving Vivian in from Dyersburg. Bill was extremely worried about her. He was talking about going to see her parents.

Vivian was only the most blatant example of the women who, the oftener they repeated their stories, the more they seemed to become unhinged. Theirs was the opposite of the common behavior of witnesses, who in most instances adjusted to the novelty of telling the truth and became increasingly comfortable with it at each rehearsal. By the time they took the stand, typical witnesses were so inured to emotion, you felt like sticking a pin in their butts. Not these. Some of the women were freaking out.

"Castleberry will have to explain to them that they're going to have to see me one on one," Al Moskowitz said. "This whole thing is already enough of a gamble."

23

Steve Parker was the first person ever in Vivian's life to talk to her bluntly, sternly, yet without rancor, to tell her that if she did not change her ways, she was not only going to die young, she was going to let a lot of people down, not least of all her daughter. She and her parents had fought for fifteen years or so; her counselor in college had advised her; Professor Owsley had given her professional guidelines and an example in his own work; the drug rehab program had promoted abstinence; Crossroads Clinic had encouraged confrontation and an understanding of herself in terms of her mother. Only Steve Parker had said, "Look, Vivian, it's up to you. It's time for you to stop blaming anyone but yourself, not even Judge Lanier. We know what's happened to you. We understand what you've been through. We'll help you get more counseling, sure. But in the long run, it's going to be your decision. I can tell you one thing, we can't use you and you can't help us if you don't help yourself first."

Those were his words and, sensing that he was getting through to her, or hoping that he was, he was not sure, he elaborated, there in his office after her last, shaky grand jury appearance. It was just the two of them, face-to-face. Parker and his wife had no children of their own. He felt as if he were talking to his own daughter, as if he were confronting the disintegration of his own family, not just another federal case.

He did think instinctively that Vivian was the key to the Lanier case, for two reasons: hers would be felony counts; and when Vivian was at her best, she was among the two or three most convincing witnesses, because of her obvious candor. But if she kept on drinking and drugging the way she was, the prosecutors would have to forget about her, would never be able to risk putting her on the stand, if she lived that long. She would be too wasted to be taken seriously.

"I understand, Mr. Parker" was about all Vivian could manage to say as she sat crying beside his desk.

"I don't want to put you through something that's going to make you worse," he said.

"No, no! I want to help!"

"Think of it this way. You're not even doing it for yourself. You'd be doing it for your daughter and for other women. You believe in God, don't you?"

"Of course I do."

"Well, I'm not trying to be a religious nut or anything, but I have to tell you, I see this case as between good and evil. I know what side you're on. We want you with us, too, but it's going to take a lot of work and a lot of courage from you."

Bill Castleberry happened to be waiting in the law library when Vivian emerged from Parker's office. She looked as if Steve had really put her through a wringer. Castleberry was about to ask her if she'd like a ride back to Dyersburg but thought better of it. Sadly, because of her reputation it would not be a good idea for him to be spotted alone with her in his car. On his part, he trusted her completely; it was what others, sympathetic to Lanier, would say. He asked her how she was feeling.

"Mr. Parker really reamed me out," she said.

"He did?"

"Well, he asked me if I wanted to live or die, in so many words. He also talked about good and evil."

"Steve's a religious guy. He wasn't bugging you, was he?"

"Oh, no," Vivian said, crying again. "The truth hurts. I ought to know."

Thanksgiving at the Forsythe house was a melancholy occasion. Vivian's brother Brad was home from Florida, where he was supposedly studying to be an airline pilot. He was stoned morning, noon, and night. He had a girlfriend with him. Vivian found it impossible to talk to her about Brad's problems, and besides, her own were on her mind, along with Steve Parker's speech to her or sermon or whatever it was.

There was another guest at Thanksgiving dinner, Brenda Castain, who had nowhere else to go. She was talking about moving to Memphis, to try to start over and get her son back. Vivian's older brother and her sister and her husband were at the table, too.

When her father started to say grace, Vivian burst into tears and hurried away to her bedroom and took a swig from a bottle she had hidden there. Her hands were bruised and so swollen that she could scarcely grip the bottle to tip it up. Medically she was aware that the drugs were making her edemic, a condition that causes fluids to accumulate in cavities and tissues of the body. She was aware of how grotesque she looked, but it was as if she were two persons, as if those were someone else's hands, as if what she was doing to herself were being done to someone else.

When she returned to the table she watched Donna feed Ashley bites of sweet potato and attend to her own children.

"You're letting your daughter down," Mr. Parker's voice admonished her in her head.

Parker and Castleberry had encouraged her to call them, and she did so, at least once a day to one or the other of them between Thanksgiving and Christmas. When she told them that, one way or another, she thought she had to get out of Dyersburg, would never be able to straighten herself out in that atmosphere with all its familiar, easy temptations, they encouraged her to leave. Her drug connections contacted her daily to see what she wanted; her friends, especially Brenda, were a mess; and Lanier was there, still in his court, still defiant and powerful and a reminder of what she was up against. All she had to do was drive past the courthouse to start shaking. Her dilemma was, if she went off on her own in her present physical and mental state, how could she cope with Ashley?

Castleberry took it upon himself to intervene, believing that it was actually a life-or-death situation for Vivian, never mind the court case.

He visited the Forsythe house and had a long talk with Mrs. Forsythe, who agreed that Vivian had to do something drastic to save herself. Castleberry had the impression that Judy did not believe, or not fully, that her daughter had been raped—another strong reason for Vivian to leave, if possible. But Judy did seem willing, even eager, to take on the responsibility of Ashley for the time being.

"You're going to have to care for your grandchild, I don't know for how long," was the way Castleberry put it. "You don't have any choice, the way I see it. I gather you're already doing so. It's the only way to save your daughter."

The sense of rivalry between Judy and Vivian was palpable, he would have to have been blind and deaf to miss it; and he had no doubt that many of Vivian's grievances against her mother were legitimate. But there was no other way to go, under these horrendous circumstances. Judy assured him that Ashley would be well cared for.

Castleberry did not enjoy the role of family counselor, which for him was unprecedented. Compared to this, bank robberies, frauds, hostage situations, armed fugitives, even homicides were a snap. He could deal with drug dealers; addicts were not his bag. *I am not a social worker, god-*

damnit, and I am not a psychologist, I thought I was an FBI agent, he kept saying to himself.

But he was the one who had roped Vivian into this case, he knew; and he felt that he bore an uncomfortably heavy responsibility for having done that. When he had first interviewed Vivian, she had been holding down a job, at least; now she could not bring herself to show up for work. He had to try to do something for her, unsure as he was of what he should do or say.

Just after the New Year, Vivian took off for Orlando, Florida, with Brad and his girlfriend. "Are you sure you want to stick that close to your brother?" Mr. Castleberry had asked her, but when she explained to him that she had nowhere else to go and thought she might help herself by trying to help Brad, too, Castleberry had no answer and wished her well and said that he and Steve Parker would be sure to keep in touch with her. As soon as they needed her in Memphis, he said to her, more to try to give her something to think about than believing that she would be able to return, the government would fly her in. He felt very sad, telling her good-bye.

He did not tell her that neither Parker, Amy Spain, nor he was optimistic about her chances, instead sending her off with plenty of "We know you'll make it!" and "You can do it, Vivian!" and other phrases that rang rather hollow in his ears. Among them, Parker, relatively speaking, held out the most hope. He prayed for Vivian every Sunday.

Castleberry was correct about one thing, the impossibility of Vivian surviving while living with Brad. She was appalled to discover the conditions in which he was existing, with bills unpaid, utilities about to be shut off, local dealers calling, and even a couple from Dyersburg on the line constantly. Explaining the situation to them, she asked and received from her parents enough for first month's rent and a security deposit on a one-bedroom in Winter Park, not far from downtown Orlando. Moved to her own place, she spent the rest of January and into February barely functioning, in bed most of the day and night.

She had a supply of pot with her. When that ran out, she was tempted to call Brad for more and to see how they could score something stronger. She had not shot up since leaving Tennessee. Instead, she remained in a state somewhere between lethargic and comatose—and so depressed that she did not answer the phone or, for that matter, even open the blinds.

The days and nights slipped by. One day she woke up and, acting more or less on instinct, showered and shampooed and went out to buy a newspaper. That was how she found out that it was almost Valentine's Day. She telephoned Ashley, had a good cry with her on the phone, and thought about scoring some dope.

Then she realized that she had gone more than a month without ingesting or shooting anything. *Let it go another day,* she thought, and went out to put a down payment on a television set—but did not, because she realized she was down to twenty dollars. *No,* she decided, *I am not calling my parents for money, not this time. What I need is a job.*

In the classifieds she saw an ad for a secretarial position at a law firm, called the number, and set up an appointment for an interview the next day. That night, trying to sleep, she heard Steve Parker's voice in her head, talking about not letting people down and about good and evil and Lanier and her responsibilities to Ashley.

She had lost so much weight, she was afraid she would look sick for her interview; but when she examined herself in the mirror that morning, she had to admit that, if anything, she appeared healthier than she had in some time, just by staying off the drugs and drink, even though she had hardly been eating anything, except the occasional hamburger. *I am going to get some orange juice,* she said to herself, carefully applying some makeup and brushing out her hair until it began to shine.

The law firm, which was one of the most prominent in Orlando, hired her that day. And that night, feeling better than she had since she could remember, she said a prayer of thanks and tried to think clearly about what lay ahead.

I have something to live for, she told herself, or God, or her pillow. *Is hate a reason to live? I hate Judge Lanier, and I want to survive to testify against him and to get him thrown in jail. No, it is not just hate, it is love, too, for Ashley, so that she won't have to go through what I've been through and so other women won't have to, either.*

She told herself the same things every night as she went through her first week and then another at work, blessing the office routine. She started showing up on Saturdays to get ahead. And she kept hearing Steve Parker's stern, emotional voice and thinking about how nice Mr. Castleberry and a few others had been to her.

She tried to avoid seeing her brother, who was sliding further down. And because she was so lonely and the telephone was no substitute for actual human contact, she began, cautiously at first, talking to people at work about what she was going through. Everyone seemed sympathetic. The partners in the firm encouraged her and were interested in the case against the judge from a legal point of view. She began to accumulate more people whom she felt she could not let down. It was as if staying off drugs had as much to do with others as with herself, and that made a difference.

She thought that she probably ought to get herself into some kind of counseling program but hesitated, afraid that it would mean raking up the past again, her problems with her mother, all that. For the moment it seemed better simply to work hard and to try to keep clean.

And every night she repeated to herself like a litany the reasons for which she was trying to survive—not for herself but to get that bastard Lanier and, for Ashley's sake, to show the world that a man cannot do that to a woman and expect to get away with it.

24

SUPPORT
OUR
JUDGE

> Don't allow a political character assassi-
> nation to happen through the power of
> the U.S. Attorney, FBI, local would-be
> political machine and a biased daily
> newspaper.

This full-page advertisement, which appeared in December 1991 in the
State Gazette, went on to urge citizens to write to U.S. Attorney Ed
Bryant protesting the prosecution of Judge Lanier and to send donations
for a defense fund. The ad, which was identified as "paid for by friends of
David Lanier," also urged people to cancel their subscriptions to the
paper. Whoever these Lanier supporters were, they were angry enough at
the *Gazette* for its coverage of the investigation to ask donors not to sub-
scribe to the paper carrying the solicitation for funds.

A few days later the *Gazette* printed a letter from one of these supporters, who linked the Lanier prosecution to actual political assassination:
"We all know how powerful the federal government can be at trying to
control any situation in our lives—we have known this since the days of
John F. Kennedy's murder in Dallas." This rather surprising analogy may
have been inspired by the just-released film *JFK,* which with comparably
wild surmise blamed the FBI, Lyndon Johnson, the Pentagon, and other
federal entities for President Kennedy's murder. It was common, as Steve

Parker commented, for all indicted politicians to cry government conspiracy; but the rhetoric in this instance was reaching new heights of paranoid, or disingenuous, absurdity.

The letter included the current Republican candidate for governor in this menacing cabal, charging him with trying to capture Lanier's Democratic scalp as a "trophy" for his "mantle" [sic]. The *Gazette,* too, must be part of this scheme, or it would not have run the story of the Laniers' divorce on page one. As for Steve Parker, he had summoned "a bigger boy from Washington to try their luck on the civil-rights laws."

The signed author of this letter, Reed Riley Sr., happened to be a private investigator employed by David Lanier. Castleberry and Champine's name for him, for Cozy Kitchen purposes, was Rikki Tikki Tavi, because they thought he looked like a mongoose, although he was the ally of a viper.

Riley's letter aside, the prosecution team had no reason to complain of coverage in the media, led by the *State Gazette,* which was now owned by the New York Times Company and gradually proved itself more influential in setting the tone of reporting than one might expect of a small-town paper. Consistently the *Gazette* got stories first and got them right. In Donna Whittle, the paper had a reporter who immediately grasped the significance of the Lanier story beyond local boundaries, as a case involving the rights of women everywhere.

Whittle's presence at the courthouse and in Memphis struck Castleberry as symbolic. She was feminine in a distinctly Southern way, soft-voiced, not overtly aggressive; attractive with straight, bobbed black hair and a very fair complexion, she dressed smartly, nearly always in combinations of red and black; the code name for her was "the lady in red." At the same time, she was manifestly the emancipated female, New South rather than Old. Perhaps a couple of the witnesses, Vivian Forsythe certainly, were as intelligent as she—but her education and sophistication set her apart from them. To the Laniers of this world, Donna Whittle was as invulnerable as Amy Spain.

When the agents showed up at the judge's chambers one morning, Donna Whittle was there with her notebook and camera. The next day her photograph of Castleberry standing beside a door marked JUDGE'S CHAMBERS with a tape measure in one hand and a pad and pencil in the other appeared on page one, accompanied by her story headed "Agents Examine Lanier's Office." Without speculating on the agent's purpose, the story and photo were enough to make any reader wonder what must have gone on in that room.

Castleberry found that the chambers measured ten by fifteen feet, small enough to feel claustrophobic but large enough to permit the actions the witnesses had described. For him it was an eerie and disquieting experience to record the dimensions of that gloomy room and to make an inventory of its furnishings. Secrets came alive in his imagination. Lurid scenes flashed through his mind as he verified how the witnesses' stories added up. More than anything else, he felt pity for the women and gratitude that they could now tell the truth.

He moved into the tiny bathroom behind the desk, noting that the small, frosted window was too small for escape. Here the full impact of the horrors descended on him. He became acutely uncomfortable. He could not help imagining himself as Vivian, spitting into the washbasin, and nausea seized his throat. When he walked out, he half expected to see Lanier sitting behind his desk adjusting his trousers.

There was no sleeping bag to be found under the desk. The judge was "out of town on business" that day, Sherry Cooper told the agents and Donna Whittle and a handful of TV reporters and technicians. "Maybe David's gone camping," Castleberry cracked to Champine, who had trouble keeping a straight face. Nor could they find the infamous "Judge Thomas robe." What a pity. Castleberry had hoped to send it to the FBI lab in Washington for analysis, but he was just as glad not to have to touch it. It would have made an unusual trial exhibit.

It was remarkable how secluded the chambers felt, and were, there in the busy courthouse. Castleberry and Champine tested to see whether they could hear each other's voices through the walls with the door shut and could not, except, faintly, in the hallway. The situation of the filing room, between the secretary's office and the chambers, made it a sound trap for any screams that might come through or under that door. Lanier had told at least two women that the walls were soundproofed. Castleberry knocked on them; they did seem unusually solid. Could Lanier have had them specially constructed?

Castleberry retraced Vivian's sequence of retreat after the first rape, from the bathroom, past the desk, quickly toward the hallway door. It was then that he noticed a framed motto that was hanging near that door. He read the printed lines:

> *Until you've been in politics*
> *You've never really been alive;*
> *It's rough and sometimes it's dirty*
> *And it's always hard work and tedious details.*
> *But it's the only sport for grown-ups.*
> *All other games are for kids.*

He did not recognize the quotation. He thought about all the hard work and tedious details that must have plagued Judge Lanier in that room—

which ought more aptly to be called the torture chamber. He opened the door to the hallway and faced again the imposing portrait of James P., and at that moment something Source had told him hit home.

David Lanier's mother had committed suicide after James P. had divorced her—to marry his secretary. Another source, an old gentleman whose wife had worked in a dress shop during James P.'s day, had said that the first Mrs. James P. Lanier had often come in with a black eye or other facial bruises when she also worked at the shop; and that everyone had talked about the time James P. had kicked another of his secretaries out of his office when he found out that she was dating someone else.

He had not merely thrown her out. He had kicked her, literally, out the door and slammed his shoe into her butt as she fell forward onto her hands and knees, and kept kicking her as she crawled down the hall toward the exit—in the same hallway where his august portrait now hung. People had stood by and watched.

Like father, like son, only David was more secretive about his ways with women. And no one had ever accused David Lanier of beating his wife. That wasn't his style, but James O.'s. There was a third son of James P.'s, but David and James O. had never acknowledged him, because he was by the second wife. Not a true Lanier, from their perspective, not a true heir.

After New Year's 1992, Castleberry found more women to interview. The number was now in excess of thirty, about half reporting direct experience of the judge's brutalities, the rest with secondhand knowledge or pleading ignorance but on the list from other sources. And there were other sorts of witnesses that kept turning up, some in relation to questionable judicial decisions and one a part-time limousine driver with his own alarming story to tell.

The young man's ex-wife had been friends with Brenda Castain, who was now living in Memphis in a drug rehab program, trying to get her son back. Around Christmas, when Brenda had been still in Dyersburg, he had received a telephone call from an unknown man who would not identify himself but sounded middle-aged and white.

The caller said that he knew the limo driver was a sociable sort and was often around certain women. Did he happen to know Brenda Castain, Linda Pickering, or another woman—whose name was also on the witness list, Castleberry noted. The caller had mentioned at least two others also, but the limo driver could not recall those names.

It was Brenda Castain who had led the agents to this informant, who said that he had repeatedly asked the caller to identify himself. The mysterious voice replied only that if the driver would do something important for him, they could meet later. If he cooperated, the job would be worth ten thousand dollars to him.

The caller asked him to have sex with as many of these women as he could, offering them drugs in exchange. He should make sure that the drugs were planted on the women afterward.

Ten thousand was a lot of money. He had seriously considered accepting the assignment. But he liked Brenda and did not want to be responsible for getting her or the others into trouble. That this was a setup was obvious. He told the caller that he did not wish to "mess with drugs." The man had not called again.

The driver kept quiet about the offer until he happened to run into Brenda on the street, and he told her to be careful, explaining about the anonymous call.

He thought he knew what David Lanier sounded like and did not think the caller was the judge. Castleberry ran other names past him, but he claimed not to know them. He felt sure, however, that he would recognize the voice if he heard it again.

Castleberry and Champine contacted all of the other women to warn them that someone might try to plant drugs on them. And the agents served subpoenas on certain people who were known to be working for the judge, Rikki Tikki Tavi among them, and alerted them that some unprincipled fellow out there was trying to accomplish some nasty business. They would be well advised to keep their distance from such behavior. What if someone confused the schemer with one of them? That would not help the judge's case, and it might end up sending somebody to jail for a long time.

Unfortunately, some of the witnesses were quite capable of getting into trouble on their own, without encouragement from Lanier or his allies. Maybe it was the early spring weather in 1992. Sometime around March, a courthouse employee quit or was fired, when the judge found out that she had made statements detrimental to him—or had likely done so—before the grand jury. The woman, whose Cozy Kitchen moniker was Valerie, was having a drink at Chequers one evening when a blond, athletic-looking young fellow walked in. She did not recognize him, but they got to talking, and when he told her he was an FBI agent, he seemed even more attractive to her.

The agent's nickname within the Bureau was Driller Jack, because he had once worked on oil rigs in the Gulf of Mexico, and for another reason. He had nothing to do with the Lanier case. He happened to be in the territory because of a completely unrelated investigation, one involving high physical risk. He was a member of an FBI SWAT team. The more she found out about him and the more time she spent with him—other agents began to spot the pair everywhere, including Memphis—the more smitten she was. Incendiary, they were.

One day late in April, just before the resumption of grand jury hearings, when Lanier himself was scheduled to testify, Steve Parker happened to see the pair in the Mud Island parking garage across the street from the Federal Building, and made a few inquiries. He knew Valerie; he knew that Driller Jack was an agent. What the hell were the two doing together?

Castleberry, who had not known about the affair, was not pleased to hear of it but was hoping it would burn itself out fast. That was not good enough, Parker told him. The relationship had to be stopped immediately. What if Lanier heard about it? He probably already had! It was a potential time bomb. Parker asked Castleberry to speak to Driller Jack at once and to tell him to stay away from any of the Lanier witnesses.

"Neither of them is married," Castleberry said. "How can I tell him what to do with his private life?"

Parker said he wanted the affair stopped now. Couldn't Castleberry understand that as long as it went on, it was like handing Lanier a trump card? He would claim that government agents were seducing witnesses to corrupt them.

"But that's not true," Castleberry said. "Jack has nothing to do with this case."

"Tell him to lay off!"

Castleberry was surprised that Parker, as a former policeman, would ask him to instruct an agent on how to deal with his love life. Cops did not do that to one another, unless they wanted to incur the contempt and resentment of their colleagues. It was part of the unwritten code, like not ratting on a colleague.

Castleberry decided on a middle course. Without telling him what he should do, he approached Driller Jack and warned him of Parker's displeasure. The agent took the news calmly and said he would break off the affair. It would not be easy, however. The woman in question had made the first moves and had been pursuing him vigorously ever since. Castleberry said that he himself was not particularly concerned about the matter, since this woman, who was among those who had changed their stories several times, would never be called as a witness at the trial. Given Parker's displeasure, however, it would make things a lot easier on everyone if Driller Jack could find himself a new girlfriend.

Castleberry had the impression that the agent would be a good sport about the conflict and comply, but a couple of weeks later, Parker again encountered the amorous pair in and around the Federal Building.

Parker summoned Castleberry again and went through the roof. Castleberry refused to take further action. He was not with the Bureau's department of internal affairs or running some sort of morals squad, and he lacked authority to do anything more, even if he wanted to, which he did not.

Parker contacted Driller Jack's supervisor, who ordered the agent to end the relationship or face suspension, a threat that proved effective. If only you had done that to begin with and not asked me to do the dirty work, Castleberry considered telling Parker, but thought better of it.

Parker and Castleberry both tried to keep in touch with Vivian, whom they would need in Memphis again soon, when and if the grand jury indicted Lanier. Over the phone she assured them that she was doing much better. She had slipped off the wagon once or twice, she said, but on the whole was okay, especially since she had limited contact with her brother. She loved her job, she said, and had already been supplied with a new computer. She was thinking of asking for a raise.

"Sundays are the hard part," she told Castleberry when he phoned her. "I call Ashley, and then I don't know what to do. But I've started reading again. It's been so long, I forgot how much I need that."

"That's what I do," he said, "when I'm not in my yard. What are you reading?"

She rattled off a slew of titles, from *Toxic Parents* and other pop psychology books to *The Human Skeleton in Forensic Medicine; The Mismeasure of Man,* by Stephen Jay Gould; Darwin's *Origin of Species;* and articles in the *Journal of Forensic Sciences* and the *Annual Review of Anthropology.* She was also reading endless amounts of law, in connection with her work, which she found fascinating.

"You sound like you're doing great," Castleberry said.

"I'm better," she said, and he could hear that she was holding back tears.

"Hang in there," he said. "We need you."

"That's all I think about, Mr. Castleberry."

Either Vivian was a remarkable person or a great actress, Al Moskowitz commented when he heard about this seemingly miraculous process of recovery. He would have to make that determination himself when he interviewed her.

25

Bill Castleberry was more worried about several of the witnesses, not just Vivian, than he let on to any of the prosecutors or even to Steve Champine. His frequent contacts with the women and, in several instances, with their families had given him a picture of people living in terror and in general emotional disarray.

To these women, David Lanier was a figure more threatening and frightening than anyone except themselves and perhaps the investigators, including Joey McDowell, could understand. You had to be in Dyersburg to appreciate the full impact of Lanier on their lives. The phone calls, the stalking, the constant threat of the judge's power had devastated their psychological and even their physical well-being. Since her appearance before the grand jury, for instance, Patty Wallace, perhaps the most stable of all, had begun clenching her teeth so ferociously in her sleep that her dentist had warned her that she was facing a major operation on her jaw if she could not somehow learn to relax.

Lanier, in his nocturnal meandering around town, wrote down the license numbers of male guests at the single women's homes and called the women to express his virulent jealousy; he managed to convey messages to all of them, warning them not to talk to anyone about him. Since the initial grand jury hearings, he had approached several of them to ask if they had been subpoenaed or contacted by the FBI. If they admitted as much, he would advise them to tell the truth—and then proceed to outline some fictitious scenario for them to provide the FBI or the prosecutors and the grand jury, one indicating that nothing sexual had ever transpired between him and them.

Many of the women believed that Lanier carried around a microcassette recorder; some had seen recording equipment in his chambers. He must have removed it before Castleberry's inspection. Because they feared being taped, the women were afraid even to say things to pacify him, because he could use that against them.

Several expressed frustration with the slowness of the legal process, and said that they would never have cooperated had they understood what would be involved. Castleberry got the idea that they would back out now, if only they could figure out how. He was all too aware that only the fear of punishment that he had instilled in them was keeping them in line; he also knew, and was counting on their not knowing, that if they simply refused to testify, there would be nothing the government could do about it, or at least would do. Throwing them in jail was hardly a realistic option; it was unthinkable. But he let them believe otherwise.

The prosecution had hoped for indictments in February. It was now April, and nothing had happened. The women had been hanging in limbo, their anxieties and troubles mounting, for several months. The chancellor was still on his bench, still in control of many of their lives. Vivian, at her mother's insistence, was about to grant "temporary" custody of Ashley to Judy Forsythe, so Judy could act on behalf of the child in case of emergency. Vivian was balking, however, at this traumatic step, largely because David Lanier would be the one to make the order. Was Lanier behind this idea, holding it over Vivian to intimidate her? This had been his threat to her all along, since he had mentioned it in the moments before the rape. Vivian agonized. Should she return to Dyersburg and risk ending up back on drugs, just when she was starting to get herself together? Castleberry urged her to stay in Orlando. He asked himself whether, in doing so, he was putting the case ahead of the welfare of a mother and child. He tried to believe this was not so, that Vivian would be flirting with ruin if she came back too soon, or maybe ever. But what did he know? Was he playing God, as selfish and calculating as Lanier himself?

Everyone was suffering. Another witness received a cassette in the mail, a recording of several telephone conversations between her and the judge. A young man reported that Lanier had told him to approach the boyfriend of another witness and inform him that the judge had numerous compromising recordings of the woman. Anything to disrupt the witnesses' lives.

The more troubled the women's backgrounds and personal lives, the more distraught Lanier could make them. Jennifer Gallagher, whom Lanier had wrestled onto the sleeping bag, had recently married for the third time—mostly, she admitted to Castleberry, to have the comfort and protection of a husband as a shield against Lanier.

At first, Jennifer did not tell her new husband about her experiences with the judge, not about how often he had phoned her, not about his obscene calls. She was still a city employee, vulnerable to Lanier on that account. She was afraid to ask Lanier for help in obtaining child support from her second husband, who had adopted her little girl, who was actually the biological child of Jennifer's first husband. She was also afraid to go to the judge for help in permitting her child to continue in an advanced class at a Dyersburg city school, even though she was now living beyond the city limits. What would Lanier ask of her, Jennifer worried, if she petitioned him? She was so confused, she was thinking of letting her parents take custody, because they still lived within the city—but Lanier would be the one to rule on that, too. Lanier was controlling her life! Every time Castleberry talked to her, she sounded hysterical or clinically depressed; he never knew what to expect. Did she have to testify, she asked him again and again. Yes, he told her, she did.

Castleberry gave Jennifer his pager number. She called it almost daily. Late one day, just as he was preparing to leave for home, she rang and said that it was an emergency. Could he come to her house right away? She had told her new husband about what Lanier had done to her. The husband had pitched a fit, was on a rampage, was swearing to kill the judge. It was no joke. He was a championship-caliber marksman. He was loading up his guns.

Castleberry jumped into his car and raced to Jennifer's house. He knew exactly where it was, although he had not been there before, because he had made a map pinpointing each of the witness's residences so that he or Joey McDowell could respond at once if Lanier resumed his stalking.

He approached the door cautiously. Jennifer's husband opened the door, a dark-faced, brooding young man.

"Hi there. I'm Agent Castleberry. Mind if I come in?"

Castleberry was taken aback by the interior. It was easy to see whose possessions were whose. What he could only think of as "country kitsch"—handmade dolls and wooden animals; quilts; bowls of potpourri and needlepoint samplers and pillows—was everywhere. It was a veritable souvenir shop. But the gimcrack Americana was scattered among the husband's collection of dead animals. On the walls and propped in corners and on the floor as rugs were not only standard hunter's trophies, deer and elk and moose heads, but numerous other creatures of the forest—raccoons, possum, rabbits, varmints of all sorts and, glowering with teeth bared beside the fireplace, a coyote—or was it a gray wolf? The place looked like the Tommy Cribbs Museum of Natural History.

"I'm so glad you could come, Mr. Castleberry," Jennifer said in her tiny soft voice, as if she had invited him for pot roast. "I'll put some coffee on." She was sorry he could not meet her daughter, who was visiting grandparents.

Her husband, who introduced himself as Richard, picked up a shotgun to resume cleaning it. Castleberry followed Jennifer into the kitchen.

She was as small as her voice, no bigger than a mouse's ear, as Joey McDowell had said of her. A brown-eyed blonde devoted to the tanning salon, she might have been Californian but for her accent and a certain abjectness in her manner that identified her as a young woman trained from the cradle to defer to men. Castleberry from the beginning had analyzed her as a type of "walking victim," the sort of defenseless creature rapists target and cops smart enough and concerned enough to care and knowledgeable enough from experience can identify at a glance as someone who has been beaten, if not by a father or a stepfather to begin with, then by a boyfriend or husband. He doubted that this husband, Richard, had touched her in that way, or not yet. They still seemed protective of one another.

In the kitchen Jennifer nattered on about being cross with herself lately because she had spoken harshly to Richard once or twice. She blamed her outbursts on a combination of two factors, Judge Lanier and, shifting the guilt to herself, premenstrual syndrome.

"It's just not like me, to lash out like that," she said.

I bet not, Castleberry thought. Did Richard spend a good deal of time out hunting, he asked, knowing the answer was obvious.

"He's away most of every weekend," Jennifer said.

"Does that bother you, I mean with your being afraid of Lanier? I mean, wouldn't it be better if your husband was here to protect you, with all those guns of his?"

"Well," she said, "I think it's good he has something to get him out of the house, you know?"

In the living room Richard, whom Castleberry silently decided to nick-name Deerkiller, was examining his arsenal. Rifles, shotguns, pistols, revolvers; muzzle loaders, carbines, semiautomatics; knives for skinning and killing; a longbow that would need plenty of muscle to pull it, with metal-tipped arrows; and a huge crossbow. Which weapon was he thinking of using to kill the judge?

Jennifer brought the coffee and the three of them sat down to chat. He would have to be going in a minute, Richard said. He was working the seven-to-seven shift at Colonial Rubber.

"I understand you're thinking about killing Judge Lanier," Castleberry said, as if referring to some ordinary target, quail or a goose. He wanted to induce the young man to reveal his thoughts, to vent his rage. If he could get him to unload his feelings, as in dealing with someone who had taken hostages, Richard might unwind.

Surely, if he confessed his intentions beforehand to an FBI agent, it was unlikely that he would act on them?

It took a bit more friendly coaxing for Deerkiller to open up, and then he really did, pouring out his anger and distress over what Jennifer had told him the judge had done to her. And the more he talked, admitting that he wanted to shoot Lanier, the calmer he became. But at length his fury transformed itself into shame. He was embarrassed at having revealed his frustrations to another man, one with more power than he had, and in front of Jennifer. She moved to comfort him, but he shrank away.

Castleberry now worried that he had emasculated the husband in front of his wife, or that Richard felt that way, his vow to kill her tormentor made empty after all. Castleberry could feel the dynamics changing between Richard and Jennifer. She was feeling sorry for him; he hated that. The next step would be for the husband to turn his frustrations onto his wife, after Castleberry left. Undoubtedly, Richard had sworn to kill Lanier to begin with mainly to impress Jennifer—to show his loyalty and bravery and to test her feelings for him. If she didn't want him to kill Lanier, did that mean that she did not care that the judge had raped her? Where were her loyalties?

"Have a cigar?" Castleberry held one out to him, a Nicaraguan second, seventy-five cents apiece, that Bill bought regularly at a Memphis shop. Richard hesitated. "Courtesy FBI," Castleberry said. Richard accepted, and Castleberry lit up with him. They let the smoke rise in silence for a while, and Jennifer lit a cigarette and asked if anyone would like a beer.

"I'll have one," Castleberry said. "We'll all have one. I tell you what," he said to Deerkiller, "how about you let me make you a promise?"

"Yessir? What would that be?"

"Can you do me a favor?"

"Yessir. I'll try."

"Wait a minute. I want your wife to hear this. Jennifer? Richard here has agreed to do me a favor."

She came in with the beer and they all took a sip.

"What I really wish you'd do," Castleberry resumed to Richard, "is let the courts handle Lanier for the time being, okay? I know how you feel, and I admire the way you want to stand up for your family. Believe me, I do. But let us handle this and let the courts decide. For the time being?"

"Yessir."

"And down the road, if it comes to that, if we don't get that man off the bench and put him in jail, for a long, long time, so he can't do anybody more harm, then it's a different ball game. Do you get me?"

"I think so."

"And if the courts don't do their job, then I will personally buy you the bullets or the arrows or whatever you need to kill Lanier. Is that a deal?"

They shook on it.

*   *   *

For the moment Castleberry had defused the Jennifer Gallagher situation, but other danger spots flared, it seemed, nearly every day, and he began to feel completely inadequate to the situation. It was not just the number of witnesses with serious emotional problems, it was that he realized that he did not know how to handle many of them. He was operating by instinct, unsure of what to say to the distressed or what to do for them. Instead of diminishing, reports of Lanier's stalking and of his hangup obscene calls increased. Two of the women talked about being afraid of ending up face-down in the Mississippi. Barry Wallace and Junior Sanders—Patty's and Sandy's husbands—the two couples had become friends—were checking under their cars each morning, for fear that a bomb was attached. Junior noticed a tin can lying close to the house in his driveway and deposited it gently in an empty lot and poured water on it, just in case.

Castleberry thought that fears of this sort of violent retaliation were unrealistic. It was true, however, that the phone calls had become even uglier, if that was possible. One witness who had originally stonewalled but was now cooperating testified that she received a call in which this same muffled male voice, breathing hard with anger, threatened to slash her face and cut off her nipples.

What to do about the calls and the stalking? To record the women's incoming calls would be to give Lanier the chance to make self-serving tapes, which would vindicate him when discovered at a trial. The phone at the Penthouse could no longer be monitored—Lanier had replaced the cordless one with a conventional model; somebody had tipped him off. From the background noise some of the women reported hearing, he might be using pay phones some of the time. By now he would suspect he was being recorded by the women.

To try to reassure the women and to satisfy his own curiosity about Lanier's nocturnal movements, Castleberry requested and received help from Memphis FBI headquarters, which sent a Special Operations Group of eight agents to Dyersburg. Specialists in surveillance, working in pairs, the agents studied a map of the town and divided it into quadrants. The idea was to box Lanier in, as with a zone pass-defense in football, with each unit keeping in touch by radio and assuming responsibility alter-nately as Lanier drove from quadrant to quadrant.

The agents did verify that Lanier was driving around town in his old pickup, which henceforth became known as "the stalking vehicle," until two and three o'clock in the morning, heading out from the Penthouse about eleven. Frequently he would stop to make a call or calls from pay phones, his favorite apparently one out on the bypass near Barham's bar-becue. But on the whole, the surveillance did not work.

It was impossible to keep track of Lanier's every movement, the agents reported, partly because of the town's irregular layout, with its twisty streets and many obscure lanes and alleyways, the ungeometric result of nearly two hundred years of habitation—and the agents' unfamiliarity with the place. Lanier by contrast obviously knew every cranny of his city, his kingdom. And he drove with a jerky kind of mania, darting here and there, hour after hour. They would need an airplane to keep up with Judge Lanier.

Castleberry called off the specialists. He tried following Lanier himself one night and quickly understood the problem. To avoid his spotting you, you had to keep a certain distance, and that was all he needed to dart into some crooked lane and disappear on his nightly rounds.

Castleberry tried again the next evening, with a picture of the Dyersburg map in his mind. He followed Lanier from the courthouse to the Penthouse, watched him climb the fire escape and go inside, and sat in his car for almost three hours, smoking and waiting. He knew Lanier was planning to prowl, because the pickup was there, parked next to the Mercedes he normally drove to and from the courthouse. Did he actually think people wouldn't recognize him in the truck, or did he reserve it for stalking out of some peculiar sense of order?

Finally he came down the fire escape and, as he opened the door of the stalking vehicle, looked this way and that, swiveling his head from side to side to see if he was being watched. It was dark in that alley, but Castleberry recognized the swivel-headed gesture because it was so characteristic of Lanier whenever he was out and about. Jennifer Gallagher had noticed it, watching him through the window of her City Hall office when he emerged from the courthouse, turning his head from left to right in a semicircle. She thought he looked like a robot.

He drove off. Castleberry followed him as far as the courthouse—and all at once something dawned on him. Later he called it an epiphany.

He let Lanier go and stopped in front of the courthouse. He stared at the big building in the moonlight. He made out the little bathroom window and conjured up the gloomy, crepuscular feel of the chambers. That was the secret.

Lanier might scare some people tonight, cruising past their houses— but he was not going to do much of anything, away from his true base. Even the Penthouse was not the real thing. This was it.

The chambers were everything, and the courtroom, and his courthouse. It was all about power. That was why he summoned the women to him there, leaping on them with his robe spread out like vulture's wings. The courthouse was the source of his perverse strength. It gave him his erection.

*   *   *

Castleberry became increasingly worried about the women, some of whose anxieties had mounted to the point of threatening to detach them from reality, so frightened had they become of the judge and of the prospect of their experiences with him becoming public knowledge. It was just as Joey McDowell had predicted: they were becoming worse as the weeks went by rather than showing signs of healing. And, Castleberry could tell, several of them and their husbands or boyfriends were blaming him for their situation.

He confessed his frustrations to Joey, who told him to get some help, now. "Don't wait for the first suicide" was the way Joey put it. "I'm telling you, somebody's going to crack. Bill, you can't handle this on your own." He described what the women were going through as an experience of continuous trauma, as if the assaults they had endured had never ended.

Through his Memphis supervisor, Castleberry put in a request for help to Robert Hazelwood, who was the Supervising Special Agent of the FBI's Behavioral Science Unit in Quantico. It was hoped that Hazelwood could assign a forensic psychologist to advise Castleberry and help with the witnesses. Unfortunately SSA Hazelwood, whose unit was best known for its preparation of psychological profiles of criminals, was out of the country, advising the Australian police for several weeks. Word came back that the Dyersburg problems would be addressed on his return and coordinated with the efforts of Al Moskowitz in Washington to locate an expert witness for the anticipated trial, someone who could explain to a jury why these women had been reluctant to come forward and had even hidden their experiences with Lanier from family and friends. Like Parker, and Spain, Moskowitz was concerned about this area of testimony because of the skepticism Anita Hill had encountered by waiting so long to come forward.

Castleberry was not sure that his supervisor or officials back east really understood what was going on with these women any better than he did. The experts at the Bureau might know a great deal about the mind of a psychosexual maniac such as the character Hannibal the Cannibal in the book and movie *Silence of the Lambs*. And they might be able to construct a plausible psychological profile of David Lanier. Might. But what did they know about how victims thought and felt? Surviving victims? Not the wolf but the lambs, who in Dyersburg were no longer silent but crying for help?

Castleberry began to be afflicted by severe pangs of conscience and slept fitfully, having one bad dream after another. His wife told him that he was thrashing about in the bed all night long.

He did not tell her about his dreams. He did not think they mattered, because the women were having worse ones, as they told him, about David Lanier. One woman said that her dreams were so vivid that she had woken up screaming, thinking that Lanier had crawled into bed with her. Others said that in their sleep they felt poisonous snakes slithering into bed with them or boa constrictors and pythons coiling around them.

One of Castleberry's nightmares kept recurring, however, and bothered him a great deal. The first time he had it, he thought, had been just after Vivian Forsythe had fled to Orlando. He had been thinking about her, worrying whether she could survive on her own, without her daughter. Then, weeks later, he had the dream again, and by late spring it was visiting him two and three times a week. It must no longer be about Vivian only, he figured, but have to do with his guilt about all the women.

It was always the same. It began with his hearing a woman's voice calling to him, "Help! Help me!" over and over. These were long, drawn-out cries, coming from a distance, like a mournful song drifting to him on the wind. He would try to move in their direction but was mired in some foggy swamp.

Finally he would see her through the fog and make a last, desperate effort to reach her as she called to him, faintly now, softer and softer. And she was on fire! The woman was burning alive!

Flames licked at her and leapt from her head and toward the heavens. He could see her flesh blackening and bubbling and peeling off, and her hair was on fire as she called to him still—but hers was not the only voice. In the background, he heard his own voice, singing, or his voice as a child.

The song he sang, or the verse he recited, was "The Gingerbread Man"—

> "Run, Woman, run as fast as you can
> But you won't catch me—
> I'm the Gingerbread Man!"

And then, invariably, Castleberry woke up, sweating, frustrated, furious at himself for not having reached the burning woman in time to save her.

He considered the dream as straightforward as it was disturbing, an allegory of current anxieties, the imagery of fear of failure. Except for the Gingerbread Man. What was he doing in the dream, and how did he fit into the symbolism of defeat?

Castleberry remembered how his mother had read the story of the Gingerbread Man to him and his brothers when they were growing up on Army bases. And he recalled also that she would bake gingerbread men for them. You always ate the smiling face last, after devouring piece by piece the legs and the arms and the brown sugary body. The face had a big smile on it drawn in frosting.

He could not get the Gingerbread Man out of his mind. He found the tale in his daughters' collection of children's books and reread it. The Gingerbread Man thought he could outrun everyone, but was caught and eaten by Mr. Fox. A story of hubris.

If dreams were prophecy, Castleberry had to conclude that he had to see himself as the Gingerbread Man, so prideful as to believe that he would escape being devoured. His smiling agent's face, the one he showed to women to make them believe in happy endings, would be chewed up and swallowed, because he would fail to save anyone. Judge Lanier must be Mr. Fox.

Believing that he had solved its riddle, Castleberry thought the dream would go away; it did not. It kept on visiting his sleep and frightening him. He began to wonder if the first psychological casualty of this case would be himself. And as much as he was unnerved by the dream, he was angry at himself for not being able to banish it, or at least to repress it—for to him, the veteran agent, it seemed a weakness.

Then one night he awakened from the dream and understood in a lurid flashback how the symbolism was shaped by his memory of another case, the most traumatic experience of his life in the FBI, the psychic residue of an incident he had managed to keep out of his mind for fourteen years, until the Lanier case triggered that memory.

In the winter of 1977 he had been working as the resident agent at Fort Leonard Wood, Missouri, an Army base hidden away in the south-central fringes of the state, in the foothills of the Ozarks. He was not actually living on the base, however, or adjacent to it. The Bureau and the Army had agreed that he and his family could live in the country at some distance from the strip joints and various honky-tonks that surrounded the barracks. Late one night at home he received a call to return immediately to the base. There had been a killing, maybe more than one.

Ordinarily the drive took less than an hour, but an ice storm blowing in from the plains that night made travel so hazardous that he was on the road forever, it seemed, the freezing rain turning the highway into a ski run. Telephone lines went down, transformers exploding in blue flames; his was the only car on the two-lane road. He kept spinning out, but he had to keep on. A call on his radio informed him that a lone gunman still at large had murdered at least three people.

After more than two hours he at last reached the base and learned that four teenagers had disappeared earlier that day. One of them, a girl, had wandered in bleeding from gunshot wounds, stumbling into head-quarters nearly frozen. She and her boyfriend and another couple had driven into the woods to party. A man in uniform had approached their car with a flashlight and a gun, had raped the girls while making the boys watch, and had shot everyone and left them for dead under a snowbank.

She had survived by pretending to be dead. Somehow she had walked more than two miles in from the woods. Soldiers had already located the bodies of her companions.

Castleberry discovered that a military policeman had asked for extra ammunition that night, claiming that he had used up his supply shooting dogs at a dump. Castleberry organized a search of the woods and found the killer at dawn.

He visited the surviving victim many times in the hospital, to prepare her for the trial. Every time she described the events of that white night, a certain incident proved beyond her ability to discuss. She became hysteri-cal in describing it.

Before shooting everyone, the rapist had forced the girl at gunpoint to perform oral sex on the other girl, who had been her best friend since childhood.

Castleberry finally told her that she did not have to repeat that part of the story on the witness stand. She could skip it, going on to the shootings and her escape. Everything would be all right and the killer convicted, he promised her, if she could manage to say that much.

Because of publicity and public outrage, the trial had to be moved all the way to Des Moines, possible because it was a federal case. The young woman took the stand and fell into a kind of trance as she began her account. It was as if she were not merely retelling the events but reliving them. And when she reached the one detail of that night that she had been told to omit, she could not stop herself.

Castleberry was sitting in the front row. The girl began to describe what she had been forced to do to her friend. He thought she would make it through, but in the middle her voice seized up and she broke down, weeping.

The judge called a recess. Castleberry went to her, helped her down from the stand and out of the courtroom. She was shaking so, he did not think she could go on—but she did, finishing her story for the court before collapsing again.

Castleberry sensed, knew, that some terrible, greater damage had been done to her that day. He could see something crumbling within her, a last chance for faith in life, a final ounce of courage spilled, never to be recovered.

Castleberry made a point of not finding out what happened to her after that. He did not want to know; it could not have been good. His guilt at having coaxed her into testifying was already acute enough.

And now he understood that this memory had become his nightmare—this and perhaps also another, still deeper memory, that of the ovens in the crematorium at Dachau. Why else would the woman in his dream vision be burning to death, while he arrived on the scene too late to save her? As on that afternoon at the death camp with his father and brothers, all he could do was stand there and imagine the horror. Dachau, Fort Leonard Wood, Dyersburg—now he was caught in another storm and swamp, rushing to save women and failing or, worse, leading the victims into fresh punishments, in the name of justice. Once again he, the G-Man Gingerbread Man, was saying, "If only you will testify, all will be well."

"Vivian Forsythe would retreat to a spot on the Mississippi . . ." Near Chic, Tennessee, August 1994. (Courtesy Richard Spoo)

"The sign proclaimed that there was a god of Chic." August 1995. (Courtesy Richard Spoo)

The patriarch, James P. Lanier. (Courtesy Linda Creighton, *U.S. News & World Report*)

Judge David Lanier with his daughters, Leigh Anne *(left)* and Robbye, Memphis, December 1992. (Courtesy Gale Cavness, *Dyersburg State Gazette*)

Vivian Forsythe *(left)*
and Amy Spain, law
library, Memphis, 1993.
(Courtesy Vivian
Forsythe)

FBI Special Agent William
Castleberry, 1993, with the Dyer
County Courthouse in background.
(Courtesy Linda Creighton, *U.S.
News & World Report*)

Sandy Sanders, in Judge Lanier's courtroom,
Dyersburg, 1993. (Courtesy Linda Creighton, *U.S.
News & World Report*)

Detective Joey McDowell, Dyersburg Police Department, 1994. (Courtesy of the author)

Patty Wallace, at the entrance t[o] Judge Lanier's chambers, 199[2]. (Courtesy Linda Creighton, *U.S. News & World Report*)

(left to right) Leigh Anne, Robbye, David, and Joan Lanier; attorney Tim Naifeh. Federal Courthouse, Memphis, 1992. (Courtesy Gale Cavness, *Dyersburg State Gazette*)

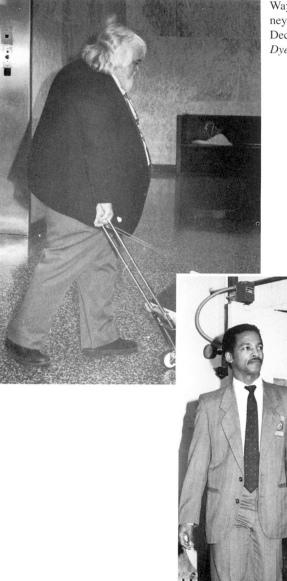

Wayne C. Emmons, David Lanier's attorney, Memphis Federal Courthouse, December 1992. (Courtesy Gale Cavness, *Dyersburg State Gazette*)

David Lanier, escorted by U.S. marshal, immediately after he was ordered jailed for violation of his bond, Memphis Federal Courthouse, February 1993. (Courtesy Gale Cavness, *Dyersburg State Gazette*)

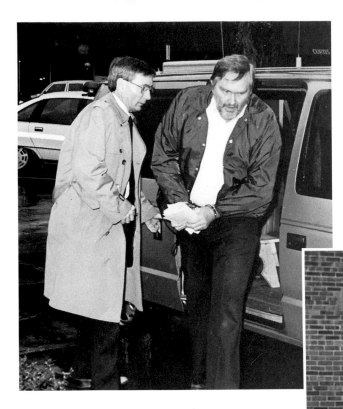

U.S. marshal escorting a hand-cuffed David Lanier from prison van to Dyer County Courthouse, February 1993. (Courtesy Gale Cavness, *Dyersburg State Gazette*)

The only entrance to Jud Lanier's Dyersburg "Penthouse," 1993. (Courtesy of the author)

The Penthouse *(4 upper windows at left)* after building's collapse, June 1994. (Courtesy of the author)

Professor Louise Fitzgerald, 1995. (Courtesy Louise Fitzgerald)

Bill Castleberry, Crowne Plaza Hotel, Memphis, after the verdict. (Courtesy Vivian Forsythe)

David Lanier, a prisoner in Memphis, 1993. (Courtesy Linda Creighton, *U.S. News & World Report*)

Steve Parker, Cincinnati, June 14, 1995. (Courtesy of the author)

Albert Moskowitz, Cincinnati, June 14, 1995. (Courtesy of the author)

Amy Spain, Cincinnati, June 14, 1995, two weeks before her death. (Courtesy of the author)

required but, Parker felt, good strategy—especially if the defendant, without his lawyer there to control his testimony, tipped prosecutors off to the nature of his possible defense.

In her story about that morning's session, which began at nine-thirty, and which was also covered by other regional papers, the Memphis *Commercial Appeal,* and the Associated Press, Donna Whittle referred to the secrecy of the proceedings but speculated that "though subpoenaed to testify, Lanier could have invoked the Fifth Amendment against self-incrimination and declined to answer questions posed by U.S. attorneys." This may have been an educated hypothesis, because that was exactly what Lanier did. He evoked the Fifth forty times in the less than an hour that he stood before the panel. At first he declined even to state his age, until Steve Parker invited him to step outside to consult with his attorney, as the rules did permit. Lanier allowed that he had been born on November 16, 1934, recited his Social Security number, and gave his address as 219 South Main, the location of the Penthouse.

Parker was not surprised that Lanier was taking refuge in the Fifth. Somewhere around fifty percent of accused persons did so at this stage; probably more than that were advised by their attorneys not to answer questions, but some could not resist talking anyway. Parker had thought, however, that Lanier might talk, because politicians most often ignored their lawyers and tried to sway the jury to their side. As Parker liked to say, politicians were used to conning people all their lives and rarely could resist trying again.

But Lanier evoked the Fifth again and again as Parker asked him, in turn, whether he had ever had any sexual relationships with each of twelve women, those for which the prosecution believed it had the strongest evidence, plus Vivian Forsythe and Jennifer Gallagher. For these two, it was only their word against Lanier's, unless he admitted involvement with either. If he did, and claimed the sex had been consensual, he might succeed in neutralizing their accusations, especially if a trial judge admitted evidence of their erratic histories and, in Vivian's case, narcotics addiction and alcoholism.

Al Moskowitz asked Lanier if he wished to take this opportunity to address the jurors "about anything at all," whether as to his guilt or innocence or his views of the investigation and its agents and prosecutors. The judge replied only, "No, sir," and also declined to offer the names of any witnesses he thought the panel should hear.

Parker asked the grand jurors themselves if they had questions for Judge Lanier. There were several. One juror asked if Lanier considered himself a fair judge, another if he was "a family man" and had any daughters, others how long he had been a judge, whether he had ever paid

26

David Lanier appeared twice before the grand jury. On the first occasion he drove into Memphis accompanied by his two daughters and his ex-wife. His family members were not permitted to be with him in the jury room, however; nor was his attorney, Wayne Emmons of Memphis, whom he had retained after Charles Kelly and other Dyersburg lawyers were subpoenaed as witnesses and after another Memphis attorney either backed out or was dismissed by Lanier, no one knew which. Only the twenty-three jurors, or enough of them to make up a quorum of sixteen, and the prosecutors were allowed inside to ask questions. Those were the rules, an aspect of the jury's power that, along with subpoenas, had led Governor Mario Cuomo of New York to comment once that a clever prosecutor and a grand jury could, if they wished, indict a ham sandwich. A defendant's protection under the law really began only with the trial process.

The family and Emmons had to wait outside the room along with Bill Castleberry, Steve Champine, and several reporters. These factions had little to say to one another. They kept to themselves in the corridor, wondering what was going on inside that room.

For Steve Parker, this was a significant moment, because he saw himself as primarily an investigator and felt that his principal skills lay in preparation of a case during the grand jury phase, which he saw as crucial and a dry run for any trial. It was during this process that he could combine what he had learned as a cop with his legal knowledge, shaping the testimony of witnesses toward the framework of a proposed indictment. He also believed, in order to demonstrate fairness to the jurors, in giving an accused the chance to defend himself before the panel, something not women for sex, whether he had ever forced sex on a woman. A final juror told him simply, "We would like to hear your side." To each of these Lanier replied only, "I've been advised not to answer any questions at this time."

He spoke with his usual air of confidence or even arrogance, and departed without comment when told he was excused. There was a surprise waiting for him, however, on the other side of the door.

Bill Castleberry greeted him in the corridor with an "instanter" subpoena, meaning that it had to be complied with immediately, or without delay, requiring him to turn over any audio or videotapes in his possession that had anything to do with any of the subpoenaed witnesses. The subpoena also commanded him to produce handwriting "exemplars" for possible introduction as evidence.

On the advice of his attorney, Lanier accompanied the agents to the tenth floor and in the law library filled four pages with his cursive script, repeating the same sentences over and over, as instructed. The words included the names and addresses of the witnesses who had recently received tapes.

Lanier admitted that he did have some tapes such as those indicated in the subpoena, but said that they were at home in Dyersburg.

"At the Penthouse?" Castleberry could not resist asking.

"At 219 South Main," Lanier said evenly. He could have them ready by tomorrow. He would hand them over to his attorney.

"That won't be necessary," Castleberry said. "We'll follow you there. Now. Let's see, it's past noon. Would you care to stop for lunch en route? We can meet you someplace."

Lanier nonchalantly suggested the Shoney's in Millington, a town about sixty miles south of Dyersburg on Highway 51.

Castleberry and Champine waited in their car in the parking lot outside the restaurant. Through a window they could see Lanier and his younger daughter, Robbye, eating their lunch. He stared at this unusual father-daughter pair. Anyone ignorant of the kinks in David Lanier's personal life might have found the obvious affection between the two touching. Who knew? Maybe it was.

Robbye, twenty-two, a tall and hefty young woman, had the look of a counterculture artist about her, something of a throwback flower child, with her long straight hair and her long, shapeless dress, a sort of beltless cotton caftan, printed with what could have been Native American petroglyph motifs. And there was her father, by contrast, judicial in a dark suit and white shirt, in every one of his many inches the picture of older generation conservatism and respectability, the teetotaling Christian elder.

They were conversing with apparent ease, Robbye staring into her father's eyes trustingly, affectionately. Castleberry had felt her hate, and her sister's, when he had handed Lanier the subpoena. Loyalties. Joan Lanier, too, had stared at the agents resentfully. He had remembered then how Stan Cavness compared them to a Mafia family.

The father-daughter bond transcended all. *I have this much in common with David Lanier,* Castleberry thought, *the love of two daughters.* Castleberry's younger one had written him a poem for his birthday expressing her love for Dad.

They lived alone together now, the judge and this daughter, in the apartment that in its nefarious way had become legendary in the minds of investigators and prosecutors, who took mordant pleasure in saying the name "Penthouse," with its ironical connotations of urban luxury and a skin magazine. Castleberry was eager to see at last the inside of this place he had been hearing about and watching for months. He had no intention of letting Lanier fetch the tapes by himself, or pretending to do so while disposing of them. He hoped that they would prove as enlightening as Richard Nixon's had been.

Lanier led the little convoy into Dyersburg, Castleberry trailing the smoking Mercedes.

"You are witnessing an unprecedented event," Castleberry told Champine. "This is the first time in history that the Federal Bureau of Investigation has tailed David Lanier without losing him."

Up Main, west a block on Cedar, right on Mill a few yards and hard right into the alley. Castleberry drew up next to Lanier in the grungy lot behind the building and got out. He did not have to tell Lanier they were going in with him; the judge knew.

Robbye went first up the fire escape and opened the door. Castleberry crawled up behind Lanier, with a view of the judicial arse. And then they were aloft and inside.

A sixties snakepit was the first phrase that came to Castleberry's mind. The next was *pigpen.*

Robbye seated herself on a mattress on the floor, staring up with curses in her eyes while her father began rummaging around for the subpoenaed tapes. Castleberry surveyed the scene. The painting of the matador on velvet, the dented suit of armor, the pool table, dirty laundry in heaps. Glasses and mugs caked with crud. Stained unraveling throw rugs. From the kitchenette the odor of spoiled milk and garbage. Frozen dinner packaging spilling out of an overturned grocery sack. A couch that would be left unsold at a garage sale.

The agents were there to receive evidence, not to conduct a search, but Castleberry could not resist a look around. Down the dark hallway off the

main pad, the three dingy old hotel rooms reminded him of the whorehouse this once had been—until during World War II the Army had told
the city fathers to clean up Dyersburg or have it declared off-limits to soldiers, and the modern era of the town's tidy and respectable appearance
had begun. Only the last room had an actual bed in it and appeared mod-
erately hygienic, the one where Dr. Warner had brought Vivian, from her
account and by his own admission. Castleberry had interviewed the doctor back in February, when he had admitted the affair and writing prescriptions for Mepergan and Dilaudid for Vivian and for Brenda
Castain—for headaches. How Vivian must have despised herself after a
visit to this place! First Lanier raped her and then Dr. Warner took her
here. Her degradation was complete, or nearly.

He walked back to the main room and its incredible juvenile clutter.
How could an adult live in a place like this on purpose? It was like the
room of an undisciplined fourteen-year-old boy.

Lanier held up some tapes in a plastic bag. He had no videotapes, he
said. Castleberry took the bag from him and noticed his pale, pudgy little
baby's hand.

That was the answer, Castleberry thought, the key to understanding
David Lanier's personality, the way everything fit together, from his family background, to his father's favoring him and spoiling him and setting
up his life for him, to his mother's suicide and his lust for power and his
King David complex. He used his chambers as a playpen, this ghastly
Penthouse as his kid's bedroom, a masturbator's hideaway. His compulsive secretiveness, the sibling rivalry that continued into middle age, his
sneaking around like a window-peeker, his flashing—it was all one picture.

The guy is a case of arrested development, Castleberry said to himself
as he dumped the tapes onto the pool table and began dating and initialing
them. *This man is like a high school kid who cannot deal with life. He has
never progressed beyond adolescence. His father's power and then his
own powerful offices have permitted him to remain in a state of perpetual
adult puberty. David Lanier is a big overgrown egotistical selfish insensi-
tive baby boy. He thinks women are his playthings, and if anybody ever
succeeds in taking his toys away from him, he is going to bawl. If he hadn't
done so much harm, I'd think he was pathetic.*

"Now, David," he said, "I want you to note that I'm receiving six
microcassette tapes and one regular cassette. Is that correct?"

"Yes," Lanier said.

Champine opened the door to leave, but Castleberry had one other
thing to say. He had been thinking about how far he was from being able
to see this case from any point of view other than that of the women.

Among them there were varying degrees of innocence, but basically this had become a master versus slave story. Usually there were more dramatic gradations in culpability. At least for his own satisfaction, he wanted to demonstrate openmindedness.

"David," he said, trying to catch Lanier's eye, but the judge was looking down and away, as he always did when Castleberry spoke to him, ever since their first meeting. "You haven't said a single thing to me in your defense. If you want to tell me something, now's the time. Is there anything I can do to be fairer to you?" Silence. "I want you to know that my interest is, I just want the truth to come out. I'd work as hard for you as for anyone else."

There was no response, except in Robbye's stare. She remained plopped on the mattress.

Outside, Champine looked at Castleberry and shook his head.

"That was some little speech, Bill. I almost gagged."

The tapes revealed nothing, except David Lanier's compulsion to record conversations. Disconnected dialogue was all there was, Lanier greeting people in hallways or on the street, in the supermarket, making an appointment for lunch on the phone. Castleberry called the material "nonsense."

There was some question of the whereabouts of additional tapes, which Lanier had supposedly turned over to his original Memphis lawyer. Steve Parker summoned the judge again before the grand jury on Wednesday, May 20, to ask about them and letters of resignation from Brenda Castain and Sherry Cooper, who had quit early that year, as well as about drug-screening results for employees. Lanier claimed that he had turned all records over to the government or to his lawyer.

Parker offered him one more chance to defend himself before the jurors. He again declined to do so. Amy Spain asked him about what had happened to any videotapes or photographs he may have had. He claimed to have no knowledge of any that had not already been produced. Parker excused the witness.

And that afternoon, the federal grand jury indicted defendant David W. Lanier on eleven counts of violating Section 18 § 242 of the U.S. Criminal Code. The indictment alleged that between 1988 and 1991, Lanier had sexually assaulted eight women who either worked for him at his chancery or juvenile courts or had a case pending before him. The women included Patty Wallace, Sandy Sanders, Cathy Kiely, Vivian Forsythe, Mary Haralson, Julia Garnett, Jennifer Gallagher, and Janet Thomasson, in that order, with two counts each involving assaults against Sanders, Kiely, and Forsythe. Julia Garnett was the woman who claimed that Lanier had exposed himself to her when she went to see him about her divorce settlement.

JUDGE LANIER FACES RIGHTS, SEX CHARGES was the front-page headline in the *Commercial Appeal,* and the Lanier story was the lead item on evening news broadcasts throughout the region. The severity of the penalties Lanier faced if convicted was of particular interest to the media. Eight of the counts against him were misdemeanors, carrying a sentence of up to one year each in prison. Three of the counts, those involving Jennifer Gallagher and Vivian, were felonies, and on them Lanier could be imprisoned for up to ten years for each. No one, including the prosecutors, expected that Lanier would receive the maximum if convicted on any or all of the charges, but that there was theoretically a possibility of a sentence of thirty-eight years in prison did catch everyone's attention.

"Maybe people will begin to get the idea now," Parker said privately, "that the charges are not trivial."

Wayne Emmons stated to the press that there had never been a case like this against a judge and that he doubted the charges would stick. Parker countered by comparing them to the successful prosecution of Henderson County Sheriff Jack Fowler, who in 1988 was convicted of raping prisoners in his jail. Castleberry, with his memories of that case, thought this an excellent analogy, particularly in relation to what Lanier had done to Jennifer Gallagher and Vivian Forsythe.

Lanier, again surrounded by his daughters and his ex-wife, read the indictment to himself on the afternoon of its issuance, as he prepared for his bond hearing before U.S. Magistrate Daniel Breen. One reporter wrote that Lanier appeared "stunned," but Castleberry, Champine, and the prosecutors detected no change whatever in Lanier's bland exterior. They believed that the judge had expected to be indicted. Several women at the courthouse had reported a meeting between Lanier and some of his more loyal employees during which he was supposed to have said, "The FBI is after me for harassment, and they have got me," or words to that effect. The timing of his divorce and its property settlement agreement also indicated that he anticipated harassment charges being brought against him.

The framing of the indictment in terms of civil rights, however, and the severity of the penalties, especially on the felony counts, must have shocked him. He and his lawyer could not have been prepared for him to be charged with violation of 18 § 242, because they could not have found any legal precedent for the application of the statute to a judge, except in the single instance of the Texas prosecution, which had failed.

Amy Spain handled the bond hearing for the government and asked that special conditions be attached to the defendant's release pending and during a trial. She contended forcefully that Lanier was likely to continue "to harass, intimidate, and attempt to manipulate victims in this case." In setting Lanier's bond at twenty thousand dollars, unsecured, Judge Breen agreed that Spain had presented a convincing argument for restrictions on Lanier and expressly prohibited him "from making contact with any victim or potential witness except through defendant's attorney and during court hours and on court business."

By Friday, two days after the indictment, Judge Lanier was back on the bench in Dyersburg, an indication that, however surprised he may have been by the severity of the charges, he was far from conceding defeat. There was no power in the state or in the nation that could force him to step down. The Tennessee Court of the Judiciary, a panel charged with monitoring judicial ethics, had received a complaint against Lanier back in February involving his refusal to recuse himself from ruling on a motion for retrial in the personal injury suit involving Mary Haralson while she was his secretary; supposedly that complaint was being investigated. But the Court of the Judiciary was not expected to begin even considering a recommendation for impeachment to the state legislature until the conclusion of any trial on the sexual assault charges. Until that happened, when and if it did, Lanier was free to remain on the bench. On his first day back, he heard fifteen cases, including divorces, adoptions, a juvenile detention matter, and a workmen's compensation settlement.

The lines between pro- and anti-Lanier factions in Dyersburg were now clearly drawn. Reporters were there on May 22 to cover his resumption of power and noted that several "well-wishers" came by to say hello before he took the bench. One asked how he was doing, and he replied, "Perfect." The executive editor of the *State Gazette,* Dannye Crouch, took a different view. In an editorial he urged Lanier to step down until the federal charges were resolved. These were criminal charges, the editorial reminded its readers. Lanier was doing a disservice to the community by clinging to office under the circumstances.

Meanwhile the prosecution worried that with Lanier still on the bench, he remained a threat to witnesses against him. Brenda Castain and at least one other woman had told the grand jury that the judge had instructed them to lie under oath. He now knew the names of each of his principal accusers. Although the media continued to protect their identities, they were listed in the public record of the indictment, of which Lanier had a copy and which anyone was free to examine.

In asking for restrictions on the judge's contacts with victims and witnesses, the prosecutors had not listed names beyond those in the indictment. It was something of a dilemma for the prosecutors, since they wished to prevent Lanier from threatening people but could hardly expect to do so without their specifying whom he was forbidden to contact. The matter of the names was resolved at the arraignment, on May 29, when Wayne Emmons requested a list of those whom Lanier was supposed to avoid, and the presiding magistrate ordered it produced. On June 16, after considerable agonizing over whom to include and whom to spare, the prosecution provided a list of twenty-one people, including the eight women in the indictment, eleven additional women, and two men, Ben Beveridge and Charles Kelly. Brenda Castain and Linda Pickering were among the others. Their charges had not been part of the indictment because technically the sex they had provided Lanier had been consensual, or was so in the eyes of the law and any likely jury. But they remained potential witnesses, had testified before the grand jury, and were certainly in need of protection.

Lanier pleaded innocent to all charges at the arraignment. A senior judge who acted as counsel to the Court of the Judiciary informed the prosecutors that he had asked Lanier to step down, with pay, until the charges were resolved, but that he had insisted on his innocence and refused the request. In July U.S. District Judge Jerome Turner of Memphis, who had been assigned to hear the case, set the trial date for September 29. Lanier remained in office. Again the *State Gazette* asked Lanier in an editorial to "excuse himself." He was innocent until proven otherwise, but "the judge is under the cloud of suspicion. No such shadow should be hanging over the powerful man dispensing justice in our local civil and juvenile courts. The integrity of those courts must be beyond suspicion." Lanier remained unmoved by such pleas.

"They'll have to drag him off the bench in chains," Joey McDowell said to Bill Castleberry, "or he'll never leave."

Lanier had become very much aware of the role McDowell had played in bringing the charges. Through his attorney, the judge complained to the prosecutors that the entire case against him had been maneuvered by McDowell and, to a lesser extent, Stan Cavness, because of those officers' resentments over the collapse of their juvenile program and subsequent run-ins with the judge and the district attorney's office. McDowell, it was Lanier's contention, would be exposed eventually as having overstepped not only the bounds of his position but various statutes, including those against illegal wiretapping. His statements to the prosecutors about Linda Pickering and the gun that Judge Lanier had asked her to recover from the police department were instances of how McDowell was engaged in a vendetta. That gun, Lanier maintained, happened to be one that McDowell had wrongly taken from Juvenile Court several years ago.

There was such a gun, as McDowell now remembered, although far from taking it against regulations or appropriating it for himself, Joey had turned it over to the evidence room at the DPD, where it was now, prop-

erly recorded and secured. He remained convinced that Lanier had tried
to intimidate Pickering and him by asking her to find it and return it.
Perhaps Lanier actually thought that everyone was as contemptuous of
the law as he was and that Joey made a habit of commandeering evidence
for personal use.

"I don't think David knows the meaning of the word honest,"
McDowell said. "I don't even know if he knows the meaning of the word
justice. Let's hope he finds out."

27

That Lanier was just as active in laying the grounds for his defense as the prosecutors were in trying to undermine it became clear during the first week in August. With the September trial date approaching, the prosecutors decided to meet with the witnesses again, to see how they were doing and to begin to determine who would testify and in what order. Rather than asking them to take off time from work to travel to Memphis, Parker, Spain, and Moskowitz chose to meet them in Dyersburg—with the exception of Vivian Forsythe, who would have to be flown in from Orlando. Moskowitz had yet to interview Vivian and remained adamant about that. As with all the victims, he was concerned about whatever degree of compliance or consent she may have shown to Lanier.

Castleberry and Champine telephoned everyone and set up meetings with each at hourly intervals over two days, in Room 130 at the Dyersburg post office. A federal building seemed a more appropriate venue than a motel. With Lanier presiding, they could hardly use the courthouse.

There were no surprises the first day, but when Jennifer Gallagher appeared at the post office at nine Wednesday morning, August 5, everyone could tell at once that something was wrong with her. She looked like a case study in paranoia and started crying as she described her latest encounter with David Lanier.

It had happened yesterday, during the noon hour at her job, in City Hall. As he usually did, the judge walked across the street from the courthouse to the main-floor lobby, where clerks stood behind a counter to receive payments for city taxes and rates. Lanier, as he often did, paid a utility bill at the counter. Jennifer had noticed him, then kept her head down at her desk, which was in a cubicle just to the left of the front door. She was expecting him to leave, because she handled utility hookups and bill transfers. He would have no reason to do business with her unless he was moving house; and he was forbidden to do so anyway, she knew, by the terms of his bond.

But he walked right over to her office, came in, and started chatting.

"What did he say?" Castleberry asked. He had the same thought as everyone else. Lanier had heard that the prosecutors were in town. Now was the time to make his presence felt by one of the witnesses against him. The brazenness of it was amazing, even for Lanier.

The judge had told her how well she looked, Jennifer said, complimenting her on her tan and on her loss of weight. He said that he had lost weight, too. That must be because they were "on the FBI diet." Only a select few got to go on this diet, he said. He added that he could not understand why the government was doing this to him. It would be different if Jennifer were a child, but this had been a matter between consenting adults. She had said nothing.

He then asked her about her personal life. She had the distinct impression that he was propositioning her. How was her marriage? Was the honeymoon over? She should give him a ring. At this point she recalled specific dialogue.

"Is your husband still working nights?" Lanier asked.

"Yes," she admitted, wishing she had kept quiet.

"Well, you can call me then. I'm at the Penthouse. I'm divorced, you know. It was on the front page of the paper." He went on to say that he had gotten rid of his cordless phone and had been assured that his calls were no longer being bugged. He had fixed that, so she should call him.

For the agents and the prosecutors this part of the conversation rang especially true, because they knew that after Lanier had found out about how his cordless calls had been recorded, he had replaced that instrument with a conventional one. He had also hired someone to "sweep" the Penthouse for electronic bugs. The technician had taken the initiative to inform Joey McDowell and to supply the receipt for his work, after the indictment was issued and he understood the possibly criminal aspects of the job.

This is it, everyone listening to Jennifer's account was thinking: *Lanier has clearly violated the conditions of his bond.* When Jennifer added that she was certain others must have seen the judge go into her office and talk to her, she estimated for about ten minutes, the likelihood that Lanier could be thrown into jail at once, there to await trial, instead of sitting on the bench and running around intimidating witnesses, seemed real.

"Was yesterday the only time you've talked to Judge Lanier since the indictment?" Castleberry asked.

There was a pause. Parker asked if Lanier had been telephoning her. She had received hangup calls, she said, but in fact she had gone to see him herself at the courthouse, about three weeks earlier. The word *Why?* escaped several mouths at the same time.

It had been about her daughter, Jennifer said, and the problem of keeping her in the city schools if she lived outside the district. On the advice of an attorney—she named one of Lanier's inner circle—she had decided to give custody of the girl to the grandparents. It was only a formality, so the child could have a Dyersburg address. But she had to have a judge sign the petition. Jennifer had tried to have the matter referred to Judge Riley, but his secretary had said she would have to see Lanier first. Before she knew it, Judge Lanier's secretary had called to set up an appointment. Her parents had gone with her. Judge Lanier had signed the order, after warning her that her parents might not want to return the child to her custody later. He had told her that she was taking a serious step.

It had been a nerve-wracking experience, Jennifer said, having to petition Judge Lanier, but she had come through it all right. She had been as pleasant to him as she could, because she had been afraid to offend him. Her daughter's welfare was in his hands, just as her problems with child support had been.

That night Amy Spain prepared a "Motion for Bond Review" and filed it the next day, charging David Lanier with having "repeatedly violated the special conditions of his release" by having "contact with a victim named both in the indictment and in the list requested by the Court." She summarized Lanier's visit to Jennifer Gallagher at work, an incident that had been verified by two City Hall witnesses. And she argued that the prior incident was also a violation, because "under the Code of Judicial Ethics, the defendant should not have ruled in a case involving a victim named in the indictment now pending against him."

Magistrate Judge Breen set the hearing for only three working days later, on Tuesday, August 11.

As Lanier's attorney, Wayne Emmons was not pleased about the short notice. He was, he told Judge Breen that morning, "absolutely irate" that he had had to cancel family plans over the weekend and "major matters" on Monday. He asked for a continuance, legal parlance for postponement, since the prosecution was actually requesting that his client be "detained," in other words, jailed.

Judge Breen decided that he would let the government have their say and then decide if the defense needed more time to respond. This satisfied

Emmons, who also had something up his sleeve. Only minutes ago he had handed Steve Parker the transcript of an audiotape labeled "Conversation Between Jennifer Gallagher and David W. Lanier in his Office Immediately After She Gave Custody of her Daughter to her Mother and Father by Consent Petition and Order." Emmons had a pretty good idea that reading this transcript—and hearing the tape itself, which he had brought with him—might make the prosecutors choke on their doughnuts and coffee and wish they hadn't bothered to disrupt anyone's weekend.

An outsider might have been misled by Wayne Emmons's appearance and background, but the prosecution never underestimated him. Whatever a lawyer is supposed to look like, Emmons did not. He was bigger than many National Football League linemen, weighing in at well over three hundred pounds, with a mostly white beard and shaggy hair that flowed down over his collar and large, sad eyes under coal-black eyebrows. He had started out as a Church of Christ minister and fifteen years later became a lawyer and a part-time country comedian, playing a character called Cousin Bubba, a bumpkin awed by the big city, who expresses his amazement at contemporary hypocrisies and excesses by writing letters home to a Cousin Luther. Emmons liked to say that with all of his experience as a minister and a lawyer and a nightclub act, he had spent more than thirty years in show business.

No member of the prosecution team had been around to observe the Reverend Emmons in the pulpit, but both Parker and Castleberry had seen his comedy act, which he had developed at legal seminars around the nation, in nightclubs on the West Coast, and now performed mostly at charity functions—and he was very funny, a raconteur in the old Andy Griffith, Minnie Pearl, and Charlie Weaver (Cliff Arquette) tradition. Like his more famous comedic antecedents, he was from a rural background and very bright, and he was able to draw on authentic country memories to put urban madness into timeless, down-home perspective. Occasionally he was able to combine his legal acumen with his comedy routine, as he had when defending some topless dancers on obscenity charges. But usually, as Parker and Castleberry knew from being on opposite sides from him in trial, Emmons was deadly serious and effective in the courtroom, an eloquent, tenacious, and smart lawyer.

In Emmons, David Lanier had ended up with an ideal advocate. If anyone could convince a Southern jury that Lanier was innocent or, at worst, only human, Wayne Emmons could. Steve Parker was already worried that jurors would conclude that if Cousin Bubba liked Lanier, the judge must be all right.

That morning Emmons objected as Parker put Castleberry on the stand and began to ask the agent what he had been told by various witnesses about David Lanier's attempts to influence their testimony. This was nothing but hearsay, Emmons complained; but hearsay was permissible in this sort of hearing, Judge Breen ruled, as Parker and Castleberry continued. Lanier had told witnesses to lie under oath, had harassed them with obscene and hangup calls, and had threatened and stalked them.

Only last night, Castleberry said, Linda Pickering had reported seeing Lanier drive slowly past her house. Since the indictment she had also observed the judge parked outside her office, sitting in his car staring at the window and at her as she left for home. He had also followed her and her boyfriend, on several occasions speeding past them, pulling around in front of them, and jamming on his brakes to frighten them.

Again over Emmons's protests that this was beyond the scope of the hearing as he had been able to prepare for it, Judge Breen permitted Castleberry to summarize his interview back in February with the limousine driver who had been asked by an anonymous caller to plant drugs on several of the witnesses. Emmons asked what the agent knew about this man's character and how he had been persuaded to talk. Castleberry admitted that the limo driver was not exactly a fine, upstanding gentleman; he had reminded him, however, of his "duty" to be truthful to a federal agent. Emmons suggested that another FBI agent could have made the call offering the ten thousand to plant the drugs. To which Castleberry replied that he doubted the FBI would do this. And in any event the man had refused the offer and was not a paid informant, so why would he make it up?

At last, in what he hoped would be decisive testimony, Parker had Castleberry summarize Jennifer Gallagher's account of Judge Lanier's recent visit to her office and her previous encounter with the judge on July 17 at the courthouse.

For this Emmons had been able to prepare. He requested permission to play a certain audiotape, on which Judge Lanier had recorded a conversation with Jennifer Gallagher, an exchange that had taken place in a room adjacent to the judge's secretary's office immediately after Lanier had granted the custody petition. Judge Breen agreed.

The tape, although a microcassette and of uneven quality, was definitely of Jennifer Gallagher talking to David Lanier. What everyone heard was, in part:

Jennifer: Can I speak to you for a minute?
Judge: Yes.
Jennifer: (Crying) There's something I'd like to say to you.
Judge: Okay.
Jennifer: That I did not want to be in on this trial. They came to me

and they made me . . . I have begged them to leave me alone—I
mean I really have. I have called and talked to Steve Parker. I said I
don't want to press charges. . . .

Judge: I appreciate that and I didn't ever think that.

Jennifer: I hope you didn't. They came and they made me, because
they said someone had told them. . . . I told them when I was questioned by them—I'm being very honest—I told them things because
they said I had to have the truth—tell the truth—but . . . I would say
one thing and it was turned around completely.

Judge: They would put your name to their words.

Jennifer: Yes, sir. . . . But I mean I wanted to tell you and this has bothered me so bad—I wanted you to know that I didn't—I was made.

Judge: I appreciate you telling me.

Jennifer: Well, it takes a big person, but I wanted you to know that.

Judge: Thank you, it'll be all right.

Jennifer: Well, you hang in there—I think it will be, too, I mean I'm
serious.

Judge: You tell the jury that and we won't have any problem.

Jennifer: Well, that's the honest truth.

Judge: That's right—that's no problem.

Jennifer: And see it was like they said, you know, did he hurt you?
And I said no. Did it feel good? Well, you know it was just like you
know what I'm saying.

Judge: You mean you told them no. They said you said I hurt you.

Jennifer: No, sir, that's what I told them. That's exactly what I told
them, see, that's what I'm saying.

Judge: It's so ridiculous.

Jennifer: It is. I went down there three or four times and I'm telling the
truth.

Judge: I believe you.

Jennifer: I mean I'm not, you know, I'm not saying anything. I did not
want to be a part of it and I'm not now. . . .

Judge: You don't have to, but they, you know, can make you do anything. They can make you say anything—that's what they can do.

Jennifer: Right. My mother's waiting on me—I—I. Good luck and you
hang in there and it'll be okay.

And that was the end of the tape. Emmons allowed a few moments of
silence before summarizing. This was the defense's proof, he said, that
Judge Lanier had done nothing wrong. It was such a powerful rebuttal of
the government's motion and tactics that in effect it said to Count Ten of
the indictment, that involving Jennifer Gallagher, "Bye-bye, out the win-

dow." Gallagher had clearly initiated this conversation. She wanted to tell Judge Lanier how sorry she was and how bad she felt for him. What did her statements mean except that she believed that both she and he were being persecuted by the government?

The tape also explained, Emmons argued, why Judge Lanier had stopped by to see her in her office three weeks later. She had been so friendly and apologetic. Why shouldn't he say hello when he went in on a perfectly innocent errand, to pay a utility bill? Perhaps this was technically a violation of his bond, but Dyersburg was a small town. Was he supposed to go around incognito? The idea of revoking his bond for this, given the prior meeting and circumstances, was preposterous. The tape amounted to "a major revelation by this lady." She had told the FBI that she had gone in to see the judge afterward to thank him for making the custody ruling. In fact, she had done much more. She had "poured out her soul" to him. She had not leveled with the FBI, because she was afraid of them. Her entire credibility was now seriously at issue.

Steve Parker, after conferring with Al Moskowitz, responded as best he could to this analysis. He had been shaken by the tape and tried not to show it, choosing to bulldog the situation out. The fact that Lanier had tape-recorded the conversation, Parker argued, showed that it was not an incidental contact but a deliberate ploy on the judge's part to gather evidence from a witness with whom he had been forbidden to speak. Nor had Jennifer Gallagher lied to the FBI. Castleberry had had only a couple of minutes on the phone to speak to Gallagher about what was on the tape.

Nowhere on the tape, Parker went on, did Gallagher say she had lied to anyone. She may not have wanted the facts to come out, because she was afraid of Lanier, as her crying and obvious nervousness in the conversation showed. Lanier had control over her child. She was crying because she was afraid Lanier would retaliate against her, so she was saying, in effect, "Judge, I'm sorry, but they made me tell the truth." Three weeks later he came into her office and propositioned her.

"Lanier thinks he is a law unto himself and nobody can control him. He deliberately violated the sanctions against him. These women are petrified. He controls their livelihood and the fate of their children." Even now he was using the power of his office to damage the credibility of witnesses against him. "He is a sex offender, not a corrupt official that took a little money on a case. He is alleged to be a criminal sex offender as in sexual battery and rape, a violent sex offender. And he is contacting his victims."

Parker concluded by saying that Lanier should not get a break because "he is a judge that sells out of his office." In this Parker was enunciating one of his major worries about the case, that one judge would go easy on another rather than admit that disgrace had fallen on the entire judiciary, in the person of Judge David Lanier. Parker asked Judge Breen to consider the victims' rights, to think of "the women in this case and what they have been going through."

In weighing Parker's plea on behalf of the women against Emmons's contention that Jennifer Gallagher's credibility had been "exploded to the sky," Judge Breen took a middle ground. He found that, at least in talking to Gallagher in her office, Lanier had violated his bond. Breen decided not to jail him but to amend the conditions of the defendant's release by ordering that he should have no contact whatever with witnesses, whether in court or out, with or without his attorney, without receiving prior permission from this court.

Breen added that if the government submitted another petition showing any evidence or proof that Lanier had contacted any victims or witnesses, he would be jailed, at once.

It was the best the prosecution could have hoped for, in view of the tape, which was a bombshell possibly powerful enough to eliminate at least one count in the indictment. Jennifer Gallagher had a lot of explaining to do if she was to remain a viable witness. "Score one for Cousin Bubba," was the consensus among the prosecutors.

There was some difference of opinion among the U.S. attorneys about what to do with Jennifer Gallagher. Amy Spain had not been present at the hearing, but when she heard the tape, she was dismayed by the tone of Gallagher's voice. It was the sort of pleading, compliant Southern female voice that set her teeth on edge, because it reminded her of girls and women she had known all her life—the ones from which she had always felt distant. Their natures seemed shaped toward one purpose alone, to placate men and to serve them. It was the kind of voice that made personal and professional life more of a challenge for Amy because, for all her reserve and good manners, she did not sound like that, and many men resented her lack of ingratiating cooing and purring and accompanying self-deprecating, ingratiating gestures. Jennifer's was the sort of voice that might say anything to please or to manipulate.

Steve Parker understood why Amy felt the way she did. Jennifer was not among the witnesses in whom he placed the most confidence, and he felt similarly to Amy about that particular Southern type. His own wife, Jackie, was a feisty, wisecracking woman who did not mind cooking and keeping house but who also drove a Federal Express truck five days a week. Parker, like Amy, found Vivian Forsythe's straightforward talk and emotion more appealing—and convincing.

But both Spain and Parker agreed with Al Moskowitz, who of the three prosecutors was the most favorable toward Jennifer Gallagher, that just because Gallagher was the sort of Southern woman she was did not give David Lanier the right to take advantage of her. Lanier targeted women with weaknesses or personal problems or both. That was why they were putting him on trial.

Jennifer's explanation for the way she had talked to Lanier was that she was afraid of him. She also claimed that she had been offended by the language of the indictment, which asserted that Lanier's acts had resulted in "bodily injury" to her. She had understood this to mean a black eye or a broken bone or the equivalent, in other words a beating, and had been afraid that Lanier would think she had lied to the grand jury.

Moskowitz pointed out that the main lesson to be learned from the fiasco of the tape was that they had to make sure that there were no other bombshells waiting to explode in relation to any of the women. Perhaps the most worrisome aspect of the hearing, however, was that the defense had as much as admitted that sex had taken place between Gallagher and the defendant. What if Lanier admitted that he had had sex with Jennifer and with Vivian Forsythe and claimed that it was consensual? That would be an extremely powerful defense, probably the best defense. It would certainly undercut the felony counts, particularly if the jury gathered that these witnesses were not exactly model citizens. Jennifer in addition to her multiple marriages had admitted taking gifts of money from a married man with whom she had been having an affair until his wife found out about it. Lanier knew about this and would probably find a way to make it public.

Gaining a civil rights conviction against a judge was proving very chancy. No wonder it had never been done.

28

Early that September of 1992, with the trial agonizingly postponed to mid-October at the defense's request, and the second anniversary of the rape approaching, Vivian, who had not seen her daughter since Easter, took her week's earned vacation to come home to Dyersburg to visit Ashley. Vivian was feeling better about herself, compared to when she had first arrived in Orlando. For more than six months she had been sober and free of drugs. She had just received her second increase in salary at the job she had held since walking in blind to the law firm and was now making about twenty-four thousand a year, not much but more, she knew, than she could ever have earned as Judge Lanier's secretary, an achievement that pleased her a great deal and that encouraged her to believe that before too long, or after the Lanier trial, she would be able to bring Ashley to Florida to live with her.

As for the coming trial and her role in it, Vivian had become optimistic, or nearly so. Her view of her grand jury testimony the previous year was that she had done very well. Many of the jurors had cried, she had noticed, as she had described the first rape and her reaction to it, how she had fled to where her father's farm had been, how she had bathed herself to try to scrub away the filth and the guilt and, to no avail, the memory of degradation.

Until Steve Parker had confronted her—that remained the biggest shock of her life and, unless she relapsed, the turning point. His sincerity, his earnestness, his bluntness, the way he had leaned across his desk toward her and fixed her with those brown spaniel eyes of his—and the way he talked about his mother. The impact on her had been enormous and, she hoped, permanent.

"My mother was an addict," he had said. "You can't know the effect that had on me." Then he had talked about the way he had drunk himself through Old Miss until his mother died and he sobered up and became a cop and what he was now, somebody who, from everything Vivian could tell, cared about justice. So much so that it scared her a little, he was so intense, a man with a mission, possessed, if that was the word, by hatred of evil, that was the way he talked. Steve Parker, from everything Vivian could tell, and she had thought about it a lot, was the first intensely religious person she had ever met who was not a hypocrite. Mr. Castleberry had assured her that Mr. Parker was no phony, and she believed everything Mr. Castleberry said, he was so kindly and sad about her and the others.

Her life, and she was aware of this, had become a different thing than ever before because she was devoted to one purpose alone, enchanted nearly, she thought, by the belief that her existence at last mattered, to defeat Lanier and to live for her daughter. Those were her thoughts when she woke up and fell asleep; those were the thoughts that made getting high uninviting.

Even her playful, edgy humor had come back, like a gift retrieved from high school days, that quality she had that had amused her black friends and put off some of the whites then, and that made the lawyers and secretaries who worked with her and the clients who visited her office laugh. Beside her desk in Orlando hung a human skeleton, or rather a model of one. Her knowledge of anatomy, acquired in college and refreshed since, served well at the law firm, as did the medical terminology she had picked up from working in doctors' offices. Personal injury cases made up a large percentage of the firm's work. If someone had suffered whiplash or a crushed bone, Vivian was ready with her skeleton to pinpoint the damage, help the client and the lawyer involved to understand the lingo and not be confused by an insurance company's expert witnesses, and to make sure that the advocate's brief was precisely framed.

"Where'd you get that skeleton?" people would ask.

"You really want to know?" she would tease them. "Well, back in Dyersburg where I come from, it's a little town in Tennessee and believe me, nothing much happens there, but I can't live there anymore for a number of reasons, I worked for a doctor once, who was real nice to me, and I even became almost like a nurse in his office. And we had an affair. His name was Dr. Lynn A. Warner. It was a mistake, but anyway, when we broke up and I had to leave his office, he gave me this skeleton because he said I knew so much about bones, and he wanted me to have it, and I've hung on to it ever since. I mean, when I left Dyersburg to come here, it was pretty funny in the car, there was my brother and his girlfriend and me and this skeleton in the backseat—I used to buy a hamburger for him!

"I'm sure people might think it's a little weird me hanging on to it as a reminder, because we did make kind of a scandal, but I don't care what people think, I'm that kind of a person, so why not? Dr. Warner's kind of a sad old guy and he really did love me and protected me, whatever people say. And anyway, guess what, it's turned out to be really useful. This way, I can point to it when somebody has, say, head injuries, and I can say, like, 'This is what happened when your head hit the steering wheel when you got creamed from behind by that pickup, see,' not just, 'Your forehead got whacked,' but, 'The force of the blow caused a fracture in the superciliary ridge, here, down to the supraorbital margin, here, putting pressure on the optic canal, here, which is why you can't see worth a damn and we're suing for eight million dollars!' "

Those who knew Vivian in Orlando were impressed by how chipper she seemed most of the time, when they heard what she had gone through and what lay ahead for her at the impending trial. She was apt to burst into tears suddenly but also to regain her composure quickly; she readily described herself as "a recovering addict and alcoholic" who by that summer was refusing even a drag on a joint. "I can't handle it," she would say, "it only makes me feel worse."

She did feel that she had built up the strength to visit Dyersburg again—but she was wrong about that. As wonderful as it was to see Ashley, it was as painful to find the child a bit shy with her, especially at first; and the attitude of her family made her wish that she had stayed in Florida. Her sister, who had been helping care for Ashley since Vivian's departure, was overtly hostile, not that anyone seemed particularly sympathetic to the role they now knew she would play in Lanier's trial. How could she have been hurt twice by Lanier, everyone wanted to know, with reference to the two felony counts. The prosecution team had asked her not to discuss her testimony beforehand, and she did not want to go into details with her family anyway. All that she could have responded to her mother, Vivian thought with some bitterness, was that "I was weak, I was desperate for a job. Daddy wanted me out of the house, and you pressured me to call Lanier back, and I was stupid enough to think I could handle him. And," she would have added, "whatever you think of me, we'll see what a jury decides."

Bill Castleberry remained in touch with Vivian by phone and thought she sounded all right, although, as Steve Parker's experience with Brenda Castain showed, drug use was easily masked, and Vivian spoke so rapidly under normal conditions that someone might think she was on speed when she was not. But Castleberry was more worried now about Jennifer Gallagher, who had become so unstrung, worrying about facing Lanier in court, that she was talking about backing out of testifying. Bill had had to give her a speech.

"Jennifer," he said to her at her office one day, "the state of Tennessee won't get rid of Lanier. The FBI and the United States government can't get rid of him. Only you can do that, you and the other women. It's up to you." And she relented, for the time being, while complaining about how unfair all this was to her husband.

Even the stronger women were suffering. Patty Wallace did have to have an operation on her jaw because of her teeth-grinding. Mary Haralson remained unemployed. Janet Thomasson looked more distraught every time Castleberry saw her. All summer long, Lanier had done everything he could to intimidate Sandy Sanders, sending her memos saying she "did not have the best interests of the Juvenile Court in mind," requiring her to have written permission from a doctor for sick leave, and making her understand that he now considered her to be on the lowest level of court employees, in spite of her supervisor's title. Meanwhile, when word spread that Sandy would be a witness, her husband's co-workers at ERMCO, a plant that manufactured transformers, razzed him mercilessly, taunting him with questions such as, "How come you let that judge put his hands on your wife?"

Junior Sanders wanted to fight back but knew he could be fired for throwing a punch. Finally he complained to his boss about the harassment, which slacked off but continued as an undercurrent. "Don't fire me if somebody shows up with black eyes," he said, but he managed to hold up, barely, under the pressure.

The disruption to family life was severe for everyone. As the trial approached, Barry Wallace kept finding his wife alone in the bedroom crying; he had to persuade her to send out Christmas cards and let him put up a tree. At school their little boy wrote an essay about what his family was going through and how God was helping them and keeping his daddy's temper under control.

How much could the victims and their families continue to endure? What would happen when the women had to stand up in court with Lanier glaring at them and the media ready to report excruciatingly intimate details? If Lanier was convicted, would it have been worth the emotional cost? And what if, an equally likely outcome, Lanier gained acquittals?

A careful consideration of these factors and risks led the prosecutors to reconsider their priorities. Which was more important, to send Lanier away for a number of years as punishment, a risky option, or to make sure that at least he was off the bench? The answer was clear-cut. It was time to negotiate a plea bargain agreement.

After lengthy consultation with Ed Bryant, the prosecutors crafted an agreement that would permit Lanier to plead guilty to some of the misdemeanor counts, resign from the bench, and serve eighteen months in jail. Presumably the disgrace would end his political career, at least as a judge. They were fairly optimistic that he would accept the offer, which also allowed him to keep his judicial pension, unless some action by the state legislature deprived him of that, an unlikely prospect. He would lose his present political power but regain his freedom by 1994. And by avoiding felony convictions, he would be able to serve his time in a minimum security prison, rather than doing hard time.

It took Wayne Emmons only a couple of days to report his client's decision. He was innocent, Lanier said, and he would accept no such terms, nor any other plea bargain. The prosecutors could either drop all the charges or be prepared to go to trial.

It was now obvious that David Lanier was confident of vindication. No one could say whether in rejecting such a generous deal Lanier was following his attorney's advice or not; the prosecutors had expected Emmons to urge acceptance of the agreement. But all that was now moot. The trial would go on. The victims would either be able to withstand the pressure or not. Among everyone involved, only the defendant seemed confident of the outcome.

Because of a flurry of defense motions, including a doctor's report saying Lanier had a sore back, the date for the trial to begin was reset for November 30. This date was firm. Judge Turner had rejected allegations by the defense that the statute was too vague to justify the charges and that the government had engaged in "outrageous misconduct" by "neutralizing" Lanier's personal attorneys from defending him, by recording his telephone calls, and by permitting an FBI agent to have an affair with one of the witnesses.

When Lanier repeated this last charge during a television interview, saying that "the FBI agent in this case has seduced my secretary," Castleberry had to explain to his wife and daughters that the agent involved was not part of the Lanier investigation, as the government pointed out in its response, and that the witness concerned had testified before the grand jury but was not even named in the indictment and would not testify at the trial.

One rather humorous note did emerge from these allusions to the adventures of Special Agent Driller Jack. Judge Lanier's present secretary, who was a reserved and proper woman of some years, had to convince her eighty-year-old mother that the secretary involved was not she but an employee who had long since resigned.

When Al Moskowitz insisted on flying Vivian Forsythe into Memphis to interview her, Castleberry exploded. He did not see the necessity of it and feared that asking Vivian to rehearse her testimony again before the trial was demanding too much of her. She would relive the rapes. She would also undoubtedly visit Dyersburg again to see her daughter, and this, too, was to risk disaster. The farther away she was from her family until the actual trial, the better.

But Moskowitz insisted. The argument, which took place in the law library at the Federal Building, was about more than Moskowitz's prerogatives and encompassed the tensions that had built up between Castleberry and the prosecutors over several matters. In truth, it was more of a dispute about personal and professional identities—and Castleberry's self-respect and longtime resistance to authority. Without saying so, even to himself, he had come to think of this as *his* case. Hadn't he unearthed it, on his own? He did not wish to tell the prosecutors what to do in the courtroom, but he thought he was in a better position than they to know how fragile many of the women were.

This dispute brought to a boil resentments that had been simmering—petty things, most of them, such as whether Castleberry's 302 reports were too detailed or not detailed enough. They added up to a conflict as to who was in charge here, the FBI or the Justice Department. The answer, of course, was Justice, but at one point in a meeting with the prosecutors Castleberry felt under attack and shouted, "I am proud to be an FBI agent!" and defended the Bureau against charges of publicity-seeking and bureaucratic calcification.

"Gee," he said afterward to Moskowitz, "you guys really ganged up on me in there. Three against one! I didn't even have Champine to help me out."

"Well, Bill," Moskowitz said dryly, "you're no shrinking violet."

To needle them, Castleberry and Champine began referring to the prosecutors by their initials, PMS. Amy Spain took the rather macho, snide wordplay on premenstrual syndrome with good humor, although other women attorneys in her office told her she should not put up with it.

When the prosecutors did fly Vivian into Memphis, ignoring Castleberry's strong objections, Al Moskowitz talked to her for more than two hours in the law library, hammering away at the question of compliance. Had she truly and consistently resisted Lanier, on both occasions? Had she not given in, if only somewhat, to placate him? It did not matter if she had, Moskowitz told her. What Lanier had done to her was still a crime. But if she had given in even a little, say, to avoid injury, he had to know. She had quoted herself as saying "No!" when Lanier first grabbed her and started kissing her. How long had she kept up her verbal protest, apart from struggling physically?

"Up to a point," Vivian said.

"What point?"

Vivian thought she had been explicit enough. What else did this attorney want from her? She had great difficulty, now, controlling the urge to break down completely in tears.

"It's not easy saying 'No!' with your mouth full of something!" she finally burst out. "You ought to try it!"

"Okay," Moskowitz said. "Of course."

Lanier had simply overpowered her, Vivian insisted. That was the truth and she was going to continue to tell it, whether everyone was convinced or not. She had done all she could do to resist, period.

"I believe you," Moskowitz at last assured her. "I just needed to hear you for myself. I do believe you, Vivian."

Castleberry and Champine drove her to the Memphis airport, after she had seen her family again, another tense visit. She was now truly afraid that her sister, Donna, was going to testify against her, appearing as a witness for Lanier.

Vivian was crying when they reached the Orlando gate. Castleberry looked out the window of the concourse waiting for her plane to leave, half-expecting to see her jump out the door.

She had waved to him as she disappeared down the boarding ramp. He could not get the look on her face out of his mind. So sad. Trying to be so brave.

That night he was the Gingerbread Man again.

Bill Castleberry met Louise Fitzgerald for the first time less than two weeks before the trial was to begin. She arrived in Memphis on the *City of New Orleans,* the train that ran from Chicago to the Crescent City and stopped on the way in Champaign-Urbana, where she was an associate professor of psychology at the University of Illinois; she met with Parker and Spain in Steve's office early on the morning of November 19. Castleberry and Champine barged into the middle of that meeting, and Dr. Fitzgerald, who was a petite blonde, a gamine who did not dress like an academic, stood up and stuck out her hand and said hello to the agents and went on talking to the prosecutors about her specialty, which was sexual harassment in the workplace. She was the author of more than fifty articles and the co-author of two books on that and related women's subjects. A year earlier she had been an adviser to Anita Hill's legal team at the Clarence Thomas hearings, where she evaluated witnesses for the lawyers, lobbied senators, and addressed a pro-Hill rally on the Capitol steps. She had planned to testify as an expert witness, specifically on the issue of why women often do not report incidents of harassment, battery, and rape, or do so only after long periods of time, but the Judiciary Committee had not permitted any expert testimony.

Parker and Spain tried to figure out how radical Fitzgerald was—whether she could persuade a jury or would alienate them. Her connection to Anita Hill was bothersome.

Al Moskowitz, who was in Washington on the day of the interview, had found Louise Fitzgerald through the feminist connections of his immediate boss at Justice, the head of the criminal civil rights section, Linda Davis. When Professor Fitzgerald happened to be in Washington to participate in a conference at Georgetown University commemorating the first anniversary of the Hill-Thomas hearings, Moskowitz invited her to his office to sound her out about becoming a witness at the Lanier trial. In addition to her expert testimony, Moskowitz hoped that she could also help Bill Castleberry with preparation of the witnesses. The FBI had been unable to find anyone to advise Bill, whose pleas for assistance became more insistent week by week.

Fitzgerald thought she was up to the dual assignment. She agreed to join the prosecution team, at a reduced fee, owing to budgetary constraints. She would end up making less than ten thousand dollars, Moskowitz estimated, for her work against David Lanier.

Moskowitz was satisfied that Fitzgerald was not too radical for a Memphis jury; nor did he think her association with Anita Hill would be a problem. But would Castleberry accept her?

Everyone went to lunch at the North End, a casual hangout favored by the legal crowd at 346 North Main, a short hop from the Federal Building. Castleberry watched Dr. Fitzgerald forcefully field questions from Parker and Spain. *You're no shrinking violet, either,* he thought as she expressed the opinion that the law favored men over women and needed to be changed, or else rape convictions would continue to be too difficult to obtain.

"We have to deal with the law as it's given to us now," Parker said, "or we won't convict Lanier." He looked somewhat uncomfortable.

Castleberry kept silent. He would have his chance at her that afternoon.

She met alone with the agents in the law library. Castleberry began by describing some of the problems the women were having. Dr. Fitzgerald explained their reactions in terms of post-traumatic shock syndrome. When a woman was physically assaulted by a man, whether physically or verbally or both, she could go through something similar to what men experience in war, what used to be called shell shock. Their emotions shut down; they withdraw; they cannot talk about their experience yet relive it constantly, actually can think about nothing else, which paralyzes them and may send them into drug and alcohol abuse and depression.

And when forced to confront their experience and to speak about it, Fitzgerald added, traumatized women might as well be going through it all over again. She had seen this happen herself over and over again in her experiences as a therapist. In addition to her academic work, she counseled patients, including victims of rape and battering, at a clinic attached to the University of Illinois.

Castleberry, as she talked, was listening but at the same time was giving her the old eyeball treatment. He was searching for some emotional feedback. He was not getting any. What he was getting was a feminist lecture, it sounded like. He intensified his gaze, blue eyes zapping away at brown.

And Louise Fitzgerald was thinking, *What the hell is it with this man? Those eyes! Is he always like this? Were all FBI agents like this? Did he pick out that blue shirt this morning to match his eyes? Is he trying to do me?*

What she was saying made sense, Castleberry finally responded, with the victims who had been raped, Jennifer and Vivian. But what about the others? Why was Patty Wallace, for instance, so distraught? She had not been raped.

"What is your definition of rape?" Fitzgerald asked him.

"Penetration. That is the definition."

"You're wrong," she said.

"I beg your pardon? What do you mean I'm wrong? That is the legal definition. Penetration."

"Uh-huh. Of the penis into the vagina, I suppose."

"Well, more or less." He was thinking, *This is a mighty forward conversation with a woman I've just met.*

"More or less? What do you mean by that? Halfway in? A quarter? An inch? All the way in?"

"I mean penetration of, if you want to know, the vagina, yes, or other orifices, in which case it's called sodomy. It's still rape, too."

"That's rape because men say it's rape."

"Without consent, of course," Castleberry added.

"What's consent? You mean she can fight him off but if she gives in to penetration that's consent? Penetration is a bullshit definition. That's rape because men say it's rape."

"Oh, come on. You're playing with words."

"And you're playing with women."

"It happens to be the law."

"And it's the law because men make the laws. Men write the laws. Did you ever ask a woman what rape is?" He was silent. "Because if you did, you might find out that rape can be a fist in the face, too, or a kick in the ribs or even an ugly, humiliating remark at work. For Patty Wallace it was a hand on her crotch in a courtroom, if I remember correctly. Wasn't it?"

"That's not a rape count. We're arguing at cross-purposes," Castleberry said.

"That's because you're arguing the law, and I'm arguing what it's like from a woman's point of view. Psychologically. Emotionally. Think about it."

"You'll have to forgive me. I've never had this discussion with a psychology professor before."

"And I've never talked to an FBI agent before, either, so we're even. I thought you wanted to find out why these women are so terrified and what we can do to help them."

"I do."

As long as he was asking questions, let her ask one, Fitzgerald said. Why was the original complaint against Judge Lanier ignored for so long?

Castleberry tried to explain—the reluctance of Brenda Castain to come forward, the disagreement between the interviewing agents, the fact that the investigation at the time was focused on corruption and on James O. Lanier, the problem of other pressing cases, the question of FBI jurisdiction.

"But you were responsible, right?" Fitzgerald asked.

"Yes."

"And you did nothing, right? For months? Until it was too late?"

"I hope it's not too late."

"It is for Brenda Castain." She let that sink in. He said nothing. "And one of the reasons you didn't act is because like most men you didn't think much of anything had happened to the woman. After all, there hadn't been *penetration,* had there? All Lanier did was jack off at her and threaten her if she didn't give in, right? Did you put that in your report?"

Dr. Fitzgerald's language startled Castleberry. He hoped he had not flinched. The last time he had heard a woman talk like that, he was arresting her for bank robbery.

Dr. Fitzgerald certainly did not have the appearance of a gun moll, even if she was talking like one. She was sitting there with her nice legs crossed demurely, wearing a suit that may have been bought for a bundle in Paris—France, not Tennessee—and if she would keep her mouth shut he might mistake her for . . . he could not say. She was no familiar type. Her accent betrayed no region, except maybe the Midwest. He could not tell her age, either. From her accomplishments she must be past forty, but could be thirty-five. Yellow hair that looked natural, cut short but cute, stylish. Tiny crow's-feet, just the suggestion of them, above prominent cheekbones that gave her a pixie slant. Good squarish teeth. An attractive female, all right, if only she'd shut up.

"I asked you a question," she said. "Did you put that in your report? Lanier's gross behavior toward Brenda Castain? A judge exposing himself?"

"I didn't write that report."

"But you knew about it? The threats?"

"That's correct."

"And you did nothing."

"Not at the time."

"Can I smoke in here?"

"We can go outside. I just want to say, Dr. Fitzgerald—"

"You can call me Louise."

"Louise, okay. We wanted Brenda Castain to call us again—"

"Oh, sure—"

"But she didn't. And when I did reread that report, a light went off—"

"A light went off. When was that? Weeks later? Months? What was it, a fifteen-watt bulb?"

"Several months, that's true."

"You really fucked up, Bill, didn't you?"

29

Much to Al Moskowitz's distress, neither Parker nor Spain approved of Louise Fitzgerald. "There is no way we can work with her," Parker said flatly. No one doubted her qualifications or intelligence. It was her aggressive manner and ideas about the law that bothered them. They feared that she would come off to a Memphis jury as a radical feminist and would shift sympathy toward the defendant. And her concept of harassment as part of a spectrum of assault, with rape an extension of it, might make sense psychologically—but legally it would sink the case. In this she sounded too much like Catharine MacKinnon, the radical law professor from Michigan whom Fitzgerald admired. To moderates like Parker and Spain, MacKinnon's views were fanatical, a denial of First Amendment and other constitutional rights that made men, not injustice, the enemy.

Only Castleberry wanted Louise Fitzgerald. He needed her, and desperately, he argued, whether she testified or not, to help him with the witnesses. He *had* fucked up, in not seeing them as victims. He absolutely had to have Fitzgerald's guidance from here on. Could she not play a dual role?

Moskowitz worked the phones to discover who else might be available on such short notice. He could find no one.

He also did not think Fitzgerald as radical as she may have appeared to Parker and Spain. A week before the trial, he told his colleagues, in effect, "Look, guys, this Louise Fitzgerald is it. If you want to have an expert witness, take her or leave her." They took her.

Moskowitz telephoned Fitzgerald and gave her his "This is the South" speech. She had to realize that they were operating in the most conservative part of the country. The female witnesses would have to prove themselves to the jury. They would not enter under the presumption that they were victims but probably, in the minds of most jurors, troublemakers.

Fitzgerald replied that she understood the South very well. She had spent most of her childhood in Georgia and had gone to college in Florida, before assuming her earlier incarnation as a dutiful wife and mother of three. Her graduate degrees were from Ohio State, but her roots were in Dixie.

She did not confide to Moskowitz—nor to feminist academic colleagues—that she had once been Southern enough to have been nominated by her sorority for Orange Bowl Queen.

Moskowitz was correct. Louise Fitzgerald was no rigid ideologue. Her passion for women's rights was not something abstract but came directly from counseling battered and raped women and from her own past experience in an oppressive marriage. But to her, being a feminist did not mean becoming man-hating, sexless or lesbian, or Marxist. At the time she was hired as an expert she had just bought herself a white Miata convertible and did not mind if somebody mistook her for a character in a Beach Boys video as she streaked through the cornfields of Illinois with the top down and the wind in her hair. She lived with her present husband, who coincidentally held the Lanier Chair of Psychology at the university, in a house that resembled a ski lodge amid the cornrows. And she was not the sort of feminist who objected if a male complimented her on her looks. If a man told her how pretty she was and that she looked much younger than her forty-eight years, she did not condemn him as an agent of oppressive patriarchy.

When Al Moskowitz sent her summaries of the women's stories, however, she reacted with the fury of a fierce advocate for women's rights. Her experience as a clinician made the women's accounts all the more vivid and convincing to her. And when she read that Vivian Forsythe had said, "I am doing this for my daughter, so that man won't be around to hurt her and others like her. I am not doing this for myself. I could run away and hide and maybe forget about it. I am doing this for all women," the words leapt off the page, and Louise could not wait to meet this person.

Louise Fitzgerald arrived again in Memphis on the evening of Sunday, November 29, with jury selection to begin the next morning. Bill Castleberry met her at the Amtrak station, and as he drove her to her hotel, she asked where the witnesses were. Still in Dyersburg, he said, except for Vivian Forsythe, who was already in town. Maybe she could have dinner with Vivian that night, Louise said.

"Difficult," Castleberry said. "She's at another hotel."

"Where is her hotel?" Louise asked.

"Pretty far out," Bill said. "We've got her hidden, so Lanier's people can't get to her."

"Who's with her?"

"Nobody. She's alone."

"Alone! I can't believe this. Bill, you have fucked up again."

Castleberry tried not to lose his temper—which quickly subsided into frustration with himself and guilt. He knew she must be right, painful though it was to admit.

They were almost to the Crowne Plaza, where Louise was staying and Bill had booked a room for himself.

"This is a complete screwup," Louise said. "Take me to see Vivian Forsythe, right now. She is coming to stay at my hotel. I want a room next to hers. And I want all the other women staying there, too, when they come in. The sooner the better."

"We can't do that."

"What do you mean, we can't do that?"

"Because it's not done. It's against procedure. You cannot have witnesses staying together. They'll contaminate each other's testimony."

"I don't care about procedure. I want them together! They've got to know they're not alone."

"Parker won't allow it. You don't understand."

"I'll talk to him. You're the ones don't understand! Now get us to Vivian as fast as you can! You can break the speed limit, can't you?"

He hurried through the light Sunday evening traffic to I–40 and headed east. From the agitated way that Louise was talking, he knew she was genuinely worried about Vivian, who could conceivably commit suicide under these circumstances and was undoubtedly thinking about it. How could he have been so dense! He had been following rules—ones that had no application whatever to this impossible, infuriating case!

Ever since the incidents with Lanier, Louise explained, Vivian would have felt totally alone in the world and powerless. That was the key factor in dealing with a rape victim. You had to understand how powerless they felt—and how the worst thing you could do was to put them into an even more helpless situation, isolated, alone. Stashing her in some strange hotel, away from any kind of support, marooned on the island of her suffering—that was the worst possible thing to have done to a victim. Vivian was an alcoholic and an addict, wasn't she?

"Where the fuck is this place?" Louise demanded. They had been driving for nearly half an hour. "Did you put her in another goddamned state?"

They were almost there. The Hampton Inn was near the intersection of I–40 and I–240, well east of the Memphis airport. Castleberry pulled up at the entrance and had to trot to catch up to Dr. Fitzgerald at the elevator. Bill had a key to her room. He started to justify the reason he had housed Vivian way out here, to hide her from Lanier, but skipped it.

They found her lying on her bed with the lights out and the curtains drawn.

"Mr. Castleberry?" came the little voice. He switched on the lights. Vivian's face was streaked with tears. Louise introduced herself and went straight to the bed and sat down and took Vivian's hands in hers.

"It's all right, sweetheart," she said. "We're not going to leave you alone anymore. Go ahead and cry, if you want to. Bill, can't you get her a Coke or something?"

Louise had dinner with Vivian in her room, which was next door to Louise's, that night at the Crowne Plaza. Bill's room was across the hall. At about eleven he was sitting listening to a tape of *Madama Butterfly*— he always brought opera cassettes along for comfort when away from home—smoking a cigar and reading one of his favorite authors, Pat Conroy, a novel called *The Lords of Discipline,* about life in a military academy based on the Citadel. He had read it before, and one passage always bothered him, as it did that night. "I have eyes that give people what they want, eyes that whore in order to please, commiserate, endorse, affirm. . . . I have the eyes of a ward politician or a priest on the make with the choirboys. I have eyes I have learned to distrust completely."

That's me, he thought. *That passage was written so that I could read it and throw up.* He poured himself another Jack Daniel's.

Then there was a knock at the door. It was Louise.

"I need a drink," she said.

They stayed up all that night talking. Bill did most of it, telling her about his guilt over all these women, how he had not known how bad it would be for them or how uncertain the outcome of the trial would be. He felt that he had misled them.

He was right to worry about Vivian, Louise said. Vivian was a mess. That big suitcase of hers—Louise had unpacked it for her. The poor girl must have packed everything she owned in it—as if she were trying to tote her identity around with her. Louise could not remember seeing a woman in such bad shape. How she would ever have the strength to testify?

And Bill should know that Vivian talked about him as if he were some knight in shining armor. As if he were the father she never had and her savior.

"She called you 'Papa Bill,' " Louise said. "Can you take that? I notice to your face it's strictly 'Mr. Castleberry,' Papa."

Bill took another drink. He got tears in his eyes. He told Louise how rough he had been on many of the women at first, when they did not want to talk. He had used nearly every technique of persuasion he knew on them. He said that he and Joey and Steve Champine had called that room in the police department the dungeon.

"You really are an asshole," Louise said, shaking her head and sighing.

The trouble was, Bill went on, that he had approached this case as if it were conventional, what he was used to and trained to investigate. He had thought of the women as witnesses, not as victims. Now he understood that they were both. Joey McDowell had warned him, but he had not listened to Joey until the women started disintegrating, just as Joey had predicted would happen.

"Maybe you need to repent," Louise said. "I'm a Catholic, or I used to be. Maybe you should ask me for absolution. I think there may be hope for you. I think behind those eyes and without that gun of yours you may actually be a closet postmodernist feminist."

"Don't tell anyone," Bill said. "And what the hell is postmodernist? I know what the closet is. You're a psychologist. How good are you at interpreting dreams?"

"Lousy," she said.

He described his recurrent nightmare. He said that if he ever wrote a book about this case, he would call it *King David and the Gingerbread Man.*

Louise said she thought he had his dream vision figured out better than he did the case. He ought to remember that this story was not about him and David Lanier. It was about these women. It was about the woman across the hall who was probably lying there awake and petrified and staring at the ceiling, or dreaming about a judge. It was about a woman burning alive.

Louise and Bill never had a cross word between them after that night. Except when they talked about Anita Hill, and Bill said that if the FBI had been allowed to do a full job, the truth about Hill and Thomas would have come out. That infuriated Louise.

Steve Parker resisted Louise's plan to house the witnesses together but relented when Bill said that he already could see that it had been a mistake to isolate Vivian. They should still be discouraged from discussing their testimony with one another, Parker said; but as many of them had already met at the grand jury, keeping them apart did seem unnecessary.

Parker also gave in, with doubts, to Louise's advice on jury selection.

He believed that women tended to judge other women more harshly than men did, and Castleberry agreed with him. But Louise insisted that this was a myth, and her strategy to try for as many women as possible became the plan. As it turned out, the way Emmons began to use his challenges indicated that the defense wanted a female jury, too. Could this be David Lanier's vanity at work, or was Emmons counting on women's scorn for women? Someone was going to be wrong.

During the voir dire (French for "to speak the truth") questioning of prospective jurors—a rapid process in federal court, where the judge controls the pace and does most of the interrogating himself—a pool of twenty-eight people answered questions individually about whether they or members of their family had been sexually assaulted, whether they could render an impartial verdict, and whether they were close to law enforcement or personally acquainted with the defendant or members of his family. Of these twenty-eight, chosen by lot from a larger pool, nineteen were men and only nine were women; but several of the men quickly disqualified themselves for various reasons: one was so old that he had trouble staying awake; another was so inarticulate that no one could make sense of his answers; a third had known David Lanier for fifty years, he said, since the days when he had hunted with James P. Further questioning revealed that he had also been married to and was divorced from Joan Lanier's twin sister. He admitted that it would be difficult for him to render an impartial judgment, although which way he might be leaning was anyone's guess.

The degree to which each may have been affected by the considerable prior publicity about the case was naturally of concern to Judge Turner, who began the proceedings by reading out the entire indictment, which began:

David W. Lanier is the only Chancellor for the 29th Judicial District for Dyer and Lake Counties in the State of Tennessee. . . . [He] handles all cases . . . including divorce petitions, child custody proceedings, child support matters, appointment and removal of guardians, and adoptions. David W. Lanier also acts as the only juvenile court judge in Dyer and Lake Counties, and as such [he] has jurisdiction over all juvenile court matters . . . All juvenile court employees, including secretaries and juvenile officers, serve at the pleasure of David W. Lanier. In addition, all clerical employees of the Chancery Court, including court secretaries and clerks, serve at the pleasure of David W. Lanier. These employees can be hired, promoted, disciplined, or fired at the will of David W. Lanier.

Whatever they had heard about the case on television or read in the papers, this was undoubtedly fresh information to the jurors, because no news report had gone into detail about the base and extent of Judge Lanier's power. Nor would most people, in an era when so many government employees are protected by civil service procedures, have known that in the late twentieth century a judge could exercise so much authority over so many people and play so determinant a role in the lives of women and their children. It was Steve Parker who had made sure that the indictment was based expressly on this premise. He had framed it himself in that form and knew that jurors would have copies of it to think about.

Some of the media material that may have affected jurors was not directly related to the Lanier case, or may have had a subtler if deliberate relationship to it. As Wayne Emmons said to one juror, "The reason we're going into certain issues is because sexual harassment is a hot issue just now."

Only that morning—could it have been coincidence, or was someone trying to send a message to jurors?—the Memphis *Commercial Appeal,* which was the only daily left in the city, carried an editorial headed in very large type, WITCH HUNT? SEX POLICE GO TO EXCESS IN PURSUIT OF PACKWOOD. Without mentioning the Lanier case by name, the piece was a strong condemnation of governmental attempts to control personal relations in the workplace, with specific reference to accusations of sexual harassment leveled by several former employees of a Republican senator from Oregon. The editorial labeled charges against Bob Packwood an "inquisition" and prayed, "Heaven help the Republic if feminist puritan witch hunts become the order of the day." It dismissed Senator Packwood's bumbling "interest in adulterous dalliance" as a joke and asked, "Has Anita Hillism dawned in Washington?"

Wayne Emmons asked each prospective juror whether he or she had seen the Hill-Thomas hearings on television or read about them thirteen months ago. Nearly all said they had; every one of them stated that he or she could not decide on who had been telling the truth—that, in other words, Anita Hill had failed to prove her allegations against Clarence Thomas beyond a reasonable doubt.

As Parker and his colleagues knew, there was no hope, nor had there ever been, of obtaining a jury the majority of whom believed in Anita Hill. The prosecution's plan was to try to counteract the impact of the Hill precedent, compounded now by sympathy for Senator Packwood, by making clear distinctions between the relatively mild accusations against Packwood and Thomas, as opposed to the far more serious charges against David Lanier.

The mood among the prosecutors, the agents, and Louise Fitzgerald was tense. Everyone was hoping that the number of witness-victims against Lanier would matter, in contrast to Anita Hill's solitary voice. Louise told everyone that there were actually at least two other women who had wished to testify against Clarence Thomas but that they had been prevented from doing so by the Senate committee. In this instance, at least, there might be greater strength in numbers, if only the women proved believable.

Louise had the feeling that she was in alien territory, far removed from the collective mind of the academic community, which overwhelmingly supported Anita Hill. She could see that she, the witnesses, and indeed the entire feminist movement were the targets of that "witch-hunt" editorial, and that in this view it was the witches and bitches who were not the hunted but the hunters. She had been away from the academic cloister for only twenty-four hours but already understood the importance of distinguishing among degrees of harassment and assault if any hope of convicting Lanier was to remain. The rest of the team welcomed her conversion and willingness to put aside feminist doctrine, theory, or insight in favor of practical necessity.

She knew that she was now an accepted member of the team when Castleberry and Champine bought a toy police badge, printed the words SEX POLICE on it, and presented it to her. She pinned it onto her jacket, behind the scenes, and felt sworn in.

And she was pleased that the jury, after a day and a half of voir dire, ended up composed of eight women and four men. All of the women had had some sort of working experience outside the home, and one of them was a professor of medical science at the University of Tennessee Medical Center and a practicing physician attached to the emergency room there. Rape victims were among her patients. Yet even she stated emphatically that she had no idea whether to believe Anita Hill or not and had no personal experience of harassment or assault.

Nothing could cheer Bill Castleberry up, however, when Steve Parker informed him that the prosecutors had decided that Castleberry would not be permitted in the courtroom during the trial. Parker's reasoning was clear. He assumed that the defense planned to attack Castleberry personally and might well call him as a witness. Charges of "outrageous government conduct" were the subject of a continuing objection by Wayne Emmons and had already received considerable publicity. Lanier had repeated his accusations before TV cameras that "the FBI agent" had "seduced my secretary" and that the women had been threatened by the government and forced to testify against their wills.

Castleberry was devastated—that was the word everyone used to described his reaction—and angry. For more than two years he had devoted nearly every waking hour, and many asleep, to the investigation, only to end up barred from observing the culmination of his work. He would not be permitted to watch as the women he had discovered and hammered at and cajoled finally came through with the truth—or did not. From his point of view, being shut out was as if the author of a play were told that he was forbidden to be present at its performance.

Parker sympathized with Castleberry but was not about to risk the case because of the agent's feelings. To have the defense charge government misconduct was one thing; to give that government a face for the jurors to contemplate, and for Emmons to point at, was another. Lanier was arguing that the case was a political vendetta against him. Better to keep the accused provocateur of this supposed vendetta out of sight. If he was called as a witness, he would come to the stand as a minor player. If he sat at the prosecution table, which would already have the three attorneys at it, and where an agent customarily sat, Castleberry was more likely to be perceived as a conspirator, whispering advice to his cohorts.

Parker, moreover, had not long ago experienced defeat in a parallel situation. It was common practice for the defense to attack the prosecution, especially when no better strategy presented itself; and Southern juries were prone to see the federal government in an oppressive, unfavorable light. In a recent trial of Parker's, the defense attorney had pointed repeatedly to the FBI agent at the prosecution table, portraying him as the representative of a menacing police state. The jury had hung, split down the middle. Afterward a juror who had talked to the agent asked Parker if the FBI man was really a nice guy after all. Yes, Parker said, actually a pussycat. "Gee," the juror said, "I kept looking into those dark eyes of his. I thought he was a real sonofabitch."

Castleberry tried to accept Parker's reasoning and did, for one minute; in the next he was cursing the prosecutor for pulling rank—that was what the banishment added up to, he became convinced. He was being told to know his place and that he was not needed anymore.

"You're just feeling castrated," Louise told him, a remark that did not raise his spirits.

"What am I supposed to do for the rest of the trial?" he asked her. "Take care of the women? What am I, a baby-sitter with a badge?"

She reminded him that he had not been barred from the courthouse, only the courtroom. He could be there to assist everyone. He countered that maybe the hotel could hire him as a liveried shuttle driver to transport witnesses to and from the courthouse.

Castleberry's fears of incipient retirement played into his reaction. He was not being forced out, he had the option of staying for another seven years, but he knew it would soon be time to go. The Bureau was changing. Everything was becoming team management. Older agents like him who worked on their own did not fit in with the modern scheme of things. The Lanier case was becoming potentially a landmark in the law and in the history of the FBI, which had played such a vital role in the enforcement of civil rights law, in spite of J. Edgar Hoover's loathing for Martin Luther King, but had been uninvolved in the women's movement until now. He knew that he had undergone, or was still undergoing, a personal conversion to the cause of women's rights. And for his troubles and enlightenment, he felt, he was being summarily kicked in the teeth.

He shut himself in his room. Louise called him and, not unlike a mother, tried to coax him out of his funk by convincing him to help her take Vivian and Jennifer Gallagher to dinner. They were the only witnesses in town so far. They were already becoming friends and gaining strength from one another. Wasn't their welfare more important than his hurt?

She suggested the North End, where they could have some drinks and play the jukebox and keep the women distracted from their anxieties. What else did he have in mind, crying in his beer in his room?

"You're being a jerk," she told him. "What opera are you playing tonight, *Pagliacci*?"

He relented.

The women chatted among themselves as Castleberry drove them to the restaurant. At dinner he drank a couple of doubles and picked at his steak and became totally withdrawn, irritating Louise, who tried kicking him under the table, but he shrank away. Jennifer and Vivian exchanged memories of Dyersburg High, where Jennifer said she had thought Vivian was the wildest thing and must have been a genius, to carry on like that and make A's. But Mr. Castleberry's brooding was too oppressive to ignore.

"What's the matter with Papa Bill?" Vivian whispered to Louise.

"Oh," Louise said loudly, "he's just feeling sorry for himself and sulking because big bad Steve Parker made him mad."

Bill pretended not to hear her.

"Maybe we should go dancing," Louise said.

"Where I'm gonna go," he said, "you can't go."

"I wonder what Mr. FBI means by that?" Louise shrugged.

Back at the Crowne Plaza he refused her suggestion of a nightcap in the lounge and went straight to his room.

Louise had one drink with Vivian and Jennifer, and everyone retired. In her room Louise turned on the television. Lanier was the lead story on the ten o'clock news. There on the screen were the judge and his family leaving the courtroom after jury selection. Until now she had not given much thought to his daughters and Joan Lanier, and as she did so her loathing for the judge increased. He was making these women suffer, too, along with the victims. His wife and daughters in their pitiful loyalty to him were also victims. Bill had told her how sorry he felt for Mrs. Lanier, and now Louise understood.

Her phone rang. It was Vivian. Jennifer was with her. They were worried about Mr. Castleberry. Louise said he'd be fine. He had had his feelings bruised, was all.

She rang his room.

"I'm going out," he announced.

"Where?"

"I just need to get away. I'll find someplace. I'm not taking my badge or my gun."

"Men's stuff? You going to fight somebody?"

"I'm not looking for a fight."

"But you wouldn't run away from one, would you?"

"No."

The truth was, he needed to get out of the hotel and, he did not tell Louise this, away from the women, if only for a few hours that night. He wanted to be by himself in some honky-tonk, listening to the music and having some beers and just thinking, alone. Okay, so he was sulking. *If I'm going to sulk,* he told himself, *I want to sulk like a man.*

"A man's gotta do what he's gotta do," was all he said to her.

"Oh, Christ. Stop by my room before you go."

He appeared at her door having changed clothes. He was wearing cowboy boots and jeans.

"Good night, Doctor," he said.

"Good night, cowboy."

30

Although the Federal Building in Memphis was a glass-and-steel block, as cold and impersonal as its Bauhaus-derived clones around the world, within it Judge Jerome Turner's courtroom was an appealing anachronism. Some architect had enough respect for tradition to know that right angles and the dispensing of justice do not mix. To spend a few hours in it was to imagine another era, to dream that you could walk outside, light up a cheroot, and stroll down to the river to find Mark Twain piloting his steamboat on the way to New Orleans.

The ceiling must have been twenty feet high, with graceful plasterwork along the cornices. Tall windows were draped with heavy, deep red velvet, and huge portraits of previous judges of the United States District Court for the Western District of Tennessee hung on the white, faintly yellowish walls. Judge Turner himself looked rather nineteenth-century in his full, reddish-brown beard. He was fifty and a Memphis native. His speech varied from the courtly to the gruff, and his mien was grave. He might have been incubated in that room.

He was known as a judge's judge—cautious, thorough, meticulous, impatient of legal innovation. Steve Parker was worried about him.

U.S. 18 § 242 had never been used successfully against a judge before and Judge Turner, with his devotion to precedent, was showing signs that he was not happy with this case. Not that he had ruled injudiciously so far on any of the motions brought by either the prosecution or the defense, but he seemed uncomfortable with the whole idea of bringing these charges against a fellow jurist and in becoming the judge of a judge. It was Turner's manner rather than any specific act that made Parker, Spain, and

Moskowitz sense that he wished this David Lanier business would just go away.

The way he fussed about how Lanier should be addressed by the attorneys and himself was a clue. Normally, Turner discoursed from the bench before bringing in the jury and asking the attorneys to begin their opening statements, if a judge practices as a lawyer in court, he or she is not addressed as "Judge," "for obvious ethical reasons." But in this instance the defendant was himself a judge and a lawyer—and a sitting judge at that. Should he not be accorded the respect due his office?

Parker quickly moved to smooth any ruffled judicial feathers. He proposed to address Judge Lanier by his title—or at least as "Judge," not going so far as "Chancellor"—because, he said, that was how the witnesses knew him and would refer to him, spontaneously. And, Parker could not resist adding, the entire case was about the abuse of power in which this judge had engaged. It seemed only proper to remind everyone, as frequently as possible, of how he had betrayed a high office.

Wayne Emmons said simply that there would not be a person in the courtroom who did not know that Lanier was a judge, so he might as well be called that. Judge Lanier he was and would remain.

Judge Turner was happy with this unanimity and took pains to tell the defendant that as a judge and a lawyer he was free to join in conferences at the bench, if he wished.

Parker controlled his disgust with all this deferential prattle, as he saw it, but he was inwardly unusually ticked off, even for him, that morning. As they stood there discussing how to show respect for a rapist, Lanier was manipulating the judicial system and state politics to what he presumed would be his ultimate benefit. A second lawyer had now joined the defense team, a man from Dyersburg whose personal background made him a very peculiar choice to defend anyone, let alone someone charged with three felonies and facing up to thirty-eight years in prison.

His name was Tim Naifeh; he was thirty-three, dark and lean, with slick black hair styled into a sort of pompadour. He smiled a lot, the dazzling grin of a lounge act emcee. He favored purple shirts and suits that bordered on the zoot. Only four months ago he had been arrested and charged with two counts of possessing cocaine with intent to deliver. A trooper had discovered the drugs when they fell out of an envelope Naifeh was carrying in his car when he had the misfortune of becoming involved in a highway crash.

Naifeh pleaded guilty to a reduced charge of simple possession of cocaine. On August 17, 1992, he was fined fifteen hundred dollars, ordered to perform a hundred hours of community service, and given a year's sentence in jail, suspended. He faced certain censure and suspension of his license to practice law by the Tennessee Supreme Court's Board of Professional Responsibility when that body got around to ruling on his case, presumably after the Lanier trial was over. But in the meanwhile, there he was, Judge Lanier's new advocate.

Anyone who knew Wayne Emmons presumed that he could not have been happy to have Tim Naifeh as his co-counsel. Cousin Bubba might be a defrocked preacher, but that career change had had to do with his divorce; he had never done anything criminal, let alone been involved with drugs. His honesty was what made him respected by prosecutors and police. Lanier must have forced him to accept this dubious assistance. But why?

Because Tim's cousin, Jimmy Naifeh, happened to be Speaker of the Tennessee House of Representatives—Steve Parker was convinced that must be the reason, could only be the reason. Lanier was, once again, being a Lanier. He was calculating that by doing a favor for one Naifeh, he would encourage another to prevent the legislature from instituting impeachment proceedings.

Parker further believed that Lanier was calculating that he would either be acquitted or, at the worst, convicted on one or two of the misdemeanor counts, get off with a slap on the wrist, and, with his leverage in the legislature assured, not have to worry about being thrown off the bench. Life in Dyersburg would go on as always.

Wayne Emmons introduced his colleague to the court, saying that Mr. Naifeh "will be our assistant" and would be in and out during the trial "doing some investigation and research," not actually participating in the proceedings. In other words, Parker thought, doing nothing.

"We're glad to have you, Mr. Naifeh," Judge Turner said. "Are you the state legislator or is that someone else in your family?"

"No, sir," Tim Naifeh replied. "That's my cousin, Jimmy Naifeh. I'm better looking than he is, Judge, I think."

"Good afternoon, ladies and gentlemen of the jury. During jury voir dire, you kept hearing the term sexual harassment. This is not a sexual harassment case. This indictment charges that Judge David Lanier used his position to assault not one, not two, but eight women. And you will hear from all eight women."

That was how Steve Parker began his opening statement, which was brief, taking less than twenty minutes to deliver, but as powerful as he could make it, which was very. When Parker spoke, all his emotional intensity and loathing for Lanier came through. Whatever the jury would decide, there was no way that they could avoid concluding that this prosecutor believed passionately in what he was saying. And the words he chose were deliberately designed to conjure up revolting images, verbs and nouns evoking specific actions and things.

"You will hear," he continued, "how he used his position to fondle them, to touch their breasts, to touch their crotches—how he exposed himself to them, how he masturbated in front of them, and how with very weak victims who thought they were going to lose their child support, lose their child custody, he coerced them to have sex with him."

Parker went on to outline Judge Lanier's powers as chancellor and juvenile court judge and how he used them to exploit two groups of women, those with cases before him and those who worked for him. He named each of the eight victims and summarized what Lanier had done to them.

And when he came to Vivian Forsythe, he was frank. One of the prosecution's major worries was that the jury would do what society has done since the beginning of time, divide the women into "good" girls and "bad" girls, based on the double standard of sexual morality as applied to women versus men. Through this distorted lens, Vivian was certainly on the bad side of the ledger. Although the prosecutor had made a motion to exclude "prior sexual conduct" as an admissible area of questioning the witnesses, Judge Turner was going to rule in each instance, as the witnesses appeared, rather than issue a blanket prohibition. Legal precedent was clear in most rape cases that a woman's sexual history was irrelevant. This, however, was a civil rights action, which gave the judge more discretion on what evidence in this potentially explosive domain and that of drug abuse to allow.

Every good trial lawyer knows that the best way to deal with potentially damaging material is to introduce it at once, rather than wait for your opponent to spring it on the jury in a context favorable to the other side. With this principle in mind, Parker told the jurors on that first day that Vivian "was a very troubled young girl."

"She came from a very dysfunctional home," Parker said. "She came from an abusive marriage. She is a very weak and vulnerable girl with a lot of problems. She may have a lifestyle you may not like. But she did have one thing that hooked her with responsibility." Parker's choice of that last verb was a slip, but he went on to refer to Vivian's love for her daughter and how Lanier had exploited that to try to get her to submit to sex and to ensure her silence.

Parker concluded by reminding the jury that the Constitution and the statute under which Lanier was being tried guaranteed to every citizen certain inalienable rights. Among them was "the right to bodily integrity."

"Everyone has the right not to have sexual battery committed upon them," and no one was above the law, not a police officer and not even a judge. "What this case is about is the abuse of power, how this man," and he gestured toward Lanier, "used his position for his own gratification."

It was not possible to deduce a clear defense strategy from Wayne Emmons's opening statement, which he made in a calm, low voice that contrasted with Parker's passion, as if to say, in effect, "We're not worried." Emmons spent most of his time extolling the long public service that David Lanier and his brother and their father before them had rendered to their community and to the state of Tennessee. Judge Lanier was now in his tenth year as chancellor, but he had not been able to occupy the bench as he normally would, in his conscientious way, for several weeks, because of the necessity of preparing for this trial.

The jury, Emmons advised, should be very attentive in listening to the witnesses against Judge Lanier, because, as would be shown, all of them had reasons of one kind or another to be biased against him and to lie about him. Any scrutiny of their motives to lie or stretch the truth should begin with the fact that none of them said anything, not for years in several instances, until approached by the government and the FBI. The Laniers were a powerful political family, with many friends and many enemies, as with all political figures. The jury would come to understand the combination of political and personal motives that had caused false charges to be brought.

Judge Lanier was not a saint, Emmons concluded. His wife of twenty-eight years, who was sitting with their daughters, Emmons pointed out, in the second row of the courtroom, had divorced him on grounds of adultery. He was not perfect, but he was "not the animal that he has been portrayed to be." The case was a complex one and would "reach right down into your guts and tear you all apart." Yet in the end the jury would find Judge Lanier a human being who had made mistakes but was not guilty as charged.

Only in these last references to Lanier's "flaws" and his having been divorced for adultery could the prosecutors discern a possible line of defense, one that would be very difficult to counteract. Was Lanier going to admit to having sex with some of the women and to having made attempts to seduce others? If he did, while denying the use of force, he could very well be perceived as nothing worse than a harmless, dirty old man, or almost old, with a weakness for younger women. Pursuing that approach, Parker, Spain, and Moskowitz agreed, along with impugning many of the witnesses' reputations, might easily convince the jury that convicting Lanier would be like saying that most of the male population over fifty should be locked up.

That was certainly how his family appeared to view the matter. Amy Spain noticed how fiercely the Lanier women glared at her, as if she were a traitor to womanhood, siding with a gaggle of conniving hussies to ruin a beloved family man.

*   *   *

That evening Bill Castleberry began to adjust to the role that fate, Steve Parker, and, to tell the truth, his own concern for the women and the case had assigned him for the duration of the trial. All of the witnesses were now staying at the Crowne Plaza. From his room on the eleventh floor he could look out at the river and at the great pyramid Memphis had built as its convention center and think that, whatever his frustrations, he could take pride in unearthing Lanier's abuses—if only the jury would now agree! His late-night excursion in search of manly solitude had done him a world of good. By the time he had found a likely looking roadhouse on the outskirts of town, he had already regained some composure. A few rounds and some football talk with good old boys had done the rest. He remained frustrated about not seeing the trial, but he could live with it.

"You see," Louise told him, "you really can act like a grown-up." She was pleased he was back, because she was going to need his help with the women. Steve Parker had estimated at first that the trial would take about a week, but Wayne Emmons was now saying that it would last at least twice that long. Judge Turner had set a four-days-per-week schedule, with Friday reserved for the attorneys to attend to other business.

The prosecutors had brought all the witnesses into Memphis at first so as to make a final determination of the order in which they would be called and to make sure that they remembered what they had said to the grand jury. Equally important was for them to meet with Dr. Fitzgerald, so that she could help them understand their anxieties and, it was hoped, adjust to the challenge ahead.

Louise brought the women together in her room, her first chance to meet most of them and an opportunity to see themselves as part of a group. She gave them a brief pep talk, emphasizing how important what they were doing was for all women and for the health of American society, as well as for themselves, their children, and their community. They were true heroines for coming forward.

She did not mention some of the gloomy talk she had heard among the prosecutors or the worries about whether some of them would be able to hold up. Nor did she confide in them some of the doubts she had about the role she herself was beginning to play.

She had signed on primarily as an expert witness, but from the moment she had arrived she had become psychological counselor, first to Vivian, then to Jennifer, now to all the witnesses—not to speak of the FBI agent! She could not have done otherwise. Her instinct to try to help women in trouble was the strongest motivation of her life. Yet was she truly helping them emotionally by preparing them for trial, or was there a conflict between her job as witness and helper for the prosecution and minister to the emotionally damaged? Louise was very much aware, from the extensive scholarship on the issue as well as from seeing the effects of the legal system on some of her clients, that facing a courtroom situation can often be nearly as traumatic for a sexual assault victim as the original incident or incidents—especially when lawyers tried to win by defaming the victim.

She decided that convicting Lanier would be worth the risk to these women. What would happen to them if he remained as judge in Dyersburg, now that he knew who his real enemies were?

She asked the women how they felt about testifying. All professed great anxiety; some described how their lives had been turned upside down for months by this case. Louise explained post-traumatic stress disorder to them, comparing the psychological effects of rape to those of a natural disaster, such as a powerful earthquake or a tornado. Prolonged assault or battering, featuring repeated incidents, could be compared to military combat. As in these kinds of experiences, the women were reacting to what Lanier had done to them the way human beings usually did to terrifying or in different degrees disturbing events that were outside the normal realm of experience. The effects could be prolonged, and they could be relived through memories and dreams, and they could involve attempts at denial. That was why many of them had not told anyone about the incidents—that and, of course, fears of his reprisal.

Some of the women, Louise told them, by way of conversation, not as a lecture, may have internalized their traumas, blamed themselves for the attacks, gone through periods of repressing their anxieties only to have them return in virulent form, or tried to cope with them through alcohol and drugs. What they had to realize was that in no case should they compound their problems by blaming themselves or seeing themselves as abnormally weak. They were reacting as victims always did, whether surviving a flood or a fire or a concentration camp or sexual assault. If they had been abused earlier in their lives, by a parent, a relative, a teacher, a husband, anyone they viewed as an authority figure or a person in whom to place their trust, Lanier's actions would be doubly damaging to them.

As Louise made this last point, not in a didactic way but gently, she was studying the faces of her listeners and saw increased unease in some of them. Jennifer Gallagher's eyes dropped; Vivian stared at her imploringly; another woman gazed out the window, or pretended to, as it only mirrored lights against the night.

There was one other point she would like to make, Louise said, and then she'd be happy to talk to any of them individually or together, as they wished. They should also know that careful research showed that the effects were always greater if trauma occurred in a place that the victim had considered safe. The shock was then intensified and recovery more difficult.

What could be safer than a courthouse? Hadn't they all thought that?

They must have believed that under no circumstances could they be in a more protected, safe place than with a judge in his courthouse.

Vivian and Jennifer were among the three women who lingered in Louise's room. Louise wished that Janet Thomasson were among them, because outwardly she appeared to be the most frightened of all, afflicted with nervous tics and twitches and obviously having trouble breathing. But the third was Linda Michaels, who was not named in the indictment but had testified before the grand jury that Cathy Kiely had told her about Lanier's assaults soon after they occurred. Michaels had also experienced one incident herself at the hands of the judge. The prosecutors were hoping that she could testify to that, but it had occurred in 1987, before the time frame of the indictment. Judge Turner might not let it in.

Vivian asked where Mr. Castleberry was. In his room, Louise said, as far as she knew.

"Is he all alone?" Vivian asked. It was getting close to Christmas. He must be thinking about his wife and children.

Louise wondered if the women felt they could speak freely before Mr. Castleberry. He had already heard everything, they said. Why not?

Louise called Bill and asked him if he could bring something to drink. He said he would go buy some and warned Louise and the others not to walk outside the hotel themselves. Memphis was dangerous. All the liquor stores in or near downtown had bars on them. The women could get themselves killed.

"You could lend us your gun," Louise said.

"You're not FBI," Bill said. "You wouldn't know what to do with it."

"You're right," Louise said. "See you soon."

By the time he arrived with the supplies, Linda Michaels was telling the story of her life. What Louise had said about previous acts of trauma had set her off. She was here as a minor sort of witness, she had said. What she had gone through with David Lanier was nothing close to what some of the other women had experienced. In the light of what Louise had said, Linda thought that she must have reacted so strongly because of her past.

One day when she was working for a Dyersburg law firm, she had been in the courthouse examining some property tax records. She was sitting on a high stool, facing the wall, poring over record books. Every day women were in there doing the same thing, and often, Linda had noticed, Judge Lanier would stroll into the room and get too friendly. He would cuddle up to the women, who were all young, and nuzzle and hug them and in general behave like some old dog.

Linda, who was in her early thirties then, did not know Lanier and thought she was safe from him for that reason. But on that day he walked up behind her, put his arm around her shoulder, started chatting about the weather, rubbed her shoulders, and let his hand drop slowly down her spine.

It was hard to convey how instantly angry she was, Linda said. The only words to describe her feeling were that she was going nuts. He began massaging the small of her back, still talking on about nothing, and finally—all of this took only a few seconds—she felt his hand on her butt. He took hold of the fullest part of her buttocks, which was hanging off the edge of the stool, and squeezed.

At that she leapt up, whirled around, and screamed, "Take your hand off of me and don't you ever touch me again!"

She caught a glimpse of him as he stood there with his mouth hanging open. Maybe no one had ever done that to him before in public. When Linda had told that part of the story to the grand jury, they had burst into applause. Steve Parker said he had never seen that happen before.

She had run out of the courthouse and back to the law office, burst right in on one of her bosses, and told him what had happened. He called in his partner. They were very understanding. They said that they knew Judge Lanier was like that, and they were trying to get rid of him, some-how, and she did not have to put up with that. But she had quit that job shortly thereafter. She did not want to have anything to do with the law in a town that permitted a man like that to hold such an important office. It made her literally sick to her stomach.

Castleberry arrived just as she was concluding this account. He had heard it before, but the way she was telling it now was especially impres-sive. She looked so proud, so dignified and calm, and self-respect glinted in her eyes. He had not had to coax the story out of her the first time, either; she had volunteered it. She was eager to bear witness.

And he knew she told the truth. He had verified her story by checking with the lawyers with whom she had then been working, who affirmed that she had come to them with her complaint.

But it was Louise's statement about how previous incidents of abuse could exacerbate the effects of new ones that had caught Linda Michaels's attention, she said, and that was what she wanted to talk about now. Why else, except for what she had experienced as a child and as a young woman and beyond, would she have reacted so strongly to David Lanier's groping? Why else, except that she had fought through her entire life to free herself of oppression, would she have had the guts then to scream at him and tell her to leave her alone?

Castleberry poured everyone drinks. Linda Michaels resumed her story. She had been born as the oldest of six children of itinerant farm workers in the river counties of Tennessee, she began. Their life had been very rough. Her father had been the one to beat the children, but usually this had occurred at her mother's direction. Her father would come home, for instance, and her mother would say whip this one or that one, he or she had misbehaved, and the father would comply, using his belt or a stick. The one thing in the house you could be sure of was that someone would be beaten every day.

One day when Linda was in high school her mother had chosen her for the beating, and her father had gone after her as if she had broken every commandment, flailing at her ribs, her stomach, working up to her head with his fists. When he had exhausted himself, she crawled to the bathroom, hung on to the washbasin to haul herself up, and saw in the mirror that her head was swelling up like a watermelon.

As always, they were living in a shack at that time, this one in Lake County, in the bottoms near the Mississippi. And it was winter. After the beating Linda told herself that if she did not find the strength to get out now, somehow, she would never leave and would end up broken or, like her mother, hateful, angry, ruined—if she survived at all.

She struggled painfully to the room she shared with two of her brothers and a sister and threw what she could into a gym bag, including her basketball uniform from school, where she was a star player. She laced up her basketball shoes and went out the window.

Snow was falling that evening. It was four or five miles to the one house she hoped would welcome her, where her boyfriend lived. They took her in. She stayed on there through the next year. Her family never asked after her, and when a county social worker came to her at school, she convinced him not to make her go back to them. They had moved on along the river as harvests required.

She graduated with honors from high school, but nobody told her about the scholarship for college she was qualified for—so she went to work as a stitcher in a Dyer County jeans factory. She married that boyfriend; he beat her. At the factory, she shunned the union and worked up to a management job, because of her labor-saving ideas.

Her life had never been easy. She had often changed jobs—but she was now free, twice divorced and separated from her third husband; the mother of two boys, yet on her own. She rarely saw or spoke to her parents. She was still trying to get up the nerve to break with them forever. She was currently an executive with a property management company, not rich but self-sufficient. No one like David Lanier would ever mess with her again.

Linda Michaels narrated all of this in a quiet, even voice. When she paused, her mesmerized audience of four—the two other witnesses, the professor, and the FBI agent—asked her more about her parents. Where were they? Was she going to see them this Christmas, which was only three weeks away? She sat there, a Sibyl become beautiful.

She responded by telling them one more story. When she was about twelve, she said, and living with her family in the bottoms, one of her brothers had misbehaved one day. He was only about four, as she recalled, or three or five. Whatever, on that day he was the ornery one. Her mother, frustrated that the man of the house was not around to deal out the punishment as usual, decided to take matters into her own hands. She would show that boy what was what.

She ordered all six children into the yard, where a plum tree grew, and commanded them to range themselves around the trunk of that tree and to lie down, like spokes on a wheel. Except for that young boy. He was to stand and wait to do as his mother directed. He waited under the plum tree's branches.

Linda remembered lying in the grass with her brothers and sisters, their feet pointed toward the trunk of the tree, and watching as her mother brought a bucket, turned it over and placed it on the ground next to the tree, and told her brother to take off all his clothes and stand on it.

He did as he was directed to do. He stripped naked and did as he was told. To this day, Linda could remember seeing her brother's white feet climb onto the bucket and the way his little knees knocked together, just downright clanged together. She watched as her mother knotted some rags and looped them around her brother's neck, tied the ends of the rags to a branch, said a prayer, and kicked the bucket out from under him.

He swung, her little brother did, from that tree, until he gargled and his penis grew erect and he began to spray his brothers and sisters with pee. At that point his mother cut him down.

He survived, Linda Michaels said. He was now a dope addict. She had not talked to him in years.

Vivian lay awake that night thinking about Linda and the plum tree. What unspeakable things people did to one another. Whatever had happened to her, nothing could be as horrible as that. And how lucky she was now, Vivian thought, that she had Steve Parker and Amy Spain and Dr. L. and Papa Bill to protect her.

But most of all, as she lay there sleepless, thinking about Linda Michaels, Vivian thought about Linda's courage and how, if a woman could survive all that and succeed in life in spite of it, there was all the more reason to have the courage to bring down David Lanier.

31

Louise kept a plate of chocolate cookies in the library for the women waiting to testify and for those who preferred to have company rather than remain at the hotel. Linda Michaels was always there. Louise anointed her, that was Castleberry's term, priestess of the women. For all of the unsettledness of her life, she represented independence of spirit; and she was the only one who could move between and was welcomed by the two distinct factions that developed.

Unfortunately the good girls/bad girls prejudice prevailed here among the sisterhood, too. Many of the women avoided Vivian as if she were tainted, because of her reputation for promiscuity and, especially, because of her affair with a married man. "They think I'm a slut, don't they?" she said angrily but with tears in her eyes to Louise, who had no answer to that question. Louise did her best with Linda's help to keep the factions reminded of their common cause, but she could see that some of the women resented her appeals to their common womanhood and humanity. They considered themselves on a higher moral plane.

The women would have been further divided had they known that the prosecutors ranked them according to their likely appeal to the jury. As would the director of a revue, they had to decide which numbers would be likely to play to the audience, opening with something solid; sprinkling the weaker performances through the middle, where they might be forgotten anyway; and closing with the most effective witness. Parker, Moskowitz, and Spain were unanimous in thinking Patty Wallace was their star and that they would save her for last. Sandy Sanders was chosen to lead off, with Mary Haralson going second and Vivian third.

Vivian was the big mystery. If she could endure what would certainly be very tough and embarrassing questions, the two felony counts attached to her could be the most important of all. What Parker had euphemistically referred to as her "lifestyle," however, might easily lead the jury to disbelieve everything she said.

When to call Louise to explain to the jury why the women had taken little or no action on their own was a decision left day to day.

For the time being, Louise continued in her role as counselor. On the morning when the first witness prepared to take the stand, Wednesday, December 2, Louise was there with Sandy Sanders, advising her to take deep breaths and to find a friendly face among the spectators on which to focus during her time. Sandy did not seem to need much coaching or help. In the witness room, a long, narrow place that was the last stop for witnesses before the courtroom, she prayed fervently before going out to face her ordeal.

Amy Spain questioned her for the prosecution. The prosecutors had decided who would question whom on the basis of personal rapport with each witness, familiarity with this or that count against Lanier, and individual strengths. Amy's cool intelligence was thought a good match for Sandy's emotional intensity, as if reason were interrogating emotion to the goal of truth. It seemed to work. Sandy was on the stand for nearly two hours and did not falter. When Wayne Emmons tried to get her to admit that Lanier had occasion to be displeased with her work, she reacted indignantly but answered precisely.

Hadn't she used a county car and gasoline card to run personal errands? Never, she replied, except with the judge's explicit permission, when her own car had broken down and she had gone to the doctor in Jackson. Emmons also tried to imply that it was Ms. Sanders who had approached the judge sexually rather than the other way around, and that her resentment of Lanier stemmed from his rejection of her. But Emmons quickly backed off this tactic when he sensed, or appeared to, that Sandy's personality made it less than credible.

The most dramatic moment of her testimony came when Amy Spain asked her to demonstrate how Judge Lanier had grabbed her breast and buttocks and for what length of time. Amy played Sandy, Sandy played the judge. First Amy pretended to be walking from the courtroom, and Sandy grabbed her by the haunch. Then Amy placed two straight chairs before the jury, and she and Sandy sat down side by side, as Sandy had been with Lanier in his chambers.

"Would you show the jury what happened?" Amy asked her, cool as could be, her serious face showing no more than if she had asked Sandy the time of day.

"He reached over and grabbed me," Sandy said.

"You can go ahead and show the jury how he grabbed you," Amy said.

As she repeated, "He reached over and grabbed me," showing great distress, she tentatively imitated Lanier's action, placing her hand on Amy's breast.

"He grabbed your breast?"

"He grabbed me."

"Did he squeeze your breast?"

"Yes, he did."

"Do you know how long he left his hand there?"

"A few seconds."

"Did you try to move his hand away?"

"Yes, I was pushing away," and her voice broke.

From what Parker, Moskowitz, and Louise could tell, this was a highly effective demonstration, not least of all because Sandy Sanders had such obvious difficulty in going through with it, spontaneously showing how distasteful she found it. That Amy of all people had come up with the idea herself was a source of some amazement to her colleagues, who would never have asked her to do it on their own. She, who had begun as the most skeptical among them, had come so far around that she was voluntarily subjecting herself to this difficult performance.

In the witness room, Mary Haralson was shaking so before she had to testify that Louise could hear the young woman's bracelets rattling. Louise told her that she did not have to look at Judge Lanier in the courtroom and advised her not to. Mary was having difficulty breathing at all, let alone taking the deep breaths that Louise told her would ease her anxieties.

In her notes to herself about each witness, Louise had made up a chart with the headings "Background," "Incident," and "Response," with subheadings under this last of "Avoidance," "Appeasement," and "Internal-External Response." She had written down that Mary among all the women had done the most to appease Lanier, without giving in to him, over a long period, perhaps two months; and she had never actually quit, waiting instead to be fired and coming to believe, the longer she appeased Lanier, that there must be something wrong with her. For all these reasons her nerves were close to shattering that day, as she prepared to do now what she had never been able to do on her own, to defy openly this authority figure, who she believed or knew was controlling her life still, since she had now been out of work for weeks.

Louise gave her one last hug, tried to steady her, wiped away her tears, and reminded her to look for a friendly face—Louise's, if she wished.

She started off shakily but soon settled down under Amy Spain's calm questioning, which gradually became more specific and dramatic.

"Ms. Haralson, I know this is difficult. When Judge Lanier came up behind you, where did he grab you?"

"He had his arms and he grabbed me around so that he had me basically like this." She hugged herself.

"Are you indicating that he had his arms around you?"

"Around me, yes."

"And you said he took his—"

"He took his pelvic area and pressed up against me."

"Pressed up against your buttocks?"

"Against my buttocks, yes."

"Did you feel anything?"

Mary Haralson hesitated. "Yes," she said.

"Ms. Haralson, could you feel his penis against you?"

"Yes, I could."

"Could you feel if it was erect?"

"Yes, it was." Her voice broke. She took a breath. "I would say I could feel it."

"Could you tell if that is what he was rubbing against your buttocks?"

"That is what he was rubbing against me, yes."

"How long do you think he did that before you yelled to leave you alone?"

"Just a few seconds. As soon as I felt it, it was just like all I could do was just jump. I just jumped."

Amy asked if Lanier still had on his judicial robe, and Mary replied that he had. This was an important question, not only for the disturbing image it conveyed but because Amy wanted to establish that this even had occurred "under color of law," as the statute required.

At Amy's invitation, Mary came down from the witness chair into the well of the court and demonstrated what she had described, after pointing out the exact location of the incident, the filing room, on a large diagram of Lanier's courtroom and its adjoining offices. Amy played Mary, Mary played the judge, grabbing Amy from behind and grinding her pelvis into Amy's buttocks. The courtroom was very quiet.

Steve Parker studied the jurors' faces as this demonstration was taking place. A few of them looked disturbed—but whether by the idea that Judge Lanier had acted in this way or by the sight of two women engaged in a sexual pantomime was anyone's guess. Amy made sure, since she and Mary were about the same size, to remind the jury through questions that Lanier towered over his secretary.

In his cross-examination Wayne Emmons tried to get Mary to admit that she had been an incompetent employee. She was obviously offended and disturbed by this imputation, including the allegation that she had worn inappropriate clothing, such as a sleeveless knit top, to the office.

"I don't own any sleeveless knit tops," she said, adding that she would certainly never wear one to work. Emmons kept at this angle, implying that she was flirtatious and that she had quit because Lanier refused her advances. She insisted that she had, on the contrary, been fired, even though her termination papers stated that she had left of her own accord.

"You were very angry at this entire episode, correct?" Emmons asked.

"I was hurt."

"I'm not talking about the allegations of being touched."

"I was hurt," she repeated, holding back tears, saying that she had tried to hang on to her job because she needed it. Her husband had quit working the late shift to have some time with his wife and son. But his new job as a surveyor depended on good weather, and the spring rains had reduced his income to about a hundred dollars a week. When she was fired, they were in serious financial trouble.

She did not mention that they were quarreling again now, and that she was running an enormous risk by testifying—that she and her husband felt every day the scorn of people who seemed to think she was betraying her hometown by standing up for her rights.

Mary Haralson managed to control her emotions until she was back in the witness room, collapsing in Louise's arms. Her husband was not there to comfort her, because she, as did all the other wives among the witnesses, felt it would be too difficult for a husband to hear such intimate details discussed before a room full of spectators and reporters. The media kept to the convention of not naming names, but that was a thin shield in a town where anyone reading either the Memphis or the Dyersburg paper or watching summaries of the testimony on television could identify the witnesses with little effort.

The *State Gazette,* which by then had printed three editorials calling for Lanier to step down, now called the proceedings "ugly but necessary." The "sordid allegations" against Judge Lanier were troubling. "It is not pleasant to see our community's name associated with such things." It would be worse to leave such allegations unresolved.

It was not that the women were without support in their town. Mary Haralson's cousin loyally stood by her and testified that Mary had complained bitterly to her about Lanier's behavior at the time it had been going on. But husbands grew impatient with the effect that the stress of testifying was having on family and sex lives; some in their rage at the judge and embarrassment over the revelations became impotent. Jennifer Gallagher's parents were especially angry at her for testifying at all, even when she tried to explain that she could not perjure herself.

*   *   *

The night before Vivian was scheduled to testify, Bill and Louise were
already into a routine they figured would last the length of the trial, taking
whichever women wanted to go out to dinner, to keep them company and
try to distract them from their anxieties. Bill knew Memphis intimately
from his days as a student and a Shelby County deputy and prided himself on ferreting out pleasant, middle-priced restaurants, especially in the
midtown area, near the medical center. When he had been a deputy, he
told Louise, when Memphis was still segregated by law and custom and
when the division between the races worked both ways—with whites no
more daring to enter black establishments than the other way around—he
had been able to visit the late-night clubs where blues musicians, then
unknown to the white world, played. His badge had been his passport,
and he had cultivated his love of jazz and blues in anonymous, funky
joints strung out along Highway 51 south of town. These black clubs,
where the music that had already begun to sweep the world fermented,
had no signs to mark them; you had to know them and, if you were the
rare white and a cop like Castleberry, be trusted to let the music roll and
ignore the pungent reefer smell for the privilege of hearing geniuses like
Memphis Piano Red or wild new groups like the Hot Nuts, who rocked
away the night clad only in fluorescent jockstraps when they weren't freeing college kids of their inhibitions on Eastern college campuses. That
secret, joyful, mournful scene haunted Castleberry now, being around
these women who blurted out their tales of loss and anger and courage
like so many cascades of blue notes. When Linda Michaels told the story
of the plum tree, he could almost hear Piano Red picking out the chords.
That week everybody sang the blues.

That night Vivian had wanted to stay in her room, but Bill and Louise
coaxed her out to Anderton's, a simple steak and seafood place that felt
like thirty years ago, a neighborhood hangout warm with talk and laughter. Even at those modest prices, Bill knew that by the end of the evening
he would be another hundred or so in the hole, especially when Linda
said she wanted "a martini as big as I am." He was covering out of his
own pocket what the government allowance, twenty-six dollars a day per
witness, did not; there would be nightcaps back at the Crowne Plaza.
When Louise found out what he was doing, she offered to split the difference with him, but he refused. She informed the prosecutors, who said
they would help Bill out of their own pockets when the trial was over.
Louise told Castleberry, but from his reaction was willing to bet that he
would never submit an accounting.

Each night, it seemed, was someone else's turn to bare her soul, usually on the eve of her testimony. Linda Michaels was scheduled for

tomorrow along with Vivian and Cathy Kiely, but Kiely did not mix much with the others and kept to her room, and Linda had already told her life history. Vivian no longer drank much, but that night she had more than usual and before long the tears were flowing and she was talking about her mother and her father and her marriage—and David Lanier.

Bill and Louise tried to calm her down, but they became a torrent, these chapters from her fragile life.

Perhaps they ought to have let her stay in her room after all, Bill said to Louise after they had more or less carried Vivian upstairs. Louise did not agree. If Vivian trusted everyone enough to unload like that, it meant she believed she had some friends in the world. It should make her stronger.

But you never knew.

32

Compared to the first two witnesses, Vivian showed by far the most evidence of panic as she waited in the witness room before testifying that Thursday morning. Part of the problem was the length of time she had to spend in there, nearly an hour while the prosecutors argued with Wayne Emmons before Judge Turner, with the jury still sequestered in its room, about whether the defense should be permitted to question Vivian about her drug use and sex life.

The defense strategy was now emerging, after only hints of it with Sandy Sanders and Mary Haralson. Whether Emmons had come to his decision himself or was being directed by his client—the prosecutors strongly believed the latter—he had decided to attempt to undercut the felony charges by destroying the witness.

In the bench conference, Emmons began by arguing for the inclusion of evidence of Vivian's drug use because, among other reasons having to do with memory loss and lack of personal control, it spoke to a contempt for the law. Not only was possession illegal but, Emmons claimed, there was evidence that Vivian had traded sex for drugs, which meant engaging in prostitution. There was also evidence, he said, that she had given her brother drugs as a birthday present, which meant she had engaged in delivery of narcotics, a separate felony.

Emmons moved on to his argument for inclusion of material concerning her sexual behavior, which would make the idea that she had been raped highly doubtful. He proposed to develop proof of "consistent, widespread, far-ranging, far-reaching totality of sexual indulgence and sexual misconduct that would penetrate to the very heart of her character."

Judge Turner asked Emmons to state what he hoped to elicit from Vivian Forsythe by questioning her. Emmons went straight to the point.

"Your Honor, I expect this witness to be shown to be called by the term 'the blow job queen of Dyer County or Dyersburg, Tennessee.' That she has bragged herself about the number of sexual escapades she has had with different men." She had "hopped in and out of one bed after another," exhibiting "a pervasive attitude of immorality that the jury, in order to examine her credibility, should be able to hear about."

Judge Turner asked Emmons whether the defense was that Ms. Forsythe had consented to sex with Judge Lanier.

"No, Your Honor," Emmons said. "The defense is denial" that any sexual act took place between Judge Lanier and Ms. Forsythe.

In that case, Judge Turner replied, to admit evidence of prior or other sexual conduct would be both contrary to law and contrary to common sense: "To take the position that, no, I didn't have sex with her, period, but look at all the other men she had sex with, fails to prove [the defendant's] position. Instead, it tends to show that they did have sex, and that it was some sort of consensual sex. But his position is that they didn't have sex at all. How this other extrinsic evidence about other men at other times, not involved in this case whatsoever, could have any relevance to a defense that it didn't happen, period, escapes me."

Judge Turner did permit, however, examination of the witness, away from the jury, to begin with at least, on the subject of her drug use. He ordered Vivian brought in.

Steve Parker intercepted her in the hallway to warn her what was about to take place. He had hoped it would not happen. Was she prepared to answer what would surely prove to be some very embarrassing questions? Vivian said she was. She did not, however, look like it.

This was exactly what Parker had feared. How Vivian was going to endure public exposure of her personal life, he had no idea. He did believe one primary thing about Vivian, however: that she was honest, painfully so. Whatever happened, she would tell the truth.

She took the witness stand and looked out over the spectators and could find no friendly face, until Louise came in through the side door and took her usual seat. She felt Lanier staring at her from the defense table and stared back at him. Steve Parker's voice broke the spell. She answered the usual preliminaries. He asked her how old she had been when she first used drugs. She said about sixteen.

"Are you currently using drugs?"

"No, I am not."

"Would you just give us a list of what drugs you have used?"

"I have used just about everything," Vivian said. "I have used marijuana. Alcohol. Valiums, Xanax. I have tripped on LSD. I have used Mepergan, cocaine. Hashish. Just, you know—"

"Would it be safe to say that at some point you were a drug addict?"

"Yes."

She mentioned various treatment programs she had been through, said that her father was an alcoholic, that she had used drugs on a daily basis, except during pregnancy, for nine or ten years. She had been off hard drugs for a year but had continued smoking pot until three months ago. She was now off everything, except for the occasional drink.

With everything now up front, Parker was ready to turn, if he could, Vivian's honesty to the prosecution's advantage by showing a correlation between her increased use of hard drugs and the incidents in David Lanier's chambers. Vivian stated that it was after her traumatic experiences with Lanier that she had "started getting really bad into cocaine. And then to come down off of cocaine, I started taking Mepergan.

"And then"—her voice began to falter—"I got really bad into running Mepergan with a needle and IV."

Here she broke down. Parker asked the judge for permission to bring the witness some Kleenex and diverted her emotions momentarily by having her discuss the success she had had in staying off drugs and in working for the Orlando law firm. When he asked her whether drugs had affected the clarity of her memories of the incidents with Lanier, however, she broke down again, because the answer was no.

Vivian had been so straightforward with Steve Parker that there was not much else Wayne Emmons could ask her about her drug use. During his cross-examination of her, David Lanier frequently summoned Emmons to the defense table to confer, after which Emmons would ask the witness questions about specific drugs—mushrooms, for instance, which Vivian allowed were one of the few hallucinatory substances she had never tried. She said that most of her experimentation had been in high school and that her heavy use of hard drugs had occurred after her experiences with Lanier.

After all this, Judge Turner barred any questions whatever before the jury about prior sexual experience or drug use. Emmons would be permitted to ask about the Bahamas trip, but not in relation to sex.

Parker believed he had scored a victory. Neither he nor Judge Turner nor Wayne Emmons, however, was taking into account the degree of Vivian's honesty.

Judge Turner ordered the jury brought in. Now came the real test.

Vivian broke down frequently as Steve Parker led her through the history of her family troubles, her divorce, her father's hostility when she did not have a job after her surgery in the summer of 1990—everything that led to her going to Judge Lanier's chambers to apply for the secretary's job and his forcing oral sex on her. Parker was excruciatingly specific with his questions.

"I know this is hard, Ms. Forsythe. When you say Judge Lanier put himself in your mouth, what did you mean?"

"He had exposed himself," Vivian said, gripping the arms of the witness chair, her voice quavering. "And he had me by the hair and he had—he had an erection and he stuck his penis in my mouth and he kept moving his pelvis back and forth."

"Did he have an orgasm?"

"Yes. Yes," she said, crying.

She described how she had gone into the bathroom afterward.

"How did you feel?"

"I felt dirty."

She explained how she had driven to her father's farm in order to collect herself before facing her family and her daughter and how she had tried to bury this and the subsequent incident and why she had not reported either.

"It wouldn't have done any good," she said.

"Why is that?"

"He was the judge. It wouldn't have mattered. Nobody would listen and I would look like a fool."

"Did you go tell the District Attorney's Office, the prosecutor?"

"God, no!"

"Why not?"

"It was his brother!"

Parker asked her why she had taken a bath after she got home that day. He knew that this action was typical of rape victims and let Vivian make the point that she had felt so dirty and defiled that she hoped she could wash the experience away.

Parker turned to what the prosecution considered perhaps the most crucial area of credibility, why Vivian had not told a soul, or had done so only indirectly. He had, of course, the Anita Hill precedent in mind.

"Why did you not tell anybody the details?"

"Because I still thought that they would blame me and that if I told people—I was embarrassed of it. I was humiliated. I didn't want to tell them that this man did this to me and that I wasn't weak—I mean, that I wasn't strong. Everybody thought I was a strong person and it would admit weakness."

She went on to describe the second incident and how she had gotten herself into that vulnerable position again because of pressure from her parents, with Parker by means of his questions eliciting from her the degree of physical harm suffered—how she had found her hair coming out afterward, the pains in her jaw, the bruises.

"Ms. Forsythe, I hate to be so graphic. Why did you have to go to the bathroom both times?"

"Because I had his—I had his in my mouth. He had an orgasm in my mouth."

"Semen?"

"Yes."

"You had to spit it out?"

"Yes," and she sobbed and covered her face with her hands.

Parker's own voice cracked at this point. He was afraid he was going to burst out crying or throw up or both, and he asked Vivian if she would like to take a break—as much for himself as for her.

"No," she said, looking up, gasping for breath, trying to straighten her shoulders. "I want to go on."

And she did, and her strength lifted Steve Parker up. He thought he could ask this woman anything and through her tears she would tell the truth. She described how frightened she had been in the ensuing weeks and months that Judge Lanier would ruin her, even more than she was already ruined, and take Ashley away from her as he had hinted he would. And she described the trip to the Bahamas with Lanier and Dr. Warner. Parker did not want to avoid that episode, only to have Emmons bring it out as he was sure to do, because Judge Turner had given him permission to do so. She described how Lanier had propositioned her on the beach and how she had rejected him and refused to solicit one of her friends to join him in Nassau.

Parker had carefully laid the groundwork for his final direct questioning of Vivian. The day before, Judge Turner had permitted Amy Spain to demonstrate physically with Sandy Sanders and Mary Haralson what Judge Lanier had done to them. It had been Amy's idea to engage in the same sort of dramatic representation with Vivian—a much more controversial tactic, since this involved simulating not only touching and grabbing but actual rape. Amy had discussed the possibility of the maneuver with other female attorneys in the office; all had advised her against it and were astonished that someone as outwardly low-key as Amy Spain would even suggest it. But Judge Turner had already accepted the tactic with other witnesses. He could hardly overrule himself now. Amy wanted to risk trying it with Vivian.

Parker and Moskowitz agreed. Something told the prosecutors that such a reenactment might have a more powerful effect on the jury than any merely verbal description—if it did not so offend them that they thought the prosecution had gone too far and had descended into mere sensationalism.

It did seem a bit too much to have Parker play the Judge Lanier role. Why not have the two women enact the demonstration, as before? Parker asked Judge Turner's permission to do so, and the judge granted it, and Amy came forward.

Vivian was crying again as Parker arranged chairs in the well of the court to represent Judge Lanier's chambers. First Vivian played herself as Amy took her by the wrist and whipped her around a space meant to represent Lanier's desk.

"Can you do this?" Parker asked Vivian, who nodded, crying. "All right. Now, switch around and let Amy be you. You do what the judge did."

The two women faced each other. They were about the same size, each with brown hair—but all at once they were metamorphosed, become man and woman, rapist and victim—as Vivian grabbed Amy by the hair.

"I was turning my head back and forth," Vivian said as she clutched Amy's hair, and Amy started twisting her head and flailing her arms as if trying to push Lanier away. "And I was crying and he was pulling my hair and then he grabbed me right here real hard," and she put her fingers around Amy's neck. Everything she said, she demonstrated as Amy wriggled in her grip. "And he started grabbing me around the neck and started reaching under my shirt and then he started fondling my breast and everything. And I was fighting, pushing, trying to push him away. And he kept trying to kiss on me. And then he grabbed me by the hair again and slammed me into the chair."

"Show us how he put you in the chair," Parker said.

Vivian slammed Amy down into the chair and stood over her, straddling her.

"And then he still had me by the hair with one hand and he started undoing himself and exposed himself." She brushed her free hand against her skirt. "And he tried to put himself in my jaws. Tried to get me open." She pressed her thumbs against Amy's jaws. Amy opened her mouth. "And then he put his penis inside of my mouth!" Vivian was sobbing now.

"Okay," Parker said. "It's okay."

"And then when he had an orgasm he stepped back and just went and sat at his desk like nothing happened. And I ran into the bathroom."

Not wishing to interrupt the momentum of this drama, Parker led the women through the second incident, asking, "Was he standing with his knee in front of Amy's knee like you have?" Who was who? The transformation was complete, no play depicting the switching of sexual identities ever more convincing, or so disturbing.

"All right," Parker said. "I hate to do this. When he had himself in your mouth, show us how he had your head."

Vivian demonstrated with Amy, who arched her neck back.

"He had me by both hands then, and he kept moving and I was just— my cheeks were like paralyzed, and he just kept on. And when I tried to rare back, he just pushed harder and he pulled my hair and he would squeeze me real tight back in the neck muscles. The more I tried to twist and turn, you know, the more it hurt worse. And I was gagging!"

"All right, Ms. Forsythe. You may take your seat."

And Amy Spain straightened her suit and returned to the prosecution table.

Parker asked a couple more questions, but he was through, and he felt weak. He could only imagine what Vivian was feeling. His strongest impulse was to walk over and hug her and apologize for what he had put her through. A mixture of admiration and compassion and guilt coursed through him. He requested a recess, which Judge Turner readily granted. Everyone would have fifteen minutes to compose themselves before the cross-examination began.

Louise didn't move. She was sitting in her seat in the courtroom crying. Then she thought she had better go help Vivian in the witness room. She saw people sitting numb and dumb and a few straggling out for a breath of fresh air. It was as if everyone had been witness to something very strange and powerful and horrible—a violent crime and its aftermath.

The marshals escorted Vivian back to the witness room. Judge Turner had instructed her not to talk to anyone about the case during the break, but Louise was permitted in to comfort her and found her curled up in a fetal position on a couch.

Steve Parker came upon the official court reporter, Sharlyn Phillips, a middle-aged woman whom he had always admired for her professionalism, sitting in her small office off the courtroom, weeping, it seemed, uncontrollably. He put a hand on her shoulder.

"Are you going to be able to go on, Sharlyn?" he asked.

She said she would get herself together.

"Vivian Forsythe was doing this for all of us," she managed to say, and blurted out that one of the reasons she was so moved was that she, too, had been raped—by a man who had stalked her for fifteen years, before she finally left her home state and moved to Memphis. She said she would tell Parker more about it some other time. Her ex-husband had raped her when she was pregnant with twins. He had nearly killed her.

"My God" was all Parker could say.

"Do you know what that man did?"

"Your ex-husband?"

"No. David Lanier. He winked at me when I came into court this morning. And when we had that bench conference?"

"Yes?"

"He was trying to rub up against me. I swear he was."

Judge Turner had closed the door on Wayne Emmons's asking Vivian about drugs; but within less than a minute after the trial resumed with cross-examination, Vivian had opened it. It was that honesty of hers again.

She responded to a question about why she had voluntarily given up custody of her daughter by replying that she had to get her life back together.

"You had to get your life back together," Emmons said. "What do you mean by that?"

"I mean," Vivian said, "that after the incidents, I got heavily into drugs, and I got—"

Steve Parker was on his feet and asking to approach the bench, but it was too late. Although Judge Turner restricted Emmons from asking anything else about drugs, he permitted him to clarify his original question and have the witness answer it. Again, Vivian volunteered that she had been heavily into drugs.

Emmons's cross-examination took about an hour and a half, which meant that Vivian spent more than three hours under examination that morning. Although she continued to choke up and cry every so often, she seemed to gain confidence the longer she was under the gun. The most difficult time for her with Emmons was when he asked her about her family background and why she had had a warrant issued for her parents' arrests on kidnapping charges one year and given custody of Ashley to her mother the next. She replied, trembling with emotion, that in spite of all they had been through, she believed that her mother loved her and Ashley and was taking good care of the child while Vivian got through this trial and tried to reorder her life in Florida.

"You have to think about money," Vivian said. She had had none. Was she supposed to take her child to a strange city and risk not being able to give her enough to eat? Sometimes you had to make hard choices when life did things to you and you made serious mistakes, as she was ready to admit she had.

In trying to answer what were probably Emmons's most damaging questions, concerning why and how she could have returned to Judge

Lanier's chambers for the second incident after he had so brutalized her, Vivian could only reiterate the pressure she was under from her parents, especially her mother, to see the judge about a job with Dr. Warner, with whom she admitted having an affair. It had been a desperate period.

"I want to ask you this final question," Emmons said. Had she not told Charles Kelly and several employees in Kelly's office, "'I hate that SOB, Judge Lanier'?"

"Did I say that?" Vivian asked.

"Yes."

"Yes, I did. I was very angry at him for invading me and taking away my rights."

"Because he wouldn't hear your custody matter?"

"No," Vivian replied, evenly this time, forcefully but coolly. "I was very angry because he forced me to do things that I didn't want to do." Her voice rose as she became vehement. "And I have my rights as a human being and as a citizen of these United States that were taken away from me! And I hate him for that!"

Her statement was so strong and so eloquent that it set the defense attorney back on his heels for a moment.

"Now," Emmons said, slowly, "the phrase you just used, your rights as a citizen of the United States. Were these told to you—was that phrase told to you by the government lawyer? Is that what he said to you?"

"No," Vivian replied. "No, it was not." She bristled, and she drew herself up as she had not had the strength to do before. "I am an intelligent woman. And I have rights as a United States citizen!" Here she started crying again. "There is a Bill of Rights! And I have those!"

"Nobody ever told you that is what this case is about?"

"Not at all. That is how I felt when I left that room. My rights had been taken away from me!"

There was a pause.

"That is all I have," Wayne Emmons said.

"Redirect?" Judge Turner asked Steve Parker.

"No questions, Your Honor," Parker said. "Thank you, Ms. Forsythe."

And all Louise Fitzgerald could think, sitting in the front row and trying unsuccessfully to hold back her tears, was, *Oh, my God.*

33

Louise tried to convey to Bill Castleberry what Vivian had been like, how she had looked, what she had said, the effect she had made—but found words inadequate. It had been a "peak experience," Louise said, nearly overcome in the telling of it. She had glimpsed Sharlyn Phillips toward the end, having heard from Steve Parker during the break how affected the court reporter had been by Vivian and Amy's reenactment of the rapes. When Vivian had spoken her defense of her rights and women's rights and the Bill of Rights and citizenship itself, a speech that ought to enter the anthologies, Sharlyn had been weeping over her steno machine—that was what Vivian had been like.

And a TV reporter had whispered to Louise afterward, "Build the gallows."

Louise was talking to Bill and to Steve Champine, who was also barred from the courtroom, in the law library, where everyone was gathered, hugging Vivian and congratulating her. Vivian herself was numb, as if she'd been sandbagging against a flood. She sat at the big table exhausted, a blank, lonely expression on her face. She did not seem to comprehend the strength she had projected in that courtroom or the truths she had summoned from her heart. She looked lost.

The rest of the day was somewhat anticlimactic. Cathy Kiely was adequate on the stand, everyone thought; Linda Michaels very strong, impressive. But Vivian, Vivian! Among themselves the prosecutors agreed that they wished they had saved Vivian for the final witness. Would the jury's memory of her fade after several more witnesses? How could they have known that the most flawed victim of all would turn out to be a gem, an orator, with the courage of a warrior?

Tomorrow was an off day, with the weekend ahead. The trial would not resume until Monday, December 7. In the meantime, everyone was scattering.

Louise embraced Vivian to say good-bye. Vivian would spend the weekend in Dyersburg and return. Of course she could stay until the verdict came in, Louise and Bill assured her. They would all meet back at the Crowne Plaza on Sunday night, along with the witnesses who had yet to testify and Linda Michaels, whom Louise asked to stick around.

It was raining when Bill drove Louise to the Amtrak station that evening. She would be home in Champaign-Urbana by half-past ten. Her husband would meet her and she would try to tell him what had happened that week.

"Do you think you can?" Bill asked her, helping her up the steps of her train car.

"I'll try," she said.

She let Bill carry her bag into the train.

She watched as he stood on the platform waving to her as the *City of New Orleans* pulled out. *Goddamn him,* she mumbled to herself. *He's wearing a trench coat and he looks like Robert Taylor in* Waterloo Bridge.

Castleberry made a point of checking up on Vivian that rainy weekend. Donna Whittle, who was attending the trial, identified her in Friday's edition of the *State Gazette* as "a 26-year-old woman" and provided extensive details of Vivian's testimony, including references to disputes with her parents over custody of her daughter.

When Castleberry reached her by telephone at the Forsythe house, Vivian said she could not talk. All hell had broken loose at home. She had not told her parents what she would say in court beforehand, but to them she was easily identifiable from the newspaper story. Everyone was in hysterics. Her sister definitely planned to testify for Lanier, to discredit Vivian, who might have to return to Memphis before Sunday, the way things were going.

"You have my pager," Castleberry told her. "Don't hesitate to use it."

He also contacted Jennifer Gallagher, who was scheduled to testify on Monday and who like Vivian was not telling anyone beforehand what she planned to say under oath. Jennifer was in a panic and asked once again to be relieved of the responsibility. Castleberry said only that he looked forward to seeing her again on Sunday.

He was in Dyersburg on business for the prosecutors, who were anxious to cover every base. Al Moskowitz reminded everyone that corroboration might be the key to the credibility of some of the victims' testimony. With a few, such as Vivian, there was none, a his-word-against-hers situation. Linda Michaels, however, had been impressive in backing up Cathy Kiely; so had Mary Haralson's cousin in saying that Mary had confided in her about Lanier. Two women, located back in December 1991, were ready to corroborate Patty Wallace when she testified about her distress on the day Lanier assaulted her. Castleberry's assignment that weekend was to locate at least one other such witness, who could reinforce Janet Thomasson's testimony.

Janet, however, had not volunteered anyone's name. It was only through the hip-pocket informant that Castleberry had discovered Thomasson in the first place, and that source had nothing firsthand to offer, only what she had heard from some unknown friend of Thomasson's.

Castleberry located the hip pocket, to whom he had not spoken for over a year. From her he got the name of Thomasson's friend, contacted her, and arranged to see her.

She ran a beauty shop. Castleberry met her there on Saturday night and drove her around as he interviewed her. The woman was frightened. She loved Janet but had a boyfriend who she was afraid would beat her up if she had anything to do with the police. She did not have to add that this particular "Billy Badass" must be involved in drugs, the reason for his insistence on privacy. He also did not care for Janet and would be furious to learn of any links among his girlfriend, Janet, the police, the Justice Department, and the most highly publicized case in the region within memory.

The woman admitted that Janet had indeed spoken to her about what Lanier had done. The conversation had taken place on the evening after the incident. Janet had been extremely upset. She had been the featured speaker at lunch that day, before some civic group or other, talking about her work with juveniles and their parents. She had gone from there to see the judge, who had treated her lower than dirt.

Castleberry got from the woman an account of what Janet had told her that squared with what Janet had told him and the grand jury. Was there anything else? He gave her his perjury speech, which applied to testifying under oath in court as to a grand jury appearance. He was sorry if it caused her trouble with Billy Badass, but she could well be subpoenaed next week.

There was something else, the woman admitted. After Janet had described the incident in the judge's office, she had pulled up her shirt and undone her bra and shown her friend some odd-looking bruises on the outer side of each breast and on her rib cage. Janet was puzzled by these, she said, because nothing Judge Lanier had done to her could have caused them. She could not figure out how she had got them.

"You saw them yourself?" Castleberry asked. The woman said she had. "Would you mind describing them?"

She said they were like scrapes. The skin had been rubbed raw. They were virtually identical on both sides of Janet's chest.

As soon as he could get to a phone, Castleberry reached Steve Parker at home and described the bruises or scrapes to him.

"Lanier raped Janet Thomasson," Parker said immediately.

"It sure sounds like it," Castleberry said.

Both men recognized the injuries as signs of an oral rape performed with the man straddling the chest of a prone victim, male or female. The marks were inflicted by the rapist's knees as he gripped the victim with his legs and thrust at the mouth.

"What're we going to do about it?" Castleberry said. "Obviously Janet hasn't told us everything."

"We better think it over before we do anything," Parker said. "I'll get hold of Amy and Al."

By Sunday night Janet Thomasson was staying at the Crowne Plaza along with Jennifer Gallagher, Linda Michaels, Vivian, Louise, and Bill. Julia Garnett, who was scheduled as the first witness the next morning, preferred to drive in from Dyersburg.

It was also the eve of Jennifer's appearance in court, as she was the second witness scheduled for tomorrow, and she was unable to stop crying, even with Vivian and Louise alternately holding her and assuring her that she would do well on the stand. She remained confused about the wording of the indictment in respect to her, Count Ten, and its reference to her having incurred "bodily injury" as the result of Judge Lanier's assault. She had not been injured, she said, as she had told Lanier when he had been recording her. She knew what it was to be injured. Men had hit her, blackened her eyes and broken her bones. Lanier had not done that. Her father had beaten her, right through high school; she knew what that meant.

Louise tried once again, as the prosecutors already had, to get her to understand what was meant in the indictment by bodily injury, in her case.

"When Lanier forced you onto the sleeping bag and had sex with you, you didn't want to do it, did you?"

"No," Jennifer said, "I was afraid of him."

"So you weren't ready. You know what I mean?"

"Yes."

Although everyone understood the implications, Louise hoped that Al

Moskowitz, who was going to question Jennifer on the stand, would be able to phrase matters delicately or scientifically enough to avoid either confusing her or frightening her and making her freak out.

Jennifer was especially horrified at the idea of discussing these matters in court because of something a woman in her office had said to her on Friday when she was back at work. Apparently it was now common knowledge in the office that Jennifer was going to testify that the judge had forced actual intercourse on her in his chambers. The woman had asked Jennifer about the size of Judge Lanier's penis. Was he big?

"How would I know?" Jennifer had said, starting to cry. "I didn't look at him and I didn't feel anything. You're disgusting to ask!"

She asked Louise if anyone would ask such a question in court. Of course not, Louise assured her.

Let's hope not, Louise said to herself.

The prosecutors suspected that Count Nine of the indictment, involving Julia Garnett, might be in trouble when Judge Turner questioned whether exposing oneself under color of law was actually a violation of 18 § 242. The judge reserved ruling on this point; the prosecutors could only hope that Garnett's account of the episode would be sufficient to show that the psychological shock resulting from this incident made Lanier's behavior a violation beyond doubt.

Al Moskowitz conducted the examination of Julia Garnett. She had known David Lanier long enough to call him by his first name, she said, when she went to him in March of 1991 to have her divorce set aside. She and her husband had changed their minds and had gone back together the day after the decree was final. The property settlement on which they had agreed was now a nuisance to both of them.

She had explained this to Judge Lanier while sitting opposite him in his chambers. When she was through with her request, Lanier had stood up. He unzipped his pants, took out his penis, which was erect, and began masturbating with both hands as he walked slowly toward her. He stopped a couple of feet from where she was sitting paralyzed with shock, and he began talking. "As long as I've known you," she quoted him as saying, "I've always wanted you to do this. Come on, touch me, feel it, go down on me, make me feel good."

She had stood up, protesting, but hardly able to believe this was happening. "No, David, I can't do that, please don't make me," she said, in several different ways.

Eventually he had put his genitals back in his trousers and zipped himself up. Then she had put an arm around him and said, "David, please don't be mad at me."

When she returned to work at Heckethorn Manufacturing, an auto parts factory where she was a machine operator, the experience weighed on her to the extent that she cried and told two of her co-workers what had happened. It was not that someone had done this to her; it was that David Lanier had done it. He was the most powerful man in town, and she had respected him. It was as if the judge had told her that she wasn't worth two cents. The experience had been shattering.

Al Moskowitz brought out that Julia Garnett's marriage, though long, had been a rocky one. She and her husband had divorced and remarried twice; in 1991 they had wanted, in effect, to marry each other a third time, but were in fact still divorced. She was now in her late forties, with five grown children, all by her ex-husband.

Wayne Emmons did his best to portray her as an unstable person with a penchant for filing lawsuits. She had made formal complaints to her bosses twice, charging sexual harassment, receiving a fifteen-hundred-dollar out-of-court settlement for one of these. Over Moskowitz's objection that it was irrelevant, Emmons also brought out that she had filed a complaint with the Equal Employment Opportunity Commission on grounds of age discrimination, but had dropped it. As was now a pattern, the defense's tactic was to portray the victim as unstable, promiscuous, degenerate, unreliable, a liar, or a publicity seeker—any combination or all of these—and to depict the government as intrusive and politically motivated.

Whether the defense would add to this strategy Lanier's admitting that he had had consensual sex with some of these women remained to be seen. That was still the one gambit most feared by the prosecution. For now, the demeaning of the witnesses, however it may be affecting the jury, was certainly having an effect on the women. Even Julia Garnett, who had been cool enough to talk David Lanier out of his erection, left the witness stand shaken and in tears and, it was a safe bet, wishing she had never been subpoenaed.

Bill Castleberry dreaded Jennifer Gallagher's turn on the stand. If frailty had ever been a woman's name, it was Jennifer's. In this one instance, Bill was relieved not to have to watch the spectacle in person. It was possible to argue that the experience of unburdening herself about David Lanier had been tonic for Vivian. Knowing she would testify had motivated her to kick her drug habit; it was not in her nature to be able to live with secrets and lies. But Jennifer had, from what Bill could observe, degenerated steadily since he had first met her. How would she endure the public airing of what she had done her best to conceal? Her entire personality, like her voice, was constructed on the premise that if you avoid unpleasantness, it will go away. Now there would be no avoiding anything.

She wept throughout as Al Moskowitz, his efforts to be sensitive overwhelmed by the sordidness of what he had to make Jennifer say, drew out of her the story of the sleeping bag and the hundred dollars she had kept, she said, because she needed it for her child. Moskowitz also had her confirm what she had told him only that morning, having concealed it until now from embarrassment, that the entire time that she had talked to Lanier in the filing room last July, when Lanier had taped her, with her mother just the other side of a door that was slightly ajar, the judge had been rubbing on her crotch. She had been too frightened to run.

Moskowitz's rationale for introducing this revelation was that it showed that even when prohibited from so much as contacting a witness, Lanier was assaulting one. But to Jennifer it was fresh humiliation to have to admit in public that she had, once again, endured sexual contact with Lanier. She had already been so ashamed of this indignity that she had concealed it even from the prosecutors as long as she felt she could.

There were other indignities revealed. Because it was relevant to her having accepted the money, whatever the circumstances of its delivery, her affair with a married man, which had begun while she was going through her second divorce, also became public record. He was wealthy; she admitted that he had become a "sugar daddy" to her, paying her rent and bestowing other gifts on her at a time when she had been desperate and hated having to rely on her parents to support her child. The affair had ended only when her lover's wife overheard him talking to Jennifer on the phone. His gifts to her had quickly diminished and then stopped. She said she had been very much in love with him—but how did her moral compromises sound, never mind to the jury, to the public?

To Al Moskowitz, who remained the most sympathetic of the prosecutors to Jennifer, none of this mattered. Her economic desperation was precisely why Lanier had preyed on her with his endless phone calls and, ultimately, with his sexual assault. Jennifer more than any other witness—at least Vivian's parents had money, though they insisted that she work—was the archetype of the Lanier victim: her life unstable, insecure, and dependent on the judge's power over divorce, child support, and custody.

But Moskowitz's primary purpose was to convict Lanier. As aware as he was of Jennifer's predicament, this case had to come first, the welfare of witnesses second, whatever his compassion for any of them.

Watching her agony on the stand and seeing the condition she was in after testifying—she looked broken—Louise Fitzgerald became as concerned about Jennifer as Castleberry was. Jennifer had cried throughout her three hours up there, especially under Wayne Emmons's unsparing cross-examination, which concentrated on her financial need and attempted to leave the impression that for several years she had been more than willing to trade sex for money. Nor did Jennifer have either the emotional or the intellectual strength to rise up at the end, or at any point, with a burst of eloquence. It was a wonder that she had managed not to collapse.

Jennifer was prepared to return to Dyersburg at the end of the afternoon. At the last minute in court, however, after Jennifer had left the stand, Wayne Emmons had attempted to recall her. He had just learned from his client, Emmons said, that a tape or possibly two tapes existed on which Jennifer Gallagher could be heard asking to visit Judge Lanier in his office. Emmons did not have the tapes available yet, but he wished to interrogate the witness about them.

Judge Turner had denied this request but left Emmons with the possibility of introducing the tapes when they were ready. It was possible that Jennifer would be recalled, so she would remain in Memphis another night.

Louise was glad of the opportunity to see more of Jennifer and try to comfort her; and Vivian was happy for the extra company and the chance to help, knowing so well what Jennifer had just been through.

There were six who set out for dinner that night from the Crowne Plaza to the North End for dinner: Bill as usual at the wheel; Louise in the passenger seat of the car she now called Big Blue; and crammed into the backseat Vivian, Jennifer, Linda Michaels, and Janet Thomasson, who would be the first witness tomorrow morning.

They were only a block or so from the hotel when it happened. Bill was joking that he was going to have a hard time returning to regular FBI duties. He was beginning to enjoy his role as after-dark chaperon to "the ladies," as he liked to call them, to bug Louise. All of a sudden he slammed on his brakes.

Everyone saw the scene at once. On the sidewalk, about fifty feet behind them now, from the point at which Bill screeched to a stop, one man was holding a gun on another.

"Do something!" Louise shouted at Bill.

He was already putting the car into a rapid U-turn. He wheeled around until the men were illuminated by the headlights and was leaping from the car as everyone saw the man with the gun, who was black, lurch backward as the other, who was white, took a swing at him and missed.

The black man tottered, drew his hands to his face, and fell to the ground, his gun skittering into the street. Bill drew his gun and ran up to within a few yards. Had the guy on the sidewalk been shot? Did the white man have a gun, too?

"FBI!" Bill shouted. "Police!"

Now the white was kicking the black in the head and fell on him, pounding with his fists—left, right, left—to his face.

"Separate!" Bill shouted. "Get up!" He was afraid the one would beat the other to death.

From the car came the sound of five women screaming.

Bill held his weapon in firing position and crept closer, shouting "Police!" He was within six or eight feet, caught a whiff of Mace, and quickly closed the rest of the distance. He pushed the white man back and told him to stay back, picked up the gun from the street, and shoved it into the back of his pants. In the background the women screamed. He could hear Louise calling his name.

He stood with one foot resting gently on the prone man, who groaned from the chemical and the blows, warning the other to keep back, identifying himself again.

"I know you," the white man said. He was the bouncer from the North End.

Bill said that it was lucky for him that they had been on their way to the restaurant. Otherwise someone would have been killed.

The doorman from the Crowne Plaza, who had watched the Chevy make the quick U-turn, came running up.

"Go back to the hotel and call 911," Bill told him. "Say there's an officer in need of assistance. Then come back here."

He took off running. Bill shouted to the women to sit tight, he was in control of the situation now. The doorman returned before the cops arrived.

"Keys are in the car," Bill said. "I want you to drive these ladies to the North End. Tell them I'll join them."

By the time Bill had finished making his report to the Memphis police and gotten a lift to the North End, the women were seriously into their cocktails. As he reached their table they stood up and cheered, "Hero! Hero! Our hero!"

"Dr. L. made me do it," Bill said.

"The only thing that pissed me off," Louise said, "was when you asked that doorman to drive us. I can drive, too, you know."

"You just want to say you drove an FBI car," Bill said, and ordered a double Jack Daniel's.

"I was worried for you, Papa Bill," Vivian said, and seemed about to cry.

"We better order some food," Louise said—and that was all that was ever discussed further about the incident. Louise directed the conversation elsewhere, on to the women themselves and ordinary things, while catching Bill's eye to make sure he knew what she was doing. He understood exactly. For maybe the first time in their lives, these women had seen a man act decisively and bravely, unselfishly and in the interest of others, and come back to be with them, taking care of them and sitting down with them as an equal. He could feel their reaction. It would not do to spoil it by dwelling on it, if for once they could see a man as their friend, as Louise wanted them to, it was obvious.

As the waiter brought their food, Janet Thomasson excused herself and headed in the direction of the ladies' room. After several minutes, she still had not returned.

"Her dinner's getting cold," Bill said. Louise went to see about her, saying she hoped Janet was all right. She was scheduled to testify first thing tomorrow morning.

When Louise reached the ladies' room she found three women standing in line complaining that someone had been in there for fifteen minutes with the door locked.

Louise tried the door. She knocked. She could hear a woman's voice in there, talking to herself, it sounded like. She called Janet's name and rattled the door.

Louise rushed back to the table and asked Bill to come with her. Janet had locked herself in the bathroom. Something awful might be going on.

Now there were four women standing in line and becoming irritated. Louise pounded on the door. "Janet! It's Dr. L.! It's Louise!"

Bill walked into the men's room. One man stood at the urinal, another was in the stall. Bill ordered them to zip up and clear out.

"What the hell is this?"

"Emergency. FBI. Everybody out. Now."

As quickly as they could, the men complied, and Bill ushered in the women as Louise continued to pound on the other door and call to Janet. The manager came up. Bill badged him and tried to explain that he was in charge of federal witnesses. One of them was having some difficulties. He would monitor the situation.

"Okay," the manager said. "The FBI's in charge of the bathrooms tonight. Jesus H. Christ."

Finally, as Bill played traffic cop, alternating pairs of men and women, Louise persuaded Janet to open the door.

She found her on the floor holding her knees, rocking herself back and forth, mumbling, crying. Louise got down with her and held her spoon-fashion and tried to understand what she was saying. It did not make sense, a word-salad, a torrent, angry and tortured, full of goddamns. A babble.

Bill had told Louise, a day ago, about the bruises Janet had shown to her friend and about what they almost certainly meant, that Lanier had orally raped her and that she was too ashamed to have told this to anyone. Or had she actually blocked that much of her experience in the judge's chambers from her memory? People did such things, or said they did—it was an area of great controversy, the whole question of whether the phenomenon of repressed memory actually exists. Was that memory what Janet was agonizing about now?

Louise had agreed with the prosecutors that it would be a mistake to confront Janet with the question of whether Lanier had actually raped her. It might help the case if she blurted it out in court—but if she had kept it a secret until now, perhaps even from herself, forcing that hideous truth from her could make her snap. For various reasons—compassion, caution, concern for her mental health—everyone agreed to leave the matter alone, unless she brought it up. In court she might not even be credible, having withheld under oath this information from the grand jury.

Louise continued to comfort her and try to get through to her, there on the bathroom floor. Then Louise heard the word "father," over and over, and "daddy" and "dad." Janet was talking to her father.

"It was always goddamn this and goddamned that," Janet was saying, blurting. "I had to be perfect. I was always supposed to be perfect." Louise kept listening, holding on to her.

"You understand what I'm saying, don't you?" Janet was talking to Louise now. "Don't you?"

"Yes," Louise said. "Yes, yes. Go ahead, let it out."

Janet's head was lying in a drain. Louise tried to move her; she sat up and asked for a cigarette.

Janet stood, walked over to a toilet, sat down, and smoked. She would be all right, she said. She needed to think for a minute.

Louise walked out of the ladies' room to find Bill still directing traffic and told him to get hold of a doctor. Janet was going to need a sedative, maybe hospitalization.

Instead, without telling Louise, Bill telephoned Amy Spain, who advised getting everyone to bed as quickly as possible. If things got worse, they should do whatever was necessary.

Bill was not sure why he had called Amy, rather than Parker or Moskowitz. In this strange world in which he found himself, one of female victims and a female psychologist, with everybody freaking out, hysterical, wounded, he did not want to rely on himself or on other men. And he did not want to end up as the Gingerbread Man, failing his charge, which he no longer even understood. It was not that he had lost faith in Louise, far from it. Everything she had advised had worked. The women, as she had insisted, needed each other for strength. And the victims were far more damaged than he had ever been able to realize, until Louise had educated him.

But Louise, on the floor of the ladies' room, was just as confused as he was for the moment, he believed. And as for him, well, he may have prevented a killing that night, and he had proved himself one hell of a lavatory attendant. But to figure out what to do next and how to balance his feelings for these women with the requirements of a very important case, he had needed the advice of another woman, one who was basically in the same business he was, that of bringing criminals to justice—a quiet, rational, reasonable woman, who from what he had heard was proving her worth every day in court—to tell him what to do. He had needed Amy.

Louise finally, it must have been an hour since Janet had disappeared, escorted her back to the table. Bill watched the women embrace each other, paid the check, and drove everybody back to everyone's home away from home. On the way, it was such a short distance, maybe eight minutes, he glanced at his rearview mirror as he passed under streetlamps and saw them entangled with one another, talking, attentive to Janet Thomasson, Vivian and Jennifer as if they had been through nothing, Linda with arms outstretched embracing all—and he looked over at Louise in the passenger seat, who gave him a thumbs-up and a shrug of her shoulders. They were on some kind of journey. This was a moment, wasn't it?

He pulled under the portico of the Crowne Plaza and got out.

"Welcome back," the doorman said to him. "Hey, Mr. Castleberry, hell of a job. How was the food?"

"Terrific," Bill said. "Here, have a cigar. Thanks for your help."

The lounge was off the lobby. To Bill's and Louise's dismay, as arm by arm they were helping Janet Thomasson toward the elevators, Vivian, Linda, and Jennifer headed straight for the bar. Those three were now wearing just-purchased North End T-shirts over their other clothes. They scurried in uniform to keep the evening alive.

Bill and Louise escorted Janet to her room.

"Janet and I need to talk," Louise said at Janet's door.

"Sure," Bill said. "Is she going to be all right?"

"I don't know," Louise said. "You'd better check on the others."

"Okay."

In the bar Vivian, Jennifer, and the designated chaperone and bastion of maturity, Linda Michaels, were behaving in a manner, Bill thought, potentially prejudicial to the case. They were not doing anything wrong, exactly, but were carrying on in the spirit, as it were, of emancipation, or New Year's Eve. Vivian was performing a solo tap dance. Linda was clapping hands, singing, and letting her body jive to whatever undefinable, heavy-on-the-beat disco music was piping through the place. And Jennifer, little Jennifer, her T-shirt like a nightshirt over her dress, was chatting to some lonely, in-the-bag traveler.

"Hey," Bill heard the man say, "who are you gals? I bet you're cheerleaders, right?"

"We're witnesses in the Lanier case," Jennifer said in her sweet, Southern, lyrical, maddeningly self-destructive way.

"Right on!" Vivian shouted.

"And that's my friend Vivian, and that's Linda, she's our den mother. And our other friend Janet and Dr. L. are upstairs for the night. We're having fun. Where you from?"

"Hey! Papa Bill is here!" Vivian called.

And they all ran to him.

Castleberry corralled the three of them into a booth and suggested that it was time to call it a night. But a middle-aged fellow obviously eager to party approached and started to slide in beside Vivian.

"Don't even think about it, buddy," Castleberry said. The man slunk back to the bar.

And the women agreed that they had had enough excitement.

34

The story of Jennifer and the sleeping bag was on page one in the *Commercial Appeal* the next morning, December 8, as it surely would be in that afternoon's *Gazette* in Dyersburg, where no one would have the slightest difficulty identifying her as the witness who worked at City Hall. She returned home later that day, since Wayne Emmons had been unable to prepare as yet the supposedly incriminating tape or tapes of her voice Lanier had provided. One could only imagine the welcome she would get from her co-workers and her already disapproving parents. As for her husband, he had so far been supportive, but how would he deal with his wife's private life unveiled in the papers and on TV, when she had concealed it from him even after they were married?

When Janet Thomasson knocked on Dr. L.'s door just before nine, on the morning after those difficult events at the North End, Louise was surprised to see her at all, let alone to find that she was ready to go to court. Louise had been expecting a phone call all morning from Janet or from one of the prosecutors or from Bill, saying that Thomasson had been excused from testifying for medical reasons. Louise had been prepared to recommend as much and had already thought that she must be compromising professional ethics by putting a law case above her client's welfare.

Wasn't that what Janet and at least three of the other women had become, her clients—or patients, as the more human terminology used to be? And friends, Louise thought, although to them she was always Dr. L.

So here Janet was in the hallway, her tall model's body perfect in a chic navy wool suit, saying in that beautiful deep voice of hers, a viola's voice as Louise thought of it, "Let's get this over with before I falter and lose my resolve, Dr. L. Is this okay?" She pointed to her face.

Was it her suffering that made her more gorgeous than ever? What was it about her this morning? Then Louise saw the key to the transformation. She had very little makeup on, some but just enough. Louise had been bothered from the moment she first met Janet at how this exquisite creature plastered her face. When Louise heard about the bruises Janet concealed—and heard her moaning about her father—she thought she understood possible reasons for the paint, this mask she wore as disguise and protection. Certainly no one could consider it an enhancement of her beauty; not even a copywriter for Revlon could bring that one off. Yesterday and last night her cheeks were not just rouged but red. She had looked like a marionette.

After she had held her on that concrete floor and listened to her as she got herself together, more or less, Louise told her that she'd better wash her face, because her makeup was streaked from her tears. When she did so and turned around from the basin, Louise seized the opportunity.

"Why, you look wonderful, Janet," she said. "It's so natural. I like it much better, to tell you the truth."

She had been listening. This morning her eyes were sapphires against that ivory, luminescent skin.

And it will make a much better impression on the jury, too, Louise was thinking, but would not have said that for the world.

Quickly she rounded up Vivian, Linda, and Jennifer, who had promised to stay through Janet's testimony, if there was any. Louise wanted her little group together as long as possible; if ever there was a time for solidarity, it was now. Janet might look great, but inside she must be on the edge. She was by nature—or by what life had done to her, who could say?—reclusive, but even she was helped by the unity among the women, it was obvious. To understand the universality of the female condition, of the physical vulnerability of women, that was the importance of this solidarity. With it a victim like Janet, who was by any standard the most attractive, could look at the others and say to herself, Maybe I am not so different after all. Maybe it's not my looks that I hate so much I want to hide them. Or my brains. Maybe we're all in this together.

Bill Castleberry stood off to one side, avuncular, inquisitive, in the law library as the women hugged Janet and told her she would do just fine. Bill was amazed that Janet had already recovered, as he told Amy, thanking her for giving the right advice last night. She hoped it was, Amy said as Louise led Janet off to the witness room.

Steve Parker conducted the examination of Janet, who sat poised on the stand and answered each question in that voice of hers with perfect diction and aplomb. Lanier had surprised her, she said, when she was getting up to leave his chambers after delivering her presentation of her proposal for parents in the housing projects, a program for which she had a federal grant. As she got up from her chair, her briefcase in one hand and her purse in the other, he had placed himself inches from her, and she bumped up against him. He grabbed her with both arms, kissed her, fondled her breast, and tried to stick his tongue in her mouth—at which point she managed to wriggle free. When she looked at his face it was smeared with her lipstick. She told him she knew her own face must be smeared with lipstick and makeup and, shaken though she was, she asked him how he expected her to leave in that condition. He told her to use the bathroom, which she did, and walked toward the hallway door.

On her way out, he had put his hand out and shoved it at her crotch. She stepped sideways and kept going.

As she reached the door, he told her that if she would come back, he would make sure her project was a success. He had the power, as juvenile judge, Janet said, to order parents to attend the classes she was proposing. She told him she would not be coming back.

Wayne Emmons tried to undercut this point. What power was she talking about? If this was a HUD grant, what did Lanier have to do with it?

"I came in to ask him," she replied, rather tartly, as if she were explaining something to a slow child, "would he please help me with this federal program. And he said that if I came back to see him, that he would see that I had all the clients I needed. Now, what do you think that means?"

Louise wanted to applaud. She was amazed at Janet's cool. Often she replied to Emmons with, "I believe I've already answered that," or silence, or, "Am I supposed to answer that? Is that a question?" And there was an edge to her voice and a narrowing of her eyes that implied that it was an impertinence for him to be asking her anything. She had risen from that floor to assume the manner of an aristocrat. Cousin Bubba was no match for her.

Emmons did keep making one point over and over that worried Steve Parker, however, what by now could have been called the Anita Hill argument—or the Clarence Thomas argument. Janet had not reported the incident. Parker believed that he had to address this point on redirect examination of the witness, even though he was very reluctant to do so because of the fragile state he knew Janet was in, underneath the composure she was affecting. She was being so cool, not to say frosty, that Parker worried that the jurors might think this woman was an iceberg and that nothing Lanier had done could have affected her in the least.

"Mr. Emmons," Parker said to her, in what he knew would be the final moment of her testimony, "about beat the horse to death about why you didn't report this." He paused. "I am going to ask you to look down deep inside. How did what the judge did to you make you feel?"

At that Janet Thomasson's composure cracked. Parker had said the one thing that could unleash her feelings. And he knew that when he asked the question she would be thinking not only about the kissing and the touching of her crotch, but—possibly, just possibly—about those bruises and what they almost certainly meant. In effect, he was trying to evoke the emotional devastation of a rape without making the victim talk about the incident.

She was sobbing. Parker was close to telling her she did not have to answer, more than that. But somehow she did answer through choking and crying:

"I went to the judge because I work in a program with a lot of under-privileged people who need an awful lot of help. And I would like to think that there would be one person that would really help me and the program that I work for. I didn't go in for myself, my salary was going to be the same regardless. I went in for six hundred people that I work for in housing, and I don't think that I should have to be subjected to that from any person in any kind of position."

It was a great answer, but it was not quite enough.

"And how did it make you *feel*?" Parker asked.

"I just felt really—degraded. And—like he evidently didn't think that I was worth very much."

That was it, that was what he wanted, that was what Lanier had done to all the women. Finally it was articulated. And Janet Thomasson was slumped over now, crying, gone suddenly from being the glass of fashion to a woman robbed of her bodily integrity, quite, quite down.

One more point had to be made, Parker thought. He felt as if he were torturing her, but he had to ask it. The jury had to be made to understand.

"Did that have any relation to why you didn't report this?"

Her words became fainter, but everyone could hear them:

"I don't think that this is something that you want to voice to too many people, or that you want too many people to know about."

After she had congratulated Janet and tried to help her get herself together, Louise went looking for Steve Parker and found him in his office with his head in his arms on his desk. When he looked up, she could see that he had been crying.

"I hated doing that," he said. "I hate myself for it."

"Getting her to show her feelings?"

"You know what she was thinking about."

"You had to do it," Louise said. "That's your job. Maybe she never faced up to her feelings before. Who knows, maybe you did her some good."

"I seriously doubt that," he said.

Bill Castleberry came in. He had heard from Amy and Al about Janet's testimony, the way she was. Not just her breaking down at the end, the whole thing.

"I thought I knew what courage was," Bill said. "I've seen men do incredible things under stress. But now, what Janet did, that is courage."

Patty Wallace did not need help from Louise in the witness room—and had never needed it or wanted it, Louise understood. When Louise peeked in to see how she was doing, Patty was there with her parents and sister. They were praying together. Louise discreetly withdrew.

And Patty Wallace did very well under both Spain's and Emmons's questions. There was doubt, of course, about whether the jury would understand why she had not left the Dyersburg courtroom as soon as Lanier began touching her. Could they appreciate her commitment to decorum?

Two women confirmed that Patty had been very upset after the incident and had told them about it immediately afterward.

With that, the prosecution rested its case. The prosecutors had already informed Louise that they had decided not to call her as an expert witness. The decision had been made after Janet Thomasson's testimony. They concluded that she and some of the other witnesses, especially Vivian, had explained very well why they had not reported Lanier's assaults. To be told again in more technical, psychological terms might make the jurors feel insulted, lectured at, and not trusted to evaluate evidence on their own. Louise disagreed, and she was disappointed. But she did believe that Steve, Amy, and Al were sincere when they told her that she had already been of invaluable help outside the courtroom.

She, Bill, Janet, and Vivian had a quiet dinner that night, back at the old North End. Vivian was afraid that she would be banished to Orlando and would miss the rest of the trial. No, Bill assured her, she could stay. The government owed her that much and more and, besides, she was still under subpoena.

The defense began its case the next morning by putting on nine witnesses, five of whom described Vivian Forsythe as a liar. The first of these, the leadoff witness for the defense, was Donna Forsythe McDivvit, Vivian's sister.

"She tells you what she wants you to know for what she thinks is appropriate," Donna said. "She is not a very honest person."

Steve Parker tried to counter this by referring to the constant turmoil in the Forsythe family. Was it not true that Vivian and her parents did not get on very well?

"I have no idea," Donna said. "My dad told me last night that Vivian was crying to him."

Parker brought up the dispute over Ashley. Donna replied that she took care of the child regularly and brought her to church every Wednesday night.

When Emmons asked her again about her opinion of her sister's dishonesty, Donna stated, "It is not really an opinion. It is a fact."

The next witness to attack Vivian was Leigh Anne Lanier Johnson, who said with heat, "She is a pathological liar. She had lied all of her life about everything." She had known Vivian since playschool, Leigh Anne continued, and they had been in the same sorority together in high school. After the ninth grade, however, they parted company, because Vivian was too "wild."

Leigh Anne took similarly dim views of others of her father's accusers. Mary Haralson was incompetent as his secretary and had worn flimsy, skimpy, and otherwise inappropriate clothing to work. Janet Thomasson had hugged the judge at the Christmas party. And as for Patty Wallace, she was known for hugging everybody. Leigh Anne had come into her father's office one day when he was sitting in a chair in the reception area. Patty Wallace had come right up to him and bent down and hugged him, pressing her chest into his face:

"If she had been Dolly Parton, he would have smothered. But she is kind of flat-chested, so he didn't."

"It's safe to say you love your father, isn't it?" Steve Parker asked her when he got his chance.

"It sure is," Leigh Anne said, "but I wouldn't lie for him."

Leigh Anne's husband, Larry Johnson, testified that he had known Vivian Forsythe for many years and had once dated a friend of hers. It was the general opinion in Dyersburg, he said, that Vivian was untruthful. To this Steve Parker simply asked him to affirm that he was the defendant's son-in-law. But when yet another witness, a former bartender at Chequers, testified that Vivian "never told the truth about anything," Parker finally lost his temper.

Even if Vivian had lied to him, Parker said, "Would that give the judge the right to grab her by the hair and throw her in a chair and stick his penis in her mouth?"

The startled young man did not have to answer, because Parker withdrew his deliberately inflammatory question, which he had hurled at the witness like a firebrand, when Emmons objected. But the jury had heard it. And when yet another witness, a woman who had worked at Forsythe's House of Fashion, said that she had known Vivian for nineteen years and that she was "an habitual liar," Parker, not wanting to blow his stack again, let Al Moskowitz ask her if she had any direct knowledge of any of the alleged assaults in this case or of anything else that had been testified to for the past week and a half. She admitted she did not.

There was one witness that day for whom everyone had pity, and that was Joan Lanier. The judge's ex-wife, a dark-haired woman whose sad and darting eyes and nervous hands conveyed consuming anxieties, said that she had divorced her husband for adultery, but that she had "detached in love," and that he was incapable ever of assaulting or sexually abusing anyone. On the contrary, he was constantly the target of women's affections, which was very upsetting from a wife's point of view.

She had been upset to find Cathy Kiely, who was very attractive, young, and divorced, working for the judge. She had told Judge Lanier to watch out for that woman. And she had seen many, many women lavishing affection on David and wearing "eye-catching outfits" around him. Patty Wallace had hugged him in friendly fashion at an Amway meeting, long after she had supposedly been bothered by him. Patty had never complained to her about David. She and Patty often saw each other at the beauty parlor.

"I know this has been tough on you, Mrs. Lanier" was all that Steve Parker said to her.

35

Vivian had been in the law library with Janet, Bill, and Steve Champine that morning when Louise came in to break the news that Donna McDivvitt had just left the stand after calling Vivian a liar. Whatever tears Vivian had left began to flow; she put her head down on the table and covered herself with her arms as if trying to hide from the world. Her own sister on the side of the man who had raped her! Could there be anything worse, short of having Judy Forsythe follow?

No one could find the box of Kleenex Castleberry had bought the day before after the supplies in all the U.S. Attorney's offices had run out. Louise remembered taking it to the witness room and leaving it there.

Castleberry and Champine rode the elevator up to the eleventh floor, passing a few reporters hanging around the halls, and through a side entrance behind the courtroom. Leigh Anne Lanier's husband was standing outside the witness room; Castleberry said he needed to go in to retrieve a box of tissues and opened the door. Inside he discovered Joan Lanier, Leigh Anne, two other women he did not recognize, and Rikki Tikki Tavi. He said hello to Mrs. Lanier, who did not return his greeting; he retrieved the box, and started to walk out with it.

He noticed that Leigh Anne and her husband were giving him a suspicious look. It was as if—in an instant Bill realized—no, could it be? They thought the Kleenex box was bugged! He walked out with it.

Leigh Anne and her husband followed the agents around to the elevator.

When Leigh Anne caught up to him she thrust her hand into the box and took out a tissue; her husband said he wanted one, too, and reached in as if to grab all that were left. Castleberry snatched the box away, held it gingerly up in the air, and said, "You can't have any. This is U.S. government property!"

Just then the elevator doors opened, Castleberry hurried inside as Champine shielded him, and the agents slipped away. They waited to tell of their adventure until Vivian had left the room, as she was not in a frame of mind to find this or anything else funny.

But that was not the end of the matter.

After the last witness had finished that afternoon, Tim Naifeh, in his first and only courtroom act during the trial, approached the bench.

"If Your Honor please," Naifeh said, "Judge Lanier has asked me to bring up a particular matter that is of interest to him. Mr. Emmons has refused at this point to bring it up, or we'll let the judge bring it up. He would like to have the record show that the FBI, in particular Agent Castleberry, entered the witness room this morning. Basically he entered the witness room with six or seven of the defense witnesses in there. He had a particular interest in the Kleenex box."

"In a what?" Judge Turner asked.

"A Kleenex box that was in the witness room."

"Wait a minute. All of you," Judge Turner said, looking rather incredulous. He excused the jury for the day. At which point Parker, Moskowitz, and Spain could no longer contain themselves. The three of them started giggling like schoolchildren. Judge Turner was not amused.

"I don't know who laughed," he said sternly, "but the three of you know better than to be laughing."

"It was us," Amy said.

"I did," Steve said.

"No, it was me, Your Honor," Al Moskowitz said.

"I try to run a low-key court, but that does not include laughing at serious matters."

"Judge," Tim Naifeh said, "I am serious about this, and I take offense at the remarks by counsel. We believe that Castleberry entered the room with the intent to intimidate our witnesses. Plus we feel that they are eavesdropping on our conversations. And the Kleenex box in and of itself, we are suspicious. We have no way to prove that it contained recording information, because he took it—"

"Where is it?" Judge Turner demanded.

"Where is it? He took it and would not let us have it."

Judge Turner said that it was inappropriate for an FBI agent to be in the witness room, not illegal but not something he wanted to happen again. He would have to hear the matter. He ordered the prosecutors to have Agent Castleberry in court first thing in the morning, prepared to testify—and with the Kleenex box.

The trial stopped dead for nearly half an hour that Thursday morning while Castleberry took the stand, before the jury was brought in, to explain his actions. Judge Turner declined the opportunity to inspect the box, which Castleberry held in his lap. Why was it necessary to retrieve this particular box, Wayne Emmons wanted to know.

"I assume there was toilet tissue available?"

"Yes, sir," Bill replied crisply.

"That can be used as a handy substitute?"

"Yes, sir." It was, however, low-grade, harsh, government-issue toilet tissue. "When we first ran out, we did raid the rest room."

"Without a search warrant, I take it?"

"Yes, sir."

Emmons had obviously seen through to the ludicrousness of the whole episode; he had not wanted to bring it up in the first place, but Judge Lanier had insisted. He, whose deviousness compelled him to record even the most inane of conversations, assumed the same mentality in others.

Emmons said that Mrs. Lanier had been particularly upset to see Castleberry. He had been just as surprised to see her there, Bill said, never having thought that Judge Lanier would put his wife on the stand.

"You might be interested to know," Emmons said, "that she put herself there at her own request."

Vivian flew back to Orlando that day. Her sister's appearance was all she could take. Had Vivian stayed, she would have learned that the defense spent more time trying to discredit her than on anything else. Four more witnesses denounced her as a liar or contradicted some aspect of her testimony; three others denounced in turn Julia Garnett, Sandy Sanders, and Jennifer Gallagher. The final witness for the defense, except for David Lanier himself, who was scheduled for Monday, was Dr. Lynn Warner. The defense had obviously decided that Vivian Forsythe was the key to the entire case and were asking her former lover, this older and married man, to strike the deciding blow against her character.

"I want that guy for myself," Al Moskowitz whispered to Parker, as Dr. Warner testified that he had hired Vivian after Judge Lanier recommended her, had conducted an affair with her in Judge Lanier's "downtown apartment," and had taken a trip to the Bahamas with her and the judge. At no time had she ever complained of the judge's having forced her to have sex; nor had she ever expressed any fear of David Lanier.

Moskowitz then asked Warner whether, when Lanier had recommended Vivian, he had implied that she would provide sexual favors for the doctor. Warner, after some backing and filling, admitted that this was indeed the idea, "in so many words." He had responded by giving her an interview and hiring her. Vivian's mother had also asked him to hire her, but obviously not for those reasons. And he admitted that Judge Lanier had set up the interview. The judge had told him that Vivian would say that she "would do anything for a job." That was supposed to be a code phrase for sex. She had indeed said it, and he hired her right away.

But, under Moskowitz's questioning, Dr. Warner admitted, after verifying that he had been Vivian's doctor since her childhood, that he had fallen in love with her—and that, at a moment in which she was "baring her soul," she had admitted to him that she and Judge Lanier had had oral sex in his chambers:

"The exact words that Vivian used were that he requested oral sex and that she performed oral sex. She did not elaborate on any words used or any actions."

This was a major breakthrough for the prosecution, since Lanier, at least so far, was denying having had sex with any of the victims. But it could also be damaging to Vivian, if Moskowitz failed to evoke more.

"She was embarrassed and ashamed and upset when she told you that, wasn't she?"

"As I see it," Dr. Warner said, "she was clearing her conscience and clearing the slate. Because she is an open person."

Moskowitz pounced.

"She is an open person, isn't she?" he asked.

"Yes."

"And she will tell you whatever is on her mind, and she will just be open about all of her faults, won't she?"

"Yes, sir," Dr. Warner said, with no hesitation. Remarkably, this star, climactic witness for the defense was singing the praises of the major witness for the prosecution. Moskowitz kept the ball rolling.

"There are a lot of good qualities about Vivian Forsythe, aren't there?"

"Oh, yeah. Yes, sir."

"She is a loving person, isn't she?"

"Yes, sir."

"She will tell you anything that is wrong about her? She won't hide anything, will she?"

"That's true."

"She's not a pathological liar, is she, Doctor?"

"I've never caught her in a lie. I can't say that she is, no."

"You wouldn't have fallen in love with her if she were, would you?"

"No. Love is something different. I probably would not."

"No more questions."

There was not much Wayne Emmons could do. The more questions he asked Dr. Warner, after Moskowitz was through, the worse a witness

Warner was, from the defense point of view, and Emmons quit after about a minute.

It was a moment as positive as it was unexpected for the prosecution—and a victory for Moskowitz's quiet skills. Dr. Warner had started telling the truth and could not stop.

The prosecution's pleasure was tempered, however, by their apprehension over the tape that Wayne Emmons was finally ready to introduce the next day as a prelude to David Lanier's taking the stand, to conclude the defense's case. Emmons had so far produced only a transcript, but the prosecutors, working late into the night, had finally found the recording itself among the seemingly innocuous tapes that Castleberry had retrieved from the Penthouse. When they originally had listened to it, all it seemed to be was a female voice on an answering machine asking for an appointment. Now it appeared that the voice was Jennifer Gallagher's and that she was asking to come over to the chambers and talking in a most friendly way to Lanier. She referred to herself as "Jennifer from City Hall," as if pretending to be on official business, when in fact she wanted to talk to him about her delinquent child support payments. Jennifer, in her testimony, had denied having made such a call.

Potentially this tape was devastating. But the prosecutors had heard a hesitation or click in the recording that they found highly suspicious.

There was no time, they thought, to find an expert to evaluate the tape. Before adjourning for the day, Judge Turner scheduled the playing for tomorrow morning. Amy Spain argued that the tape had been altered and was in fact two conversations spliced together, to give a misleading impression.

Lanier, however, was saying that this tape had been made on the very day that Jennifer came to his chambers and had sex with him. He was making at least one exception to his defense strategy of denial. He was admitting sex with Jennifer Gallagher. This tape, he was arguing, in which she referred to her financial difficulties, was actually a proposition to him. He had given in to her—and later paid her the hundred dollars, which she had already admitted accepting.

To add to these complications, Jennifer was so upset after her testimony, which her daughter had been asked about at school, that she refused to return to Memphis to explain her version of what the tape meant. If necessary she could be subpoenaed again, but to have her forced to testify this time would be very risky, perhaps impossible given her emotional state.

It was Louise who insisted that there must be an expert in Memphis willing to evaluate the recording that very night and to come in to testify on Friday. Judge Turner had decided to forgo his previous practice of recessing the trial on the last day of the week; he wanted to conclude matters as quickly as possible. Louise got on the phone to try to make use of her academic contacts, although the prosecutors told her she was wasting her time.

She happened to know the head of the counseling service at Memphis State, a woman she had met at conferences. From her she learned that there was a speech pathologist and audiologist at the university's Speech and Hearing Clinic, a Dr. Walter Manning. Neither his office nor his home phone answered.

Louise convinced Bill that they should not give up. She and Steve Champine piled into Big Blue and Bill drove them to the university, where they banged on the door of the clinic. A graduate student, somewhat startled when Bill and Steve showed their badges, said that Dr. Manning was at a basketball game. It was now nearly eight o'clock.

Louise had missed her train home to Illinois. She took a taxi to the airport to catch a flight to St. Louis, where she could just make the last commuter flight to Champaign-Urbana, while Bill and Steve proceeded to the Memphis State basketball game and had Dr. Manning paged.

When he agreed to try to help, Bill called Amy Spain and had her bring the tape to the clinic. Amy and the agents stood by as the professor hooked the tape into an oscilloscope and other equipment. It would take him a couple of hours, he said, to evaluate it.

36

Dr. Manning testified the next morning, out of the presence of the jury, that he was certain that the tape had been altered and that his opinion was that it was actually two tapes that had been recorded separately and joined together on this one. He illustrated his points with spectrograms, printouts he had produced from his experiments the previous night. Louise Fitzgerald's frantic search for an expert had not been in vain.

Judge Turner ruled, however, that portions of the tape still had such probative value that he would allow them to be played for the jury. The prosecution would be able to bring Dr. Manning back on Monday during their rebuttal, at which time they would also try to have Jennifer Gallagher on hand to explain her words, or try to.

And, at last, the jury was brought in, and David Lanier took the stand.

Wayne Emmons led Judge Lanier through the highlights of his career in public office, with copious references to his distinguished father and brother, emphasizing the political rivalries and resentments that such a long family political history would naturally engender. When asked to name people who might hold grudges against him, Lanier mentioned the former district attorney, Jim Horner, first, but placed special emphasis on Chief Bobby Williamson, Stan Cavness, and Joey McDowell. He described the officers as incompetent and vindictive, and he repeated the disproved accusation that Cavness had been involved with an underage girl. Lanier went over all this material in the rather blasé manner that was his normal way of conversing—as if all these charges against him were so much pap, the complaints of disgruntled employees spurred on by fired policemen.

Lanier called himself "a hugging kind of guy"—and to an outsider he may indeed have come across as a harmless sort of paternal figure. He had lost about twenty pounds in the last few months, was less porcine in appearance, not at all intimidating in a casual beige tweed jacket and tie. Women came on to him constantly, he said, probably because of his eminence. He knew how much this hurt and upset his dear ex-wife—at which point he choked up, and Emmons asked for and received a recess.

When he resumed, however, Lanier admitted having had a consensual sexual encounter with Jennifer Gallagher, at which point Emmons played the contested tape for the jurors. It had all been her idea, Lanier said, and he had paid her. He was very ashamed of having done so. He had taped the conversation beforehand because "if you can't trust people, it might be good to have something on record. When someone tells you she needs a sugar daddy, you wonder."

For the rest of the afternoon, Lanier described this or that character defect or incompetence in his other accusers, whom, he said, he had never done more than hug in a harmless way. He had done everything he could for these women. Recommending Vivian to Dr. Warner had been typical of his generosity.

Emmons led Lanier through six of the eight names that day; his defense in relation to Janet Thomasson and Patty Wallace would have to wait until he resumed testifying on Monday. He reemphasized that, although he did have sex with Jennifer Gallagher once, he had subsequently tried to help her with her legal problems, which was why she had come to him to thank him and to express her regret over testifying against him before the grand jury. She had mentioned that she had been threatened with a jail sentence if she did not cooperate with the government.

LANIER DENIES SEX CHARGES, SAYS HE'S A "HUGGING TYPE" was the headline in the *Commercial Appeal;* Donna Whittle's *Gazette* account was headed LANIER SAYS WOMAN AGREED TO RELATIONSHIP. And, in addition to the Associated Press, national publications began covering the trial. The *New York Times* ran a lengthy account in its edition of December 15, noting that "parallels between the charges that Judge Lanier misused his power and accusations against Senator Bob Packwood and Judge Clarence Thomas are not lost on people here." The *Times*'s story, however, focused on the effects of the trial on Dyersburg, where, a local lawyer was quoted, the *State Gazette* "'is rated "R" these days, and you have to hide it from your kids.'" And the director of the chamber of commerce lamented "'the tragedy of it all. Here is a person who many think ought to be on a pedestal, and it seems to be crumbling.'"

The *Times*'s angle caught exactly the reaction of most of the people of Dyersburg, who regretted the negative publicity that the trial brought to their town. No one mentioned the tragedy of the women.

*   *   *

By the time Lanier took the stand again on Monday, Bill Castleberry and Louise Fitzgerald were on their way up to Dyersburg to try to convince Jennifer Gallagher to accompany them back to Memphis so that she could testify once again about the damaging tape, which, even though the Memphis State professor would tell the jury that day that in his opinion it had been altered, remained a source of worry. With Jennifer, Lanier had taken the one defense position that had all along seemed the most worrisome to the prosecutors, claiming consensual sex; and now they were concerned about a spillover effect on the other counts. But Jennifer had flat-out refused to budge from her house.

In the car Louise distinguished among the victims in terms of the effects Lanier had had on each. All had been traumatized, but there were degrees. Jennifer and Vivian, and probably Janet Thomasson, had been severely damaged, she hoped not permanently, but that was possible, whereas the others would be able to heal on their own. Vivian had exhibited resilience and strength of heroic proportions. Not one woman in a thousand could have done what she had already accomplished in facing down her tormentor. Jennifer, however, was showing signs of disintegration that seemed to be accelerating as she returned home. One of the reasons Louise agreed to help bring her back was that she wanted to evaluate Jennifer, to get her into some appropriate therapy.

Bill said that he hoped Louise understood that he was now very much aware of the effects of assault, having begun from a point of relative ignorance and insensitivity. Just three months ago, during a lull in the Lanier case in mid-September, he had put some of what he had learned into action. The sheriff of Lauderdale County had been the subject of numerous civil rights complaints, most of them racially based. He was allegedly beating up prisoners as a regular thing. When a female prisoner's grandmother and mother reported to the FBI that they had visited the woman in jail and that she had shown signs of being beaten and had told them that the sheriff had assaulted her, Castleberry went to investigate.

The woman was charged with aiding a fugitive from the law; he was black, and she was white. At the jail Castleberry talked briefly to the sheriff and noticed a big stick leaning against a corner—one that instantly reminded him of a weapon used by the sheriff in the movie *Walking Tall*. When he alluded, pretending amusement, to the film, the sheriff just grinned. Castleberry then interviewed the woman being held.

She absolutely denied having been beaten. Before the Lanier case, that would have been that. But now, with his experience of the reluctance of victims to talk, from fear or shame or both, he persisted. It took about an hour. He went so far as to promise the woman that she would never be harmed for talking to an FBI agent—a pledge he knew he would have to fulfill somehow, without knowing how at that point. He went so far as to promise her that if it was true that the sheriff had beaten her, she would be out of jail that night. Why had her mother and grandmother complained? Why was she so nervous? Finally she broke down.

When she was brought into the jail, she said, the sheriff had ordered the handcuff removed from her left hand. He had then taken hold of the other handcuff, swung her around, hit her in the mouth with his fist, and knocked her down. He grabbed her by the throat, threw her down on the floor, picked her up and threw her into a chair, and called her "a yellow-nigger-loving-bitch" and other epithets. He was enraged that a white woman loved a black man. He had thrown jail clothes at her, said, "Here, put on these nigger clothes," and hit her in the back with his elbow as she tried to get into the bathroom to change.

Castleberry did get her out of jail within a few hours, after talking to her attorney, on the basis of a faulty warrant. A month later, the sheriff admitted to having beaten the woman and resigned. Castleberry considered his experience with the Lanier victims the key to achieving this swift ouster. Nor did Louise have to point out to him the obviously sexual nature of the sheriff's attack on the woman: racism, sexual aggression, abuse of power, all of these factors combined with hatred and contempt for women, none alone the single cause, the lot of them an explosive mixture.

Bill's story made a profound impression on Louise, not only for its grotesque horror but paradoxically for the hope it gave her. If this man could come so far so quickly in his understanding, perhaps the gap between the sexes was not as wide as many feminists believed.

On his part Bill wanted Louise to understand how far he had come and that he and she were on the same side. He presumed to believe that she, too, was learning something about how men and women could work together, that there were men out there like Parker, Moskowitz, and himself who could be as valuable in the fight for women's rights as anyone else.

"I think you'll find this house interesting as to symbolism, Doctor," Bill said as they walked up to Jennifer Gallagher's door.

Jennifer, alone at home that day, did not seem especially glad to see them but told them to come in. Louise let the ambiance soak in, trying not to overreact. Because it was Christmastime, the clutter was greater than when Bill had been there before. Jennifer had brought the mounted animals into seasonal motif, tying colorful bows on them and hanging ornaments from their antlers. One deer's head had a bow stuck onto its nose.

"That's a cute touch," Louise said, "those decorations on the animals."

"Richard doesn't like it," Jennifer said. "He hates it. He said it's not masculine or something."

"Did he shoot all these things?" Louise asked.

"Yes. He must've killed fifteen deer or so this season."

"My goodness. You must know every recipe for venison there is."

"Richard won't eat venison," Jennifer said. "He hates the taste of it."

"Tell you what," Bill said, "let's go get some lunch."

At Barham's, where Bill talked Louise into her very first barbecued baloney sandwich, they persuaded Jennifer, not without considerable effort on Louise's part, to return to Memphis with them. By the time they checked her into the Crowne Plaza again, however, the prosecutors had decided she was not needed.

Bill was furious with the prosecutors, but Jennifer was much relieved. Unfortunately, she soon learned from TV news and the newspapers that Lanier had spent a good portion of his time on the stand that day talking about how Jennifer had clearly enjoyed having sex with him. "It wasn't so pleasant that I went back," he said, "but it was an experience. She acted like she enjoyed it. It wasn't like it was one-sided sex."

By the end of the day, Jennifer remained the one victim with whom Lanier admitted having had sex. For this he described himself as a sinner but hardly guilty as charged.

This, Monday, December 14, was the last day of the trial proper, after which closing arguments would precede jury deliberations. It was Al Moskowitz who would make the closing argument for the government and who cross-examined Lanier, his precise and quietly tenacious manner best suited for those important assignments. Although he did not succeed in breaking Lanier down—no one had ever thought that possible—his questions, short and vividly phrased, had the effect, in the opinion of most observers, of making Lanier's defense difficult to accept.

Moskowitz spent more time asking Lanier about Vivian than about any of the other victims. Moskowitz's rhetorical weapon of choice was irony, which he used several times like an interrogative stiletto. He concentrated on the unseemly spectacle of two aging men, the judge and the doctor, conspiring to use Vivian for sexual purposes. To Lanier's insistence that he had felt sorry for Vivian and had resisted her attempts to trade sex for a job, Moskowitz painted an alternate version of events.

"You certainly wouldn't take advantage of that young woman that day, would you?"

"No, sir," Lanier said.

"Instead, showing such great self-restraint, you passed her off to your doctor friend, Dr. Warner, didn't you?"

"No, sir."

"And you two old men were passing that young woman around like she was so much meat, weren't you?"

How Lanier inwardly reacted to this kind of questioning was anyone's guess. There was general agreement among the prosecutors, the agents, and Louise Fitzgerald that Lanier's view of the law and of women was so much an extension of his ego that he conceived his power to be a justification in and of itself, a Tennessee version of *L'état, c'est moi*. For this reason he must have believed that women enjoyed sex with him, and that their resistance was only part of the pleasure. Or, to paraphrase Joey McDowell, if you're going to remove the king, you can't reason with him, you have to kill him.

Steve Parker took it upon himself to turn the jury's attention to this indifference on the part of Lanier to reasonable argument or behavior. It was Parker who had the final word for the government, because he gave the prosecution's rebuttal to Wayne Emmons's closing argument. Emmons stressed the political motivation of the prosecution, together with the flawed characters of many of the witnesses. Parker wanted the jury to think about the victims as individuals helpless before Lanier without the intervention of the federal government. He cited as his final example Vivian Forsythe and risked sickening the jury by phrasing her suffering in the most vivid possible way.

"You heard Vivian Forsythe's testimony," Parker told the jurors. "I am going to be blunt. I hope this doesn't offend you. But while Judge Lanier had his penis in her mouth, she was crying. How can a man stay aroused when that is going on—unless it turns him on? But if you don't think he broke the law by doing this, send him back. Send him back to the bench."

By ten-thirty the next morning, Wednesday, December 16, the jury retired to deliberate. They returned about an hour later to ask for clarification on one of the instructions Judge Turner had given them, having to deal with definitions of "willfulness" and "implied consent." At what point should they draw the line, in terms of what the defendant thought he was doing, or what he believed an alleged victim consented to in the way of a sexual advance or act? It was, of course, a question nearly impossible to answer and one that had already inspired debate all over the country in relation to codes of sexual behavior at colleges and universities. The most notorious of these, promulgated at Antioch College, required a series of questions and answers for consenting adults to review during stages of sex that were so elaborate as to make one wonder whether the person or persons who had prescribed them had ever actually experienced sexual intercourse or anything approximating it.

Judge Turner thought his instructions were clear enough, and he assumed the jurors' common sense.

Steve Parker and Al Moskowitz agreed between themselves that this question about "willfulness" was significant, coming as it had during the first hour of deliberations. Presumably the jurors were beginning by considering in order each count in the indictment. Count One was Patty Wallace. What the jurors must be trying to decide, Steve and Al speculated, was whether the longer Wallace permitted the judge's hand to remain on her leg, the more it implied consent—on the analogy, say, of a boy in a movie theater testing his date's willingness to progress from one sexual level to the next. Hence the metaphor of getting to first base, second base, and so on.

What it sounded like was that the jury would acquit on Count One. At the same time, if they believed the gist of what the women had said about the incidents, this could also mean convictions on other counts. No one could say for sure.

As the jury deliberated again, Judge Turner heard a new motion for mistrial by the defense. Astonishingly, to the prosecutors at any rate, it involved the matter of the Kleenex box again. Emmons, who continued to appear most uncomfortable with the entire issue and may have been following the instructions of his client, brought in Leigh Anne's husband, Larry Johnson, again, who said he was "terrified" of the FBI and that Agent Castleberry had carried the box of tissues "like it was a porcelain vase" and refused to let him inspect it. Leigh Anne confirmed her husband's account and asked why, if he had purchased them himself, had Castleberry said that the tissues were the property of the U.S. government? Joan Lanier described how Castleberry "strikes terror in my heart because month after month he has come into Dyersburg each week terrorizing and threatening the women. When I saw him walk in, he scares me to death. I watched him. It was like his eyes never left my face."

The defense also argued for a mistrial on the basis that Dr. Louise Fitzgerald had not been retained as an expert witness, because she had not testified, but to coach the witnesses, in which role she had behaved improperly. To permit her to defend herself and the government's decision not to call her to the stand, Amy Spain brought Louise in to explain her actions. She had not told the witnesses how to testify, Louise said, but only how to retain composure, to the degree that they could. She had neither made gestures to them from where she had been sitting in court nor discussed their testimony with them beforehand. When Wayne Emmons asked her if her function was basically to keep witnesses under control, she replied rather sharply:

"Mr. Emmons, I am a psychologist, and what I do for a living is to work with victims. And I have an ethical obligation to protect human welfare. And if I could alleviate discomfort within the bounds of my ethical role as a consultant, you bet that's exactly what I was going to do."

Judge Turner denied the motion for mistrial. Now there was nothing to do but wait out the jury.

When the jury failed to return a verdict on Thursday, Louise went home to Illinois. Much to her chagrin she was not there on Friday morning, December 18, when the jury foreman, who was a resident of Germantown, held a master's degree in forestry, and was employed as the director of statistics and quality control for the International Paper Corporation, sent word to Judge Turner that verdicts had been reached on all counts.

The jury had only ten of the eleven original counts on which to decide. Judge Turner had already dismissed Count Nine, that involving Julia Garnett, on the grounds that in exposing his genitals to the woman, Lanier had not committed actual assault. To the prosecutors this was an excessively narrow view of the law, but they decided they could live with it.

The jury had spent about eleven hours altogether in deliberations over two days, not long considering the number of counts and usually a bad sign for the defendant. At close to eleven that morning, with a cluster of reporters and all of the principals except the witnesses, Castleberry, Champine, and Fitzgerald present, foreman Raymond Freeman stood in the jury box and read out the first verdict:

"On Count One of the indictment, that on or about July 12, 1988, in the Western District of Tennessee, David W. Lanier, while acting under of color of law of the State of Tennessee, did willfully subject Patricia Wallace, an inhabitant of the State of Tennessee, and an employee of the Circuit Court of Dyer County, to the deprivation of rights and privileges which are secured and protected by the Constitution, and the laws of the United States, namely, the right not to be deprived of liberty without due process of law, including the right to be free from willful sexual assault, that is, by willfully touching Patricia Wallace on and near her crotch and otherwise molesting her, all in violation of Title 18, United States Code, Section 242, we the jury find the defendant not guilty."

The jury had acquitted Lanier on the Patty Wallace count, as Parker and Moskowitz had expected. The second count, they and Amy Spain knew, would be the real test of whether the jury would convict on any of the misdemeanors and would be a good indication of how they had decided on the three felony counts, also. Count Two was the first of those two involving Sandy Sanders, this one her accusation that Lanier had grabbed her breast, as she had demonstrated with Amy in court to the jury. Had Amy's strategy worked, or had the jury been less than impressed?

Foreman Freeman began the lengthy formulation of the indictment's charge again, concluding with "that is by willfully grabbing the breasts of Sandra Sanders and otherwise molesting her . . ." and announced that the verdict on Count Two was "guilty as charged."

The first great challenge had been met, and it seemed highly unlikely that the jury would convict on only one count, since several were so similar to this one. It looked as if Lanier would be off the bench at last.

Count Three, however, was an unpleasant surprise for the prosecutors. On the charge that Lanier had grabbed Sandy Sanders's buttocks "in or about May through August, 1989," the jury had reached a second not guilty verdict. It was difficult although not impossible to see the panel's logic, since Lanier had grabbed Sandy's breast within the confines of his chambers, where she was essentially confined. The buttocks-grabbing had occurred as she was leaving Lanier's courtroom, so in the strict sense she had not been deprived of liberty on that occasion. This was a jury capable of making fine distinctions, it seemed, making it more likely that their verdicts would hold up on appeal—but one misdemeanor count was hardly satisfactory. It could mean little or no time in jail for Lanier at all, and he could soon be back in Dyersburg, even if off the bench, to make life hell for the women again.

The prosecutors stopped worrying when the foreman announced guilty verdicts on Counts Four, Five, Six, and Seven, the latter two being the most important, the felony counts against Lanier for having coerced Vivian Forsythe Archie to engage in sexual acts, "resulting in bodily injury" to Vivian, and carrying a jail sentence of as much as ten years on each.

Lanier, whatever he was thinking, betrayed no emotion whatever at what must have been for him these devastating felony verdicts. As Parker sat there trying to catch a glimpse of Lanier without being obvious about it, he whispered to Amy that he could not wait to telephone Vivian. This was her day, perhaps even more than any of the other brave women, although, as everyone now realized, none could have done it alone.

The jury also brought in guilty verdicts on Counts Eight and Eleven, those involving Mary Haralson and Janet Thomasson. The jurors had not, however, been entirely convinced by the testimony of Jennifer Gallagher. On her count, Ten, they voted not guilty, undoubtedly, as the prosecutors discussed afterward, finding reasonable doubt on the question of Jennifer's degree of consent. It seemed unlikely, as later proved true, that they had believed Lanier's version, that the sex between him and Jennifer had been entirely consensual; but Jennifer's having kept the money the judge threw on her desk probably had not helped her credibility, unfair though it was to blame a woman in her circumstances.

Jennifer, like the other two women on whose counts the jury had acquitted Lanier, would be very upset, no doubt. But the general message the jury had sent was one of overwhelming condemnation of David Lanier. Among them the seven guilty verdicts carried a total possible prison sentence of twenty-five years. And in the federal system, the concept of parole had been abolished. Whatever sentence Judge Turner determined would be served in full.

Judge Turner set a date for sentencing of March 26, 1993. The prosecutors, while not surprised by this delay of three months, were not pleased about it. Lanier would remain free on bond during that time.

Technically, hard as it was to believe, Lanier was still in office, although a special panel of the Tennessee Supreme Court had ordered him to step down until the charges against him had been resolved. Legal scholars doubted, however, that that high court had the power to enforce that order. It remained strictly up to the state legislature to remove him. And he would continue, in jail or out, to receive his eighty-two-thousand-dollar annual salary until the legislature acted against him. He showed no signs of wishing to resign voluntarily.

In discussing the verdicts afterward with reporters, one member of the jury, Dr. Lynda Park, stated that there never had been any question of Lanier's guilt in anyone's mind. "Everybody," she said, "thought that the judge had committed wrongdoing either ethical or moral on all the charges." The acquittals had evolved around the meaning of "coercion" as it appeared in the indictment. Before retiring Thursday night, the jurors had requested further definition of the word from Judge Turner. Where coercion had not taken place beyond a reasonable doubt, the jury had decided on not guilty verdicts, even though all disliked what Lanier had done in each instance.

Subsequent discussions with jurors revealed that at the beginning of deliberations, the four men had all wanted to convict the judge on each of the ten counts before them; what doubts there were had been voiced by women. Whatever this did or did not reveal about how women and men think about one another, eventually they had come together to condemn David Lanier's acts.

When Steve Parker telephoned Vivian with the news, he found her back at work in her Orlando office. Of course she wept, but this time from gratitude and relief that, no matter what, twelve people whom she had never met believed her and had publicly endorsed her honesty. It would have been nice if her own family had had that much faith in her, but she was not bitter about that, or was trying not to be. She felt sorry for

Jennifer Gallagher, who must be in agony that, in the end, she had not fared as well. He would try to explain to Jennifer, Parker said, that this was really only a technical difference. Good luck trying to convince her of that, Vivian said.

She added that she was very disappointed that Lanier would still be free for months on bond. He could do a lot of damage in that time, she warned, and she would not rest easy until he was locked up. That was going to happen, wasn't it? For how long?

That, Parker said, would be up to Judge Turner.

37

Of the women whom the jury had found Lanier not guilty of assaulting, Patty Wallace took the news the most calmly, realizing perhaps better than the prosecutors had that conviction on her count had been a long shot. Her husband, Barry, however, was less sanguine and less willing to accept that the actual goal of the trial had been accomplished. He was so angry when he heard the news that he attacked a tree in the yard with a metal baseball bat, destroying the tree and the bat in an outburst of monumental frustration. Judge Turner had better come up with a stiff sentence for the bastard, Barry said, or he still might have to consider vigilante justice. Bill Castleberry went to see him at the UPS depot to try to calm him down.

Julia Garnett was also irate that Judge Turner had dismissed the count involving her. Since when was it not a crime for a judge to expose himself and masturbate in front of a woman? He agreed with her, Steve Parker said, but his recourse to legalisms did nothing to assuage her.

Nor could he or Castleberry, as Vivian had predicted, repair Jennifer Gallagher's shattered psyche. No matter what anyone said, everyone she knew, including her family, would interpret the verdict as a condemnation of her. When Louise called her, Jennifer for the first time talked about suicide.

When Vivian also predicted that Judge Lanier would find some way to make trouble as long as he was out on bail, she had not been thinking of herself but of the other women, all of whom except Brenda Castain were still in Dyersburg trying to resume their lives. Vivian, after all, was a thousand miles away.

Shortly after the New Year, on January 6, 1993, Vivian was at home with the flu, sleeping on that Wednesday morning, when her answering machine recorded a message from Dyersburg. It was Dr. Warner calling, asking her to ring him back.

She was very surprised to hear from him, having had no contact with him whatsoever for months, perhaps for more than a year, she could not remember the last time. Nor was she sure she wanted to talk to him, ever again. But she remembered that, according to what the prosecutors had told her, Dr. Warner's testimony at the trial had been complimentary toward her and had ended up confirming her honesty—had been one of the two or three most important factors in convicting Judge Lanier, contrary to what the defense had expected when they put him on the stand. Perhaps Dr. Warner merely wished to say hello. Maybe he wanted to apologize for any suffering he had caused her. She telephoned him at his office. Just punching out those numbers brought back some very disturbing memories, but she stayed on the line.

They exchanged friendly greetings. Vivian told Dr. Warner that she was trying to figure out a way to keep her job and go back to college, perhaps at night. Then Dr. Warner said that the reason he was calling was because he had talked to Judge Lanier yesterday. The judge was adamant that things between Vivian and him had not happened, or not in the way Vivian had testified. Lanier wanted to know if, now that she had had some time to think about it, she would be willing to come forward and change her testimony, since she had been responsible for his being convicted of two felonies, which could cause him extra time in jail and the loss of his pension. Would she consider that?

Vivian exploded. What right did Dr. Warner have, asking her to do such a thing? She had told the truth. Twelve people had believed her, no matter what Lanier or anyone else said.

The more she talked, the more hysterical she became, damning Lanier for not having accepted a plea bargain just to force the victims to endure a trial, as she believed. That man had ruined her life, and now he was asking for help from her? Asking her to lie for him, to commit perjury?

He was just relaying a message, Dr. Warner said. Vivian hung up on him.

She lay there in bed, furious and also frightened. Judge Lanier's tentacles had reached her even in the haven she had found for herself! She did not know what to do.

During the next few days, Vivian became more ill. She began throwing up. A week later, she forced herself to go back to work, but her boss sent her home again and told her to call a doctor. *That's all I need,* she thought. *One already called me.*

She recovered sufficiently to return to work but could not stop thinking

about Dr. Warner and Lanier. At last, on January 19, she telephoned Bill
Castleberry.

Castleberry lost no time when he heard that Lanier had tried to contact a
witness to try to get her to change her testimony—and Vivian, of all of
them! She had sounded hysterical, terrified, on the phone. She had
reached him at home in Jackson. The next day he appeared at Dr.
Warner's office and heard the background. Warner said that he had been
feeling guilty about his testimony, if that could be imagined, because it
had hurt his friend, and he called Lanier to apologize. Lanier had taken
the opportunity to suggest to Warner that he call Vivian; at Lanier's suggestion, Warner obtained Vivian's home and work numbers from Tim
Naifeh, who evidently had thought it a fine idea for him to contact her.

    After hearing Vivian's reaction, which surprised him by its vehemence,
Dr. Warner had gone to lunch with Charles Kelly, who told him that he
had made a serious mistake that could get him into trouble and land
David Lanier in jail ahead of schedule. Until then, Dr. Warner said, he
had not thought he had done anything wrong.

    You are going to find out different, Dr. Warner, Bill Castleberry
thought. *We have been waiting for something like this.*

    He called on Charles Kelly with a specific purpose in mind. Not only
had Lanier contacted Dr. Warner, he had also, as Castleberry discovered
and Kelly would be surprised and no doubt chagrined to learn Bill knew,
written a letter to his former attorney, asking Kelly to contact several witnesses.

    "I'll need that letter you just received from Lanier," Castleberry told
Kelly in the lawyer's office.

    "How in hell do you know about that?" Kelly asked.

    "I'm an FBI agent."

    "You're an asshole."

    Kelly turned the letter over. It was written in Lanier's hand on a folded
note card on the front of which was an engraving of the Dyer County
Courthouse. Dated January 5, 1993, it read:

Dear Charles,
You can still help me if you want to. You're off the list of people I
can't contact, so I am contacting you. I need lots of names on petitions but I especially need some that you can get for me. I need for
Vivian to tell the truth that I did not hurt her and you could probably
get Judy to get her to do that. I'm losing my family, my job, my law
license and my freedom, thanks to her, but she could save my pension for me. . . .

*   *   *

After this request to have Vivian's mother pressure her into changing her testimony, the letter, signed "David," suggested other people for Kelly to contact to persuade Jennifer Gallagher, Cathy Kiely, Mary Haralson, and two women who had testified before the grand jury to sign a petition on the judge's behalf. A copy of this petition was enclosed, and it was headed:

We, the undersigned citizens and residents of the United States of America, do hereby respectfully petition the honorable Jerome Turner to carefully consider probation or house arrest for David W. Lanier in lieu of incarceration since it is his first offense and he has served as a good, honest, law-abiding public servant for his city, county and state for the past 27 years, and he has maintained his innocence of all charges throughout.

Kelly also provided a copy of the letter he had written to David Lanier in reply. Dated January 8, it warned David that to act as he wished would constitute a breach of the conditions of his bond and would cause him to be "incarcerated immediately." "It is my understanding," Kelly continued, "that Dr. Warner has contacted Vivian concerning possible 'recanting' of her testimony. I am sure, as well as you are, that this conversation was taped by her."

Castleberry soon learned that Lanier had also written on courthouse notepaper to Charles "Bubba" Agee with a similar request to that attorney, this one asking him to get Janet Thomasson, Linda Pickering, Jennifer Gallagher, and another woman to sign the petition requesting leniency. He obtained a copy of that from Agee. Agee had not replied to it, considering even that much contact with Lanier improper under the circumstances.

When Castleberry presented him with the evidence, Steve Parker moved swiftly to request a new hearing for revocation of Lanier's bond. Judge Magistrate Daniel J. Breen set the date for Friday morning, February 5, in Memphis.

Al Moskowitz flew in from Washington for the event. The small magistrate's courtroom was filled with reporters. Louise Fitzgerald was there, but none of the victims was present. They did not wish to risk being disappointed.

Castleberry was the first witness for the government, giving an account of how that frantic phone call from Vivian had led to this morning's hearing. Parker referred to Lanier as a "convicted violent criminal" who was still hiding behind his position. Sitting in the front row with her sister, Robbye Lanier bristled and walked out, only to return shortly afterward. Dr. Warner was questioned as at the trial, by Al Moskowitz. When David Lanier took the stand to defend his letters to the lawyers and the phone call to Vivian, which he claimed had been Dr. Warner's idea, Steve Parker attacked him so vehemently that Wayne Emmons asked Judge Breen to restrain Parker from getting into Judge Lanier's face.

Joan Lanier said that calling Vivian had been Dr. Warner's idea, because he had telephoned the Lanier family home first, to get David's apartment phone number. Al Moskowitz asked her if she still had affection for her husband and did not want to see him go to jail. She replied with a torrent of words that seemed to imply that she and her family were the victims of some vast conspiracy, American degeneracy, and foreign forces, mentioning Scud missiles, "nameless faces," and "faceless names," and alluding frequently to her religious faith. She was starting a new job at a mental health center, she added.

Although Al Moskowitz had the last word for the government that morning, arguing in his usual quiet, careful way that David Lanier had clearly violated the conditions of his bond, it was Steve Parker's summation that rang in everyone's ears afterward. Parker evoked the suffering of the victims and their right to be free at last from David Lanier's attempts to intimidate them. Shouting, pointing at Lanier as he sat beside Wayne Emmons and continued to evade Parker's eyes, Parker let loose a tirade, which Judge Breen did not restrain:

"The fact that a *sex offender* is trying to pressure his victims into changing their testimony is absolutely atrocious. He is the center of the universe. He can't use his power anymore, so he tries to play on sympathy. I lose my pension, how am I going to support my family? I'm *sorry,* Your Honor. *He didn't think about his family when he raped Vivian Forsythe!* He was thinking about himself. *He is a selfish perverted sex offender,* who abused his position, and he should be in *jail!*"

Judge Breen ruled that the evidence left him no choice. He saw no conditions that he could set that could protect witnesses from Judge Lanier's contacting them or that could force him to abide by the conditions of his release.

"And I therefore," Judge Breen said, "revoke bond and detain him."

The words, spoken softly and almost without inflection, left behind them a strangely powerful silence. More even than at the moment of the guilty verdicts, everyone in that courtroom could feel that something profound had just happened. A man who for nearly ten years had spent his professional life judging others and wielding power over their lives and liberties was now about to be deprived of that most precious thing on earth, the foundation stone of the American republic, his personal freedom. With one sentence from Judge Breen, David Lanier was going from the status of judge to that of a federal prisoner, and all because he had contempt for the very thing that he had sworn to uphold and administer, the law.

There was something oddly and powerfully symmetrical about that scene as two U.S. marshals, dressed inconspicuously in tan uniforms, came forward from where they had been sitting unobtrusively at the side of the bench and approached David Lanier, who stood up. He knew what was coming, the handcuffs and shackles. He who had enjoyed and abused all the power of the law was now to be subjected publicly to its demeaning implements.

The marshals helped him off with his jacket. In her seat, Joan Lanier buried her head in her hands and cried. Leigh Anne and Robbye could not bear to let their father endure this moment of humiliation alone and rushed forward, crying, to embrace him. The marshals waited as he kissed his daughters good-bye and gazed toward his ex-wife, as if still seeking a sign of recognition from her or even endorsement or sympathy, it was impossible to say. And, most peculiarly, he still wore that odd, lopsided grin of his, surely now out of habit more than self-satisfaction. But who would presume to have fathomed this man?

The marshals pulled his unresisting arms back and cuffed his wrists together behind him. They shackled his ankles together, so that when they led him out the door and off to jail, he walked with short, awkward, rattling steps.

38

It was difficult to believe that David Lanier was finally off the bench, especially because technically he was not. He might be in jail, held in the Federal Correctional Institution in Memphis, but he had not resigned, and the legislature had not impeached him or voted on his removal, had not even considered the question. And he was still receiving his salary, which by 1993 had risen to more than eighty-five thousand dollars a year. Outrage about the situation spread throughout the state, with numerous newspapers demanding his ouster. The *Commercial Appeal* called for the legislature to act now and "just get rid of him." But House Speaker Jimmy Naifeh said he preferred to wait until the Tennessee Court of the Judiciary ruled on the case. Two Memphis legislators, both Democrats, sent a letter to Lanier asking him to resign and made it public, but he refused.

The Court of the Judiciary had filed charges against Judge Lanier in January but did not schedule the formal hearing on the matter until February 24. This body, consisting of fourteen members, most of them judges, others lawyers and lay citizens, met twice a year in different court-houses around the state. By coincidence the first meeting of 1993 had already been scheduled for Dyersburg. David Lanier announced from his cell that he would attend and would represent himself. He then asked the entire panel to resign, saying that they had already shown bias against him by giving credence to the federal indictment against him and his conviction. They did not act on his request. Lanier countered by saying he wished to call a total of forty-eight witnesses, some on his behalf, others including all the women who had testified against him before the grand jury and at his trial last year. He would be examining them all himself, he announced.

The idea that Lanier would be able to confront his accusers again and

subject them to what would undoubtedly be harsh questioning was as hor-
rifying a prospect as it was bizarre. Steve Parker contacted the presiding
judge of this different sort of state court to try to explain the situation to
him. Louise Fitzgerald wrote a long letter to the Court of the Judiciary
detailing the suffering these women had already gone through and giving
her opinion as a professional psychologist and in her capacity as a member of the prosecution team that it would be a disaster should the women
have to appear.

Only days before the hearing, the presiding judge agreed that the purpose was not to permit Lanier to retry his federal case before this other
court. The women would be excluded from testifying. What exactly the
purpose of the hearing actually was remained to be seen. On the basis of
it, apparently, the Court of the Judiciary would decide whether or not to
recommend to the legislature that Judge David Lanier be impeached. Was
there not already more than sufficient evidence for that?

What was actually going on could only be understood in the light of
American history. It was another battle, being fought this time without
guns, over states' rights versus federal authority. No state, or not this
Southern one at any rate, was going to be told by the federal government
when to remove one of its judges. And so the hearing went forward.

Louise Fitzgerald returned again from Illinois. She would not have
missed this spectacle for anything, even if on some level she was as puzzled as anyone else as to why it was taking place. She and Bill drove up
from Memphis; Steve Parker and Amy Spain arrived that morning in
Dyersburg, too.

Louise had seen a bit of Dyersburg before, when she and Bill had gone
on their mission to retrieve Jennifer Gallagher for her recall to the stand
that never happened. But Louise had never seen the courthouse, that
impressive, stately building, that center of the Lanier universe and the
navel of the entire case, from the inside. Lanier himself, the deposed or
almost-deposed king, had yet to arrive from his Memphis cell, as Louise
mounted the steps.

The hearing was to be held in the second-floor circuit courtroom,
which was larger than Lanier's old chancery court, where a retired judge
appointed by the state Supreme Court had been handling Lanier's duties
for the past few months. But before taking them upstairs, Bill escorted
Louise, Amy, and Steve into Lanier's old offices. Until now the others
had seen only photographs and diagrams of the place on which their
imaginations had been fixed for so long, so intently.

His name was still on the door. Inside the chambers his books were
still on the shelves, the furniture remained as the women had described it.
And the bathroom. Bill watched as Louise stepped into it and quickly left,

her eyes lowered, her mouth turned down in disgust, shaking her head. As had been his experience, Bill could tell, everything was all too hideously real now for her inside that place.

Bill was fascinated by Louise's powerful reaction. Even though she had spent her career studying women's problems, even though she had talked to scores of clients, heard their tales of misery, she had not experienced before the impact that a visit to an actual crime scene can have. It was the reason people made pilgrimages to holy places. Only then could the unimaginable become real, the suffering become flesh.

Then Joey McDowell poked his head in. Lanier had arrived. They could watch through the window in the filing room.

Louise, Amy, and Steve hurried to the window that gave a view of the courthouse lawn and the driveway where prisoners were customarily unloaded, to be brought into basement holding cells.

And there he was!

Only Bill stood back. For the moment he was more interested in Louise's reaction than in seeing Lanier. He knew what Lanier would look like, more or less. He would look like a federal prisoner.

Steve, Amy, and Louise gazed down into the driveway. The prison van had just pulled in. Lanier, dressed in a maroon prison-issue nylon windbreaker, eased himself out the back door that was held by a marshal and with difficulty stood up.

He was handcuffed and shackled. He looked very different from the last time any one of this group had seen him. His hair was long, shaggy, seemed grayer than before, and he had grown a grizzled beard. He had lost a lot of weight, looked almost gaunt.

What must he be thinking—brought back in irons to the place over which he had held sway for so many years, and his father before him? Was James P. also watching from somewhere, his portrait still hanging in the hallway? And James O., doubtless with more satisfaction than pity?

They led Lanier into the basement, out of sight.

Bill kept his eyes riveted on Louise. When she turned away from the window, she was pale. He had thought she would be.

"I'm shaken," Louise said. "I was not prepared for this. This isn't easy. It's not what I expected." She shivered.

How complicated this thing called justice is, Bill was thinking. There was no need to say it.

Of all of them, Amy Spain seemed the most matter-of-fact about seeing Lanier in his changed conditions—she who had begun as the skeptical one about the women. Now she was adamant.

"He still looks arrogant," Amy said, turning away from the window.

And Bill knew she was right.

*   *   *

Joey led everyone to the second-floor courtroom. About halfway up the crowded stairs, they made way for Leigh Anne, Robbye, and Joan Lanier, who scowled at the intruders from Memphis. As Leigh Anne passed through, Amy lost her balance, gripping the handrail.

"I can't believe it," Amy said under her breath. "Robbye hipped me! I guess she wanted to knock me down the stairs."

Joey said that the sheriff had laid on extra security, afraid that Barry Wallace might seize the opportunity to attack Lanier or that Jennifer Gallagher's husband might decide to play sniper. Barry had been vocal about his hatred, especially after the acquittal on Patty's count.

But no—there was Barry at the top of the stairs, looking tense but acting like his normal cheerful self. Bill took him aside and reported that he was fine. He seemed to have derived satisfaction from seeing Lanier in chains. He was apparently the only family member of the victims present; none of the women were there.

Sitting in the second-to-the-last row of the courtroom, Bill and Louise heard the clock atop the building strike eleven. The Court of the Judiciary filed in.

The scene was medieval. Twelve stony-faced judges in their black robes took their seats in the jury box. A thirteenth, Judge Jerry Scott of the Court of Appeals, ascended to preside behind the bench. A fourteenth, retired Judge Lloyd Tatum of Henderson, the only robeless member, stood at the prosecutor's table.

Only the presence of five women among the seven men in the jury box struck a contemporary note. Otherwise, all was indeed medieval ecclesiastical, the crowd that filled every seat pious in their stiff silence, the jurists in their vestments there to determine whether to defrock one of their own. A week ago the state Supreme Court had suspended Judge Lanier's license to practice law. Today he would defend himself before his colleagues and the people of Dyersburg, acting *pro se* or for himself, as the term was. The law retained more Latin than the Church of Rome.

Journalists scribbled in their notebooks. Donna Whittle, the lady in red, sat directly behind the Lanier family. Joey McDowell and Stan Cavness stood to one side at the rear.

And then through a door beside the jury box strode Judge Lanier, escorted by a pair of bailiffs. Unbound, he was still in that jail-issue jacket. Lanier, still with his smirk. Was it only habit, or was he pleased to again be the cynosure? He ambled with what was perhaps affected nonchalance to his place alone at the defense table.

What Lanier was still fighting for, improbably, was to retain his title and his salary, even if he had irretrievably, barring the success of his

appeal, lost his power. There were two issues before the Court of the
Judiciary. Lanier's convictions under the federal indictment were one; the
other was his failure to have recused himself back in 1991 from ruling in
favor of a new trial in the accident case involving his then-secretary,
Mary Haralson. This court had already censured him for the latter, which
was one basis on which he was condemning these jurists as having
already declared their bias against him.

Judge Tatum entered both matters as evidence on the question at hand,
namely, whether the court should recommend Lanier's removal from
office. In response, Lanier, more forbidding in appearance than before,
with his longish hair and grizzled beard and prison garb, as if no prison
could hold him after all, moved for the entire court to recuse itself.
Approaching the jury box, he asked each of his berobed colleagues to
admit his or her bias against him. Each individually declined to do so.

"I accept this," Lanier said. "It's hard, but I accept it." His tone was
decidedly petulant.

He then made his rather outrageous request to call no fewer than forty-
eight witnesses in his defense, more than had testified for him during his
entire federal trial. He complained about how difficult it had been for him
in jail to obtain their addresses for subpoenas. Judge Tatum countered by
arguing that Lanier's federal conviction made calling any of the witnesses
from that trial superfluous. This court was not about to retry that case.
Judge Scott agreed.

Lanier refused to give in. He said that the women who had testified
against him had been intimidated by the FBI and the U.S. attorneys. He
had been persecuted. He singled out Vivian Forsythe and characterized
her as a pathological liar.

Finally Judge Scott ruled firmly that Lanier would be permitted only
character witnesses on his behalf, not to call his accusers.

Lanier's grin was now, even behind his beard, overtly a smirk of contempt. He looked around at his family as if to say, "You see? They're all
against me."

The hearing went on for two surreal days. Lanier called some twenty witnesses. A banker testified that he had loaned the judge large sums without
collateral and always received the money back with interest; a fish dealer
spoke of knowing the Laniers for fifty years and admiring them. The
Master of the Dyer County Court, Sissy Nale, stunning in a black, gold-
embroidered pantsuit, in office the past thirteen years, was fidgety on the
stand—and the federal prosecution team knew why. She had tried to
remain loyal to her long-time employer, but during the trial Lanier had
pushed her too far, asking her to swear out an affidavit saying that Agent

Castleberry had seduced her, or tried to, and that Mary Haralson had been an incompetent employee. She had refused and had told Castleberry about the requests for her to perjure herself. "Maybe now you know who the good guys and the bad guys are," Bill had told her. Here, wiggling her foot and clutching a gold purse, she did her best to say that Lanier had been a fine judge and a fair employer.

"She hated my guts," Bill said to Louise, "but I always liked her. She's a hell of a woman."

Louise remained tongue-tied. There were so many layers to this story! And so many women! Some victims, some not; some who complied, some who did not but survived unscathed; some who lost everything, some who profited. This wasn't a law case, it was a nineteenth-century novel! And then the women of the Lanier family.

He called each of them to the stand.

"Are you my daughter, Robbye?"

"Yes, Daddy," the witness replied.

"What kind of a father am I?"

"Everyone should know how trustworthy you are. You never lost your temper. You taught me not to jaywalk. You've always gone out of your way to be good to everybody."

Leigh Anne's voice broke when she said that in twenty-six years her father, who stood before her, prisoner and advocate for himself, had never yelled at her. A gentle man.

And Joan Lanier. After extolling her ex-husband's kindly demeanor, Mrs. Lanier suddenly erupted into a diatribe against the federal government, a Gestapo police state that had persecuted her family. She attacked the women who had accused him. "Is there no law against prostitution in this country?" She spoke of devils and invoked Jesus Christ.

When she was through, Joan Lanier, sad, frantic, rushed down the aisle of the courtroom to take her furious leave. All heads turned as she passed. She reached the rear door.

It was locked! It had been secured against some violent intruder, and now it was preventing Mrs. Lanier from getting out of what for her must have been a torture chamber. She rattled and pounded on the door, shouting for someone to open it, as everyone watched, not moving. Finally a deputy released it from the outside, and she fled.

"Now I know what this is all about," Louise whispered. "This is like a Greek tragedy the community performs to ritualize their frustrations and expiate guilt."

"That's good, professor," Bill said. "Except there's no tragic hero."

"Heroines, then," she said.

*   *   *

It was expected that the Court of the Judiciary would take at least a month to decide whether to recommend impeachment to the legislature.

Meanwhile, on March 26 in Memphis, Judge Lanier appeared back in Judge Turner's courtroom for sentencing. This time everyone was there, including Vivian from Florida. Most of the victims wanted to be present for this event, but just to be sure, Steve Parker had them subpoenaed. He asked them to fill the first two rows of the right-side benches, where Judge Turner had to see them. Parker had no quarrels whatever with the way Judge Turner had conducted the trial, except for his dismissal of the Julia Garnett count. But the prosecutor wanted to do what he could to persuade the judge not to lean toward leniency for his fellow jurist.

He had determined, Judge Turner said, that federal guidelines as mandated during the past few years by Congress called for him to sentence Judge Lanier to twenty-five years in prison: one year each on the misdemeanors, ten years each on the felonies. He was troubled by this. In fact, he was "somewhat amazed" that the guidelines, a complex system of calculation in which extra points are added for the use of force in the commission of a crime and for lying on the witness stand, added up to what amounted to a life sentence for Lanier, who was now fifty-eight.

"I don't make light in any way of the situation these victims found themselves in," Turner said. "The conduct in this case warrants a high sentence. The question is, how high?"

Parker asked the judge what he considered "high." Ten years was a substantial sentence, Turner replied; so was fifteen. But twenty-five? The federal system offered no possibility of parole, only fifty-four days a year time off for good behavior.

Parker reminded the judge of the severity of the crimes and, to illustrate, read out portions of Vivian Forsythe's testimony. Vivian, who was sitting between Jennifer Gallagher and Linda Michaels, could not help crying all over again.

Judge Turner postponed sentencing for eighteen days. He invited both the defense and the prosecution to submit arguments for why he should or should not deviate from the federal guidelines.

On April 12, they were all together again. Gathered in the library beforehand, they speculated about what Judge Turner would do. Most thought he would opt for twelve years or thereabouts, although it was highly unusual and an invitation for reversal on appeal for a federal judge to deviate from the sentencing guidelines established by Congress. Parker, Moskowitz, and Spain had no idea what Turner would do. Neither Bill nor Louise had a clue. Of the women, only Vivian was willing to bet that the sentence would be twenty-five years. "I have a feeling," she said. "I hope I'm right."

It was time to go in. Previously the women had entered the courtroom through a side door, to avoid the press and others. Now Vivian said that she was tired of hiding.

"I'm not going in some back door," she said. "I'm going in the front door. Who's coming with me?"

"I am," Louise said immediately, and Linda Michaels and Jennifer Gallagher came forward also.

At the main entrance to the courtroom the four women joined hands. Vivian led them down to the front row as everyone stared at them.

Judge Turner had a good deal of public rumination to accomplish before he got around to announcing what Lanier's sentence would actually be. He complained at length again about the rigidity of the federal sentencing guidelines and about how, if Judge Lanier had been tried in a state court, his sentence would have been far less than twenty-five years. This disparity created the appearance of unfairness or at least disparity in the justice system, Judge Turner said, and he did not like that.

"I have struggled with the sentencing phase of this case for weeks now," Judge Turner added. "I looked at these guidelines for a long time. I was dismayed when I was given reason to believe that the government had offered, and the defendant had turned down, a prospective settlement of the case for something in the neighborhood of eighteen months on a plea of guilty."

As much as he worried about the severity of the sentence mandated by the guidelines, however, he wanted to be clear that he was not minimizing the seriousness of the crimes: "Judge Lanier, despite your denials, the jury has found that you did engage in the conduct charged in this case, and in Vivian [Forsythe] Archie's case, found that you used force to impose yourself on her. Accepting that verdict as returned, it was a terrible infliction of demeaning sexual abuse by force. And as to the other victims, this is simply obvious degradation, that you [could have] not only belittled them but did, I think, substantial damage to the faith that a lot of people have in the justice system, of which you were such a distinctive part."

Twenty-five years was a "terribly long" sentence, he said, "and for this individual it was going to be even longer because of his age. But when I think about what an appropriate sentence would be for physically forcing a woman to have oral sex . . . I can't conclude that ten years is too long." That it happened a second time was "even more egregious." For these reasons, and because he had no room otherwise under the guidelines, Judge Turner sentenced Judge Lanier to ten years each on the felony counts and a year on each of the misdemeanors. Twenty-five years without parole it was.

And Judge Turner went further, levying a twenty-five-thousand-dollar

fine, payable immediately, and ordering that if indeed David Lanier was
eligible for a state pension, fifteen hundred dollars a month was to be for-
feited from it for the duration of the sentence toward the cost of the prisoner's incarceration.

There were no outward reactions in the courtroom, except that most of
the women, who were holding hands across the two rows in which they
sat at the front, squeezed one another and drew each other close. As for
the defendant, he remained his usual enigmatic self.

Steve Parker stood before the women in the law library afterward and
asked if he could say a few final words to them.

"I want to thank you on behalf of all my colleagues and myself," he
said, "for all you have done and all you've endured. We know what
you've been through." He had tears in his eyes. "You're my heroines, and
I love you all."

Most of them cried, some loudly. Vivian, Jennifer, Linda Michaels, and
Brenda Castain, who was there to show her solidarity, hugged one
another. One or two, including Janet Thomasson, quickly hurried away, as
if to try as soon as possible to escape a nightmare.

"A victory for women?" Bill asked Louise.

"Not only that," she said. "I think it's a triumph of the human spirit."

Louise noticed Steve Parker standing in a corner, looking oddly glum,
staring at his shoes. She went to him and asked him what was the matter.
Shouldn't he be feeling as if he'd won a great victory?

"I was thinking about all the hurt that's been done to these women,"
Parker said. "By Lanier, of course. But by all of us. It's called the price of
justice. Justice is emotionally very expensive."

Louise demurred. These women had done something heroic. For the
rest of their lives, they had something to be proud of.

Parker agreed about the heroism. But he had been around the victims
of crime long enough, he said, to know that they had lost something, too,
and forever. David Lanier had taken something from them that they could
never recapture. Call it innocence, call it faith in life, the ability to sleep
peacefully, whatever. It was gone. That was why twenty-five years was
not too long a sentence for a man who had turned some hearts to stone.

Louise felt her own heart sink at this realism.

"Their lives will never mend," Steve Parker said. "They may improve.
Some of them may learn to forget, most of the time. But in the middle of
the night, or when they send a child off to school or into the world—oh,
God. There's no solution, Louise. There's no perfection when this kind of
harm is done, and there are no new lives. There's only justice."

39

The Tennessee General Assembly finally acted, on April 21, 1993, on the recommendation of the Court of the Judiciary, to remove David Lanier from office by unanimous votes of both the House of Representatives and the Senate. Before the tally was taken, Lanier informed the legislature that he had already sent a letter of resignation to Governor Ned McWherter. If Lanier had wished to avoid this ultimate political disgrace, as President Nixon had by resigning before he could be impeached, he lost his nerve, or retained hope of vindication, or chose to remain contemptuously defiant. The governor's office sent word that no such communication had been received, and the vote went ahead. For the first time in nearly sixty years, no Dyersburg Lanier any longer held elective office in the state.

The issue of federal versus state jurisdiction remained a factor until the end, when one senator finally overcame his reservations about ousting a state official on the basis of a merely federal conviction and made the verdict unanimous. He resolved his misgivings only because he could see himself as acting on the advice of the Court of the Judiciary, not the feds. By then, however, it was no longer politically prudent to support David Lanier, whose case, with the national publicity attached to it, had become an embarrassment to Tennessee. Momentum gathered in support of a statute forbidding sexual harassment in the workplace; the governor soon signed the bill into law. Whether such legislation would have prevented someone with Lanier's power from acting as he had, without federal intervention, remained doubtful.

Early in May, marshals transported David Lanier from Memphis to the Federal Correctional Facility in Talladega, Alabama, a medium-security prison situated about fifty miles east of Birmingham and a hundred miles west of Atlanta, where he became one among nine hundred and forty-five inmates. In Memphis he had been isolated for his own protection; as a former judge, he was in danger of assault. He found the solitude unbearable, however, and at his request was placed among the general population at Talladega.

There he worked on his appeal and initiated various other legal actions, including a complaint against Charles Kelly, charging incompetent representation. It was Kelly's belief that the source of Lanier's resentment was Kelly's having turned over to the FBI Lanier's letter asking the lawyer to contact witnesses. Kelly, of course, had had no choice in the matter, since Bill Castleberry had already known of the letter's existence; concealing it might well have landed Kelly in prison, too. But Kelly by then was no longer acting as Lanier's counsel. Maybe David wants company, Kelly remarked, exasperated that until the complaint was resolved or dismissed, he could not be licensed to practice across the river in Missouri, where riverboat gambling was about to be legalized. David had his ways of getting back, even from behind bars.

From his cell Lanier issued at irregular intervals a "newsletter," each issue some two to three thousand typed words, photocopied and distributed to family members and supporters on the outside. The issue of December 7, 1993, was typical. Datelined "Pearl Harbor Day," Lanier's message was that veterans of World War II who had fought, been wounded, and died in the cause of freedom would be horrified to see that their country had become "a police state [such] as the ones they were fighting against." He predicted that juries in federal cases would soon be abolished, since they had become nothing but rubber stamps for the FBI and the prosecutors anyway. He reaffirmed his innocence. He was not trying to justify having committed an immoral act, but he was not a criminal, he insisted.

The remainder of the Pearl Harbor Day issue consisted of a diatribe against Vivian Forsythe, rehashing her drug addiction and going into stories about her sexual promiscuity, all secondhand of course, in steamy and hostile detail. He had only felt sorry for her, Lanier wrote, and had never been physically attracted to her: "In fact," he wrote preposterously, "I had heard that she had AIDS."

Obviously his hatred of Vivian, whom he blamed, and with good reason, as the key instrument of his downfall, remained so intense that he was eager to try to hurt her again from prison, by reminding people of her former problems and by spreading new, false, and vicious rumors about her. As he wrote on and on about her, however, the salacious nature of his interest in her would have been apparent to any but the most psychologically obtuse reader. His was a sensibility in which sex, hate, and the lust for power were so intertwined as to be indistinguishable.

His ignorance of himself, on the evidence of the newsletter and his pride in it, was equally apparent. The Pearl Harbor Day issue, which suggested that if the federal government could defeat the Germans and the Japanese, what chance had he, was among those he forwarded, like any aspiring writer, to New York literary agents. In his cover letter he announced that he was seeking representation in the interest of "getting my book published and my movie produced." As one recipient of this literature, a man who knew little more about the former judge than what could be deduced from these carefully typed, grammatically errorless outpourings, remarked, David Lanier appeared to be a man whose self-pity was rivaled by his self-deception.

In other newsletters he described prison life, alluding to the menace of assault against him because of his former profession, commenting on the quality of the food (not bad), and complaining of the unpleasantness to which he was being subjected. Citing the amount deducted from his pension by Judge Turner's order, he referred indignantly to the small size of his cell and to the gross inconvenience of having to share living space with another inmate. He was sure, he said, that at this rent he could secure better accommodations on the outside. (Despite his removal from office, he remained eligible for the pension.)

He informed his readers, in a bland, even tone very different from that of the typical inmate, about his routine and his surroundings, expressing pessimism about the status of his appeal, saying that if it failed, his attorney was ready to "hang up his spurs." He worried about his safety and stated that the chief source of trouble among inmates involved disputes over the highly restricted telephone privileges. Prisoners were permitted only fifteen-minute calls, after standing in line to enter their names on a reservation list. His most serious, nearly violent altercation so far, he wrote, had been with an inmate who had "stolen" six minutes from him.

As certain targets of his calls attested, Lanier was making actively malicious use of his privileges to cause anxiety among those he regarded as enemies. Taking advantage of a call-forwarding service, he would ring up a certain former mistress of his who remained loyal to him and use her to connect him with third parties, including women who had been witnesses against him. In this way, no record was left for prison authorities to check, except the number of the mistress in Dyersburg.

Specifically to avoid unwanted calls, Jennifer Gallagher had installed an answering machine. One evening during the first week of October 1993, however, she heard an unfamiliar female voice on the machine asking to speak to her, and she picked up the receiver:

"Hello. This is Jennifer."

The woman gave her name and continued, "Jennifer, everyone knows you're living alone with your daughter. How is she?"

"Fine. Why do you ask?"

"Wouldn't it be a shame if she was taken away from you?"

To imply such a threat, Jennifer knew, the caller must have known that, legally, her parents retained custody of the child.

"Why are you saying that? What do you want?"

"I have someone here who needs to speak to you."

"Who?"

"I'll put him on."

Then came the voice Jennifer dreaded and feared most in the world.

"Hello, Jennifer," David Lanier said. "I understand you've lost weight. That's wonderful news. I bet you're looking just beautiful."

She was in shock. The impulse to hang up was immediate, but it was as if she were paralyzed in a dream. In horror and fright, she continued listening a moment longer.

"Jennifer," Lanier went on in that calm, sinister tone of his, "it's a shame what they made you do. They've ruined your life, haven't they, and your daughter's life? You know, we didn't do anything wrong. It was consensual, we know that, don't we? You didn't have to say those things they made you say, did you?"

"All I did," Jennifer said, beginning to cry, "was say the truth!"

"Now, we know that's not so. All you have to do, to make things right, is tell everyone that it was consensual. I've admitted it. Now, all you have to do is admit it, too. Then we'll both be better off, don't you see?"

Jennifer hung up, ran into her daughter's bedroom, and hugged the child, crying and waking her up.

"Mommy, Mommy! What's the matter? What can I do for you?"

"You could murder me!" Jennifer cried out, hysterical. "You could murder me! Oh! What have I said! I'm sorry! I didn't mean to say that! Oh! Forgive me!"

In panic for the next few days, Jennifer was sure David Lanier was about to get out of prison and would come back and take her daughter away. Foolishly, irrationally, she told no one about the call. But when the woman's voice came on the speaker again one night, she did not answer, got an unlisted number the next day, and told a friend about the calls. He immediately informed Steve Parker, who verified from records that Lanier had indeed called the woman in Dyersburg that evening, and many other evenings. Prison authorities managed to put a stop to Lanier's malicious game.

The relentlessness of Lanier's sadism seemed limitless. Since the jury had acquitted on Jennifer's count anyway, there seemed little reason for him to be calling her except malice; perhaps he received a sexual thrill from it, also. Or did Lanier actually think that Jennifer's recanting her testimony would cause a reversal on appeal? It was possible.

Parker already knew that Lanier was prepared to go to any length to further his appeal and that mentally he was bizarre enough to resort to absurd, even comical gambits. On the day of his sentencing he had sent a long letter, about fifteen hundred words, to the President of the United States, appealing to Bill Clinton as a fellow Democrat—did Lanier perhaps hope for sympathy from a public official who had also been accused of sexual misconduct?—and asking him to instigate an investigation by the Justice Department and the FBI. The U.S. Attorney's office in Memphis, he said, had manipulated the grand jury, had failed to disclose evidence favorable to the defense, and had permitted Special Agent William Castleberry to intimidate witnesses. All of this was a vendetta against a "lifelong Democrat" by people appointed by Republicans. He referred to himself as "not guilty" and as "innocent on all counts in my own mind."

"Please let me hear from you one way or the other," the letter to the President closed. But it was forwarded from the White House to the Justice Department, where a spokesman replied to "Judge Lanier" that no comment from the President would be proper while an appeal remained in progress.

The United States Court of Appeals for the Sixth Circuit issued its decision on August 31, 1994. A three-judge panel unanimously rejected Lanier's petition, affirming the verdict "on all counts."

Wayne Emmons had appealed on behalf of his client on fifteen separate grounds. One of them was the argument that the twenty-five-year sentence was "grossly disproportionate" to Lanier's crimes. The Sixth Circuit thought otherwise. "Defendant was convicted of seven of the eleven counts in the indictment," the opinion stated. "These seven counts involved sexual assaults on five women, two of which were felony counts involving defendant's forcing a woman to perform oral sex on him on two occasions, resulting in bodily injury to her. Further, in committing these crimes, defendant misused his power as a state judge to gain access to, as well as silence from the victims . . . Thus, defendant's claim that his sentence of 25 years is so grossly disproportionate to the crime he committed as to suggest an Eighth Amendment [the prohibition of "cruel and unusual punishment"] violation has no merit."

After this defeat, Wayne Emmons asked for and received permission from the Court of Appeals to withdraw from the case. Lanier, however, had not given up. Early in 1995, acting as his own attorney, he filed a second appeal, a document of twenty pages that began by stating, accurately, that his was "a case of first impression in the United States where a state employee has been indicted, tried, and convicted under a violation of 18 USC §242 in which the accusers were not in custody of any kind . . ." The rest of the brief, however, was, in the opinion of Parker, Moskowitz, and Spain, riddled with fanciful, inaccurate, and in some instances odd assertions. In a move that the prosecutors thought peculiarly self-defeating, Lanier attacked the integrity of Judge Ted Milburn, who had presided over the three-judge panel that had rejected his appeal of the previous year, on the peculiar grounds that Milburn "had been a personal friend," or so Lanier alleged, "of this defendant for 37 years," or since their days in law school together, and ought on that account to have recused himself. Since Milburn had voted against the defendant the last time around, it was difficult to imagine how the appeals judge had been swayed by any conflict of interest based on friendship. Surely Lanier was not suggesting that to know him was to be prejudiced against him?

Among the several arguments Lanier mounted in his own defense, the most peculiar, to anyone who knew the attorneys, were accusations of misconduct against Amy Spain and Al Moskowitz. "AUSA Amy Spain," Lanier charged, "reportedly called [a female witness before the grand jury] a 'fucking liar,' during questioning of her."

No one had ever heard Amy use obscene language; imagining her doing so, particularly in a professional situation, was so contrary to her upbringing and personality as to be ludicrous in its incongruity. Steve Parker recalled how troubled she had been initially by the necessity of verbalizing the sexual acts involved in the charges, how difficult it had been for her at first to bring herself to utter the word "penis" in public.

Equally absurd was Lanier's complaint against Moskowitz: "The Washington lawyer reportedly used sexual remarks toward [a female witness] and told her [that] her blue eyes mesmerized him and wanted to know if she would come to work for the government and seduce men to get information from them." The idea of the scholarly, impeccably correct Moskowitz, who by then was acting head of the criminal section of the Civil Rights Division, making indecent proposals as a pimp for the Justice Department inspired a good deal of mirth.

However remote its chances of success, the Court of Appeals did agree to hear Lanier's new appeal, setting a date in the summer of 1995 to consider the matter *en banc,* that is to say with all of the circuit's sixteen judges in attendance at its Cincinnati headquarters. By this action they automatically vacated their 1994 opinion, although with the option to reinstate it, as most legal observers anticipated would happen. The prosecutors fully expected to prevail again, as Lanier's arguments appeared more likely to irritate the judges than to persuade them.

40

Just as the Court of Appeals was considering Lanier's appeal in 1994, three months before issuing its denial, his Penthouse collapsed. That is to say, the building that housed it, the old Palace Hotel, fell in—or the entire front of it did, and much of one side. "Time and old age are the apparent culprits," Bill Castleberry read on May 30 in the *Jackson Sun*, under the front-page headline PART OF BUILDING COLLAPSES IN DOWNTOWN DYERSBURG. The structure had stood at the corner of Cedar and Main "since the turn of the century," the story said, without mentioning its previous functions as a whorehouse and Judge Lanier's retreat. In a color photograph it appeared as if an earthquake had struck.

I've got to see this for myself, Castleberry thought, and jumped in his car and headed northwest over the familiar roads, past Alamo and into Dyersburg.

He was in his last year with the Bureau, he had decided, reluctant as he was to let go of a life he loved. Out of sentiment he was still driving the same Chevy in which he had racked up over a hundred thousand miles along the triangle of Jackson, Memphis, and Dyersburg, the perimeter of his work for the past four years.

At fifty-two he had the option of remaining with the FBI another five years, but he had concluded that it was time to go. If he waited much longer, it might be too late to begin life anew; he was already worried about the period of adjustment, which for him, so completely had his role as an agent defined his adult life, would amount to creating a new identity. He had come to an agreement with the University of Tennessee at Martin, an hour's commute from Jackson, to teach criminal justice courses full-time beginning in the fall of 1995. By Christmas this year he would have turned in his badge; his colleagues, as was the tradition, would frame it for him, along with his credentials, to hang on his wall. He had begun to imagine what it would be like to go around badgeless and unarmed and did not care for the sensation, which was like walking naked.

However much of a maverick he had been, his loyalty to the Bureau remained fierce. He knew, as internal counselors were now warning older agents, that FBI retirees had an alarming tendency to depression and early death. Many of them seemed not to know what to do with themselves. One he knew had improbably become a golf caddy, in return for playing privileges at an exclusive club, a prescription for self-loathing, boredom, depression, and general giving up if there ever was one. Retiring would be like getting off a fast horse, to make the rest of the way on foot.

But he had to leave now, and teaching seemed a good way out, a means of making use of what he had learned and of putting shape to his ideas about criminal behavior and social response to it. The Lanier case, he sensed, had drained him, taken a toll on his will to act and left a residue of confusion, anger, and guilt that was not healthy. He needed a new life, which would include becoming closer to his wife and daughters.

Louise Fitzgerald encouraged him, saying that he would make a wonderful teacher, and advised him about how to adjust to an academic environment. The two were already collaborating on a scholarly article based on their experiences with the Lanier case. It would be called "Working at Cross-Purposes," analyzing how the victims had become retraumatized through the criminal justice system.

The Lanier case seemed never to end, which exacerbated Castleberry's difficulties in resolving his own emotions about it. Several of the women were still having problems. Brenda Castain, in Memphis, had yet to kick her drug habit completely. How much of that was Bill's responsibility, he worried guiltily, for not having acted immediately after her first interview? Jennifer Gallagher, who perhaps never should have testified at all, given the fragility of her emotions, remained the worst off, still spiraling downward.

How often had Bill raced to Jennifer's house during the past year at the word of some fresh crisis, usually in the middle of the night? Late one evening he had driven her around aimlessly for hours, out into the countryside, down to the river, calming her down, talking her out of killing herself. Louise had obtained psychiatric help for her in Jackson and Memphis; she would attend counseling sessions a few times, then quit in hysteria and despair. Jennifer was so paranoid about Lanier, especially after his phone call to her from jail, that Louise had spoken to Steve Parker about getting her into the federal government's witness protection

program, at least until she could stabilize. Of the three women whose testimony had been either dismissed by Judge Turner or rejected by the jury,
only Patty Wallace seemed to have the inner strength—and the solid marriage—to hold her head high and resume a normal life. Jennifer's life had
never been normal, by any standard, to begin with. Now she was drown-
ing in self-loathing.

What good am I? Why should I live? she asked Bill over and over,
insisting that her daughter would be better off with her dead. Her
responses to him during the hours and hours he spent with her veered
from abject appreciation for his trying to help her—"You're such a wonderful man. You try to be so tough, but you're not, you're so sensitive!"—
to lashing out at him in resentment for having convinced her to testify.
"Don't you see that before Mr. Castleberry came along," she wailed to a
friend, "nobody knew what happened. *Nobody knew about me and
Lanier! I was safe!*"

If he had any doubts, he was convinced of the seriousness of her condition when she began to talk about herself in the past tense: "I wasn't a bad
person. I tried, but I failed," as if she were already dead. "What good am I
to my daughter? Judge Lanier killed me, he finished me off." If she could
make it look as if she had died in an accident, her daughter would not feel
abandoned, would she? That was the answer, to aim her car for a telephone pole. "I am dead. Mr. Castleberry, let me die!"

Her third marriage broke up in a flurry of violence. Her husband struck
her with his fist, she said, and as her face was black and blue, with one
eye swollen shut by the time Castleberry and Joey McDowell could
respond to her call, they had no reason not to believe her. Her parents
came to see her the next day and berated her, she reported, for her failures, her father so enraged that he picked up a Bible and beat her over the
head with it. Black eye, bruised face, sore head and all, on the following
Saturday she drove her daughter to Nashville, where the child participated in a statewide academic competition.

When Jennifer moved out of her house, her husband pursued her to
berate her as a slut, accusing her of having been married five times before
him (it was twice) and of having AIDS. She filed charges against him for
battery. In circuit court he told Judge Riley that she should not be
believed, as she was one of Lanier's victims and crazy.

Castleberry tried to calm him down, pacifying him by returning to him
a rubber plant he claimed Jennifer had stolen from their house.
Castleberry understood how and why the young man had become violent.
Even someone without the young man's propensity to kill things might
have been driven over the edge watching his wife spin out of control in
the aftermath of a situation about which he had known nothing before

marrying her. Perhaps Judge Riley felt the same way, releasing him with a warning. One thing was clear, that the marriage was over.

Castleberry made a point of dropping by her office often to visit with her and remind her that he had not forgotten about her. "Hi, babe," he would always greet her, a little joke between them, and sit down in the chair beside her desk. One day they were passing a few minutes talking about nothing much of anything when she saw him take off his glasses and rub his eyes and noticed that there were tears on his cheeks.

"I really do wish I hadn't put you through all this," he said, his voice breaking slightly. "If I'd known, somehow, I'd—I don't know—I would have found another way."

Linda Michaels found Jennifer an apartment, arranging a discount on the rent, and helped her and her daughter move in; behind the scenes, Louise Fitzgerald paid the first and last months' bills, with Linda telling her that "a special government program" had supplied the money. "I love you so much," Jennifer told Linda. "You and Mr. Castleberry and Dr. L. are the only ones who care about me! Oh, Linda, I'd ask you to marry me, if only you had a penis!"

Linda, who had done all she could and was reaching the end of her patience with poor Jennifer, did not wish for any anatomical enhancement. She watched, for a while, as Jennifer grew, if anything, more irrational. One evening news came over the television that a woman Jennifer knew had been murdered by her husband, a cocaine addict, who had stuffed the body behind a wall in their house. This event further deranged Jennifer.

After a sleepless night, from her office the next morning she began telephoning people asking them how she could find the murdering husband, who was still on the loose, to get him to come and kill her, too. Someone called the police. Joey McDowell hurried over to her office, where she sat weeping at her desk, and told her she had to come with him, refusing to take no for an answer. Castleberry arrived. The two men took Jennifer home to get her things, arranged with her parents to take care of the daughter, bundled the trembling, babbling woman into the FBI car, and drove her to Memphis, where they checked her into the Midsouth psychiatric hospital.

She remained there for nearly a month, sedated and receiving counseling, but against the advice of her doctors then discharged herself. Back in her apartment, she began a compulsive routine of running for miles beginning at four A.M. every morning. Castleberry worried for her safety in the dark at that hour.

"Don't worry, Mr. Castleberry," she told him, "I am never going to be raped again, because I will fight so hard that either I'll fight him off or I'll be dead. If I was raped again, I wouldn't want to live. Hell, I don't even want to live now."

It was at this point, feeling that he could do no more for her, that Bill Castleberry withdrew, at the same time that he decided that the time had come for him to retire from the FBI. He had to begin to establish a distance.

Perhaps, he felt, he had already done more for her than he should have, permitting her to count on him too much. He had acted out of compassion and guilt, but who was to say that he hadn't ended up doing more harm? He ought to have known how futile his attempts had been, despite Louise's encouragement. That Jennifer had become too dependent on him was obvious from the recurrent dream she had written him about.

In it Judge Lanier was chasing her with a gun, firing at her, hitting her again and again as she fell bleeding. Suddenly, as she lay dying on the ground, Mr. Castleberry appeared out of nowhere to chase Lanier away. She would get up, her wounds miraculously healed, free at last, Mr. Castleberry forever her hero.

It was unnervingly a mirror image of his own nightmare, and he was nobody's hero, Castleberry knew, not in this situation. Again Louise told him that he must stop blaming himself; he had done the best he could.

"Wait a minute," Bill said to her over the phone, "you were the first person to show me how I'd fucked up, Dr. L.!"

That was then, she assured him. He had made up for a lot. He wasn't so sure. He wasn't sure about much of anything anymore, except that he was glad Lanier was gone.

He reached the corner of Cedar and Main that bright May morning to view the collapsed building. Heaps of bricks, plaster, lumber, shattered washbasins, and a couple of toilets littered the sidewalk and pavement. The smell of dust and rotten wood filled the air. At the rear the Penthouse was still aloft, as if suspended in time. But the entire front of the building was gone, leaving exposed beams and floorboards sagging, the structure torn open as if it had imploded, its face ripped off. It made Castleberry think of photographs of buildings bombed in war.

The city had already condemned it, but a question remained of who would foot the bill to tear down the remains and remove the debris. According to the deed filed at the courthouse, David Lanier still owned the place; but if this had passed to his ex-wife, along with the rest of his property in the divorce, without anyone's having bothered to correct the documents, would Joan Lanier be responsible, or her daughters? Was this an addition to the judge's legacy to his family?

Castleberry drove over to the police station to call on Joey McDowell.

They were still working together on corruption cases. Bill's goal was to achieve as many more convictions as he could during his final months with the Bureau. As had Parker, Moskowitz, and Spain, he had received a commendation from the U.S. Attorney General, Janet Reno, for his work on the Lanier case, citing his extraordinary attention to the welfare of the victims, among other good deeds. That was gratifying, but he would take still greater pleasure in leaving the Bureau after twenty-five years having put his territory in order. He was hoping to achieve the indictment or at least the resignation of two other corrupt judges; evidence of abuse of migrant farm workers, forced to live in conditions amounting to slavery, angered him. He would do what he could and then, on his last day on the job, drive his Chevy to the levee, eat a baloney sandwich, drink a beer, bid the river au revoir, and head off for the groves of academe.

The demise of the Penthouse set Bill and Joey to reminiscing. They recited the names of David Lanier's victims. Jennifer was alive but as desperate as ever, now out of a job. Janet Thomasson had recently written Louise Fitzgerald a sad, somewhat bitter letter, full of disillusion about men. Louise, however, interpreted it as showing progress, since it indicated that Janet was prepared to rely on herself, not on a man. Others of the women reported still having nightmares about Lanier and experiencing continued hostility from some townspeople. Patty Wallace's boss at the courthouse had ordered her to stop talking about the case after she and Sandy Sanders gave interviews for a feature article that, it was felt, had brought renewed discomfort to Dyer County. Jennifer and Vivian Forsythe had been especially upset by that article, too, because it characterized the victims as divided between "good girls and bad girls"—a distinction encouraged by Wallace and Sandy Sanders, who were anxious to be classed with the former.

Everyone, however, was pleased that Lanier's successor on the bench, appointed by the governor pending a new election, was an honest and fairminded person. The new chancellor, Steven J. Stafford, a former city judge, had immediately ordered the wall closing off the chambers from the filing room torn out, to signal a new openness. Sledgehammers uncovered triple-thick insulation—the soundproofing of which Lanier had boasted. Courthouse records showed that Lanier had ordered the wall built shortly after assuming the judgeship.

As for Vivian, friends of Bill's and Joey's had visited her recently in Orlando and reported that she was doing quite well, with a new, more responsible job at another law firm, at an increased salary. She had not lapsed back into drugs; at dinner one night she had drunk one daiquiri, declining another or wine; she had resumed her readings in anthropology and was talking again of going back to school.

She had not, however, regained custody of Ashley, although she had hired a lawyer to that end and claimed to be capable now of single motherhood. The child visited Orlando often, usually in the company of her grandparents, and Vivian went to Dyersburg for holidays.

Vivian had somehow forgiven her sister for having testified against her; relations with her mother, who was now the director of a psychiatric clinic, were also less volatile, in spite of their dispute over Ashley. Vivian insisted that no matter what, she was determined to make her future a peaceful and successful one. She had written letters to Amy Spain and Steve Parker, thanking them for "changing my life" and making a new one possible.

There was something about Vivian that made Bill and Joey willing to gamble that, against all odds, she would make it. Her guts, her defiance, her strength, her basic goodness—whatever she had, it seemed to promise that she would remain one of the undefeated. Steve Parker and Amy Spain agreed, dared to hope that Vivian's days of depression and helplessness were over. Her only truly bad days, she said, came every September, immediately before, during, and after the anniversary of that fatal visit to Lanier's office or, as she always bluntly referred to it, the rape.

At the police station Bill told Joey that every time Vivian came to mind, a vague image recurred of how she had acted after that first rape. The idea of what she had done was somehow very moving, although he could not distinctly picture it. She had fled to her father's farm, she had said, or where it had been. Bill had thought about this. She could have run home, or have gone to a friend's. Instead she had gone to those fields, which must have meant a great deal to her. Where were they?

Bill had often tried to imagine the location, her father's place where a daughter had fled after she had been raped. He had never asked her where it was. Around Tylersville? Heloise?

"Chic," Joey said. "Chic, Tennessee," the words came warmly from his lips, and with the hint of a smile, "is where old B.A.'s place used to be. Where he met Judy."

Bill had to admit that he had no idea where Chic was. As for Judy Forsythe, she had baked a birthday cake for him last year. He had donated it to the Dyersburg Police Department.

For four years Bill had combed Dyer County. How could he have missed Chic? He located it in the book of Tennessee county maps he kept handy, which had a scale of one mile to the half-inch, where Chic remained nearly invisible, a tiny name without even a dot beside it. Joey, who knew his native grounds as well as any Chickasaw, offered to escort Bill to the spot. No one ever went there, Joey said, anymore. It might be worth a visit.

Bill drove. Joey navigated west through Finley to the Big Levee Road, or the Great River Road—locals called it the former, he said. On the way Bill talked about how much he was looking forward to spending time with his family on their five acres, where his pecan trees would soon be yielding a crop, and taking trips with his wife. Yet he admitted that in a way he envied Joey, who thanks in part to Bill's recommendation would be spending most of the summer at Quantico, in an FBI training session designed for outstanding police officers from around the country. It would be arduous; Joey had dropped fourteen pounds to get in shape for it. But Bill knew the satisfaction his friend would feel on graduating and qualifying for promotion—something tangible.

"Didn't you ever want to be anything besides an FBI agent?" Joey asked.

"No. Well, yes. A Texas Ranger. I used to imagine myself slapping leather out on the range, corralling desperadoes."

"Well, make a right turn here, Ranger Bill," Joey said, indicating the sign painted red with gold lettering that pointed to the Church of God of Chic.

And then they were on the half-slab, as Joey explained it was named, and on to the end and the washed-out bridge.

They got out of the car. Only faint wisps of clouds in a high sky, but there was water everywhere after heavy rains, and the air was heavy, with no breeze.

"Must've flooded," Bill said.

"Always floods," Joey said in a rough whisper, as if not wishing to disturb something. "So this is where Vivian went."

After that they did not speak. They trod their way around the standing water, where tiny sprouts of beans struggled skyward through the mud, and climbed atop the Little Levee to look down at the river.

So quiet! The Mississippi was high, a mile wide and deceptively placid. Bill, who had fished it maybe a hundred times over the years, knew what that current could do.

Watching the river go about its business, smelling those familiar moist, fecund smells, hearing a fish or maybe a frog go plop—he let his mind drift, and his thoughts became a tumult. "I talked to myself and I talked to God," he heard Vivian's quavering, anxious voice saying—and felt as if she were standing with them now. He would not have known what to say to her.

For so many months he had been trying to figure out what this entire passage meant, to resolve his emotions about the Lanier case and everything it had dredged up. A legal milestone, yes; a precedent, maybe a deterrent. Certainly a victory for truth, but so much else, too. Love and hate; vanities; sex; illusions and disillusions; euphoria and despair; women clinging to one another and scorning each other; women cleaving to men and shrinking from them. A sense of accomplishment and of futility. Today, when he had come again to Dyersburg and stood on its streets, he knew that many of its citizens resented him, and he looked forward to the day when he would leave them alone at last—yet he knew as well that as many or more were grateful to him for having scoured their courthouse clean.

He had never known what to make of it all. There was something disturbingly primitive about it, achieving justice at the price of human sacrifice, men in war, women this time around.

Just last week, after driving along the edge of Reelfoot Lake one day and stopping at Boyette's, his favorite place for fried catfish, he had arrived at some vague realization. He had begun to conclude that the entire Lanier case lay beyond comprehension or resolution in any commonplace sense of the words.

He had often taken his wife and daughters to Boyette's. Alone this time, content from his meal and with a certain sense of continuity, he had lit a cigar and was on his way again along the lake shore, observing birds, headed for an interview with an informant, when all at once it had come to him, or he believed it had. Maybe the closest he would ever get to a revelation.

He was driving past the entrance to a campground beside the lake and caught sight of a large sign there that proclaimed the legend of Reelfoot. He had read about it; now he was reminded of it. And all at once it meant something new.

The Chickasaws believed that this vast, deep lake, the hundreds of acres of it, had been created in an act of vengeance by the Father of Waters. This much was certain, that during the cataclysmic earthquakes that rocked the region in the winter of 1811–12, the Mississippi flowed backward. The epicenter of those three quakes, each of which the scientific people had lately calculated at well above eight on the Richter scale—the most powerful ever to hit the North American continent—had been at New Madrid, Missouri, about seventy miles north as the crow flies from Dyersburg.

When the river reversed itself and tore south again, a landlocked tidal wave, a force of nature beyond imagining, it had jumped its old eastern bank and rushed along a fresh declivity to form a new lake in Tennessee. That event was historical fact.

The Indians, however, had an explanation for it, a version that gave the lake its name. Reelfoot, chief of the Chickasaws and so named because of the clubfoot that gave him his Byronic walk, loved a Choctaw maiden, who rebuffed him because of his deformity. His ego affronted, the chief ordered his braves to kidnap the maiden and bring her to him for his satisfaction. They rode south to raid the Choctaw village and bring her back.

Reelfoot enjoyed her through that night. He raped her.

And then, as the chief and his braves celebrated with a great feast, the quake hit, the earth dropped sixteen feet, and everyone drowned, including the hapless woman—as the Father of Waters worked his wrath and flooded the huge hole that became known as Reelfoot Lake.

The Chickasaws commemorated the event in legend as a cautionary tale. Reelfoot's abuse of power had enraged the river god. As it happened, and as the story struck Castleberry on that catfish afternoon, the chief's abuse of power had been, prophetically perhaps, against a woman.

Past and present merged in Castleberry's mind. He, in blindly pursuing Lanier, beginning with little more than a feeling that wrongs had been and were being done, no matter what the law might say, had become no more yet no less than an instrument of impersonal, unsparing justice. People cry out for justice, and then it comes, unstoppable as an earthquake or a great river in flood, and no one is spared.

The thought was humbling, yet it also gave him a certain peace. And watching that treacherous river now, with Joey at his side and with Vivian's melodious, rushing, valiant voice in his head, Castleberry considered that maybe, possibly, he had figured out where he and everyone else stood in the order of things.

Epilogue

Neither of the principals in this story, Vivian Forsythe and Bill Castleberry, was present when the United States Court of Appeals for the Sixth Circuit met *en banc,* or as a whole, to hear oral arguments in the matter of David Lanier's renewed appeal of his conviction. I was there, though, and have decided that the best way to convey that experience and its aftermath must be in the first person.

What happened placed the Lanier case and the entire story I have been telling into a wider perspective. Suddenly it became easier to see the events of Dyersburg and the trial in Memphis as what they always had been, anything but local or isolated phenomena, not the ordeal of certain women in a backwater, but something representative, unfortunately so, of the plight of citizens who endure injustice because they have nowhere to turn for help.

Indeed, it would now take an unusually obtuse person not to understand what occurred in drowsing Dyersburg in an inclusive context, that of society in general and of women's inferior position within the justice system. This picture is a disturbing one, and it is painful to contemplate.

The sixteen judges of the Sixth Circuit, four of whom are women, have jurisdiction over appeals emanating from trials that have taken place in Kentucky, Michigan, Ohio, and Tennessee. I happen to have had personal experience with this body of worthies in the spring of 1993, and as a result I had every reason to think well of them. They had overruled, with a stern admonition on behalf of my First Amendment rights, a federal judge from the mountains of Kentucky who had banned my then just-published book, *A Dark and Bloody Ground,* from distribution in all fifty states and had forbidden me from promoting it. For a week, until the Sixth Circuit, in effect, restored my American citizenship, I had a taste of what it would be like to live without certain freedoms; and I was grateful for the speed with which the Court of Appeals affirmed mine. I was therefore not surprised when, a year later, judges from that same court ruled in favor of the rights of the women of Dyersburg and against their oppressor, David Lanier.

Early in 1995, when the Sixth Circuit responded to Lanier's second appeal by setting June 14 as the date for an *en banc* hearing, I was tempted to travel to Cincinnati for the event, but hesitated because the outcome seemed so predictable. Steve Parker had characterized the judges' 1994 ruling against Lanier as the most vehement rejection of an appeal that he had ever read; Lanier's new brief raised no substantive issues that either I or the prosecution team could see as conceivably persuasive. Indeed, the document designed to sway the judges appeared disorganized, rambling—so much so that I was not alone in speculating that confinement had unhinged the former judge.

The only question seemed to be why the Sixth Circuit had decided to grant an *en banc* hearing, an unusual procedure when a three-judge panel has already rejected an appeal. By so doing the court automatically vacated, or rendered null and void, its previous opinion. The judges could eventually reinstate their rejection—a likely possibility but only one among several.

In scheduling an *en banc,* a federal appeals court may and usually does inform the attorneys of the issues it wishes discussed. In this instance, however, the chief judge's letter announcing that a date for the hearing had been set contained nothing specific as to the reasons for granting the defendant a fresh opportunity, except to indicate that a majority of the judges had voted in favor of it. The prosecutors were somewhat puzzled, since all of the major constitutional issues—whether David Lanier had acted "under color of law," whether the "right to bodily integrity" or freedom from sexual assault was an established right, and whether Lanier's sentence was "cruel and unusual"—appeared to have been settled.

One judge among the three on the 1994 panel, it was true, had expressed certain reservations based mainly on the novelty of the case, which in legal terminology was defined as one "of first impression," that is to say unprecedented, in that no judge prior to Lanier had ever been convicted under a criminal federal civil rights statute, let alone for aggravated sexual abuse including rape. This appellate judge, Harry W. Wellford, a senior member of the court who happened to come from Memphis, had questioned whether the felony charges involving Vivian Forsythe ought to have been tried separately and had raised doubts about her credibility, on account of her drug use. Wellford had also pointed out that all previous convictions under the statute had involved "custodial" situations, as with a policeman and his prisoners or school authorities and juveniles. The drift of Wellford's separate opinion was to suggest that prosecution under civil rather than criminal statutes might have been more appropriate. Wellford noted that the trial judge had instructed the jury that to convict, they must find that "physical force, mental coercion, [and] bodily injury or emotional damage which is shocking to one's conscience" had occurred. Wellford was skeptical that these conditions had been met on all counts. Nevertheless, he wrote, "despite these reservations, I concur in the affirmance" of the conviction and sentencing of David Lanier.

Could Judge Wellford have lobbied his colleagues in the interim, so that when Lanier submitted his new appeal, a majority were persuaded that the issues were worth reconsideration by the entire court? If so, which issues?

Amy Spain speculated that because the Lanier case could offer precedent for future convictions of abusive judges, the Court of Appeals wished to sharpen its definition of the issues, with an eye toward an eventual ruling by the U.S. Supreme Court. It was conceivable, Amy thought, that the felony charges would stand up but the misdemeanors, or some of them, might not. If all the misdemeanors were thrown out, Lanier would have five years subtracted from his sentence but would still remain incarcerated until around 2012.

I made my decision to attend the hearing when I learned that Al Moskowitz would be in Cincinnati for the occasion and that Amy Spain and Steve Parker were flying up from Memphis. I knew that Parker had wanted to argue the government's case himself, or have Moskowitz do it—but that was not how things worked at Justice. There were government attorneys who did nothing but argue appeals, as one lawyer had successfully against Lanier's attorney, Wayne Emmons, the previous year. That same specialist would appear again on the government's behalf, this time—since Emmons had withdrawn—opposing a court-appointed attorney from Nashville, who would plead Lanier's case. Parker, Spain, and Moskowitz would be present in an advisory capacity. If they felt it important enough to go, I felt that I ought to be there, too, if for no other reason than to interview the prosecutors one last time.

The hearing was set for nine o'clock Wednesday morning. I checked into the same downtown hotel where the prosecutors were staying on Tuesday afternoon, June 13, and left a message for Steve Parker, asking to have a talk with him and Amy. When he called and invited me to dinner, I was

surprised, as I had never developed anything more than a highly businesslike relationship with any of the prosecutors, who were so conscious
of proprieties that they had never accepted so much as a cup of coffee
from me. Parker and Spain did have permission from the U.S. attorney in
Memphis to talk to me, but only within certain limits, which they had
been careful not to overstep. As for Al Moskowitz, I had not been able to
interview him at length until a year after the trial, when Lanier's appeal
was denied. I took the dinner invitation to mean that as far as the prosecutors were concerned, the Lanier case was essentially over, and they would
no longer have to watch every word they spoke.

When I met Parker, Spain, and Moskowitz in the lobby, they had the
appeals specialist from Washington with them. I sensed that he had no
idea what I was doing there and was unsure of how to deal with me. He
was not unfriendly, just edgy as he introduced himself—"I'm Tom
Chandler. Who'd you say you were?"—and looked me over. As for himself, he gave every appearance of efficiency, with each carefully trimmed
dark hair in place. He wore an impeccable navy blazer and was the only
man among us in a tie on that balmy evening in the Queen City.
Moskowitz, who I thought never removed his dark suit, was wearing a
sweatshirt and looked as if he might be going camping, or had been.
There was some joking about whether Al would be permitted to enter the
bistro Chandler recommended.

The mood was jovial, except for Chandler's continuing uneasiness
about my presence. As we walked the few blocks to the restaurant, he
seemed concerned about my being a writer and by the prospect of his
name's appearing in my book. I told him honestly that at that point, I had
no idea whether there would be reason to include his name or not.

The restaurant was rustic Norman in decor, rough-hewn dark wood
and whitewashed walls, with a casual, lively atmosphere. Al whispered
to me that Tom Chandler was always nervous and that I should not take
it personally; and the pleasant ambiance and Amy Spain's soothing
Southern voice and manners did seem to make Chandler relax a bit. She
began talking to him about Vivian Forsythe—how intelligent Vivian
was, how brave she had been, how her addictions, far from being only a
sign of weakness, had become an index of strength, because she had
overcome them in order to testify. I had the sense that Amy, out of some
instinct that Chandler, whom she had never met before, needed to understand this personal aspect of the case, was trying to encourage him to
reveal or to open up his emotional responses to the women. He listened
and regarded her curiously, I thought, as if what she was saying was all
very interesting but hardly germane to the argument he had prepared for
the court tomorrow.

Chandler removed his tie and expressed confidence that the government would prevail; and the conversation turned to "color of law" and "bodily integrity" and other constitutional issues the lawyers expected would arise.

"You know," Steve Parker said, "the funny thing is, I'm the guy who's always worried. I'm a worrywart. But right now, I'm not worried at all. I don't see anything to worry about."

By coffee the next morning, Parker was displaying a different frame of mind. He said that he had not slept at all that night. At two A.M. he had given up trying and watched CNN until dawn. Parker was such a transparently emotional person, you could see the anxiety in his eyes.

What Amy Spain was feeling, I could not tell. She managed to look both professional and chic in a tailored linen suit. Tom Chandler had gone over to the courthouse early, Al Moskowitz said, the way a ballplayer might arrive at the park hours before a game, to psych himself up. He had been coaching him for a month, Al said, so Chandler was certainly well prepared. Al himself was as usual quiet, his studious, somber face betraying nothing.

We walked over to the Justice Potter Stewart Courthouse, where the security, as in all federal buildings since the Oklahoma City bombing of just two months before, was tight. We took an elevator to the fourth floor.

The courtroom was an elegant one, carpeted in a brilliant red, with plenty of richly stained wood, including a carved eagle behind the bench, which was actually a semicircle that arced from one side of the room to the other. I counted fifteen large chairs behind it; nameplates identified the places for each judge, with one missing. The absentee was Judge H. Ted Milburn, the Tennessean who had written the rejection of Lanier's first appeal and whom Lanier had this time asked to recuse himself, on the grounds that they had been friends since law school.

I asked Steve Parker why Milburn had complied with Lanier's request, which seemed to me based on curious grounds, and recused himself. Was it customary for the author of a vacated opinion not to participate in a new one? Parker did not think so, and he agreed with me that Milburn had already demonstrated his lack of bias in favor of Lanier forcefully by condemning his behavior in the 1994 opinion. On the other hand, if Milburn and Lanier had indeed once been friends, Milburn might not wish people to suspect that he had been so harsh in his judgment of the defendant merely to prove impartiality, now that Lanier had raised the issue of their friendship or alleged its existence. Whatever the reasons behind it, Milburn's departure meant one less vote certain for the government and against Lanier.

"Hear ye, hear ye!" the clerk called out. "The United States Court of Appeals for the Sixth Circuit is now in session. All rise."

From a door behind the bench the judges filed out and seated themselves, with Chief Judge Gilbert S. Merritt, a Tennessean, in the center and the others in descending order of seniority fanned out to either side of him. I settled into my seat at the end of the second of four rows of benches, and as I did so I noticed David Lanier's two daughters, Robbye and Leigh Anne, sitting down with their mother, Joan, across the aisle. The daughters' loyalty to their father, who could have elected to be present but had not, was striking. As for the ex-Mrs. Lanier's constancy, that was notable, too, considering all the speculation about whether her divorce was a sham to protect assets.

Chief Judge Merritt announced that each side would have twenty-five minutes to present its argument, with five minutes reserved for rebuttal of the government's case by the defendant's attorney. He commended Lanier's advocate, Alfred H. Knight, for accepting appointment by the court "in the highest tradition of the profession." Less from the words he uttered than from the manner in which he uttered them, I thought that Judge Merritt was exceptionally complimentary of Mr. Knight at this point, even given the fulsome traditions of Southern courtesy. My reaction may have had to do with my unfamiliarity with accepted decorum at this high jurisprudential level, but I could have sworn that I detected in the Chief Justice's tone a subtextual message, something to the effect that Mr. Knight would learn that he had not wasted his time coming all the way from Nashville. I did not learn until later that the two had at one time been law partners together—perhaps what I was hearing was nothing more significant than a greeting from one old friend to another.

Knight argued that Judge David Lanier had not been acting "under color of law" when and if he had assaulted women; that Lanier's conduct had been of a private, personal nature and had therefore not been in violation of 18 U.S. § 242; and that this statute was too vague in its references to "rights" to be applicable in this case. Knight sailed along in soft, gentle, courtly cadences, bending over the lectern with his back to the audience, sounding so sweetly reasonable that I had only one thought—how removed this scene was from the realities of the David Lanier case!

Where were the women who had risked so much and suffered so intensely, who had sacrificed themselves or, as Bill Castleberry worried, had been sacrificed in the cause of justice? We were sitting through this orderly, mannerly proceeding, so far away from Memphis, light-years as it were from Dyersburg and the dark interior of Judge Lanier's chambers! A young woman sitting next to me, a law student perhaps, was taking neat notes on a legal pad; occasionally she peeked over, as if we were in a schoolroom, to try to read what I was scribbling onto the small spiral notebook on my knee. Other young women were among the judges' clerks at a table to the right of the lectern—scholarly looking young women, they were undoubtedly from very good schools, with fulfilling, remunerative careers ahead of them. David Lanier would have been too shrewd, or too cowardly, ever to have attacked women such as these, who would not hesitate to sue any assailant immediately and who could undoubtedly slice him to ribbons with words. Could these women understand what had happened in Dyersburg?

I thought of Amy Spain and how she had changed her views, how she now referred to this case as her "education." And I bet that she, sitting just in front of me in the first row, was thinking about that, too, and that Steve Parker was wishing he could jump up and shout, "Your Honors, David Lanier is a convicted rapist!"

Judge Merritt interrupted Alfred Knight's monologue to ask several questions—which I thought were less questions than rhetorical extensions of Knight's arguments. I asked myself whether I might be misinterpreting what was going on, but what I thought I was hearing was that the chief judge was encouraging David Lanier's attorney and agreeing with him. If this was true, I wondered, how much influence did Merritt have over his colleagues? When another senior, male judge asked a similarly concurring question, strengthening Knight's argument rather than challenging it, I sensed a worrisome pattern emerging. And then Judge Merritt asked:

"Is your position that these indictments never should have been brought or that, having been brought, they should have been dismissed by the district court?"

I was stunned by the sweeping nature of that inquiry, in fact astonished that such a broad, complete rejection of the entire Lanier case could or would even be considered, let alone by the chief judge, whose tone, I thought, had a note in it of condescension toward the total concept behind the prosecution of David Lanier. I thought Alfred Knight was stunned, too—as if he had never considered before that moment that he might actually win a reversal.

"Well, yes, yes, Your Honor," he finally said. "That is our position, that the indictments should have been dismissed."

I had no idea what the other judges were thinking, because up until now, nearly all of them had kept silent. When Tom Chandler took his place at the lectern and began to speak, all that changed. Chandler had not gotten through two or three sentences before Judge Merritt interrupted with a question, clearly a hostile one this time:

"What constitutional right has Judge Lanier violated? We want to get this clarified, if that's possible. What is the government's position on that?"

"The right to bodily integrity," Chandler replied.

"Where does the Constitution guarantee that right?"

Chandler argued articulately and cogently that this right derived from Fourth Amendment protections against unlawful search and seizure, from the "due process" clause of the Fourteenth Amendment, and from extensive case law. He cited the most important relevant Supreme Court decision, that in a 1945 case called *Screws v. United States* (commonly and aptly, with regard to David Lanier, referred to simply as *Screws*), in which the court held that § 242 was not unconstitutionally vague, since "rights" were defined specifically by majority court opinions. Chandler went on to cite a Fifth Circuit case from 1985 and another from the Seventh Circuit in 1994 as defining specifically the right to bodily integrity.

"Can you cite any *Sixth Circuit* case?" a senior, male judge asked.

Chandler was nonplussed, and rightly so.

"Just one, from this circuit," Judge Merritt said. "That's all we're asking."

Tom Chandler could not name one because there was none. The Sixth Circuit had heard very few civil rights cases over the years, the largest number of which had been filed in the Fifth, based in New Orleans and covering several Deep South states. Not being myself a lawyer, I could not imagine what difference this happenstance would make. To argue that what had become law in one federal circuit did not apply to another was to take, it seemed to me, a rather provincial view of the American legal system. What about *e pluribus unum* and all that? But I was not a lawyer.

Tom Chandler was never able to get back to his prepared statement. Several of the senior male judges and one woman, also a senior judge, Cornelia G. Kennedy, peppered him with questions.

Judge Kennedy, a handsome woman who reminded me of the headmistress of a preparatory school, made only one brief comment but a telling one, I thought, in terms of her attitude to the case. Hers was less a question than a statement. She indicated that she thought it absurd for the trial judge to have instructed the jury that to convict, they must find Lanier's acts "shocking to one's conscience."

"Whose conscience?" the judge asked rhetorically. "Is one person's conscience the same as another's?" She did not seem to require an answer to what was really something of a philosophical or religious argument that, if taken to its logical conclusion, undermined the concept of moral conscience itself. It was as if she were saying, or I took it that way, that the law and not personal moral repugnance ought to be the sole measure of any judgment made in a courtroom. Personally I found this argument unacceptable, as I believe all law, the Fourteenth Amendment for instance, to be based on agreed-upon concepts of right and wrong, instinctively felt. But it was not so much Judge Kennedy's philosophy that alarmed me, as that it seemed to imply that there was room for doubt about whether what David Lanier had done was repugnant or not, or that it did not matter, one way or another, legally speaking. Could she really mean that?

Perhaps she was revealing a misunderstanding about the basis for Judge Turner's having so instructed the jury. She may have believed that Turner had improperly borrowed a concept from the civil law to apply to this criminal case. She could have been thinking, one had to surmise, because she did not explain the matter, that Turner had been thinking of obscenity statutes, which may vary in their standards from one locale to another, and had used that principle in trying to guide the jury. If she believed that, then she was saying that the jurors had been left to deal arbitrarily and subjectively with the question of Lanier's guilt or innocence. And if she did believe that, she was clearly skeptical of the verdict.

But far from trying to make it easier for the jury to convict, Judge Turner had introduced the "shocking to one's conscience" requirement for precisely the opposite reason, namely, *to raise the burden of proof,* to make it more difficult to convict by adding this element. He did so not with reference to obscenity or any other civil statutes but from the venerable concept of a jury as the collective conscience of a community, with each juror's moral conscience a part of the whole. This instruction, moreover, was, of course, only one of several standards that Turner required each juror to meet in reaching verdicts on the various counts.

I wished Chandler had been able to convey some of this to the doubting judge, but he may have been right in letting the matter pass without much of any comment. To begin debating moral relativism at this stage would have invited chaos. And things seemed to be going badly enough already.

These considerations flitted through my mind as Judge Kennedy voiced her misgivings and as, after her, the discussion descended to a lower level. Another senior judge, this one male, expressed approval of what I had already thought was a distressingly inappropriate analogy drawn by Alfred Knight. To be fair to Mr. Knight, he had prefaced, during his argument, this analogy by saying that by invoking it, he in no way meant to "trivialize" what the victims of David Lanier had suffered. Unfortunately, as is the rhetorical inevitability when someone says "I don't mean to" and then goes on to say it anyway, the result was that the trivialization that Knight professed to abjure was indeed effected. With all due respect, as one pretends in court, it was a bit like saying, "I don't mean to trivialize slavery, but at one time the practice was universal." Therefore, who's to worry?

Attempting to disprove the idea that Judge Lanier had been acting "under color of law" in assaulting women in chambers, while threatening some of them with loss of children and other serious consequences if they did not sexually comply, Knight compared Lanier to a policeman stealing an apple. If a cop, the analogy went, walks into a market, in uniform, and steals an apple, does that make him guilty of a federal crime?

Picking up on this analogy, between a judge who sexually assaults women and a policeman who steals an apple, senior judge David A. Nelson, seemingly content with the idea that a woman's bodily integrity might suitably be compared to the price of a red Delicious, was pleased to suggest an analogy of his own:

"Supposing I went down to Riverfront Stadium," Judge Nelson said, alluding to the home of the football Bengals and the baseball Reds, "and beat up a ticket scalper because he charged me too much. Does that mean I've committed a federal crime, because I'm a judge?"

"If you're wearing your robe," Chief Judge Merritt interjected drolly, undercutting with this jest one of the principal supports of the government's argument that Judge Lanier had been acting "under color of law."

"Oh, yeah." Judge Nelson picked up the joke. "Sure, if I'm wearing my robe!"

Was this a courtroom, or had the scene suddenly cut to the men's locker room at some golf club?

Soon Judge Merritt and one or two of the others were bandying about references to the enduring Senator Robert Packwood, whose sexual peccadilloes, slight in comparison to David Lanier's violent acts, had threatened, like the Anita Hill–Clarence Thomas controversy, to cloud issues in the Lanier case since the day of jury selection at the trial. As Steve Parker had said in his opening statement, "This," the Lanier case, "is not a case of sexual harassment." It was a case about sexual assault and rape. Parker's passionate admonition, I could see, was no more. The judges, by bringing up Packwood, were revealing their lack of understanding, or their refusal to confront what Lanier had done. Everything that Parker had feared and, with Spain and Moskowitz, had obviated in Memphis was coming back to trivialize the issues in Cincinnati.

Nothing could be more frustrating for the prosecution than to have Lanier's acts perceived as harassment rather than the violent assaults they actually were. If this was true back in 1992, when Parker, Moskowitz, and Spain were concerned that the Lanier case would be confused with the Hill-Thomas hearings and the accusations against Senator Packwood, it was an even bigger worry now. Although sexual harassment was still very much in the news—the number of complaints filed with the Equal Employment Opportunity Commission increased every year, and Anita

Hill remained a heroine to the feminist movement—there was also a considerable backlash against the issue and, to the dismay of many, ridicule of it. By 1995, as an indication of the lightness with which the matter was regarded in many quarters, you could walk into any novelty shop and purchase a parlor game called "Harassment, You Be the Judge," in which participants could laugh about various court rulings. The prominence of older male Tennesseans on the Sixth Circuit, moreover, was the legacy of conservative Republican former senator Howard Baker and did not suggest any particular receptivity to what was essentially a liberal cause. Finally, at least one member of the court had had harassment complaints filed against him.

Other than Judge Kennedy, the women on the bench remained silent. Of the other males, only one, Nathaniel R. Jones, tried to help Tom Chandler, citing one Sixth Circuit case as possibly relevant. And as for Chandler, while I in no way could blame him for not being able to fend off this barrage from the jurists, I did believe that Amy Spain, Steve Parker, or Al Moskowitz would have done a more passionate and, possibly, effective job. The problem was that Tom Chandler, as Amy had instinctively grasped in the restaurant the night before, had not been in that Memphis courtroom when Vivian Forsythe had stood up to assert her rights as an American citizen and as a woman. He had not been there when Amy and Vivian acted out the rape, nor had he listened to the other women tell their stories. He had not heard Steve Parker's moral indignation nor Al Moskowtiz's slashing interrogation of Lanier, when Al compared Judge Lanier's and Dr. Warner's treatment of Vivian to the exchange of a piece of meat. He had not, like the twelve Memphis jurors, been so affected by testimony as to be certain, unanimously, that David Lanier had violated the standards of his office and the federal law.

In this splendid, lofty courtroom, human lives and sordid human acts were becoming abstractions. The very impersonality and objectivity for which the appeals process strives were creating their own distortions. Furthermore, the impartiality of the appeals court was a myth, as it was obvious that at least some of the judges had come to this hearing with their minds already made up and loaded with assumptions, biases, prejudices, and sexual politics as common as those manifest every night in pool halls.

Alfred Knight did fill his allotted five minutes with rebuttal of the government's case. He did so after acknowledging, graciously, that the judges had already done a fine job of stating his arguments for him.

I followed Parker, Spain, Moskowitz, and Chandler back to the hotel. They stopped for coffee along the way.

Amy appeared the most shaken. She had a look in her eyes that to me spelled disillusion, and she did not speak. Parker and Moskowitz discussed what might happen next. The court would not get around to writing and issuing its opinion for weeks, perhaps months. It could be Christmas before the ruling came down.

Was it possible that they would dismiss the entire case? That did not seem conceivable. But some modification in the conviction and sentencing was inevitable now.

Would they have to retry Lanier? I do not recall who brought up that. I might have, during a silence.

"I'm ready, if it comes to that," Parker said, but no one responded. To me the idea was as painful as it was inconceivable, and I know I shut up after it was broached.

"I can't believe," Al Moskowitz said, "that this court would rule that there is no such thing as a constitutional right to bodily integrity. That would be like legalizing rape."

"You guys are too gloomy and pessimistic," Tom Chandler said. "I thought things went rather well this morning, all things considered."

I could not figure out whether Chandler was trying to put the best face on a calamity or whether, on account of his distance from the history of the case, able to see it only on pages of transcripts, he had not realized what a change had taken place. In the Memphis courtroom the women had been human beings. Here they were merely figures of jurisprudential speech, with no more reality to them than characters in a text, to come alive or not as judges or journalists determined.

"We need eight votes," Steve Parker kept saying, whistling some Dixie, I am sure he knew. When only one judge had spoken out in favor of the government and at least one female judge had manifested concern that, forget the women, a judge may have suffered injustice, the odds against the prosecution's winning over eight judges were too long to handicap. The Sixth Circuit was going to do something on David Lanier's behalf, no one knew what.

The last of any of them I saw in Cincinnati was Al Moskowitz. At the hotel we rode the elevator up to our rooms to pack. Al was so lost in thought that he missed his floor and got off at mine to wait for a ride down again.

"Tell me something, Al," I said. "How do you feel right now?"

"Shaken," he said. "Deeply shaken."

The Court of Appeals acted more swiftly than anyone had anticipated. On the next day, June 15, they issued an order releasing David Lanier from prison.

Just like that, he was free.

By the time I heard the news that Thursday afternoon, Lanier was on his way home to Dyersburg. Nine to six in favor of his immediate release, that was how the vote had gone. He was on his own, under his own recognizance, without bond. In order to reach this decision, the majority of the court had to have determined that Lanier was not a danger to himself or to his community and was not a threat to flee. In so deciding, the court ignored the ruling of the federal magistrate who, back in 1993, had determined that Lanier had violated conditions of his bond by contacting and trying to persuade women who had been witnesses against him to recant their sworn testimony. But all that was moot because, in releasing him, the Court of Appeals had also determined that Lanier had expectation of success on his appeal.

Of one thing there was no doubt: the message was clear. His conviction and sentence were being reversed. On what grounds the Sixth Circuit had acted, no one knew. Their written decision, in which everything would be spelled out, doubtless accompanied by dissents, might not appear for weeks or months.

Steve Parker and Amy Spain phoned all the women to inform them of the defeat. The first person I phoned was Bill Castleberry, whose first thought was for the women but who, as he was used to doing, kept his true feelings, which I could tell were mostly angry ones, under wraps. It's the way things happen, was about all he said. I could not and cannot imagine the complexity of his emotions, given his ambiguities about persuading the women to testify to begin with. I remembered that he had told me, more than once, that within the criminal justice system, there are no winners. I also recalled that, before now, he had never lost a case that had gone to trial, nor ever had one overturned on appeal. But on the phone, all he talked about was how the women must be feeling. It was a bitter irony, we agreed, that the person who of all seemed to have been the most unhinged by the case, Jennifer Gallagher, whom everyone had written off as beyond help, was the one who had predicted that David Lanier would get out of jail and return to Dyersburg to haunt her.

Vivian Forsythe was not at her office when I telephoned. She had gone home for the day, a secretary told me, and I did not have to ask why.

I hesitated to call her at home. She had trusted me with her life's story, spilled out over so many days and nights during the past two years or so. Now she might regret her candor, with Lanier again on the loose and, I knew she must be thinking, on the prowl. Still, I had to let her know that my wife and I continued to believe in her, no matter what this court had ruled. I tried to rehearse an uplifting speech; it was false. The only halfway positive thing I could think of was that Lanier—I got out my calculator—had served twenty-seven months in prison, nine months longer than the plea bargain he had rejected. That sounded pretty hollow, too. He was out, that was what mattered, having admitted to nothing and, no doubt, feeling vindicated, a martyr resurrected.

When Vivian took my call I had little chance to say anything. She unleashed a vehement, sobbing attack on the justice system:

"This isn't about justice, Darcy, this is about some goddamned old men who don't care about what a woman suffers, and they sit there in some courtroom with their big salaries and their nice homes and their pensions and everybody fawning over them and all they do is debate nitpicking little legal points that aren't about the Constitution but, you know, are about protecting one of their own, don't you know that? What do they care about women? Nothing! Do they care that that bastard Lanier is going to be after me again? Do they care that I've just got my life together and I've just started to be able to live with what he did to me and just got Ashley back so I can love her like a real mother and—" She broke down. When she recovered, all she could talk about was her fear of David Lanier.

She should contact someone immediately, was all I could think of to say, if Lanier tried to get in touch with her, not wait two weeks like the last time—but it was no good. Whom should she contact, the FBI all over again?

"How is Papa Bill taking this?" she asked suddenly.

"I don't know. Not real well, I wouldn't think. He's worried about you."

"I want to talk to him. I want to tell him it's not his fault, what's happened. He tried. Steve and Amy and Al, and Dr. L., they all cared, didn't they?"

I assured her that they had cared and still did and were eager to talk to her, if she needed "bolstering," as Parker had told me.

"I just want to get on with my life," Vivian said.

When I talked to Louise Fitzgerald, she said that what Vivian had said about wanting to get on with her life was the most encouraging thing in all this mess.

By the next day word had trickled out from the Court of Appeals—one clerk told a friend of hers or his, who told another, and so on—that the majority had determined that David Lanier should never have been prosecuted. Apparently the judges were taking the position that the Sixth Circuit had never itself specified in any case that the right to bodily integrity was something protected by the U.S. Constitution. Therefore, so the hypothetical ruling was said to run, Judge Lanier had had no "notice" that he was in violation of the Constitution, and acting "under color of law," in assaulting women, as far as the federal law was concerned. The court supposedly was going to rule that Lanier ought to have been prosecuted by the state, possibly on civil rather than criminal grounds.

There were various opinions on how the court might word its decision. One was that the Sixth Circuit might affirm that the right to bodily integrity does exist, in conformity with the findings of other circuits, but not retroactively, thereby reversing Lanier's conviction. An equally strong possibility was that the Sixth would deny the existence of this right, absent any Supreme Court affirmation of it. Either way, Lanier would be free.

However it chose to formulate its opinion, the judges seemed bent on saying, explicitly or implicitly, that Lanier's prosecution ought to have been brought by the state, not the federal government. Anyone with the slightest knowledge of the realities of politics in western Tennessee when the Laniers were in power would find the logic of this argument, as Bill Castleberry delicately phrased it, "elusive."

When the circumstances of David Lanier's release reached national women's groups, the reaction was one of outrage.

"The Lanier case," said Lynn Hecht Schafran, director of the National Judicial Education Program to Promote Equality for Women and Men in the Courts, "is a woman's worst nightmare about the justice system: to be literally raped in the courthouse by an all-powerful judge with authority to take away your children. Then to be figuratively raped by another judge who thinks this no different from his beating up a ticket scalper for charging too high a price."

After his release, David Lanier lay low for weeks at the house on Starlight, uncharacteristically silent. It was the consensus among citizens that, although out of office, he remained an embarrassment to Dyersburg, whatever the Court of Appeals ruled. His family and his cadre of supporters may have felt justified, but they remained subdued, giving no interviews—except to say that for now, they were grateful. If Lanier had ideas of regaining his judgeship, he would have to wait for nearly eight years to try, as his appointed successor had won election to his own term as chancellor by an overwhelming vote in 1994.

Joey McDowell had been on vacation with his family and friends when he heard the news of Lanier's release. "It kind of spoiled the holiday," Joey said in his laconic way. Linda Pickering, who was along on the trip with her new husband, the man who had been by her side when she confessed her relationship with Lanier to McDowell and Castleberry, was very upset at the prospect of having to return to a Dyersburg that included David Lanier, but Joey thought she would be able to manage. The reactions of others of Lanier's victims ranged from anger to depression. Jennifer Gallagher, who had never emerged from what her doctors had called a borderline psychotic state, was predictably the most seriously affected.

The important thing to remember, Joey McDowell emphasized, was that Lanier was off the bench. That much had been accomplished.

According to the prosecutors, the possibility of appealing the Sixth Circuit's ruling to the Supreme Court still remained, and they were committed to doing so, if a way could be found. Parker, Moskowitz, and Spain took solace in the belief that they had done what was morally right. Justice, as Parker said, had been done, even if it had been undone.

It seemed the best view to take. Even Vivian came around and admitted that if Bill Castleberry had never asked to hear her story, she would have "crumbled," as she phrased it, beneath her addictions and her sense of helplessness. In that sense good had evolved from evil, and from her weakness there had come strength.

The moment of justice had been evanescent. If the time ever came when justice triumphed for more than an instant, for longer than the wink of an eye, it would never happen on this earth. "Only a fool would believe otherwise," Vivian said. "I did get help when I needed it most. Now I've got to depend on myself. Every woman has to learn self-reliance."

It was only at night that her anxieties returned, even in faraway Orlando, when she was afraid to pick up the phone or to peek out the window. And then came those terrible dreams.

As with justice, so with life. "Life is brief, like the falling of a leaf," goes the old Protestant hymn. "Be in time, be in time." The sudden death of Amy Spain, on June 30, 1995—only two weeks after her last effort on behalf of her beliefs—brought this truth home forcefully and painfully.

Amy's fiancé—they had been going together for about a year and had not set a date for their wedding but were thinking about sometime in the fall—was driving her from Memphis to visit her parents for the Fourth of July weekend. At about three o'clock that Friday afternoon on I–40, a violent thunderstorm hit, and the car, traveling at about fifty-five miles per hour, suddenly hydroplaned, shot across the median, and slammed into an oncoming eighteen-wheeler truck.

Amy, who had been lying down on the rear seat because she had a headache, was killed on impact. Her fiancé and the driver of the truck survived.

Amy, who had become a leader in civic groups as well as within her profession, was so respected and loved that some twenty-five hundred people came to view her body that Sunday in Jackson. As Donna Whittle said, not in the *Gazette* but to a friend, "Amy Spain was a wonderful person. She touched a lot of lives." In the weeks before her death, Amy had been leading a probe into a vote-buying scheme in Dyer County, letting honest citizens know that, once again, they were not without recourse. On Monday afternoon, St. Andrew's Methodist Church proved too small to accommodate the number of mourners, including Amy's colleagues from the U.S. Attorney's Office in Memphis, which closed in her honor. It was striking and affecting to see so many young people at the service.

Al Moskowitz was there from Washington. Bill Castleberry and Louise Fitzgerald sat together at the rear of the church. They watched the red-rose-covered coffin wheeled slowly in as thunder rolled and hail pelted the wooden roof. Delayed by the storm as they drove in from Dyersburg, Joey McDowell and his wife found places on folding chairs in the jammed foyer.

Joey's emotions veered from grief to anxiety over the absolute silence that Lanier had continued to maintain since his release. If Lanier, as criminals often did during extended confinement, had learned self-discipline in prison, he could become more dangerous than ever before, now that he was free. It had been only his reckless arrogance that had led to his downfall three years earlier.

Other than her fiancé, her parents, and her brother, perhaps the most devastated person in that church was Amy's mentor and friend, Steve Parker. He had spent several of the previous twenty-four hours with her family; now he was one of the pallbearers and looked as if he, too, had lost a sister or a daughter. And he and Al Moskowitz vowed to their colleagues that they were more determined than ever to appeal the Lanier reversal to the Supreme Court, for justice's and for Amy's sake.

The minister, a middle-aged man who choked up frequently during his eulogy as he recalled Amy's many accomplishments during her thirty years, managed to strike the right note, or rather the only comforting one.

"The worth of a life," he said, remembering how seeing and talking with Amy had always filled him with hope and joy, "can never be judged by its length."

Sources and Acknowledgments

This book derives primarily from personal observations and interviews conducted during several extensive visits to Tennessee and other locales during 1993–95. Official documents of various kinds, including court transcripts and other materials relating to the investigation and trial of David W. Lanier (*United States of America v. David W. Lanier,* U.S. District Court No. 92–20172; U.S. Court of Appeals for the Sixth Circuit No. 93–5608), have also been important. Other printed sources have included newspapers and periodicals referred to in the text and books, especially Louise F. Fitzgerald et al., *No Safe Haven: Male Violence Against Women at Home, at Work, and in the Community* (Washington, D.C.: American Psychological Association, 1994). Dr. Fitzgerald also generously supplied articles, conference papers, and her own analyses of the causes, effects, and prevalence of psychosexual violence against women. I am also indebted to former Queens County, New York, prosecutor Alice Vachss's *Sex Crimes* (New York: Random House, 1993) for enlightenment on the difficulty of obtaining convictions against rapists and other sex offenders, a major theme of this book.

My wife, Suzanne O'Brien, who first suggested that I write this book and who joined me on several research trips, assisting with many and conducting some interviews on her own, joins me in thanking the many people who helped us and offered hospitality. We cannot hope to repay their generosity but hope that the book is worthy of the encouragement they gave to us.

In view of current and not unreasonable public cynicism about arrangements between authors and their sources, it may be worthwhile to affirm here that no person has received, nor does any oral or written contract exist, nor has anyone been offered or promised, any payment for his or her cooperation in the writing of this book. It should be added that among the more than fifty persons interviewed, only two requested payment; both cooperated fully when I explained how such transactions can raise questions about the integrity of a work. I should add that neither of the persons initially requesting payment had any connection whatever to law enforcement.

At their requests, or for reasons of discretion, or both, I have substituted the following names for their originals: Ben Beveridge, Brenda Castain, Jennifer Gallagher, Julia Garnett, Mary Haralson, Cathy Kiely, Linda Michaels, and Janet Thomasson. All other names are those of the actual persons involved.

David Lanier did not respond to a written request, addressed to him in prison, for an interview, nor to informal requests I attempted to relay through third parties. In portraying him I have drawn on a variety of sources, including personal observation of him during his court appearances in Memphis and Dyersburg in 1993, before and after his bond was revoked and he was jailed. I have also drawn on my own interviews, many of them conducted with my wife's assistance, with the following: Lanier family members and friends, and business and professional associates of David Lanier, including some who have known him since youth and during his university days; investigators, prosecutors, and witnesses against him, supplemented by court and, when those closed proceedings were made available to me by witnesses themselves, as is permissible, grand jury testimony; and attorneys who practiced in his court, including those who knew him socially and others who had the perspectives of disinterested out-of-town observers. I have also made use of print and videotaped interviews he did grant to various journalists from Dyersburg, Memphis, and Jackson before, during, and after his indictment, trial, and conviction, the last being one he granted to Channel 13 (Memphis) in prison early in 1995. I have also drawn on his portrayal of himself, his feelings, and his opinions as he has expressed them in several issues of the "newsletter" (his own term) he issued from prison to family members, supporters, and others from whom he has attempted to elicit support.

I have also, in portraying Lanier and giving voice to his views, drawn on the civil action he filed, acting as his own attorney, on May 27, 1994 (U.S. District Court for Western Tennessee, Civil Action No. 94–2611), against Ed Bryant, Steve Parker, Amy Spain, Al Moskowitz, Bill Castleberry, Steve Champine, Bobby Williamson, Joey McDowell, Stan Cavness, and others for alleged misconduct, specifically illegal wiretapping, asking for ten million dollars compensatory and fifteen million dollars punitive damages; and on his brief filed March 7, 1995, also acting as his own attorney, with the U.S. Court of Appeals, Sixth Circuit, containing accusations of misconduct against Al Moskowitz, Amy Spain, Bill Castleberry, and other federal officials. In these documents, as in his newsletter and interviews, the consistent theme has been allegations of a conspiracy by the federal government against him. He sounded the same note in his letter of April 12, 1993, after his conviction but on courthouse stationery identifying him as "David Lanier, Chancellor," addressed to "President Bill Clinton," of which I have obtained a copy.

I am grateful to the persons listed below for granting interviews and for help in other ways; I have given cursory identification to those not already introduced in the text: Charles "Bubba" Agee; Roger Atwood, M.D., of Tulsa; Jerry Bastin; Donald M. Brawner, M.D., of Tulsa; Stan Cavness; Bill Castleberry; Charles B. Clement, Jr., attorney, of Chicago; Tommy Cribbs; Linda Creighton, photographer and correspondent, *U.S. News & World Report,* Washington; Dannye Crouch, Editor, *Dyersburg State Gazette;* Stanley Crouch; Representative Carol Chumley, Memphis, Member, Tennessee State House of Representatives; Special Agent Joseph DiBaggio, FBI, Memphis; Laura Emerson, reporter, *Dyersburg State Gazette,* for historical and real estate records; Tod Eames, attorney, of Tulsa; Tom Elam, attorney, Union City, member, University of Tennessee Board of Regents; Louise Fitzgerald; Judy Forsythe; Vivian Forsythe (Archie); Jennifer Gallagher; Robert Greenup, historian, Tulsa; Mary Haralson; Jim Horner; Lyman Ingram; Roy Thomas "T. J." Jones, Dyer County Circuit Court Clerk; Charles Kelly; Hazel Kight; James E. Lanier; Leigh Anne Lanier; Laura Madonna, William Morris Agency, New York; Belinda Maples, Office of Public and Congressional Affairs, FBI, Washington; Joe McDowell; Joey McDowell; Special Agent I. Ray McElhaney Jr., Unit Chief, Office of Public and Congressional Affairs, FBI, Washington; Linda Michaels; Al Moskowitz; Professor Douglas Owsley; Steve Parker; Sharlyn A. Phillips; Junior Sanders; Sandy Sanders; Gailard L. Sartain, actor, Los Angeles, for help with Southern culture; Amy Spain; Chancellor Steven J. Stafford; Sandy Vice; Barry Wallace; Patty Wallace; Donna Whittle, now managing editor, *Dyersburg State Gazette;* Douglas W. Wilkerson, attorney, Dyersburg; Chief Bobby Williamson.

I also wish to thank Susan Moldow, publisher, New York, for encouragement and advice in 1993.

I am grateful once again to my literary agent, Robert Gottlieb, Executive Vice President and Member of the Board of the William Morris Agency, for his vigorous advocacy; he knows the depth of my appreciation for his loyalty and skill. I must also thank Erica Spellman Silverman, Vice President of the Morris Agency, for her counsel and timely actions, as usual.

Diane Reverand, editor in chief, vice president, and associate publisher at HarperCollins, and my editor, has helped in various and vital respects and has saved me from defects in characterization, structure, and clarity. I am pleased to admit that I have embraced her suggestions with gratitude and enthusiasm. I wish to emphasize here my thanks for her help and support.

I am also grateful to Ms. Reverand's assistant editor, Meaghan Dowling, with whom I am pleased to share a certain heritage and whose intelligence and sensitivity have been a lifeline.